Knowledge and the
Study of Education:
an international exploration

This book is dedicated to
Dr Harry Judge
Educator, scholar and friend

Knowledge and the Study of Education:
an international exploration

Edited by
Geoff Whitty & John Furlong

Oxford Studies in Comparative Education
Series Editor: David Phillips

SYMPOSIUM
BOOKS

Symposium Books
PO Box 204, Didcot, Oxford OX11 9ZQ, United Kingdom
www.symposium-books.co.uk

Published in the United Kingdom, 2017

ISBN 978-1-873927-97-7

This publication is also available on a subscription basis
as Volume 27 Number 1 of *Oxford Studies in Comparative Education*
(ISSN 0961-2149)

Printed and bound in the United Kingdom by Hobbs the Printers, Southampton
www.hobbs.uk.com

Contents

Preface

GEOFF WHITTY & JOHN FURLONG

The project from which this book arose originated in an encounter between its two editors at the annual conference of the British Educational Research Association (BERA) in Manchester in September 2012. John Furlong was making a presentation about his then forthcoming book *Education – an Anatomy of the Discipline: rescuing the university project?* (Furlong, 2013). In responding to that presentation, and welcoming John's book, Geoff Whitty pointed out that although the book mined UK history for alternative models for the study of education, it said little about alternative models that might exist in other parts of the world. We therefore agreed to work together on a project that might help to fill that gap.

Initially this was with a view to influencing current English debates about the role of universities in teacher education and about possible futures for education as a university subject in the event of teacher preparation being made the responsibility of schools, as seemed possible at the time (Whitty, 2014). We realised that even the close connection between teacher preparation and the study of education, which has dominated the field in the UK, was not universal. We therefore designed a small research project to examine how the field of Education was constituted in other jurisdictions with a view to placing a wider range of possibilities on to the agenda for English universities.

Our project, which was partly funded by the British Academy (small grant no. SG131230), was entitled 'Educational Studies: the university project in different jurisdictions', and it sought to understand how the study of education was configured in different countries. Limited funding for travel meant that we worked largely with countries that we were already visiting at that time or where we had good existing contacts. We nevertheless wanted to include a range of countries with different histories and traditions. After undertaking some broader background investigations, we decided to focus on six countries – Australia, China, France, Germany, Latvia and the USA.

We undertook background interviews with key informants in these six countries, a total of 21 interviews in all. These semi-structured but wide-ranging interviews covered such matters as:

- the context for educational studies in each country;
- the traditions of scholarship underlying provision;
- the nature and level of courses in Educational Studies;
- the focus of research in Educational Studies;
- any links with teacher education and school improvement;
- the extent of links between Educational Studies and other disciplines;
- any links with other national traditions; and
- the status of Educational Studies in the academy.

After analysing the transcripts of our interviews and identifying some key issues for further clarification and discussion, we invited representatives from each of our focus countries and other scholars with a particular interest in the nature of Educational Studies to a seminar at Green Templeton College, University of Oxford, in July 2015. This event, together with presentations at the universities of Sydney and Oxford, helped us to refine our thinking and to scope this publication.

During the course of the project we realised that we had a wealth of comparative data on the nature of Education as a field of study that, to our knowledge, had never been brought together in a single publication before. Even the project that led to Judge et al's *The University and the Teachers: France, the United States, England* (1994) was geographically more limited in scope than ours and had a particular emphasis on the role of universities in teacher preparation. Nevertheless, that book did provide us with inspiration for our project, and hence the dedication of this volume to our colleague and friend Harry Judge.

As a result of interest in our work from around the world, we have planned the current publication not just as a contribution to debates about the future of teacher education in England and other parts of the UK, but as a contribution to the comparative history of the study of education more generally. We hope that it will encourage less parochial thinking about the field, not only in England but also elsewhere.

The book consists of four sections. The first section is an introduction by the editors that attempts to map the different traditions in the study of education identified during the course of the project. The second section provides six case studies of education written by contributors from our focus countries. The third section contains two chapters that seek to provide conceptual frameworks for understanding the dimensions on which the various traditions in the study of education differ and two chapters that attempt to compare traditions in different countries. The final section is an attempt by one of our project advisers, David Labaree, a historian of US teacher education (Labaree, 2004), to make sense of what our contributors have provided and identify future prospects for the study of Education in universities.

References

Furlong, J. (2013) *Education – an Anatomy of the Discipline: rescuing the university project?* London: Routledge.

Judge, Harry H., Lemosse, M., Paine, L. & Sedlak, M. (1994) *The University and the Teachers: France, the United States, England.* Oxford: Symposium Books. https://dx.doi.org/10.15730/books.31

Labaree, D. (2004) *The Trouble with Ed Schools.* New Haven, CT: Yale University Press.

Whitty, G. (2014) Recent Developments in Teacher Training and their Consequences for the 'University Project' in Education, *Oxford Review of Education*, 40(4), 466–481. https://doi.org/10.1080/03054985.2014.933007

Part 1. Introduction

CHAPTER 1

Knowledge Traditions in the Study of Education

JOHN FURLONG & GEOFF WHITTY

SUMMARY The chapter draws on evidence from a number of different jurisdictions in order to clarify the range of intellectual traditions and practices that collectively constitute the field of Education today. Specifically, it asks what can be learnt about the current construction of the field by looking comparatively at 'the Education project' in seven different jurisdictions – England and six case-study countries: France, Germany, Latvia, Australia, China and the USA. What are the similarities and differences in the ways in which knowledge in the field is traditionally constructed and the ways in which it is currently contested and is changing? Three main clusters of knowledge traditions across these seven countries are identified: academic knowledge traditions; practical knowledge traditions and integrated knowledge traditions. Each of these clusters includes a number of distinctive, but sometimes overlapping, traditions within it. In conclusion, it is argued that asking questions about knowledge in Education is important because whatever the 'settlements' of the past, they are now being called into question by politicians and practitioners around the world. University and school systems are increasingly being drawn into a world of competitive international performativity, raising, in ever sharper terms, questions about the value of the study of Education that challenge the field as a whole and each of the various traditions identified here.

As Harry Judge, to whom this book is dedicated, richly documented a generation ago (Judge, 1982, 1990; Judge et al, 1994), Education [1] as a field of study has developed in markedly different ways in different countries. Even though there have been some signs of convergence in recent years, many of those differences are still apparent today. In Germany, for example, which established its first chairs of Education immediately before the First World War, Education was something of a latecomer to the modern research university (Schreiwer & Keiner, 1992). As a result, the first generation of educationists inevitably felt compelled to pattern the new subject on the examples provided by the wide range of highly academic disciplines that pre-existed it in the powerful faculties of philosophy. This was then followed in the 1920s by a period of intellectual and institutional consolidation which led to Education becoming a largely autonomous and coherent academic discipline. The study of Education in elite universities was and to some extent remains largely separate from initial teacher education, though teacher education itself has now become fully integrated into the university sector in its own right, though primarily in 'non-elite' institutions (Terhart, 2016).

The story in France was different. The formation of elementary and later primary school teachers was always seen as something quite separate from universities, with the 'normal school' (originally schools that trained teachers) tradition going back to the seventeenth century (Hayhoe & Li, 2010). The subject entered the university system 30 years before it did in Germany, with the first courses launched in 1883 and the first chairs appointed in 1887. But in the twentieth century, rather than becoming an autonomous subject, Education became closely intertwined with other disciplines, such as philosophy, economics, sociology and, later on, psychology. As a result, Education did not become a formally instituted university discipline until the 1970s. Moreover, even today, despite early successes by Durkheim, teacher education in France is only partially integrated with the university system, and the study of Education as a whole remains institutionally and intellectually fragmented (see van Zanten, 2009; Malet, 2017 in this volume).

All of this is in sharp contrast to the history of Education in the English-speaking world. From the very beginning, as has been noted by others (Labaree, 2004; Furlong, 2013), Education in England, the USA and other anglophone countries such as Australia has usually been intimately tied up with the training of school teachers. Unlike in France, it has a strong institutional identity, but, unlike in Germany, it has generally been an applied field rather than a recognised discipline in its own right. In many ways it is this engagement with initial teacher education that continues to shape its destiny in such countries today.

But the aim of this introduction is not simply to focus on the history of the study of Education, nor to provide a systematic country-by-country analysis. Rather, our purpose here is to draw on evidence from a number of different jurisdictions in order to clarify the range of intellectual traditions and practices that collectively constitute the field of Education today. Specifically, we ask what we can learn about the current construction of the field by looking comparatively at 'the Education project' in seven different jurisdictions. What are the similarities and differences in the ways in which knowledge in the field is traditionally constructed and the ways in which it is currently contested and is changing? We draw on evidence from six countries that are the subject of case studies within this book – France, Germany,

Latvia, Australia, China and the USA. In addition, we draw on evidence from the UK and more specifically from England. This is not only because we ourselves are more familiar with England as a policy context, but also because we have not included a separate chapter on that country in this volume.[2]

In our view, asking questions about knowledge in Education is important because whatever the 'settlements' of the past, they are increasingly being called into question around the world. As university and school systems become drawn more and more into a world of competitive international performativity, it raises, in ever sharper terms, questions about the value of the study of education. 'How, if at all, does the study of education help to improve the practice of education?' is a question that is increasingly posed in narrow utilitarian terms (even in Germany!). In some countries, particularly England but also in others, the answer to that question from politicians is often that it makes little or no contribution. In these countries, particularly in relation to teacher education, the traditional contribution of universities to the field of Education has therefore become increasingly marginalised from officially sanctioned definitions of legitimate Educational knowledge. In other countries, however, different settlements have been proposed. Our hope is that by increasing our understanding of knowledge traditions and practices in different jurisdictions, education academics will be more able to understand the challenges they currently face and thereby perhaps develop more appropriate responses.

The Nature of Knowledge Traditions in Education

But what are knowledge traditions? In our analysis, we take a broad and inclusive view of Education as a field, seeing it as made up of a collection of different traditions, each of which has its own distinctive conception of educational knowledge and which may vary from country to country. Traditionally, disciplines are discussed from an epistemological point of view where debate focuses on questions such as the nature of knowledge, on research methods and on protocols for the establishment of 'truth'. While epistemological questions are important, we also recognise that knowledge traditions have a sociological dimension as well. They are expressed in institutional arrangements; they are challenged, debated and defended and change over time. Knowledge traditions therefore have a political life – they are social projects. Both the existence and the character of the field of Education have been contested within and between countries ever since it first entered the university in the late nineteenth century, and the intensity of that contestation has increased markedly in recent years.

Sociological Questions

In looking at knowledge traditions sociologically, we suggest that within any one jurisdiction there will be multiple social sites which may embody different conceptions of educational knowledge. Each of these sites has its own history and traditions and may change over time.

In our analysis, the main social sites we recognise in each jurisdiction are as follows:

- academic institutions (universities, teachers' colleges, etc.) which have their own traditions embodied in established professorships, lectureships, qualifications, etc.;
- national regulatory frameworks (legislation, national 'criteria' for initial and ongoing teacher education, for research assessment, for research grants, etc.); and
- academic/professional networks (learned societies, professional institutes, conferences, etc.).

In all of the countries we have examined, since the 1990s there has been one dominant *academic institution* focusing on the study of Education – the university. However, in reality, despite the common name, the university sector is increasingly differentiated, with different universities to some extent drawing on different histories and different forms of Educational knowledge in order to serve different sectors of the educational market.

In recent years a significant factor in defining Educational knowledge within a growing number of countries has been the development of powerful government *national regulatory frameworks*. In England in relation to initial teacher education these have been particularly significant with their insistence on a strong commitment to practical work in schools and the consequent suppression of more traditional forms of Educational theory. Another example is the USA, where in the early 2000s the federal government, through its commitment to the 'No Child Left Behind' policy, prioritised a particular scientific conception of educational research knowledge. In addition, in both Australia and the UK, there are now powerful regulatory frameworks associated with national research assessment processes that have also significantly shaped educational knowledge. These latter regulatory frameworks can sometimes be in tension with those imposed in relation to teacher education.

Academic institutions and national regulatory frameworks are particularly important in that they can formally institutionalise particular conceptions of Educational knowledge. In addition, though, in every country there are also various powerful *networks* that help to shape Educational knowledge. Although these networks seldom have the power of institutions or regulatory frameworks, they are nevertheless important in helping to embed particular conceptions of knowledge. For example, many national and regional research associations (BERA, AERA, AARE, EERA) were, as McCulloch documents in this volume, specifically established to embody broad and eclectic approaches to Educational knowledge, though, as he also notes, they were also motivated, at least in part, by the 'allure' of the promise of interdisciplinarity. By contrast, bodies such as the American Psychological Association or the Mathematical Association were always predicated on a much more specific conception of Educational knowledge which in some cases has become a powerful regulatory framework for professional accreditation. In addition, there are a range of advisory bodies, think tanks, supranational organisations (e.g. the Organisation for Economic Co-operation and Development [OECD]) and private corporations (e.g. McKinsey) that can at times have a powerful, if usually indirect, influence on the shaping of Educational knowledge in particular jurisdictions.

Thus, in order to answer our questions about different knowledge traditions in the study of Education we need to begin by recognising that within any one particular jurisdiction there will be *a range* of key sites, each of which may embody its own distinctive approach to Educational knowledge. These different conceptions may change over time, and within any one jurisdiction they may be consonant with each other or they may be in tension.

Epistemological Questions

Knowledge: 'sacred' or 'profane'? In addressing the epistemological dimensions of different knowledge traditions it is helpful, in the first place, to distinguish those that are 'sacred' from those that are 'profane'.

As we have already noted, Germany established Education as an independent discipline earlier than other countries. Perhaps even more importantly, traditional German Educational theory has not been concerned with influencing the world of practice in a direct way; its concerns historically have been primarily philosophical and ultimately moral (what Schriewer [2017] in this volume characterises as a form of 'self- cultivation'), with most researchers focusing on what Stokes (1997) would characterise as 'pure basic research'. By contrast, many other (but by no means all) Educational traditions see it as an applied field; there is an aspiration to link 'theory' and 'practice'. In Gilbert Ryle's (1949) terms, that means not just 'knowing that', but 'knowing how' as well. Or, to put it another way, the aspiration is both to 'understand' and to 'make a difference' at the same time. As Keiner (2010) has argued, it is this aspiration, an aspiration that has been particularly strong in the English-speaking world, that has fundamentally shaped Education as a field of study and contributed to its relative political instability.

But despite the common aspiration to make a difference, it is important to recognise that in some intellectual traditions the links to the world of practice are made more easily than in others. This is because, in some traditions, the forms of disciplinary knowledge involved (as in, for example, the economics of Education or the psychology of Education) are often different from the forms of knowledge that circulate in education as a field of practice. In other traditions (e.g. the 'normal college' tradition), the knowledge involved in the study of Education is more closely related to everyday practical knowledge in circulation in schools and colleges.

Bernstein (1999), drawing on Durkheim, sees this as a basic distinction between knowledge that is 'sacred' and knowledge that is 'profane' – or, to use Bernstein's own terms, between vertical and horizontal discourses. As Hordern (2017), writing in this volume, reminds us, for Bernstein, vertical discourses are 'specialised symbolic structures' which are 'systemically principled'; they are based on context-independent knowledge and conserved through intricate social formations (such as academic communities) that enable abstract conceptualisation, conjecture and hypothesis-building, taking the thinker beyond their immediate experience. By contrast, horizontal discourse is 'local, context dependent', 'everyday' and 'common sense' knowledge. That is not to suggest that it is not sometimes 'inflected' with elements of academic knowledge – ideas that are borrowed, translated, applied – nevertheless, horizontal discourse, for Bernstein, is always 'contextually specific', 'consumed by that context' and circulated and exchanged through fluid and unsystematic social processes.

There are clearly value positions implicit in Bernstein's characterisation of these different discourses; vertical discourses are presented as more appropriate for serious analysis of a field like Education. Young and Muller (2014, 2016), to whose work we will return at the end of this introduction, also see them as more powerful than horizontal discourses.

As we will see, though, there are some intellectual traditions and practices involved in the study of Education that, if not actually 'profane', are more closely related to the world of practice than others. And those in these traditions would dispute the suggestion that they provide no basis for thinking beyond immediate experience. Historically, the 'normal college' tradition of teacher education (particularly strong in both France and China) is an example of a practice-focused tradition based on craft knowledge – though again sometimes with diverse elements of academic knowledge unreflectively embedded within it. A more contemporary example would be the current interest in what we might call 'Networked Professional Knowledge' (see, for example, Hargreaves, 1999). Yet other traditions – for example, the practitioner enquiry movement and some forms of 'clinical practice', which we discuss later – are based on practices that explicitly try to bring both academic and practical knowledge together. A key question for different traditions, therefore, is the extent to which they are located in vertical or horizontal discourses or whether they explicitly attempt to integrate the two in some way.

And if they are located in vertical discourses, based on academic knowledge, it is also important to ask how, if at all, they aspire to link 'theory' and 'practice'. In both France and Germany, for example, there was historically no such aspiration; the dilemmas of theory and practice were 'resolved' by the establishment of very different types of institution based on different conceptions of Educational knowledge. Practically based teacher education has been, and to some extent still is, seen as separate from the academic study of Education in elite universities and policy institutes such as the Institut de Recherche d'Économie de l'Éducation (IREDU) or the Laboratoire de Sociologie de l'Éducation. Similar distinctions exist in China, with the most elite (non-normal) universities focusing only on research rather than on teacher education, at least until recently (see Wen & Xie [2017] in this volume). In contrast, in the UK in the second half of the twentieth century, following the early arguments of Hirst (1966), the assumption was that disciplinary knowledge, however abstract in itself, could be a direct guide to practice.[3] As a result, universities attempted to *impose* a highly theoretical conception of Educational knowledge based on the (sub-) disciplines of Education – sociology, psychology, philosophy and history. One consequence of this imposition was that parts of the teaching profession, and later many politicians, saw university-based knowledge as largely irrelevant to the day-to-day concerns of the school system.

Education: 'objective' or 'normative'? A further distinction concerns the degree to which knowledge in any particular tradition is seen as 'objective' as opposed to 'normative'. By the term 'objective' we are not simply referring to notions of 'positivism'. Rather, we are referring to all of those traditions focused on the development of knowledge that is contestable through accepted protocols within particular epistemic communities. What counts as knowledge and the protocols for testing claims to knowledge will be different in the philosophy of Education from those in sociology of Education or the history of Education. Despite these fundamental differences, what unites them is that each, in their own way, will be concerned with the development of supposedly 'objective' knowledge. 'Normative' approaches to knowledge in Education are different in that they tend to start from an explicit (or at least clearly identifiable) value position. For example, some traditions are based on explicit values about how or what *pupils* should learn. The traditional conception of German theory, which we discuss in more detail below, is an obvious example here. Others, such as the religiously based teacher colleges of the nineteenth century, emphasised what *teachers* should learn. Yet others are based on clear values of how Education should contribute to the development of *society*.

In summary, therefore, we propose that it is possible to identify three broad clusters of knowledge traditions in in the study of Education. Inevitably these clusters are not pure; there is often considerable overlap between them and decisions as to where to place any one tradition are to some degree arbitrary. Nevertheless, as a heuristic device we have found it helpful to group clusters of traditions in this way. The first cluster brings together those knowledge traditions that foreground academic knowledge; these traditions are often (though not always) distant from the knowledge that circulates in education as a field of practice. A second cluster brings together those traditions that are based primarily in the world of practice, even though they sometimes draw, unreflectively, on disparate elements of academic knowledge. A final cluster includes those traditions that explicitly attempt to bring these very different forms of knowledge (academic and practical) into some kind of relationship with each other. In each of the clusters, there are specific traditions that aspire to be primarily 'objective', while others contain strongly 'normative' elements.

In the remainder of this introduction, we set out what we see as some of the major knowledge traditions in the study of Education, drawing our examples from across the seven different jurisdictions we have examined. We begin by looking at the first cluster, 'academic knowledge traditions', then go on to examine the second and third clusters – 'practical knowledge traditions' and 'integrated knowledge traditions'. In so doing, we draw on Bernstein's typology of singulars, regions and generics, as discussed in Hordern's contribution to this volume (Hordern, 2017). In Figure 1 we summarise the major traditions we will be examining below, following the order denoted by the numbers on the chart.

Cluster 1: Academic knowledge traditions	
'Singulars' within the field of education 1. Disciplines of Education/*Sciences de l'Éducation* 2. German Educational Theory	*Education as a 'region'* 3. 'Applied' Educational Research and Scholarship 4. The 'New Science' of Education
Cluster 2: Practical knowledge traditions	
5. Education as a 'generic' – competences and standards 6. The 'normal' college tradition of teacher education 7. Liberal education + craft knowledge 8. Networked professional knowledge	
Cluster 3 Integrated knowledge traditions	
9. *Pedagoģija* (Latvia) 10. Practitioner enquiry/action research 11. Research informed clinical practice 12. Learning sciences	

Figure 1. Knowledge traditions in the study of Education.

A. Academic Knowledge Traditions

Education as a 'Singular'

In examining academic knowledge traditions in the study of Education, we begin by returning to the work of Bernstein and, this time, to his distinction between 'singulars' and 'regions'. As Hordern (2017) explains, in Bernstein's analysis, a 'singular' is a body of specialised knowledge that has a discrete discourse with its own intellectual field of texts, practices, rules of entry, etc., and is protected by strong boundaries and hierarchies. In some of these singulars, the knowledge structure will be relatively unified and hierarchical (they have a strong 'grammar'), with well-agreed procedures for the testing of new knowledge. Maths, as Tatto and Hordern (2017) in this volume make clear, is an obvious example. Other singulars will have a more eclectic knowledge structure, with different sub-groups adopting different methodological and epistemological assumptions. The prime example here would be sociology. Whether the knowledge structure is unified or not, most singulars gain their strength, at a sociological level, from being strongly bounded, with clear procedures for entry and training and strong hierarchies. Importantly, unless there is a strong community of practice that subscribes to the same knowledge assumptions (as Tatto and Hordern show is the case in mathematics education), the knowledge they produce is likely to be of a different character from the knowledge that circulates in the adjacent field of practice. In these cases, the challenges of directly linking theory and practice are often significant.

1. The Disciplines of Education/Sciences de l'Éducation

Perhaps the best-known tradition of 'singulars' in the study of Education is what is called 'The Disciplines of Education', or what the French call '*Sciences de l'Éducation*'. Traditionally, the approach embraces a number of sub-disciplines – the sociology, psychology, philosophy and history of Education – though it can also include a range of other perspectives, such as economics, anthropology and applied linguistics. What is distinctive about this tradition is that it is indeed made up of a collection of quite separate singulars – a multidisciplinary set of discourses, each of which is broadly oriented to educational questions addressed from distinctive epistemological perspectives. The strength of the tradition is that each sub-discipline potentially provides a rigorous intellectual framework. Because each draws its epistemology and methodology from its parent discipline, it provides what Bridges (2006) has called 'the discipline of the disciplines'.

The Disciplines of Education model is widespread internationally as an intellectual tradition, though it has been particularly strong in the English-speaking world. In the UK it emerged in the 1960s under the influence of Richard Peters and Paul Hirst, who led the debate on the search for 'degree worthiness' as initial teacher education moved out of the old teachers' college system into the mainstream higher education system. From the 1970s onwards, the BEd degree that replaced the old Teachers' Certificate had a common structure across *all* validating universities in the UK. At its heart was the study of the sociology, psychology, philosophy and history of Education – the 'foundation disciplines'. In line with the social democratic ideals of the day, the academic study of the disciplines was justified as part of the liberal education of the well-rounded teacher, 'the scholar who happened to want to be a teacher' (Bell, 1981, p. 13), and (outside teaching practice) courses often became insulated from the world of schools.

Institutionally, the establishment of the new degree gave rise to a range of specialist appointments, and stimulated specialist research programmes and a number of specialist academic networks (e.g. the Philosophy of Education Society of Great Britain, established in 1964, and the History of Education Society, founded in 1967).

Similar moves have happened in many other English-speaking countries and the approach is still dominant in Australia and many parts of the USA (see Paine [2017] in this volume). In France, *Sciences de l'Éducation*, based on a similar group of Education sub-disciplines, was formally established in universities from 1968 onwards, but was and remains largely separate from initial teacher education (see Malet [2017] in this volume). China also recognises what it calls the 'educational sciences', which have, since the end of the Cultural Revolution, developed a strong place in both elite research universities and some 'normal' universities (see Wen & Xie [2017] in this volume).

In some countries the Educational disciplines today have their own institutional base, separate from university Faculties of Education. For example, France has a number of specialist educational research institutes based on different disciplines. The Institut de Recherche d'Économie de l'Éducation (IREDU) was created in 1971 and the Laboratoire de Sociologie de l'Éducation was created a year later. Both undertake specialist academic research in either economics or sociology and are linked to the powerful Centre National de la Recherché Scientifique (CNRS), which was established in 1939. Other institutional approaches involve the study of education within other faculties – within faculties of history or economics or psychology. In all of these cases, Education is conceptualised as part of the parent discipline, which functions as a 'singular' in its own right.

However, most Education 'singulars' take place within schools, departments and faculties of Education themselves. In Australia, the UK and the USA, Educational psychology often follows this approach, as does applied linguistics. Epistemological assumptions are drawn from the parent disciplines with academics seeing their work as sharply distinguished from other intellectual traditions in Education. That distinctiveness is often supported by powerful social networks – learned societies such as the British Association of Applied Linguistics or the American Psychological Association. As well as providing intellectual and professional networks, such societies also sometimes function as regulatory bodies. For example, the national psychological societies in the UK, the USA and Australia all use entry requirements and curriculum specifications to define the nature of the knowledge that needs to be studied in order to become a qualified educational psychologist.

Despite the strengths of this approach, it does give rise to a number of difficulties. First, while it is generally accepted that each specific discipline can only provide exploration of educational issues from its own theoretical perspective, there is little sense of how these different theoretical perspectives combine. The approach, as McCulloch (2017) points out in this volume, remains firmly *multi*disciplinary rather than *inter*disciplinary. Indeed, some see this as axiomatic. As Tibble (1966, p. 16) put it in his classic book *The Study of Education*:

> 'Education' is a field subject, not a basic discipline; there is no distinctively 'educational' way of thinking; in studying Education one is using psychological or historical or sociological or philosophical ways of thinking to throw light on some problem in the field of human learning.

As we will see below, in this regard, the Disciplines of Education model stands in marked contrast to both German and Latvian traditions, which are premised on the assumption that there is a way of thinking that is distinctively 'Educational'.

A second tension concerns the relation to practice. Although there is a general 'orientation' to the world of practice, how links are to be achieved often remains problematic. The disciplinary discourses generated by these disciplines are in most cases substantially different from those employed within the field of educational practice. For the most part, the assumption would seem to be that policy and practice can be influenced by the provision of methodologically robust 'expert technical knowledge'. Yet, as Kuhlee and Winch (2017) argue in this volume, such expert knowledge often has a problematic relationship with the world of practice; without the existence of appropriate mediating institutions and practices (some of which are considered in a later section on 'integrated traditions'), that expert knowledge potentially transforms the practitioner or policy maker into a 'technician'.

It is the failure to confront these issues that has led growing numbers of governments around the world to question the utility of the discipline-led approach to Educational research and favour randomised controlled trials (RCTs), as discussed later. This has been coupled with the move to a more competency-based conception of teacher education in England (Whitty & Willmott, 1991), in parts of the USA and most recently in Australia (see Paine [2017] and Groundwater-Smith & Mockler [2017], in this volume). In England it has resulted in a substantial reduction in the numbers of specialist courses and specialist professorial and lecturing posts in the Education disciplines. By contrast, Scotland, which has a different regulatory framework for initial teacher education, has maintained disciplinary perspectives as a necessary component of professional preparation.

2. German Educational Theory

Our second example of a 'singular' in Education is the traditional conception of Educational theory that was, until relatively recently, dominant in Germany (see Schriewer [2017] in this volume). Traditional German Educational theory is distinctive in a number of key respects. In contrast to the Disciplines of Education tradition, for example, it is strongly normative in approach; it is also explicitly distanced from the world of practice, concerned primarily with questions that are philosophical and ultimately moral.

As Biesta explains, there are at least two different, but interrelated elements to traditional German Educational theory: *Erziehung* and *Bildung*. While *Bildung* is essentially concerned with the formation of the student self through subject matter referred to as *Didactiks*, *Erziehung* is a more broadly based concept of learning which takes in educative relationships between adults and children in a variety of contexts in school, family and society; these processes are termed *Pädagogik*. What these foundational concepts immediately make clear are important differences between German and English-speaking constructions of the field. In the German tradition, the study of Education 'does not start from "other" disciplines and their perspectives on Education, but is depicted as a field in its own right' (Biesta, 2011, p. 184); the analysis starts and ends with processes that are distinctly Educational.

A second distinctive feature is that it is explicitly normative both at the level of society, where there is a concern with the importance of Education in the creation of a 'moral' community, and at the level of the individual learner. Groothoff (1973), for example (quoted in Biesta, 2011), argues that a theory of *Erziehung* needs to encompass the following elements: (1) a theory of becoming a human being; (2) a theory of interpersonal interaction; (3) a theory of emancipatory learning; (4) a theory of contemporary social life and its perspectives on the future; (5) a theory of the ends and means of education and their interrelationships; and (6) an account of the specific ends and means in the context of the different domains and institutions (Groothoff, 1973, p. 74).

These types of questions, rather than being studied empirically, are addressed through philosophico-hermeneutic reflection. *Pädagogik* in particular is phenomenological in approach; it focuses on re-interpretations of historical and philosophical theories of Education with the explicit aspiration of building a secular morality. The ambition is to articulate ultimate educational aims and, more importantly, educational aims that were, at least in the early stages of the development of the field, considered to be universally valid. More recent interpretations, following the intervention of Dilthey (see Biesta, 2011), suggest that the aims of Education are always relative to and internal to particular socio-historical configurations, but that, nevertheless, despite this relativistic stance, there remains a normative commitment – to clarify what the aims of education 'should be' in any one particular context.

Deliberately distanced from the world of practice, the study of the aims of education with core concepts such as *Bildung, Didactiks, Erziehung* and *Pädagogik* has historically formed a central part of the academic curriculum for the preparation of Gymnasium (secondary) teachers; primary, technical and vocational teachers were educated in different, more practically focused institutions. Given its distinctive approach, it is perhaps unsurprising that, as Schriewer (2017) documents in this volume, Educational researchers in Germany, supported by the German Educational Research Association (Deutsche Gesellschaft für Erziehungswissenschaft) have until recently formed a relatively closed academic community, with comparatively few international networks outside northern Europe (see also Ertl et al, 2015). However, in recent years an increased interest in more empirical approaches to the study of Education (*empirische Bildungsforschung*) has taken hold in almost all German universities and research institutes, with the re-definition of numerous chairs and lectureships. This is arguably a manifestation of the influence even in Germany of what Sahlberg (2015) terms the Global Educational Reform Movement (GERM).

Overall, we can see that 'singulars' hold a significant place in the educational landscape. Each, be it the history of Education or traditional German Educational theory, has its own distinctive approach to educational knowledge and functions as a relatively closed intellectual community, working nationally and often internationally through specialist networks, conferences and journals. Research is seen as a technical activity that can only be undertaken by those with the appropriate training, whether that be in philosophy or economics or psychology. And the outcome of this tradition of thinking is Educational knowledge that is indeed primarily academic in nature, often sharply distinct from the forms of everyday knowledge that circulate in schools.

Education as a 'Region'

Bernstein's second type of academic discourse takes place in what he characterises as a 'region'. 'Regions', as Hordern (2017, in this volume) argues, are different from singulars in two ways. First, they are made up of a number of singulars that are re-contextualised into larger units; second, they 'face both ways', operating both in the intellectual field of disciplines and in a field of practice. Medicine, engineering and architecture are examples of regions, as are cognitive science, management and business studies. Held together by their engagement with a specific field of practice, sociologically they function to some degree as a single discipline, even though they are in reality made up of a number of different sub-disciplines. However, as Hordern (2014) emphasises, some regions are more strongly 'bounded' than others; they have a stronger sociological identity and therefore have the capacity to influence knowledge production in their various sub-disciplines.

Medicine would again be an example of a strongly bounded region; social work a weakly bounded one.

3. 'Applied' Educational Research and Scholarship

Education includes a number of different intellectual traditions that function to some degree as 'regions' or 'sub-regions'; indeed, the largest intellectual tradition, what we characterise as 'Applied Educational Research and Scholarship', can be seen in this way. Within this group we are referring to those bodies of research and scholarship that are united by their focus on particular substantive educational topics, such as early years, assessment, comparative and international education, etc. The range of these different groupings is extensive, as is illustrated by the fact that BERA currently lists 30 special interest groups (SIGs), most of which are substantively focused; AERA has several hundred such groups.

Epistemologically, most of these different 'regions' or 'sub-regions' are highly eclectic in that they draw their conceptions of knowledge, their theories and their methodologies from a wide variety of different sources. Some, such as policy studies, are strongly influenced by sociology; others – early years, for example – by developmental psychology. Most, however, see themselves as explicitly multi-disciplinary. Crossley and Watson (2009), for example, characterise comparative and international Education as multi-disciplinary, which they see as an advantage: 'Not only does a multi-disciplinary perspective convey the complexity and demands of such work, but it also reflects and encourages the creative involvement of a diversity of scholars' (p. 635).

Sociologically, these traditions can take different forms. Comparative and international Education and leadership Education would be examples of sub-regions that are sociologically relatively strongly bounded with well-established learned societies such as the Comparative and International Education Society (CIES) and the British Educational Leadership, Management and Administration Society (BELMAS); many of our case study countries also support a number of strong master's degree programmes in these specialist areas. Other areas of applied Educational research – for example, teaching and teacher education – are much more open communities, perhaps finding existence only through networks such as special interest groups and journals. In addition, in both the UK and Australia there are growing numbers of undergraduate degrees in early years education, and established master's degrees in policy studies and gender and education. Many of the universities offering these degrees now have established lectureships and chairs in these specialisms. And finally, the approach is also recognised in the national regulatory frameworks developed for research assessment in the UK and Australia, to which we alluded earlier. For example, in the UK, the 2014 Research Excellence Framework panel for

Education set out a multifaceted definition of Educational research covering different sectors, such as: 'early years, primary, secondary, further, higher, medical, workplace, adult and continuing education' and different substantive areas: 'curriculum, pedagogy, assessment, language, teaching and learning'. In each case, the assessment panel was required to make judgements of quality in relation to the cannons of excellence established within each of these very different sub-communities of research.

One strength of these different intellectual traditions is that they are applied. Most take their research questions directly from the field of educational practice and then draw on a wide range of intellectual resources – theories and methods – in order to explore those questions. In the UK over the last 10 years there has been a growing practice of researchers in these traditions drawing practitioners directly into the research process itself, an approach that has been encouraged by the growing importance of 'impact' in the national assessment of research quality (Higher Education Funding Council for England [HEFCE], 2014). Because of their broadly applied nature they are often seen by practitioners as more 'relevant' to their needs than other forms of academic research.

However, a weakness is that without any consistent epistemological and methodological framing of the type provided by the disciplines of Education, they are immensely variable in terms of quality. In any one of these 'sub-regions' there will be examples of high-quality rigorous research and scholarship; at the same time, however, there will be many other examples of work that is relatively weak.[4] The lack of any agreement about epistemological assumptions also means that knowledge within any one topic area is seldom cumulative, with different researchers bringing their own theories and methods to bear on their chosen topics. In their analysis of this situation, Lawn and Furlong (2009) write with some regret of the loss of the 'disciplines of the disciplines', which they see as in the past providing more rigour. Today, they suggest, the disciplines are merely 'ghosts' of the past:

> in the current world, ghosts don't have much time to linger as the speed of reformation, sub-disciplinary groupings, interest-based developments, and utilitarian, sponsor-based work re-shapes the field constantly. Journals arrive without a past, reflecting (often creatively) new areas of work, and old journals linger on, supplied by the necessity of research audit publication. The internationalisation of fields of study and the growth of cross border study creates hybrids of different disciplinary histories and their production, or micro-studies which avoid the problems of the past while looking to the future and action. Without conversing with the past, and recognising how it was populated, can we recognise our disciplinary responsibilities before we decide to reject or develop them? (Lawn & Furlong, 2009, p. 550)

4. The 'New Science' of Education

Our second example of a 'region' has emerged, or more correctly re-emerged, in recent years, partly in response to the perceived lack of rigour in the Applied Educational Research and Scholarship tradition. It is what we call the New Science of Education. It is an approach that is increasingly powerful in many countries around the world, promising as it does significant improvements in educational outcomes by finding out 'what works' through the application of 'rigorous research' – typically defined as RCTs and/or systematic reviews.

> I think there is a huge prize waiting to be claimed by teachers. By collecting better evidence about what works best, and establishing a culture where this evidence is used as a matter of routine, we can improve outcomes for children, and increase professional independence. (Goldacre, 2013, p. 7)

The idea that Education might be studied as a science, with methods borrowed from the natural sciences, has a long history. The Scottish educationalist Alexander Bain published his book *Education as a Science* in 1879; his work subsequently stimulated the development of a network of like-minded 'scientific' researchers based in Scotland, Europe and the USA. As John Nisbet put it in the very first presidential address to BERA in 1974, in the 1920s and 1930s there was a widespread aspiration to use science to improve the quality of education. It was based on the faith that:

> if only one could design a good enough experiment, with effective controls, precise evaluative measurement and appropriate sensitive statistical analysis, it should be possible to establish objectively the one best method, the ideal curriculum, the optimum period of instruction, the correct use of aids to learning.
> (Nisbet, 1974, p. 3)

In the second half of the century, this approach was eclipsed by the development of the Disciplines of Education model based on different methodological assumptions. But as Nisbit commented with considerable foresight, the scientific method always has an initial appeal to each new generation of researchers, as indeed it has for each new generation of politicians.

Today, stimulated by international competition and particularly league tables such as the OECD's Programme for International Student Assessment (PISA), the emphasis on scientific methods in Educational research has resurfaced as a powerful approach. Its aim, once again, is to undertake rigorous evaluations of educational practices in order to determine 'what works', to help education leaders understand how to make their school system 'come out on top' (Mourshed et al, 2007). Methodologically, the new model has a particular focus on the use of RCTs.

The re-emergence of the Science of Education model has been supported through powerful regulatory frameworks. As has already been noted, in 2000, the USA federal government sought to impose such a model on Educational research in the USA through its 'No Child Left Behind' initiative. Under these regulations, federal funding for new initiatives was linked directly to rises in student achievement, which had to be rigorously demonstrated by statistical evidence. In England, all educational research funded through the Education Endowment Foundation, which was established with a grant from the coalition government in 2011, is expected to consider whether RCT methodology is an appropriate part of its evaluation strategy. And the model was reinforced in the 2016 White Paper *Educational Excellence Everywhere*. Similar developments are observable in the USA and internationally (Lingard & Gale, 2010).

Institutionally there is also growing support for such approaches. There are, for example, growing numbers of specialist research centres and networks working in this tradition in a range of countries. In England there is the Centre for Evaluation and Monitoring at Durham University and the Institute for Effective Education at York; at the European level there is the Evidence Informed Policy and Practice in Education network with links across France, Germany and the UK. Schriewer (2017, in this volume) also provides evidence that in Germany national concern with PISA has stimulated significant numbers of established chairs of Education, previously focusing on *Pädagogik*, to be redefined to be based on empirical studies in Education – *empirische Bildungsforschung*. Recent developments in China and the USA, as documented in this volume, tell a similar story, and in Latvia, the Science of Education model has emerged recently as a strong rival to the traditional Pedagogical Sciences approach (see below) to teacher education.

The strength of this knowledge tradition is indeed its methodological rigour, though as Paine (2017, in this volume) eloquently argues, it brings with it a reductive conceptualisation of complex educational processes. But its principal weakness is that despite its general orientation to the world of practice, its methods are highly technical in nature and necessarily result in forms of knowledge that are significantly distant from the forms of knowledge that circulate in Education as a field of practice. Although its aspiration is to guide practice, this tradition's way of doing that can sometimes seem to provide expert technical knowledge, which reduces the scope for professional judgement and thereby turns teachers into technical functionaries.[5]

In what follows we examine a range of other traditions that are based on very different conceptions of knowledge: those that are explicitly located in the world of practice, and those that aspire to integrate both academic and practical forms of knowledge.

B. Practical Knowledge Traditions

As we have already indicated, the language used by Basil Bernstein in his discussion of knowledge traditions is far from neutral. Academic discourse, whether it takes the form of a singular or a region, is seen as 'sacred'; it is a discourse that is principled, that enables abstract conceptualisation, hypothesis building, 'taking the thinker beyond their immediate experience'. By contrast, the discourse that all of us inhabit in our everyday educational practice is characterised as 'profane'. Of course, Bernstein is not alone in making such judgements. Peters (1964) famously described much of what he saw in the practically based teachers' colleges of the 1950s as 'undifferentiated mush that is often perpetrated under the heading of educational theory' (Peters, 1964, p. 140).

In reality, the distinction between 'sacred' and 'profane' knowledge is not as clear-cut as this characterisation would suggest. There are many examples where everyday, 'profane' knowledge is 'inflected' with elements of academic knowledge – ideas that are borrowed, translated, applied, albeit perhaps implicitly and unreflectively. For Bernstein and his followers, this is seen as potentially limiting their potentiality for rigorous thought. Such judgements, however, overlook the fact that there is an important cluster of knowledge traditions in Education that are closely linked to the world of practice – knowledge traditions that have a deep history and are perhaps of growing significance today. These include 'competences and standards', the 'normal college' tradition, 'liberal Education + craft models of teaching' and 'networked professional knowledge'.

5. Education as a 'Generic': competences and standards

For our first example of a practical knowledge tradition, we return yet again to the work of Bernstein, who coined the term 'generic mode' to describe a particular form of knowledge that is constructed and distributed outside and independently of disciplinary traditions. Generics are usually led by external agents such as governments or employers who may have little interest in disciplinary knowledge production. Instead, they are performance oriented, focused on the maximisation of productivity, drawing on local, organisational and workplace discourses. As Hordern (2017, in this volume) puts it, generics are 'produced by a functional analysis of what is taken to be the underlying features necessary to the performance of a skill, task, practice or even area of work'. Generics can therefore be seen to sit directly in opposition to the disciplinary cultures and practices of both singulars and regions; indeed, disciplinary knowledge may be seen as 'anachronistic or irrelevant, standing in the way of the fundamentals of completing a task or undertaking an occupation efficiently and effectively' (Hordern, 2017, p. 197).

The example of a generic that Bernstein gives is the competency methodology that was developed in the 1970s and 1980s as the foundation of a new approach to vocational qualifications in the UK. More contemporary examples would be the competency or 'standards' frameworks that underpin teacher education in so many English-speaking countries around the world. Rather than beginning from a disciplinary perspective, these frameworks, developed by bodies such as the National Board of Professional Teaching Standards in the USA or the Australian Institute for Teaching and School Leadership, start from an analysis of the task of a teacher and then proceed to define, often in mandatory terms, the knowledge, the understandings and above all the practical skills that new teachers need to develop. As a consequence, nationally defined standards now frame or 'discipline' both the knowledge and practical experiences to which prospective teachers are exposed; the standards become the curriculum, which is explicitly intended to integrate (highly selective) elements of theoretical knowledge and practical skill.

In England, where the focus on practical skills has been particularly strong, the standards approach has effectively squeezed out any substantial references to disciplinary-based knowledge. As we have already noted, there are significant tensions between the conceptions of knowledge embedded in these standards and those underlying the research assessment frameworks in the UK; similar tensions are now being experienced in Australia as well. Moreover, the imposition of standards has also had a major impact on the field of education more broadly. As Lawn and Furlong (2009) have argued, because education in England has historically been so bound up with initial teacher education, once disciplinary perspectives were expunged from teacher preparation, it meant that the field as a whole changed. Some chairs and lectureships in 'the disciplines' of Education were not replaced and in many cases the research agenda itself became more practically focused (Furlong, 2013).

6. The 'Normal College' Tradition of Teacher Education

Our second example of practical knowledge traditions focuses on the 'normal' college tradition of teacher education. Formal teacher education in Europe has at least a 300-year history and from its inception it was both practically based and strongly normative at the same time. Jean Baptiste de la Salle established the first *école normale*, focused on the training of teachers, at Reims at the end of the seventeenth century. Stimulated by the rise of mass schooling and the need to prepare large numbers of new teachers, the idea of using specially designated schools (rather than elite universities) for their training spread across France, China and the USA. The attraction of normal schools over the universities was that they offered the possibility of strong moral and political control by the Church and the State – something that was seen as essential in the development of new school systems.

Many of these normal schools then changed to become local normal colleges in the later nineteenth and early twentieth centuries, though in

China they continued as normal schools right up until the end of the Cultural Revolution. Despite the name change, government control remained strong. Normal schools and colleges were for the most part focused on the preparation of elementary school, and later primary school, teachers. However, the expansion of secondary schooling during the twentieth century meant that prospective secondary teachers were also in need of preparation; this was most frequently offered in universities. Based in different institutions, secondary programmes were often of a very different character from those offered to primary school teachers; in the UK, for example, they were based on the principles of liberal education rather than narrow training (Furlong, 2013). America led the move to integrate the normal colleges into the university system from the 1940s onwards, a move that was followed in the UK from the 1970s and in Australia from the 1980s. France did not make the change until the 1990s, and even today the integration remains only partial.

As Hayhoe and Li (2010) make clear, the term *normal* in English can only be properly understood with reference to its French roots, where it means 'setting a moral standard or pattern'. However, this normative emphasis was only one of a range of ways in which the normal school and later college was different from the traditional university; normal schools and normal colleges had a fundamentally different conception of Educational knowledge. Figure 2 shows how Hayhoe and Li set out those differences.

University	Normal college
Theory	Practice
Specialised disciplines of knowledge	Integrated learning areas
Value neutral approaches to knowledge	Morally directive approaches to knowledge
A relatively impersonal environment	A nurturing environment with strong mentorship ties between teachers and students
The liberal pursuit of all questions/intellectual curiosity	Action-oriented and field-based knowledge
Academic freedom and autonomy	State control and professional accountability
An orientation to deep-level understanding and long-term change	A craft orientation towards high standards of practice

Figure 2. Comparison of university and normal college (Hayhoe & Li, 2010, p. 2).

Bell (1981) vividly documents how, in England, teacher education institutions were based on these principles right up until the 1960s. They were often isolated communities, primarily focused on the 'moral formation' of the prospective teacher. In the nineteenth century that moral focus was the inculcation of religious values; by the mid-twentieth century an equally strong moral focus concerned a particular child-centred approach to primary teaching. They were also very close to the world of practice, with Education tutors frequently taking demonstration lessons in local schools with 'their' small group of students whom they nurtured throughout their course.

A similar story emerges in the normal college tradition in France, with an *école normale* for preparing primary school teachers established in every department until the 1980s. The very different approach to teacher education enshrined in this tradition is perhaps well illustrated by the selection criteria used right up until that time. Successful applicants had to pass a competitive examination made up of three parts. The first consisted of two written comprehension tests each lasting two hours, one of which had a scientific dimension; the second part consisted of a test of the candidate's ability to teach physical education, including swimming; for the third part the candidate had to produce a work of art or craft.

As Malet (2017, in this volume) explains, since the early 1990s, teacher education in France has been formally linked with the local university system through the establishment of the IUFM (University Institutes for Teacher Formation), which were reformed in 2014 to become the ESPE (Écoles Supérieures du Professorat et de l'Éducation). These institutions, which are often based on the campuses of the old *écoles normales*, are expected to cooperate with their local university for the provision of both primary and secondary teacher education. However, in most cases the actual teaching is carried out not by university staff but by those employed by the ESPE itself. China operates a somewhat similar system, with regional colleges that focus mainly on in-service teacher education.

Why this history is relevant today is that, again as Hayhoe and Li (2010) argue, many of those intellectual and moral traditions have become embedded in some parts of contemporary university systems and not just in France. Despite the common name of 'university', institutions in countries such as the USA, the UK, China and Australia are in reality highly differentiated, addressing different 'markets' and often based on different forms of educational knowledge. In the UK and to a lesser extent in Australia, the highly selective research assessment processes of recent years have rendered those differences more visible. It is the traditional, elite universities that have been most successful in research assessment terms. The newer universities, many of which evolved out of, or incorporated, teachers' colleges, have been far less successful in developing international research profiles. As institutions they see themselves as being much more closely integrated with their local communities, including their local schools, focusing on more immediately relevant forms of practical knowledge. Similar distinctions are also visible in both the USA and China, though in the latter case these distinctions are formalised, with different missions for different categories of university – elite research-based universities do not engage in initial teacher education, and local and regional universities focus mainly on in-service education, while normal universities cover all three – research and both initial and in-service education.

7. Liberal Education + Craft Knowledge

Knowledge in this next tradition has two distinct elements – personal liberal education and craft knowledge. Although they are distinct traditions, we are discussing them together in that they are frequently combined in a number of contemporary policy initiatives in several of the countries we have examined.

The idea of the centrality of personal liberal education to those who would take up a profession such teaching has a long history. It is an idea that is perhaps still most eloquently expressed by John Newman in his Discourses on the 'Idea of a University'. This is from his Discourse 7 – 'Knowledge Viewed in Relation to Professional Skill':

> (The) general culture of mind is the best aid to professional and scientific study and educated men can do what illiterate cannot; and the man who has learned to think and to reason and to compare and to discriminate and to analyze, who has refined his taste and formed his judgment and sharpened his mental vision, will not indeed at once be a lawyer ... (or a teacher) but he will be placed in that state of intellect in which he can take up any one of the sciences or callings I have referred to ... with an ease, a grace, a versatility and a success, to which another is a stranger.
> (Newman, 1853, p. 6)

For Newman, therefore, professional Education had no place in the modern university; indeed, it was not necessary. Liberal education, presumably accompanied by practical experience, was all that was needed. Despite Newman's protestations, universities, even his own university of Oxford, did become involved in the study of Education, but for the first half century what the new departments of Education offered, at least in the UK, was Education that was still fundamentally liberal in intent. This example of an exam question from the first examination in Education at Oxford University in 1898 illustrates the point well:

> Paper IV Special Subjects: Discuss the assertion that Comenius overestimated the importance of knowledge. How far and why was there a predisposition to this in his time?
> (Examination in the Theory, History and Practice of Education, Oxford University, 1898)

This form of professional education was largely only on offer to elite teachers – those intending to teach in secondary and private schools. In both France and Germany as well as the UK, elementary and then primary teacher education took a different tack. First, as we have already noted, in teachers' colleges it was strongly practically oriented, and then over the first half of the twentieth century it came to focus more and more on pedagogy (see Schriewer, 2017, in this volume). The struggles between the pedagogically oriented primary school teacher education and philosophically informed gymnasium teacher education are still observable in Germany today.

But why is the liberal education perspective relevant today? It is relevant because when combined with notions of craft knowledge it still holds sway both in public discourse on education and in a number of key educational policies in each of the countries we observed.

Significantly, conceptions of craft knowledge are deeply divided. Carr (2007), for example, takes a reductive view, talking of a long history of craft approaches to teaching where in the nineteenth century what teachers learned 'was a range of teaching skills and a body of practical knowledge that derived from a mixture of tradition, maxims, dogma and rules of thumb'. Much more positively, Kuhlee and Winch (2017, in this volume) talk of the craft of teaching as involving 'contextual knowledge', 'implicit knowledge', 'embodied knowledge', 'knowledge that cannot be put into words'. Each of these is a key part of educational practice – both at the personal level of the teacher and at the institutional level. Rather than dismissing 'craft knowledge' as something reductive, Kuhlee and Winch see it as an essential but not sufficient dimension of being a professional.

But whether one takes an expansive or reductive conception of craft knowledge, it is this conception of teaching that, combined with liberal education, has come to dominate some parts of teacher education policy in many countries. In England, where, under the influence of the New Right, this discourse has been particularly influential (Whitty 1991, 2016), state schools that are academies, like private schools, no longer need to recruit trained teachers if applicants are (liberally educated) graduates with what the school considers to be appropriate skills. In addition, teacher education itself, under the government's controversial 'School Direct' policy, is in large part now led by directly funded schools rather than by universities. There is an explicit focus both on attracting the 'best' academically trained graduates into teaching (those with a first class degree can receive a bursary of up to £30,000) and on increasingly practically based training. As the Minister of Education who pioneered the scheme, Michael Gove put it, 'Teaching is a craft best learned by observing a master craftsman or woman.'

A broadly similar approach is also visible in many states in the USA (see Paine [2017, in this volume]) and through the 'Teach for All' international network, which supports teacher education programmes based on these principles in 38 countries around the world. Schemes include Teach for America, Teach First (England and Wales), Teach for Australia, Teach for China, Teach for France, and Teach First Deutschland. These programmes focus on recruiting the most academically successful young graduates – those with evidence of having had a strong personal liberal education – and placing them after very limited initial preparation in schools facing the greatest educational need, where they are expected, through their direct teaching experience, to develop the 'skills, mindsets and knowledge needed to maximise impact on student achievement' (teachforall.org). The discourse of liberal education + craft knowledge may not be heard much in university common rooms or committees, but it is certainly strong in key policy contexts around the world.

8. Networked Professional Knowledge

Our final example of a practically based knowledge tradition is what we term 'Networked Professional Knowledge'. Again, we draw on evidence of this approach from England, but there are other examples around the world, particularly in the USA.

The intellectual history of this model of knowledge production originates in the work of Gibbons et al (1994) and what they called the 'new production of knowledge' (see also Delanty, 2001; Nowotny et al, 2001; Nowotny et al, 2003). They argued that universities, for so long the home of science, are no longer the only places in modern societies where knowledge is produced. Stimulated by the intensification of international competition in our increasingly technical society, Gibbons et al (1994) see both a growing demand for specialist knowledge and the expansion of the numbers of potential knowledge producers (as a result of the massification of higher education). This, they were arguing back in 1994, meant that in many sectors of society conditions were now set for the emergence of a new model of knowledge production – what they called Mode 2. Mode 2 research is, in principle, very different from Mode 1:

> In Mode 1 (which for many is identical with what is meant by science), problems are set and solved in a context governed by the, largely academic, interests of a specific community. By contrast, Mode 2 knowledge is carried out in a context of application. (Gibbons et al, 1994)

Mode 2 knowledge is therefore generated in the process of providing solutions to problems which have been identified on the ground, in the context of application. As a result, the process of knowledge production is different; it involves transdisciplinarity, heterogeneity, flexibility, and permeability of institutional boundaries.

> In comparison with Mode 1, Mode 2 is more socially accountable and reflexive. It includes wider, more temporary and heterogeneous sets of practitioners, collaborating on a problem defined in a specific and localised context. (Gibbons et al, 1994)

And the outcomes are different, too. While Mode 1 knowledge is hierarchical and tends to preserve its form, Mode 2 knowledge is more heterarchical and transient. While it may incorporate elements of more formally produced academic knowledge, overall it is more context specific, more frequently located within individuals themselves and their particular working context than in scientific journals. In short, it is what Bernstein would characterise as a 'horizontal discourse' – in other words, it is 'profane'.

Over the last 20 years, David Hargreaves, drawing on Fullan's (2005) work on sustainable school systems, has led the proselytisation of this approach to knowledge production in England. In his seminal paper on 'The Knowledge-creating School' (Hargreaves, 1999), he argued that it is now a commonplace in reviews of Educational research that there is a division between Educational researchers and practitioners, and that teachers and policy makers find too little of what researchers produce to be of practical relevance to, or applicable in, practice. One alternative, he argued, was to treat practitioners themselves as the main (but not the only) source of the creation of professional knowledge.

Initially, his focus was on the knowledge-generating potential of individual schools (Hargreaves, 2003). Then, in collaboration with the National College of School Leadership, he contributed to a number of projects focusing on the benefits of collaborative networks for school improvement. As he notes, England has probably led the world in the development of such networks as a result of the commitment of successive English governments to the decentralisation of the school system, with schools now responsible for a whole host of functions that were previously centrally provided by local or national government. These include directly managing finance, staffing, buildings and in many cases (in academies and free schools) the curriculum as well. They are also almost entirely responsible for teacher professional development and for a growing proportion of initial teacher education as well. This multitude of initiatives has given rise to what has been called a 'mass localism' in English education. As Bunt and Harris (2010, p. 5) put it:

> Mass localism depends on a different kind of support from
> government and a different approach to scale. Instead of assuming
> that the best solutions need to be determined, prescribed, driven
> or 'authorised' from the centre, policymakers should create more
> opportunities for communities to develop and deliver their own
> solutions and to learn from each other.

Critically, that means the development of networks; networks that can support and facilitate innovation, overcoming the 'traditional isolation of schools and challenging traditional hierarchical system structures' (Jackson, 2002). Indeed, Greany (2014, p. 7) has argued that since 2010 the development of networks and partnerships has become the '*the defining* feature' of the English government's approach to educational policy.

Significantly, in this new world, 'traditional hierarchies', including universities with their commitment to disciplinary-based research, are seen as part of the problem. As Jackson put it, these institutions:

> are more effective at buttressing the status quo than
> initiating/supporting change or transferring knowledge across the
> system. We know that school development benefits from external
> facilitation (Fullan and Miles, 1992), but it is also evident that

> what is needed is not outmoded institutions not geared up to the task, but more creative and responsive patterns of working within and between schools. (Jackson, 2002, p. 2)

Instead it is argued that schools need to take ownership of problems and innovation, seeing solutions as available from within the school system. And they need to collaborate in order to get better. It is for this reason that Hargreaves has focused much of his more recent work on exploring the nature of effective networks (Hargreaves, 2011).

It is hard to overstate the significance of this new approach to the production of Educational knowledge in England; it forms the background assumption to a host of substantive educational policies – from the development of academies and multi-academy trusts to the development of 'school-led' initial teacher education. In all of these innovations it is assumed that networks of schools will increasingly work together, developing a knowledge base for problem solving and innovation that is more directly relevant to their own situation than that provided by traditional knowledge hierarchies of the university-based research and scholarship (even though these schools are required to have a university partner). Even more radically, this approach is now being harnessed for the wholescale reform of education in Wales. Networks of 'pioneer schools' across Wales, with only minimal external support, have been given the responsibility of taking the lead in the development of a fundamentally different national curriculum and assessment framework for the country. As such, this practically based tradition is increasingly making a significant challenge to more conventional knowledge traditions in Education.

C. Integrated Knowledge Traditions

So far we have examined knowledge traditions that are either primarily academic or primarily practical in their genesis, though, as we have also noted, in practice the distinctions between these knowledge traditions are far from straightforward. Practical knowledge traditions often draw, however implicitly, on knowledge that has originated in an academic context. At the same time, a majority of those working in more formal academic traditions see Education as an applied discipline; there is a strong commitment (often *ex post facto*) to finding ways of linking disciplinary knowledge to the worlds of policy and practice, usually through the provision of expert knowledge. There are, however, some knowledge traditions where these links are not something to be achieved implicitly or after the event; rather, they are seen as central to the process of knowledge production itself. These we call 'Integrated Knowledge Traditions', and they form our final cluster to be examined. Specifically, we look at four such traditions: *Pedagoģija* (Latvia); practitioner enquiry; clinical practice; and learning sciences.[6]

9. Pedagoǵija *(Latvia)*

Our first example of an integrated tradition is pedagogical science, or *Pedagoǵija* as currently practised in Latvia. Intellectually, it is a strongly bounded multidisciplinary tradition that is held together by its normative commitment to a particular vision of educational practice. As Zogla (2017, in this volume) explains, the study of *Pedagoǵija* in Latvia has a long history. Initially, at the beginning of the twentieth century, it was strongly influenced by German philosophical theories of '*pädagogik*', and then, in the interwar years, when Latvia became independent, by American progressivism and particularly the ideas of Dewey. Finally, in the post-war period of Soviet occupation, the ideas of Vygotsky came to the fore. Today, its conception of *Pedagoǵija* is an amalgam of all these historical influences. From German traditions it draws a strongly philosophical and normative stance. Today that normative stance involves a commitment both to a child-centred view of teaching and learning (drawn from the work of Dewey), and to a Vygotskian conception of learning as a profoundly social process, taking in family child-rearing practices, the community, as well formal and informal aspects of schooling.

Latvian *Pedagoǵija* is therefore a rich intellectual tradition – a multidisciplinary science that is held together by its normative views on both teaching and learning. In some ways it therefore fits Bernstein's characterisation of a 'region'. What makes it different from other educational regions, however, is the fact that engaging directly with the world of practice is seen as central. Its aim, according to Zogla, is to become a form of 'philosophy-in-use'. As Zogla (in this volume) explains, *Pedagoǵija* works at two levels:

> First, it is formal, related to the structure of thought embedded in a pedagogical message; second, it is a philosophical generalisation of a holistic phenomenon which relates to all human dimensions and is a guide for practice. (Žogla, 2017, pp. 107-108)

In other words, *Pedagoǵija* is both an intellectual and a practical framework at the same time. It is through this sort of two-way engagement that disciplinary foundations are 're-written' and the world of practice is constantly re-interpreted through this distinctive intellectual frame.

Throughout Latvia, this approach to the study of Education has been strongly institutionalised; until the 'political re-direction' of 1990 it was the only approach available in Latvian universities and teachers' colleges. Courses and qualifications in pedagogy were recognised at every level from undergraduate studies to doctorates. Since independence, stimulated by the international comparative studies and the increasing mobility of academics, there is now a growing interest in the 'Educational Sciences/Disciplines of Education' model described earlier, which has established itself as an officially accepted alternative intellectual tradition. It, too, now offers courses and qualifications at every level, though to date the pedagogical tradition remains the strongest.

10. Practitioner Enquiry/Action Research

Our next example of an integrated tradition is also strongly normative in that it takes as its starting point the need to challenge the distinctions between the researcher and the researched. During the past 30 years, action research has become well established in the field of Education. In the UK and Australia it is particularly associated with the work of Stenhouse and his followers (Stenhouse, 1981; Elliott, 1985; Carr & Kemmis, 1986); more recently, it has been given a new twist by being reconceptualised as practitioner enquiry (Groundwater-Smith & Sachs, 2002; Groundwater-Smith & Mockler, 2009) and has developed a strong following in the USA (Cochran-Smith & Lytle, 2009). However, action research is, in fact, a much older tradition and much more varied (Lewin, 1948; Hodgkinson, 1957; Wallace, 1987; Whitehead & McNiff, 2004); it is a broad church with many different interpretations and, indeed, disagreements about its core principles.

Nevertheless, there is agreement in the literature that action research is *situational*; it implies drawing on existing literature to design interventions that respond to specific practical issues in specific contexts. In most, though not all interpretations, there is also agreement that action research should be *collaborative* and *participatory*, with practitioners themselves having an active role in the research. Finally, in most interpretations, action research is *self-evaluative*. Because the ultimate aim is to improve practice in some way, the context under study is continuously evaluated, and practice, as well as the research design, constantly modified as the project moves forward. In short, therefore, action research is different from other traditions in that it is constituted first and foremost through a particular set of *practices*. It is those practices that in turn have important implications for the forms of knowledge that are generated – primarily for practitioners themselves.

In many universities today in Australia, the USA and the UK, particularly those that are strongly professionally oriented, practitioner enquiry has become a major strand in their teaching and research agendas (Cochran-Smith & Lytle, 2009; Groundwater-Smith & Mockler, 2009). The approach has also at times, though never very securely, found its way into various national schemes. In Scotland, the Chartered Teacher Scheme was a school-based master's programme for experienced teachers that ran for 10 years from 2003 (Christie, 2006). In England, a national master's in teaching and learning based on these principles was launched in 2009 by the outgoing Labour government, though it was subsequently withdrawn after three years (Burton & Goodman, 2011; Furlong, 2011). Most recently, the Welsh government's master's in education practice was a national scheme for newly qualified teachers based on similar principles; however, it too was short lived, running only from 2013 to 2017.

11. Research Informed Clinical Practice

> One of the perennial dilemmas of teacher education is how to integrate theoretically based knowledge that has traditionally been taught in university classrooms with the experience-based knowledge that has traditionally been located in the practice of teachers and the realities of classrooms and schools. (Darling-Hammond, 2006a, p. 307)

Our next example of an integrated tradition is what has been termed 'research informed clinical practice' (Burn & Mutton 2015). Intellectually, this approach has much in common with the practitioner enquiry tradition outlined above; where it differs is that it has been specifically developed over the last 30 years to support novice teachers rather than experienced practitioners.

As Burn and Mutton (2015) note, the recent 'practicum turn' in initial teacher education (Mattsson et al, 2011) places a much greater emphasis on the role of practical or 'field' experiences in the process of learning to teach. The move has been advocated both by external critics, frustrated by the perceived shortcomings of overly theoretical or academic programmes (DfE, 2010), and also by internal critics within the university sector, who have been critical of the fragmented, uninspiring or superficial nature of traditional approaches (Hagger & McIntyre, 2006; Darling-Hammond, 2010). While the external critique has given rise to a variety of alternative options focusing on providing 'on-the-job' training, the internal critique has inspired the development of more innovative programmes, including 'internship' models aimed at strengthening the partnership between schools and universities and achieving a better integration between different sources of knowledge.

Although the precise terminology varies, the notion of 'research informed clinical practice' (and the emphasis is on 'research informed' rather than mere personal reflection) essentially conveys the need to bring together knowledge and evidence from different sources, through a carefully sequenced programme which is deliberately designed to integrate teachers' experiential learning at the 'chalk face' with research-based knowledge and insights from academic study and scholarship. Inspired by the medical model, the goal is to refine particular skills and deepen practitioners' knowledge and understanding by integrating practical and academic (or research-based) knowledge, and to interrogate each in light of the other.

> ... a key to dramatically successful preparation of teachers is finding ever more effective ways of connecting the knowledge of the university with the knowledge of the school. The more tightly integrated the learning experiences of novices, veteran teachers, and university faculty can become, the more powerful the influence on each other's practices and capacity for constant improvement. (Darling-Hammond, 2006b, p. 185)

As Burn and Mutton (2015, p. 219) explain, 'for beginning teachers working within an established community of practice, with access to the practical wisdom of experts, "clinical practice" allows them to engage in a process of enquiry: seeking to interpret and make sense of the specific needs of particular students, to formulate and implement particular pedagogical actions and to evaluate the outcomes'.

Importantly, by making explicit the reasoning and underlying assumptions of experienced teachers, student teachers are encouraged to develop and extend their own decision-making capacities or professional judgement – what Kriewaldt and Turnidge (2013, p. 106) refer to as 'clinical reasoning', which serves to describe the 'analytical and intuitive cognitive processes that professionals use to arrive at a best judged ethical response in a specific practice-based context'. The intention of clinical practice, as Burn and Mutton (2015) put it, is to 'facilitate and deepen the interplay between the different kinds of knowledge that are generated and validated within the different contexts of school and university'.

Significantly, what is being described here is a *set of practices*; practices that place the novice teacher at the centre, responsible for developing and refining their own personal 'theories' of education through their active engagement with different forms of professional knowledge. In other words, it is a set of practices that has profound implications for the forms of knowledge that are generated.

In recent decades, as Burn and Mutton (2015) demonstrate, a number of leading institutions in the USA, the UK and Australia have adopted this approach. The best known in the UK has been the Oxford Internship Scheme, established some 30 years ago; more recent UK examples include the Scottish Teachers for a New Era programme in Aberdeen (Livingston & Shiach, 2010) and the Glasgow West Teacher Education Initiative (Conroy et al, 2013). In the USA, a number of different partnerships have come together over the years to establish new, hybrid institutions. Professional Development Schools, for example, were developed as sites for both pre-service and in-service professional learning, where 'practice-based and practice-sensitive research can be carried out collaboratively by teachers, teacher educators, and researchers' (Darling-Hammond, 2006b, p. 162). Similarly, the Teachers for a New Era initiative (Carnegie Corporation of New York, 2001) focused on the use of research evidence to inform its programme design and on 'the alignment of key ideas and goals across coursework and clinical work' (Hammerness, 2006, p. 1244). As well as influencing developments in Scotland, the US model of clinical preparation and practice has also served as an important guide for the two-year Master of Teaching (MTeach) developed by the University of Melbourne in Australia, where alternative clinical models are also being developed (Gore, 2016).

12. Learning Sciences

Our final example of an integrated tradition, 'Learning Sciences', is relatively new, having emerged only in the 1990s, though it can perhaps best be understood as a development of the 'New Science of Education' tradition described above. It began with the establishment of the Institute of Learning Sciences at North Western University in the USA under the directorship of Roy Pea. Today, there is a range of broadly similar centres in a number of universities across the USA as well as in Australia, the UK and Germany (and in other countries, such as Singapore). There is also a strong international learned society – the International Society of Learning Sciences – as well as several specialised international journals. Given its relatively short history, it is perhaps unsurprising that learning sciences is still subject to considerable variation in interpretation in different centres. Nevertheless, it does involve a commitment to a number of core principles that distinguish it from other traditions.

First, it is strongly interdisciplinary in approach, bringing together researchers from a range of different fields, including education, computer and information science, cognitive science and psychology, artificial intelligence, linguistics, sociology and anthropology. While the actual contributing disciplines vary, there is in each of them a strong emphasis on the ways in which new technologies can support and enhance learning.

A second distinguishing feature is that learning is broadly conceived. As the *Journal of Learning Sciences* puts it:

> Relevant settings can include schools, higher education, community settings, museums, workplaces, play spaces, and family life, as well as online and virtual worlds... Domains of learning can include subject areas, such as literacy, history, science or mathematics, as well as other domains, such as teaching expertise, medical diagnosis, or craft knowledge. Research that problematizes disciplinary boundaries is also welcome. Work that foregrounds the design of innovative technologies for learning is a priority for JLS.[7]

But perhaps Learning Sciences' most distinguishing feature is that it is a 'design science' in ways that make it similar to engineering and computer science. It insists on an engagement with the real world, with empirical investigations of learning as it occurs in a wide variety of settings. The explicit aim of those investigations is to improve learning outcomes by the use of a 'design-based research methodology' where interventions are conceptualised, implemented, observed and then revised. In some ways this cycle of development – trial, observation and revision – has something in common with action research or practitioner enquiry. Those traditions, too, have a commitment to the improvement of practice though engagement in real-world learning settings and adopt a similar circular strategy. Where learning sciences differs, however, is both in its explicit commitment to draw on particular disciplinary perspectives and in its commitment to 'rigorous' research methods. In ways that are similar to what we have termed the 'New Science of Education', the research methods used are predominantly statistically based, with a particular emphasis on RCTs. As the International Society for Learning Sciences expresses it in its vision statement:

> ISLS is committed to application in context (not only in laboratories), to rigorous empirical research (not simply philosophy), and to design and application (not only theory). (International Society for Learning Sciences, 2009, p. 1)[8]

D. Discussion

As we indicated earlier, our aim in this exploration of different knowledge traditions in Education was not intended to be formally comparative; rather, it was to draw on examples from the seven different jurisdictions we studied in order to clarify what particular traditions there actually were. Nevertheless, at our conclusion it is appropriate to ask whether traditions do indeed vary between jurisdictions. Does the study of Education mean something different in Germany from what it means in the USA, or England, or Latvia? Our answer is both 'yes' and 'no'.

What we have found is that there are a small number of knowledge traditions that are quite distinctive. 'Traditional German Educational theory' and Latvian '*Pedagoģija*' are both examples of unique knowledge traditions that are not visible in other countries; and 'networked professional knowledge' is a tradition that is largely confined to England and the USA, stimulated by the growing enthusiasm for devolved educational policies. But beyond these three cases, what we learned is that most of the knowledge traditions we have identified are, to different degrees, visible in each of the seven jurisdictions we examined. The 'normal college' tradition was widespread across the world in the nineteenth and early twentieth centuries and its legacy can still be seen in subtle ways in many countries. Today, 'Disciplines of Education/*Sciences de l'Éducation*' is a tradition that is visible in all the jurisdictions and has been for many years. By contrast, the 'New Science of Education' is a relatively recent innovation; it may not have a long history, but is of growing significance globally.

At the same time as there is this strong degree of commonality, we have also learned of the profound organisational differences in different countries. For example, France has a highly fragmented institutional structure, with different specialist institutions based on different knowledge traditions. England, Australia and Latvia each have a unified institutional structure – the university – though there are subtle differences between different universities in terms of both their status and the knowledges they pursue. In the USA, China and Germany, universities are also the dominant institution, but here there are formal divisions between different types of university which help to institutionalise different conceptions of Educational knowledge. Therefore, despite the common ground across many knowledge traditions, because of these organisational differences, the experience of studying Education may in reality be decidedly different in different countries.

And what have we learned about the epistemological issues facing Education that we introduced at the beginning of this introduction? One question concerned the issue of whether the study of Education is normative or objective. Of course, from its very inception, Education was always seen, at least in part, as a 'moral' discipline, particularly in relation to teacher education. As mass education spread across the world, it was the promise of gaining control over the moral formation of the teaching profession that first encouraged the establishment of teachers' colleges and then the involvement of the universities in teacher education. What we have found interesting is the fact that some intellectual traditions are still strongly normative in their basic assumptions. This is so particularly in traditional German Educational theory and Latvian pedagogical science, but is also evident in other traditions, too. Action research/practitioner enquiry, for example, is often strongly normative in its insistence on the primacy of the practitioner in any research endeavour and in its commitment to social justice.[9] Research informed clinical practice often has a similar normative inflection as well. There are also normative elements amongst the descendants of the normal college tradition with their commitments to working in a directly practical way with their local and regional communities. What is notable to us is that this normative strand in Educational knowledge is today so rarely commented on, so rarely discussed, and where it is still in use, so rarely justified.

But the biggest issue we need to comment on concerns our question about whether knowledge traditions are based on knowledge that is close to or distant from knowledge as it circulates in Education as a field of practice. This we would suggest is perhaps *the* fundamental question in the shaping of the field, and not just in the English-speaking world where 'utility' has always had a key role.

We can gain some purchase on these differences first by returning to the work of Stokes (1997), and more particularly his discussion of Pasteur's quadrant. Rather than simply positing a distinction between scientific knowledge that is either 'pure' or 'applied', Stokes proposes a threefold distinction between 'pure basic research' (here he uses the example of Bohr, the twentieth-century atomic theorist), 'pure applied research' (Edison, the inventor, is his example here), and 'use inspired basic research', Pasteur's quadrant. Unlike either Bohr or Edison, Pasteur was interested both in solving practical problems for the wine industry in France *and* in the development of germ theory.

From our own exploration of knowledge in the study of Education it is clear that some disciplinary traditions are indeed focused on pure basic research. Many academics working in the Education 'singulars' (history of Education; psychology of Education) see themselves as making a contribution to pure basic research. Their aim is to advance the understanding of educational phenomena as an end in itself. It was the importance of the maintenance of this tradition that Whitty chose to highlight in his BERA presidential address in 2006. He characterised the distinction as between 'Education research', where social scientists study educational processes in and for their own sake, and 'Educational research', which is concerned to 'make a difference' (Whitty, 2006).

We can also identify examples of 'pure applied research'. Like Edison, for those in the action research and practitioner inquiry traditions, the first concern is to make a contribution to the advancement of educational practice rather than to science itself. One of the perennial criticisms of action research is that it is insufficiently concerned with contributing to scientific knowledge – that its findings are often highly localised and seldom cumulative.

But what of Pasteur's quadrant – 'use inspired basic research'? Are there examples of this in Education? Certainly those in the learning science tradition would hope to be characterised in this way. There is a clear aspiration both to develop practical applications for their work as well as to advance scientific understanding at the same time. But in reality this is the only example we have found. While many of those working in disciplines of Education would *claim* to be both of practical use and contributing to the academic development of their field, it is clear that this aspiration is not always delivered in practice. As we have argued, unlike at least the popular perception of engineering or medicine, in the vast majority of cases the forms of knowledge developed within these 'singulars' remain firmly located within disciplinary knowledge. As a result, the sociology of Education speaks primarily to sociologists, the history of Education mainly to historians and the philosophy of Education primarily to philosophers. At best, this means that Educational researchers can only offer 'specialised expert knowledge' to practitioners and policy makers. Unsurprising, then, that so many practitioners consider such knowledge irrelevant to their day-to-day lives. Whatever their aspirations, much of the educational knowledge produced in the Disciplines of Education tradition would seem to be more appropriately characterised as 'pure basic research' than something that Pasteur would recognise.

Stokes's (1997) re-presentation of the 'pure/applied' dichotomy does therefore take us some way in analysing knowledge traditions in Education. It is, however, insufficient in one key respect. That is that it sees disciplinary knowledge as the primary source of knowledge production. Even Edison, working on the phonograph, the motion picture or the light bulb, drew first and foremost on the scientific developments of his day. What is challenging about some of the knowledge traditions in Education today that we have identified is that they do not seem to do this – at least explicitly; their source of generation is not disciplinary knowledge but primarily the field of educational practice itself. This is particularly true of what we have called 'networked professional knowledge', but it is also true in other powerful knowledge traditions, such as competencies and standards. In order to understand these forms of knowledge production, rather than drawing on Stokes, we need to turn to Gibbons et al (1994) and their much more radical notion of Mode 2 knowledge production.

As we have already discussed, Gibbons et al's (1994) starting point is that the university and its disciplinary knowledge is increasingly challenged, increasingly de-centred. And the result, as they have powerfully described it, is a very different form of knowledge, knowledge that is less hierarchical, more transient, more context specific, and more frequently located within individuals themselves and their working context than in scientific journals. As we said earlier, this form of knowledge is what Bernstein would characterise as a 'horizontal discourse'.

Gibbons et al's (1994) task was first and foremost to try to capture this new form of knowledge that they predicted would become ever more powerful in the twenty-first century; at that stage at least they were less concerned with evaluating it. But it is clear that, however powerful it is in a sociological sense, epistemologically, Mode 2 knowledge does have significant weaknesses. The most significant of those weaknesses is that it has a problematic relationship with other forms of more formal disciplinary knowledge. For example, in the networked professional knowledge tradition in Education, it is unclear where ideas come from. Practitioners may get together to share, document and codify their experience of, for example, how to develop an effective strategy for assessment for learning (AfL), or how to develop a curriculum for digital competency (DC).[10] In that sense, they are sharing knowledge that is indeed context specific, less hierarchical and more transient; it therefore has an immediate use value. But the question remains of how practically and epistemologically that practitioner-based knowledge relates to the vast literature that already exists in relation to AfL or DC. Without clarification on this point, it is hard either to test the robustness of the knowledge that is produced, or for such knowledge to be cumulative.[11] As a contributor to an Internet discussion on Stokes's (1997) thesis put it:

> Without the Bohr quadrant, the Edison quadrant ended at the phonograph, the tube radio – arguably, the cat's whisker radio – and the movie projector. No lasers, no semiconductors, no internet. The Edisons of today would be nothing without the Bohrs of yesterday.
> (https://judithcurry.com/2013/05/15/pasteurs-quadrant/)

E. 'Powerful Professional Knowledge?'

It is precisely these issues that have been addressed in recent years by Michael Young and his various collaborators. For a number of years, Michael Young (2008) has argued that we need to 'bring knowledge back in' to education, especially in the context of the mainstream school curriculum. He uses the term 'powerful knowledge' to characterise the sort of subject-based knowledge that has, in his view, too often been hollowed out of the school curriculum in recent years, especially for disadvantaged students. In his more recent work with Muller (Young & Muller 2014), Young has extended these ideas to a discussion of the education of the professions, where, drawing on the work of Bernstein (2000), he has begun to develop a theory of what we might call 'powerful professional knowledge'.

Although he has said little directly about teacher education, his broader critique of vocational and professional education is nevertheless relevant. Young takes issue with a tendency in the past 30 years or so to move away from the idea that preparation for the professions requires initiation into received public forms of knowledge developed in the academy and towards attaching greater value to trans-disciplinary and applied knowledges developed in non-university contexts, including the workplace and the community.

Young and Muller therefore question the shift away from what Bernstein calls 'singulars' (pure disciplines) and even from 'regions' (multi- and inter-disciplinary applied fields like medicine and education) to 'generics'. Accordingly, they are critical of Gibbons et al's (1994) work on Mode 2 knowledge, and of that of Schon and others who place 'reflective practice' at the heart of professional education (Young & Muller, 2014, 2016). These they see as examples of horizontal discourses that lack the structure of disciplines and treat knowledge as infinitely pliable for different local and context-dependent purposes. Hordern (2016), who takes a similar position, even implies that they somehow constitute 'fake' knowledge that lacks the 'inherent value' of disciplinary knowledge forms (p. 367). This charge resonates with Bernstein's view that connections between the world of practice and the inherent structures of disciplined knowledge get lost in 'generic modes' (e.g. through a focus on 'core' or 'functional' skills). This, in turn, can make such knowledge open to manipulation by governments and employers and potentially destroy the identities (and autonomy) that professionals traditionally acquire through immersion in disciplinary knowledge. It thereby facilitates a shift from professional education to professional training, which may at least as well be undertaken 'on the job' as in the academy.

Yet even if the arguments for a knowledge-led approach to schooling are accepted, there is no reason why the same design principles should necessarily be applied to professional education. Furthermore, as with 'powerful knowledge' itself, there are questions about in what sense 'powerful professional knowledge' is 'powerful'. Traditionally, professional knowledge has often been merely esoteric knowledge that distinguishes its possessors from others, rather than knowledge with greater predictive power or greater practical efficacy. Professional knowledge is certainly an area where Young's earlier critique (1971) of the school curriculum as reflecting and protecting the 'knowledge of the powerful' could be applied. Beck and Young (2005) themselves mention that Talcott Parsons once described the American

Medical Association as a predatory conspiracy against society, although they also suggest that the idea of the 'inner dedication' associated with traditional models of medical education is 'more than a self-serving myth' (p. 188).

Clegg (2016), who is herself sympathetic to the social realist position of Young and Muller (and Wheelahan, 2010, 2013), suggests that their Bernsteinian roots nevertheless blind them to the importance of 'regional knowledge' in two senses – one drawn from the above Bernsteinian sense of knowledge regions, the other referring to knowledge generated outside the academy and indeed outside the 'global north'. She points to the 'contextual nature of professional practice' and, though critical of 'voice discourses' in some respects, insists that new actors and social movements beyond the academy 'can and do challenge academic knowledge' (p. 457). In the field of Education, 'networked professional knowledge' would presumably be an example of such 'new knowledges'.

In their writing, Young and Muller and their associates do therefore reassert the importance of initiation into disciplinary knowledge in professional contexts, although not necessarily to the exclusion of other knowledges. But, in our view, the key challenge in professional fields is surely to establish precisely how this disciplinary knowledge, which may indeed be epistemologically strong, articulates with other knowledge forms and how it can thereby have an impact on practice. Thus, there is a crucial pedagogical element to this. How can disciplinary knowledge and other external knowledges be brought together with professionals' reflective practice and practical theorising in professional arenas to produce really powerful professional knowledge and learning? Hence the significance of what we have termed 'integrated knowledge traditions'. At present, these seem to be relatively limited in number and their status within the academy remains questionable. Nevertheless, we would suggest, the search for the development of integrated traditions is of vital importance for the future of the field as a whole. As Maton (2014) – another thinker heavily influenced by Bernstein, but more inclined than Young and Muller to move beyond his attachment to disciplinary knowledge forms – puts it, powerful knowledge 'comprises not one kind of knowledge but rather mastery of how different knowledges are brought together and changed' through what he terms 'semantic waving and weaving' (Maton, 2014, p. 181).

In conclusion, perhaps the most significant thing that we have identified in this survey is the very diversity of different traditions that make up Education as a discipline. Education as a field of study does face serious challenges as it tries to respond to the ever-increasing demands made on it in the increasingly globalised, competitive world of school and university systems. But despite those challenges, real though they are, what we have come to recognise is the huge intellectual resources enshrined in the different traditions we have identified. By rendering those different traditions visible, our hope is that those with a commitment to the study of Education, from whatever perspective, will be better able to contribute to the debate about the future of this vitally important area of scholarship.

Acknowledgements

We would like to thank Jim Hordern, Susan Groundwater-Smith, Nicole Mockler and Emma Wisby for their helpful comments on earlier versions of this introduction.

Notes

[1] In this introduction, we capitalise the term Education/al where appropriate to indicate that we are discussing the nature of knowledge within the field of Education, rather than the nature of all the educational knowledge that is transmitted by schools, colleges and universities. This distinction is not consistently adopted in the other chapters in this volume.

[2] For an extensive discussion of Education in the UK, see Furlong (2013).

[3] Hirst eventually came to take a very different view with the development of his concept of 'practical theories' (see Hirst 1996), where practical knowledge is tested against 'the best that is known' from theory and research.

[4] The 2014 UK research assessment process (HEFCE, 2014) reported that in Education, the quality of research drawn from 'the theoretical disciplines' was more consistently of higher quality than the much larger quantity of research that was sector based (e.g. early years, teacher education) or issue based (e.g. children and young people, inclusion and special education).

[5] This was a common academic criticism of the early approach of the Education Endowment Foundation (EEF) in England and Social Ventures Australia (SVA), but a more nuanced approach is evident in their more recent work (e.g. Collins & Coleman, 2017).

[6] It might be argued that some 'critical' perspectives (critical pedagogy, critical scholarship, etc.) as well as 'activity theory', all of which have their roots in various forms of Marxist thought, are also examples of integrated knowledge traditions; they are conceptualised in ways that are explicitly intended to 'make a difference' by encouraging practitioners themselves to draw on disciplinary knowledge as a basis for practical interventions. While we would accept this claim, and while we noted examples of lively academic networks supporting these traditions, we found little evidence in the seven countries we considered that these knowledge traditions were at present strongly institutionalised (through, for example, established chairs, qualifications, or national regulatory frameworks) across the country as a whole as opposed to in particular institutions. It may be that in other countries (particularly in Europe) they have become more established.

[7] http://www.tandfonline.com/action/journalInformation?show=aimsScope&journalCode=hlns20#.V6RTtDVJjIU

[8] Interestingly, Arthur Levine, former president of Teachers College, Columbia University and subsequently an outspoken critic of conventional approaches to teacher preparation in the USA, now has a project at MIT which seeks to apply such an approach to the design and implementation of teacher education itself (Sanchez, 2015).

[9] Some of the less institutionalised traditions we have not discussed in detail, particularly 'critical' perspectives and activity theory, are also strongly normative.

[10] Both of these are examples of work that is currently being undertaken by 'pioneer schools' in Wales as part of the Welsh government's strategy for developing a new vision for curriculum and assessment in Wales.

[11] While this is a general issue for horizontal discourses, it is also an issue in some vertical discourses, especially those that, in Bernstein's terms, have 'horizontal' as opposed to 'hierarchical' knowledge structures. Some singulars within Education, including sociology of Education, have horizontal knowledge structures and therefore substantial incommensurability between different traditions (see Bernstein, 2000, chapter 9).

References

Beck, J. & Young, M. (2005) The Assault on the Professions and the Restructuring of Academic and Professional Identities: a Bernsteinian analysis, *British Journal of Sociology of Education*, 26(2), 183-197. https://doi.org/10.1080/0142569042000294165

Bell, A. (1981) Structure, Knowledge and Relationships in Teacher Education, *British Journal of Sociology of Education*, 2 (1), 3-23. https://doi.org/10.1080/0142569810020101

Bernstein, B. (1999) Vertical and Horizontal Discourse: an essay, *British Journal of Sociology of Education*, 20(2), 157-173. https://doi.org/10.1080/01425699995380

Bernstein, B. (2000) *Pedagogy, Symbolic Control and Identity*, rev. edn. New York: Rowman & Littlefield.

Biesta, G. (2011) Disciplines and Theory in the Academic Study of Education: a comparative analysis of the Anglo-American and continental construction of the field, *Pedagogy, Culture & Society*, 19(2), 175-192. https://doi.org/10.1080/14681366.2011.582255

Bridges, D. (2006) The Disciplines and Discipline of Educational Research, *Journal of Philosophy of Education*, 40(2), 259-272. https://doi.org/10.1111/j.1467-9752.2006.00503.x

Bunt, L. & Harris, M. (2010) *Mass Localism: a way to help small communities solve big social challenges*. London: NESTA. https://www.nesta.org.uk/sites/default/files/mass_localism.pdf

Burn, K. & Mutton, T. (2015) A Review of 'Research-informed Clinical Practice' in Initial Teacher Education, *Oxford Review of Education*, 41(2), 217-233. https://doi.org/10.1080/03054985.2015.1020104

Burton, D. & Goodman, R. (2011) The Masters in Teaching and Learning: a revolution in teacher education or a bright light quickly extinguished?, *Journal of*

Education for Teaching, 37(1), 51-56. https://doi.org/10.1080/02607476.2011.538271

Carnegie Corporation of New York (2001) Teachers for a New Era: transforming teacher education. http://carnegie.org/fileadmin/Media/Publications/PDF/Carnegie.pdf

Carr, W. (2007) Educational Research in the 21st Century: confronting the postmodern challenge. Unpublished paper.

Carr, W. & Kemmis, S. (1986) *Becoming Critical: education, knowledge and action research*. London: Falmer Press.

Christie, D. (2006) The Standard for Chartered Teachers in Scotland: a new context for the assessment and professional development of teachers, *Studies in Educational Evaluation*, 32, 53-72. https://doi.org/10.1016/j.stueduc.2006.01.001

Clegg, S. (2016) The Necessity and Possibility of Powerful 'Regional' Knowledge: curriculum change and renewal, *Teaching in Higher Education*, 21(4), 457-470. https://doi.org/10.1080/13562517.2016.1157064

Cochran-Smith, M. & Lytle, S. (2009) *Inquiry as Stance: practitioner research in the next generation*. New York: Teachers College Press.

Collins, K. & Coleman, R. (2017) Evidence-informed Policy and Practice, in P. Earley & T. Greany (Eds) *School Leadership and Education System Reform*. London: Bloomsbury.

Conroy, J., Hulme, M. & Menter, I. (2013) Developing a 'Clinical' Model for Teacher Education, *Journal of Education for Teaching*, 39, 557-573. https://doi.org/10.1080/02607476.2013.836339

Crossley, M. & Watson, K. (2009) Comparative and International Education: policy transfer, context sensitivity and professional development, *Oxford Review of Education*, 35(5), 633-649. https://doi.org/10.1080/03054980903216341

Darling-Hammond, L. (2006a). Constructing 21st-century Teacher Education, *Journal of Teacher Education*, 57(3), 300-314. https://doi.org/10.1177/0022487105285962

Darling-Hammond (2006b) *Powerful Teacher Education: lessons from exemplary programs*. San Francisco: Jossey-Bass.

Darling-Hammond, L. (2010) Teacher Education and the American Future, *Journal of Teacher Education*, 61(1-2), 35-47.

Delanty, G. (2001) The University in the Knowledge Society, *Organization*, 8(2), 149-153. https://doi.org/10.1177/1350508401082002

Department for Education (DfE) (2010) *The Importance of Teaching*. White Paper. London: DfE.

Elliott, J. (1985) Educational Action Research, in J. Nisbet & S. Nisbet (Eds) *Research Policy and Practice*. London: Kogan Page.

Ertl, H., Zierer, K., Phillips, D. & Tippelt, R. (2015) Disciplinary Traditions and the Dissemination of Knowledge: an international comparison of publication patterns in journals of education, *Oxford Review of Education*, 41(1), 64-88. https://doi.org/10.1080/03054985.2014.1001350

Fullan, M. (2005) Professional Learning Communities Writ Large, in R. Dufour, R. Eaker & R. Dufour (Eds) *On Common Ground*, pp. 209-223. Bloomington, IN: National Education Service.

Fullan, M.G. & Miles, M.B. (1992) Getting Reform Right: what works and what doesn't, *Phi Delta Kappan*, 73, 745-752.

Furlong, J. (2011) The English Masters in Teaching and Learning: a new arena for practitioner inquiry?, in N. Mockler & J. Sachs (Eds) *Completing the Circle: practitioner inquiry for and with teachers and students. A Festschrift in Honour of Susan Groundwater-Smith*. New York: Springer. https://doi.org/10.1007/978-94-007-0805-1_8

Furlong, J. (2013) *Education – an Anatomy of the Discipline: rescuing the university project?* London: Routledge.

Gibbons, M., Limoges, C. & Nowotny, H. (1994) *The New Production of Knowledge: the dynamics of science and research in contemporary societies*. London: SAGE.

Goldacre, B. (2013) *Building Evidence in Education*. London: Department for Education. http://media.education.gov.uk/assets/files/pdf/b/ben%20goldacre%20paper.pdf

Gore, J.M. (2016) Reform and the Reconceptualisation of Teacher Education in Australia, in R. Brandenburg, S. McDonough, J. Burke & S. White (Eds) *Teacher Education: innovations, interventions and impact*, pp. 15-34. Singapore: Springer.

Greany, T. (2014) *Are We Nearly There Yet? Progress, Issues and Possible Next Steps for a Self-improving School System*. London: Institute of Education.

Groothoff, H.-H. (1973) Theorie der Erziehung, in H.-H. Groothoff (Ed.) *Pädagogik*. Frankfurt: Fischer Taschenbuch Verlag.

Groundwater-Smith, S. & Mockler, N. (2009) *Teacher Professional Learning in an Age of Compliance: mind the gap*. Rotterdam: Springer.

Groundwater-Smith, S. & Mockler, N. (2017) The Study of Education in Australia: shifting knowledge interests, in G. Whitty & J. Furlong (Eds) *Knowledge and the Study of Education: an international exploration*. Oxford: Symposium Books. https://doi.org/10.15730/books.100

Groundwater-Smith, S. & Sachs, J. (2002) The Activist Professional and the Reinstatement of Trust, *Cambridge Journal of Education*, 32(3), 341-358. https://doi.org/10.1080/0305764022000024195

Hagger, H. & McIntyre, D. (2006) *Learning Teaching from Teachers: realising the potential of school-based teacher education*. Buckingham: Open University Press.

Hammerness, K. (2006) From Coherence in Theory to Coherence in Practice, *Teachers College Record*, 108, 1241-1265. https://doi.org/10.1111/j.1467-9620.2006.00692.x

Hargreaves, D.H. (1999) The Knowledge Creating School, *British Journal of Educational Studies*, 47(2), 122-144. https://doi.org/10.1111/1467-8527.00107

Hargreaves, D.H. (2003) *Education Epidemic: transforming secondary schools through innovation networks*. London: DEMOS.

Hargreaves, D.H. (2011) *Leading a Self-improving School System*. Nottingham: National College for School Leadership.

Hayhoe, R. & Li, J. (2010) The Idea of a Normal University in the 21st Century, *Frontiers of Education in China*, 5(1), 74-103. https://doi.org/10.1007/s11516-010-0007-0

Higher Education Funding Council for England (HEFCE) (2014) Research Excellent Framework 2014: overview report by Main Panel C and sub-panels 16 to 26. http://www.ref.ac.uk/media/ref/content/expanel/member/Main%20Panel%20C%20overview%20report.pdf

Hirst, P. (1966) Educational Theory, in J.W. Tibble (Ed.) *The Study of Education*. London: Routledge & Kegan Paul.

Hirst, P. (1996) The Demands of Professional Practice and Preparation for Teachers, in J. Furlong & R. Smith (Eds) *The Role of Higher Education in Initial Teacher Training*. London: Kogan Page.

Hodgkinson, H.L. (1957) Action Research: a critique, *Journal of Educational Sociology*, 33, 137-153. https://doi.org/10.2307/2264741

Hordern, J. (2014) Regions and their Relations: sustaining authoritative professional knowledge, *Journal of Education and Work*, 29(4), 427-449. https://doi.org/10.1080/13639080.2014.958653

Hordern, J. (2016) On the Making and Faking of Knowledge Value in Higher Education Curricula, *Teaching in Higher Education*, 21(4), 367-380. https://doi.org/10.1080/13562517.2016.1155546

Hordern, J. (2017) Bernstein's Sociology of Knowledge and Education(al) Studies, in G. Whitty & J. Furlong (Eds) *Knowledge and the Study of Education: an international exploration*. Oxford: Symposium Books. https://doi.org/10.15730/books.100

International Society for Learning Sciences (2009) ISLS Vision Statement. https://www.isls.org/images/documents/ISLS_Vision_2009.pdf

Jackson, D. (2002) *The Creation of Knowledge Networks: collaborative enquiry for school and system improvement*. London: National College of School Leadership. http://www.innovationunit.org/sites/default/files/Creation of knowledge networks.pdf

Judge, H. (1982) *American Graduate Schools of Education: a view from abroad*. New York: Ford Foundation.

Judge, H. (1990) The Education of Teachers in England and Wales, in E. Gumbert (Ed.) *Fit to Teach: teacher education in international perspective*, pp. 7-28. Atlanta: Georgia State University Press.

Judge, H., Lemosse, M., Paine, L. & Sedlak, M. (1994) *The University and the Teachers: France, the United States, England*. Oxford: Symposium Books. https://doi.org/10.15730/books.31

Keiner, K. (2010) Disciplines of Education: the value of disciplinary observation, in J. Furlong & M. Lawn (Eds) *The Disciplines of Education: their role in the future of education research*. London: Routledge.

Kriewaldt, J. & Turnidge, D. (2013). Conceptualising an Approach to Clinical Reasoning in the Education Profession, *Australian Journal of Teacher Education*, 38, 103-115. https://doi.org/10.14221/ajte.2013v38n6.9

Kuhlee, D. & Winch, C. (2017) Teachers' Knowledge in England and Germany: the conceptual background, in G. Whitty & J. Furlong (Eds) *Knowledge and the Study of Education: an international exploration*. Oxford: Symposium Books. https://doi.org/10.15730/books.100

Labaree, D. (2004) *The Trouble with Ed Schools*. New Haven, CT: Yale University Press.

Lawn, M. & Furlong, J. (2009) The Disciplines of Education in the UK: between the ghost and the shadow, *Oxford Review of Education*, 35(5), 541-552. https://doi.org/10.1080/03054980903216283

Lewin, K. (1948) *Resolving Social Conflicts*. New York: Harper & Row.

Lingard, B. & Gale, T. (2010) Defining Educational Research: a perspective of/on presidential addresses and the Australian association for research in education, *Australian Educational Researcher* 37, 21-49. https://doi.org/10.1007/BF03216912

Livingston, K. & Shiach, L. (2010) Co-constructing a New Model of Teacher Education, in A. Campbell & S. Groundwater-Smith (Eds) *Connecting Inquiry and Professional Learning in Education: international perspectives and practical solutions*. London: Routledge.

Malet, R. (2017) From Science to Sciences de l'Éducation in France. Past and Present in the Construction of a Discipline, in G. Whitty & J. Furlong (Eds) *Knowledge and the Study of Education: an international exploration*. Oxford: Symposium Books. https://doi.org/10.15730/books.100

Maton, K. (2014) Building Powerful Knowledge: the significance of semantic waves, in B. Barrett & E. Rata (Eds) *Knowledge and the Future of the Curriculum*, pp. 181-197. London: Palgrave Macmillan.

Mattsson, M., Eilertson, T. & Rorrison, D. (Eds) (2011) *A Practicum Turn in Teacher Education*. Rotterdam: Sense.

McCulloch, G. (2017) Education – an Applied Multi-disciplinary Field? The English Experience, in G. Whitty & J. Furlong (Eds) *Knowledge and the Study of Education: an international exploration*. Oxford: Symposium Books. https://doi.org/10.15730/books.100

Mourshed, M., Chijioke, C. & Barber, M. (2007) How the World's Best Performing School Systems Come Out on Top. McKinsey and Company. http://www.mckinsey.com/clientservice/socialsector/resources/pdf/Worlds_School_Systems_Final.pdf

Newman, J. (1853) Newman Reader – Idea of a University Discourse 7. Knowledge Viewed in Relation to Professional Skill. www.newmanreader.org/works/idea/discourse7.html

Nisbet, J. (1974) Educational Research: the state of the art. Inaugural Presidential Address, BERA Conference, Birmingham. https://www.bera.ac.uk/researchers-resources/publications/1974-john-nisbet-bera-presidential-address

Nowotny, H., Scott, P. & Gibbons, M. (2001) *Re-thinking Science: knowledge and the public in an age of uncertainty*. London: Polity Press.

Nowotny, H., Scott, P. & Gibbons, M. (2003) 'Mode 2' Revisited: the new production of knowledge, *Minerva*, 41(3), 179-194. https://doi.org/10.1023/A:1025505528250

Paine, L. (2017) Framing Education: cautionary tales from the USA of the relationship between education studies and teacher education, in G. Whitty & J. Furlong (Eds) *Knowledge and the Study of Education: an international exploration*. Oxford: Symposium Books. https://doi.org/10.15730/books.100

Peters, R.S. (1964) *Education as Initiation*, in R.D. Archambault (Ed.) *Philosophical Analysis and Education*, pp. 87-111. London: Routledge & Kegan Paul.

Higher Education Funding Council for England (HEFCE) (2014) Research Excellent Framework 2014: overview report by Main Panel C and sub-panels 16 to 26. http://www.ref.ac.uk/media/ref/content/expanel/member/Main%20Panel%20C%20overview%20report.pdf

Ryle, G. (1949) *The Concept of Mind*. Chicago: University of Chicago Press.

Sahlberg, P. (2015) Manifestations of the Global Educational Reform Movement, in S. Jokila, J. Kallo & Rinne, R. (Eds) *Comparing Times and Spaces*. Jvaskyla, Finland: Finnish Educational Research Association.

Sanchez, C. (2015) A Vision for Teacher Training at MIT: West Point meets Bell Labs. National Public Radio, Morning Edition, 17 June. http://www.npr.org/sections/ed/2015/06/17/414980239/a-vision-for-teacher-training-at-mit-west-point-meets-bell-labs

Schriewer, J. (2017) Between the Philosophy of Self-cultivation and Empirical Research: educational studies in Germany, in G. Whitty & J. Furlong (Eds) *Knowledge and the Study of Education: an international exploration*. Oxford: Symposium Books. https://doi.org/10.15730/books.100

Schriewer, J. & Keiner, E. (1992) Communication Patterns and Intellectual Traditions in Educational Sciences: France and Germany, *Comparative Education Review* 36(1), 25-51. https://doi.org/10.1086/447080

Stenhouse, L. (1981) What Counts as Educational Research?, *British Journal of Educational Studies*, 29, 103-114. https://doi.org/10.1080/00071005.1981.9973589

Stokes, D.E. (1997) *Pasteur's Quadrant: basic science and technological innovation*. Washington, DC: Brookings Institution Press.

Tatto, M.T. & Hordern, J. (2017) The Configuration of Teacher Education as a Professional Field of Practice: comparative study of mathematics education, in G. Whitty & J. Furlong (Eds) *Knowledge and the Study of Education: an international exploration*. Oxford: Symposium Books. https://doi.org/10.15730/books.100

Terhart, E. (2016) Review of John Furlong: *Education – an Anatomy of the discipline: rescuing the university project*, *Journal of Education for Teaching*, 40(5), 633-688.

Tibble, J.W. (1966) (Ed.) *The Study of Education*. London: Routledge & Kegan Paul.

van Zanten, A. (2009) From Critical Intellectuals to 'Idea Brokers'? Traditions and New Development of Links between Research and Policy-making in Education in France, *Nordisk Pedagogik*, 29(1), 53-60.

Wallace, M. (1987) A Historical Review of Action Research: some implications for the education of teachers in their managerial role, *Journal of Education for Teaching*, 13(2), 97-115. https://doi.org/10.1080/0260747870130201

Wen, W. & Xie, W. (2017) The Development and Characteristics of Educational Studies in China, in G. Whitty & J. Furlong (Eds) *Knowledge and the Study of Education: an international exploration*. Oxford: Symposium Books. https://doi.org/10.15730/books.100

Wheelahan, L. (2010) *Why Knowledge Matters in Curriculum: a social realist argument*. London: Routledge.

Wheelahan, L. (2013) Babies and Bathwater: revaluing the role of the academy in knowledge, in R. Barnett & P. Gibbs (Eds) *Thinking about Higher Education*, pp.125-138. New York: Springer.

Whitehead, J. & McNiff, J. (2004) Ontological, Epistemological and Methodological Commitments in Practitioner-research. Paper presented at the BERA 04 Symposium, 'Have We Created a New Epistemology for the New Scholarship of Educational Enquiry through Practitioner Research? Developing Sustainable Global Educational Networks of Communication', 17 September, Manchester.

Whitty, G. (1991) Next in Line for the Treatment? Education Reform and Teacher Education in the 1990s. Inaugural lecture, Goldsmiths, University of London, 14 May.

Whitty, G. (2006) Education(al) Research and Education Policy Making: is conflict inevitable?, *British Educational Research Journal*, 32(2), 159-176. https://doi.org/10.1080/01411920600568919

Whitty, G. (2016) *Research and Policy in Education: evidence, ideology and impact*. London: UCL IOE Press.

Whitty, G. & Willmott, E. (1991) Competence-based Teacher Education: approaches and issues, *Cambridge Journal of Education*, 21(3), 309-318. https://doi.org/10.1080/0305764910210305

Young, M. (Ed.) (1971) *Knowledge and Control: new directions for the sociology of education*. London: Collier-Macmillan.

Young, M. (2008) *Bringing Knowledge Back In: from social constructivism to social realism in the sociology of education*. London: Routledge.

Young, M. & Muller, J. (Eds) (2014) *Knowledge, Expertise and the Professions*. London: Routledge.

Young, M. and Muller, J. (2016) *Curriculum and the Specialisation of Knowledge*. London: Routledge.

Zogla, I. (2017) Pedagoģija and Educational Sciences: competing traditions in the study of education in Latvia, in G. Whitty & J. Furlong (Eds) *Knowledge and the Study of Education: an international exploration*. Oxford: Symposium Books. https://doi.org/10.15730/books.100

Part 2. Studies from Six Jurisdictions

CHAPTER 2

From Science to *Sciences de l'Éducation* in France: past and present in the construction of a discipline

RÉGIS MALET

SUMMARY The focus of this chapter is the history of the development and institutionalisation of the Sciences de l'Education in France. From its birth as a discipline, Sciences de l'Education has been subject to many different pressures: social demands, political injunctions, tensions with nearby disciplines, as well as the internal imperatives of scientific structuring. As such, Sciences de l'Education in France can serve as an 'observatory' of the tensions experienced within every human and social science. Although the international approach proposed in this book demonstrates many similarities between Sciences de l'Education and developments in other countries, it is argued that the particular context in which the discipline emerged in France has been quite distinctive. In particular, the discipline's relative distance from teacher education, from which it emerged at the turn of the nineteenth century but from which it then successfully distanced itself, means that today the institutionalisation of the discipline is quite different from that of many other countries in the world.

Introduction

As Blanckaert (2006, p. 48) noted in a contribution on the history of academic disciplines, the 'disciplinary world' is very recent. Numerous studies, such as Stichweh (1984, 1994), show that this model of the production, organisation and dissemination of scientific knowledge was only established very gradually during the nineteenth century. In the crossroads of powerful social, political, professional, cultural and economic demands, internal differentiations in the fields of knowledge took place, generating a specialisation both among institutions, knowledges and scholars. It is on this basis that disciplinary specialisations grew on different levels:

- institutional anchoring (disciplines, university chairs and academic positions, curricula);
- structuration of the production of scientific knowledge (corporations and disciplinary communities of research, epistemological and methodological foundation and renewal);
- organisation of the dissemination of knowledge and education (researchers' associations, congresses, seminaries, scientific journals, doctoral schools and research centres).

This process of institutionalisation concerned the 'hard sciences' but also the 'soft sciences' – the human and social sciences – throughout the nineteenth century. This process of institutionalisation through specialisation suggests a process of 'disciplinarisation' (Hofstetter & Schneuwly, 2014). According to Blanckaert (2006, p. 148), Durkheim was the first, in 1890, to use the term 'discipline' to indicate these new domains of scientific research (Favre, 1985; Becher, 1989; Bourdieu, 2001; Weingart, 2001; Hofstetter & Schnewly, 2004).

Disciplinarisation is never a completed process; it is one moment of structuring the scientific field, which remains very dynamic and uncertain in its evolution (Malet, 2005). It has been and remains subject to all sorts of powerful external pressures, connected in particular with the sociocultural, economic and political contexts, and with every discipline established with regard to the others, even against the others in a movement of ceaseless reconfiguration, including, in essence, 'interdisciplinarity' (Charle et al, 2004; Fabiani, 2006). This characteristic is particularly sensitive in the case of the *sciences de l'éducation*, and perhaps in France more than anywhere else.

The Slow 'Disciplinarisation' of Education: the positivist movement of the science of education

The case for education to be recognised as a scientific field of knowledge was made long before the nineteenth century. From the beginning of the seventeenth century, Comenius (1592-1670) had already evoked the necessity of an 'experimental pedagogy'. Two centuries later, succeeding Kant in the Chair of Philosophy and Pedagogy at the University of Königsberg, Herbart (1776-1841) formulated the same ambition when he set out to promote an 'experimental school' affiliated to the university.

In France, the expression '*science de l'éducation*' appears in 1816 in Marc-Antoine Jullien de Paris's book *Esquisse sur l'éducation comparée*. The author intended to collect systematically information on the state of education in various countries of Europe – to produce 'collections of facts and observations, tidied up in analytical boards, in order to compare them, and then to deduct from this study principles and determined rules, so that education becomes a science more or less positive'.

Nearly half a century later, Cournot sought to elevate pedagogy to the rank of the experimental disciplines. This he set out in his 1851 contribution, *Essai sur les fondements de nos connaissances*. A similar ambition can be seen in Compayré's work, which refers to the legitimacy of establishing a science of education based in the psychology of the child. In his *Histoire critique des doctrines de l'éducation* (1879), Compayré pleads for the constitution of a 'scientific pedagogy' and a 'science of education' that derived from the moral sciences and from psychology.

A few years later, in 1883, the 'science of education' made its entry into faculties of arts. The first complementary courses in the 'science of education' opened in Lyon, Bordeaux and Paris. The course at the Sorbonne grew into a Chair in 1887, and Henri Marion became the first Professor of the Science of Education in France. Ferdinand Buisson succeeded him in 1896, Émile Durkheim in 1902. Altogether, fifteen courses in the science of education were created in faculties of arts between 1883 and 1914 and almost all of the professors in charge of these were philosophers. Certain faculties delivered these courses continuously until 1914: in Bordeaux, in Paris-Sorbonne and in Lyon.

But this happened just after new laws established free, *laïc* ('non-religious') and compulsory education, supported by the influential *Ecole Normale d'Instituteurs* (primary teachers' training colleges). This was not a coincidence, and the birth of the science of education, just like its later development as the 'sciences of education', was very much related to the role of the State in the provision of schooling and teaching in France.

Consequently, the objective of the first courses in the science of education was explicitly defined by the administration of State education: it was a question of addressing the 'professional education' of future secondary teachers. Later, these courses were supposed to cater for both primary and secondary teachers, with the intention of acculturating them into the very republican '*morale laïque*' project.

It is important to note that the relationship between the administration and the teaching profession was not harmonious. The actors in the primary school system – teachers, teacher trainers, inspectors, directors of the *Ecoles normales* founded after 1830 – thought that the professional training of future teachers should take place in the institutions where pedagogy had already been introduced in the 1850s, prior to the creation of a 'science of education' in universities. By contrast, secondary teachers and inspectors – as well as most university professors – felt that academic training in the disciplines and the competitive *agregation* examination for secondary education, created in 1808, were enough to guarantee the quality of secondary school teachers (Gautherin, 2002).

Thus, the science of education in the university responded to a number of ambitions: scientific, moral and political. They mobilised new knowledges, from psychology or sociology, and this combined with the political and ideological goal – Republicans trying to legitimise their political objectivies through university efforts to promote the *morale laïque* and national cohesion (Gautherin, 2002; Hofstetter & Schneuwly, 2002).

As a consequence of these features, the academic and institutional status of the science of education within the university was weakened. This was because:

- its goal was not to construct, apply and transmit scientific theories to inform and improve educational practice, but to develop social cohesion and political allegiance through the diffusion of a '*morale laïque*'. The teaching was mostly philosophical and abstract with some psychological and sociological dimensions, provided mostly by philosophy professors;
- it was the result of direct state intervention and not of the initiative or demand of university faculties that only accepted it both because of strong state pressures and because it brought them new financial resources. It was not conceived as a traditional discipline but as a '*cours complémentaire magistral*' together with a 'practical conference'. It had a mixed non-academic audience composed both of future primary school teachers (and later secondary school teachers) as well as of high-society women and girls (Gautherin, 2002).

In his inaugural science of education lesson at the Sorbonne, Henri Marion (1883) set out very clearly the ambition to develop the 'bases of a rational culture for the universality of the people', assuming the moral and political dimension of its purpose. Eventually, the consolidation of the nation-states at the end of the nineteenth century cemented the role of education within the process of modernising the state (Popkewitz, 1996). Schools and teachers had a central role to play in this unification of national identity. As Pierre Bourdieu put it: 'it is through schooling, with the generalization of the elementary education throughout the nineteenth century, that the unifying action of the State develops on the matter of culture, which is the fundamental element of the construction of the nation state' (Bourdieu, 1994, p. 115).

The Advent of a *Science de l'Éducation*: at the crossroads of social change projects and scientific affirmation

From the end of the nineteenth century to the start of World War I, the development of education as a discipline was observable in a scientific and a political sense. In France, Binet was one of the leaders in this early development. His experimental research was one of the precursors of scientific research in the field of education, in three main domains: curriculum, teaching methods, and children's capacities (1898). At the same time, Émile Durkheim established the study of complex dynamics of education and schooling from a historical sociological perspective.

Thanks to the rise of new scientific disciplines such as psychology and sociology, advocating the necessity for and the possibility of scientific approaches to analysing individual and social phenomena (Blanckaert et al, 1999), researchers interested in child development and education acquired a new scientific legitimacy. This new field gradually shaped itself around different disciplinary canons, allowing specialisation, differentiation, and eventually professionalisation of the educational research field. Thus the *sciences de l'éducation* built up in France in relation to professional fields and around a set of disciplines, akin to what Hofstetter and Schneuwly (2014) identify as 'secondary disciplinarisation'.

In France, from the beginning of the nineteenth century, the influence of the emerging social sciences, in particular in psychology and sociology, was key to the theoretical, ideological and institutional developments that gave rise to the brand-new Chairs of *Science de l'Éducation* between 1883 and 1914 (Compayré, Durkheim, Dumesnil, Fauconnet, Marion). These were also strongly marked by philosophy, producing in the process an educational vision of society (Charle, 1990).

The link with teachers' education was also decisive in the construction of a science of education, combining the objectives of social change and ambitions of scientific affirmation. With the extension of the education system and the construction of the *Etat-enseignant* at the turn of the century, the professional associations of education and teaching grew in number and specialisation (Nóvoa, 1987; Gautherin, 2002; Hofstetter, 2010; Hofstetter & Schneuwly, 2014; Wentzel et al, 2015). The consolidation of the education system itself came along with a growing demand for teachers' professional training, which generated the need for academic institutions mandated to provide the training and certification. In this regard, the demand for the professionalisation of teachers had a major impact on the 'disciplinarisation' of education (Nóvoa, 1987).

Later on, these various influences on the science of education grew into a desire for a new era, built through the application of scientific principles and the growing aspiration to educate a 'new man' (Hameline et al, 1995). This was particularly pronounced following World War II. It was reflected in the title of the first research journal of the science of education, *Pour l'ère nouvelle* (i.e. For the new era), which was created in 1922 (and later became *Les sciences de l'éducation – Pour l'ère nouvelle*).

From *Science de l'Éducation* to *Sciences de l'Éducation*: a process of recognition and universitarisation starting after the Liberation

At the moment of the Liberation, as France began to rebuild its economy, its political system and social cohesion, the question of education reform rose to the fore; the reform commission of schooling and teaching (*Commission de réforme de l'enseignement*), created in 1945, gave rise to the famous Langevin-

Wallon project, which established the foundations of a new education system. The educational movements of *Education Nouvelle* multiplied alongside (Freinet, Cousinet, CEMEA, GFEN). Yet, concerns remain about problems of organisation, innovation and adaptation of the Department of Education to French societal renewal and growing civilisation.

Research on education was reinvigorated, mainly through 'experimental pedagogy' projects in the fashion of Binet's research. Human and social sciences had already benefited from a new prestige after World War II. After the war, there was also a rapid development and transformation of universities. Psychology was introduced as a formal discipline in 1947 and sociology in 1958, and that same year Faculties of Letters became Faculties of Letters and Human Sciences. It was not though until the late 1960s that the 'new' discipline – the sciences of education – was promoted within French universities. The institutionalisation of the human and social sciences had been encouraged through the creation of the *Centre national de la recherche scientifique* (CNRS) in 1939, but the CNRS did not consider education to be a discipline at that stage.

The 'experimental pedagogy' projects that flourished throughout the 1950s, and the various conferences that followed them, contributed to the progressive structuring of the sciences of education. The congresses of Caen (in 1956 and 1966) pushed for the development of educational research; the congress of Amiens (1968), entitled 'For a New School, Teacher Education and Research in Education', was also decisive (Hofstetter & Schneuwly, 2004, 2014). The creation of associations was another way to strengthen the legitimacy of the field and its unity in order to defend its interests.

The sciences of education were formally introduced into universities as an autonomous discipline in 1967, through the creation of a '*maîtrise*' degree, first opened at the universities of Bordeaux, Caen and Paris-Sorbonne, driven by three key academic figures in the discipline – Debesse, Mialaret and Château.

While specialists from different disciplines as well as specialists in pedagogy co-existed within these new faculties – which became, after 1968, *Unités d'enseignement et de recherche* (UER) and later *Unités de formation et de recherche* (UFR) – research on education was still conducted within research centres that remained strongly discipline-oriented. This included the *Institut de Recherche d'Economie de l'Education* (IREDU), created in 1971, and the *Laboratoire de Sociologie de l'Education* at Paris V University, created in 1972 and linked to the CNRS (Laot & Rogers, 2015).

Other significant developments included the creation of the *Institut pédagogique national* (IPN) in 1956, which later became the *Institut national de recherche pédagogique* (INRP) and, more recently, the *Institut Français d'Education* (IFE). The purpose of the IPN was to inform policy and practice in the educational system, through documentation, experimentation, innovation and research. This institution never became a place for the coordination of educational research as was at some point envisaged, but it had other important impacts on the discipline of education:

- contributing to the assimilation of the profile of educational researchers as researchers close to policy-makers or to practitioners;
- drawing educational resources for research away from universities;
- becoming a major place for research dissemination through the publication of major generalist and specialised journals in education, such as: *Revue française de pédagogie, Repères, Histoire de l'éducation, Recherche en didadictique des sciences et des technologies, Recherche et formation* and *Education et societies.*

At the Crossroads of the Human and Social Sciences and Education Practices

At the point of the institutionalisation of the 'sciences of education' in the university, pedagogy was very much the responsibility of the *Ecoles normales*, through what was called *psychopedagogy*; in the university, which educated the secondary teachers, these educational questions were marginal compared with disciplinary knowledge. The organisation of the sciences of education in the university was thus led in parallel with – and not in co-ordination with – primary teacher education in the *Ecole normale*.

The pursuit of scientific status meant that the discipline was at once connected to educational practice but also distant from it and from professional schools for teachers. Mialaret, one of the eminent founders of the discipline, recalled that the research community rejected the term *Bachelor of Pedagogy* in preference for the concept of *Bachelor of Sciences of Education* (Mialaret, 2006). This identification marked a strong distinction from teacher preparation and the identification of the discipline around teacher preparation – focusing instead on the pursuit of an autonomous academic field based on scientific research.

The sciences of education were inspired first and foremost by psychology, sociology, history, economics and philosophy. Every founder member and promoter of the discipline came from one or other of these disciplines.

The sciences of education shaped their research around plural approaches, by mobilising different disciplines. They proceeded to build up original spaces of scientific research on education, not reducible to the other foundation disciplines: analysis of teaching practices, evaluation and assessment, didactics, comparative and global education. Even if their epistemological and methodological unity remained fragile for some (Vigarello, 1994) (though one could apply this to other plural disciplines, such as psychology or anthropology), the sciences of education developed specific modes of research, and influenced other social sciences, doing so also by the construction of specific objects, in particular praxeological ones. It is very much this internal plurality that is asserted so positively by the plural in 'sciences of education'.

A strong characteristic of the sciences of education has also been the simultaneously strong connection with practice and distance from it through the epistemological and methodological tools of scientific reflexivity (Hatano-Chalvidan, 2008). In this way, professional practice feeds, stimulates and benefits from research in the sciences of education: practitioners are at the same time the partners, the sponsors, the users and the objects of the research. This specific configuration results in an organisation and an orientation of educational research that articulates, according to Hatano-Chalvidan (2008), professional practice as well as academic and disciplinary knowledges.

Contemporary Issues

Segmentation and Competition between Disciplines

Originally constituted by a juxtaposition of objects and approaches, the sciences of education won their autonomy as an academically coherent field by becoming emancipated from canonic disciplines (in particular philosophy, psychology and sociology), while protecting their plural identities and their internal diversity in the process. The advent and development of this disciplinary field was thus closely implicated in the evolution of the other human and social sciences. The sciences of education integrated the contributions of other social sciences while renewing them, allowing the emergence of new domains, objects and problems among which some are very specific to the sciences of education. At the same time, these affiliations and disciplinary borrowings raise fundamental questions about the dimensions of the discipline, among which is the question concerning its autonomy, in reference to its epistemological coherence as much as in reference to its ambition to influence professional practice, in particular in the field of the didactics and the education of teachers.

Simultaneously, the proponents of pedagogy as a unified educational discipline have now almost totally disappeared as members of the last generation of researchers who founded 'educational sciences' faculties and departments have now died or retired. Furthermore, a strong segmentation remains between the two main disciplines, psychology and sociology, that contributed to the initial development and recognition of research in education, together with philosophy. Traditional divisions between psychology and sociology have been reinforced by the insertion of psychology in the CNRS department of 'Sciences of Life and the Earth' and of sociology in the Human and Social Sciences' department, and have been recently heightened still further by the increasing importance of cognitive psychology.

Funding and Internationalisation

Research on educational questions is conducted within but also, at least as much, outside faculties of education. Most of the funding from the national agency for research (ANR) and, even more, from the EU or international agencies goes much more frequently to researchers and research groups outside university faculties of education unless the latter have research centres associated with the CNRS.

With respect to training, a main obstacle for the institutionalisation of 'educational sciences' is the fact that initial teacher education has until now been mostly conducted outside faculties of education. Until 1990, as indacated, the initial training of primary school teachers was conducted in the *Ecoles normales*, while secondary school teachers were trained in universities, with a small professional training in centres controlled by the government. The creation of IUFM (*Institut Universitaire de Formation des Maîtres*) in 1991 formally embedded teacher education into universities. It gave way to a unique training institution for all teachers, but in fact maintained the separation between university professors and other teacher trainers as well as between future primary and secondary school teachers.

The creation of ESPE (*Ecole Supérieure du Professorat et de l'Education*) in 2014 has given more influence to universities but not to faculties of education, which only provide a limited set of courses with respect to those provided by other university departments and the former IUFM trainers. Continuous professional development for teachers has to date remained undeveloped in France, with no links with promotion or mobility within or outside the educational system, and under the control of regional and local educational authorities and not of universities. Finally, while to varying degrees the foundation disciplines (psychology, economics, sociology, history, philosophy) have become increasingly internationalised through publications, international research teams, and participation in international conferences and seminars, educational research has often remained parochial due to the profile of its researchers and the higher education institutions in which they work, but also due to the nature of their research studies. The *Ecoles Supérieures du Professorat et de l'Education* are mandated both for initial and continuous teacher education, and are much more part of the university than the IUFM was, which permits it to speed up both the universitarisation of the curricula and their internationalisation.

Competition between Research Knowledge and State Knowledge

In France, there is a long tradition of production of 'state knowledge' to inform and legitimise policy decisions. In the area of education, in addition to the *Institut français d'éducation* (IFE), two bodies have played a major role in this area:

- the general inspectorate: initially created to inspect teachers, its missions have evolved since 1989 to encompass the qualitative evaluation of schools, local educational authorities and policies;
- the department of evaluation at the Ministry of Education, which is expected to provide data on the education system and its agents and on the effects of specific policies.

The knowledge developed by these two bodies has not been strongly influenced by research despite growing interaction between them, especially the DEPP (*Direction de l'Evaluation, de la Prospective et de la Performance*), and researchers, and its dissemination is strongly controlled by the Ministry of Education (Pons, 2010).

The State generally views researchers as intellectuals whose expert judgement might influence the ways in which problems are framed but seldom specific decisions, and whose role, through individual consultations or participation in various types of committees, is also frequently that of legitimising policy choices (van Zanten, 2008).

The Role of the Media

The media, especially the general and specialised press, but also radio and TV and increasingly the Internet, have also come to exert an important influence:

- on the ways in which educational questions are framed as 'social problems' or not for the general public;
- in the fabrication of 'media researchers' – educational researchers who are continuously invited to make comments on these 'educational problems' and on public policy solutions, whatever their initial area of speciality;
- in the selective circulation, presentation and interpretation of state knowledge and sometimes research knowledge.

Conclusion: the sciences of education as an archetype of the renewal of the disciplinary paradigm?

Are the French *sciences de l'éducation* an exception in the arena of academic disciplines or an iconic and emblematic example of their dynamics and their renewal? The history of the institutionalisation of this discipline, continuously caught between social demands, political injunctions, alternate cooperation and tension with nearby disciplines, and finally internal imperatives of scientific structuring, somehow makes the *sciences de l'éducation* an exemplar of essential tensions within every human and social science discipline (Fabiani, 2006).

If the object of this chapter is to set out the development of the discipline of education in France, the cross-country comparative approach of this book allows us to see that the evolution of the sciences of education is not specific to France, but very much a global movement which in the post-war decades has been evident in many European countries, and in western ones more widely.

The specificity of the development of the *sciences de l'éducation* in France perhaps lies in its relative distance, compared with other European countries, from teachers' education – from which it emerged at the turn of the nineteenth century, but from which it distanced itself as it moved into the university. For institutional reasons (the *école normale* was separate from the university) and for epistemological ones (the ambition not to reduce the discipline to a practical discipline focused on the professional preparation of teachers), the *sciences de l'éducation* distanced itself from teacher training, to establish university faculties.

One can also see the movement, through the history of the discipline in France, towards the assertion of a plural identity. This plurality was at some point denied because of the influential model of the other disciplines (philosophy, psychology and sociology). An ideal of closure characterised indeed the modern conception of the disciplinary fields (most often in spite of their objective internal plurality).

This assumed internal plurality of the *sciences de l'éducation* and this constitutive opening to all the human and social sciences were able to be considered, at one stage of their development, as a weakness or a fragility of the discipline. It is not certain, with regard to a growing call for interdisciplinarity on one hand, and for the linkage of the researches in social sciences to contexts and professional concerns, on the other hand, that the *sciences de l'éducation* would not prefigure the future of the disciplinary worlds, called to be less marked by an ideal of closure than by a concern to approach social objects by mobilising all the resources of interdisciplinarity and cross-disciplinarity.

References

Becher, Tony (1989) *Academic Tribes and Territories: intellectual enquiry and the culture of disciplines*. Buckingham: Open University Press.

Beillerot, J. (1987) Les sciences de l'éducation: histoire comparée avec les sciences politiques et la géographie, *Les sciences de l'éducation pour l'Ere nouvelle*, 5, 75-99.

Blanckaert, Claude (2006) La Discipline en perspective. Le système des sciences à l'heure du spécialisme (XIX-XXe siècle), in Jean Boutier, Jean-Claude Passeron & Jacques Revel (Eds) *Qu'est-ce qu'une discipline?*, pp. 117-150. Paris: Editions EHESS.

Blanckaert, Claude, Blondiaux, Loïc, Loty, Laurent, Renneville, Marc & Richard, Nathalie (Eds) (1999) *L'histoire des sciences de l'homme: Trajectoire, enjeux et questions vives*. Paris: L'Harmattan.

Bourdieu, P. (1994) *Raisons pratiques – Sur la théorie de l'action*. Paris: Éditions du Seuil.

Bourdieu, Pierre (2001) *Science de la science et réflexivité*. Paris: Raisons d'agir.

Buisson, F. (1911) *Nouveau dictionnaire de pédagogie*. Paris: Hachette.

Charle, C. (1990) *La naissance des 'intellectuels' 1880-1900*. Paris: Les Éditions de Minuit.

Charle, Christophe, Schriewer, Jürgen & Wagner, Peter (Eds) (2004) *Transnational Intellectual Networks*. Frankfurt: Campus.

Compayré, G. (1879) *Histoire critique des doctrines de l'éducation en France depuis le 16e siècle*. Paris: Hachette.

Fabiani, J.-L. (2006) A quoi sert la notion de discipline?, in J. Boutier, J.C. Passeron & J. Revel (Eds) *Qu'est-ce qu'une discipline?* Enquête, Editions de l'Ecole des hautes études en sciences sociales, pp. 11-34.

Favre, Pierre (1985) Histoire de la science politique, in Madeleine Grawitz & Jacqueline Gautherin (2002) *Une discipline pour la République: la Science de l'éducation, 1882-1914*. Berne: Peter Lang.

Gautherin, J. (2002) *Une discipline pour la République: La Science de l'éducation en France 1882-1914*. Berne: Peter Lang.

Hameline, D., Helmchen, J. & Oelkers, J. (Eds) (1995) *L'Éducation nouvelle et les enjeux de son histoire*. Berne: Peter Lang.

Hatano-Chalvidan, M. (2008) *Dires sur l'interdisciplinarité scientifique. La référence à l'interdisciplinarité dans le discours de chercheurs en sciences exactes*. Doctoral thesis. Centre de recherche sur la formation, CNAM, Paris.

Hofstetter, R. (2010) *Genève: creuset des sciences de l'éducation*. Genève: Droz. https://doi.org/10.3917/droz.hofst.2010.01

Hofstetter, R. & Schneuwly, B. (Eds) (2002) *Sciences de l'éducation 19e-20e siècles. Entre champs disciplinaires et champs professionnels*. Berne: Peter Lang.

Hofstetter, R. & Schneuwly, B. (Eds) (2004) The Role of Congresses and Institutes in the Emergence of the Educational Sciences, *Paedagogica Historica* (Special Issue), 40(5 & 6).

Hofstetter, R. & Schneuwly, B. (2014) Disciplinarisation et disciplination consubstantiellement liées. Deux exemples prototypiques sous la loupe: Les sciences de l'éducation et les didactiques des disciplines, in B. Engler (Ed.) Disziplin – discipline, pp. 27-46. Fribourg: Academic Press.

Lobrot, M. (1968) *Vers une science de l'éducation*. La Loupe: Rouillier.

Marion, H. (1883) Cours sur la science de l'éducation – Leçon d'ouverture, *Revue Internationale de l'Enseignement*, 6, 1259-1277.

Mialaret, G. (2006) *Sciences de l'éducation: aspects historiques, problèmes épistémologiques*, Paris: PUF.

Nóvoa, A. (1987) *Le temps des professeurs*, 2 vols. Lisbon: INIC.

Pons X. (2010) *Évaluer l'action éducative. Des professionnels en concurrence*. Paris: PUF.

Popkewitz, T.S. (1996) Rethinking Decentralization and State/civil Society Distinctions: the state as a problematic of governing, *Journal of Education Policy*, 11(1), 27-51. https://doi.org/10.1080/0268093960110102

Stichweh, Rudolf (1984) *Zur Entstehung des modernen Systems wissenschaftlicher Disziplinen. Physik in Deutschland 1740-1890*. Frankfurt am Main: Suhrkamp.

Stichweh, Rudolf (1994) *Wissenschaft, Universität, Professionen: Soziologische Analysen.* Frankfurt am Main: Suhrkamp.

Van Zanten, A. (2008) Régulation et rôle de la connaissance dans le champ éducatif en France: du monopole à l'externalisation de l'expertise? *Sociologie et societies,* 39(2), 69-92.

Vigarello, G. (1994) *Discipline et sous-discipline en Sciences de l'éducation,* in A. Jeannel, P. Clanché & E. Debardieux (Eds) *25 ans de sciences de l'éducation,* pp. 77-88. Paris: Institut National de Recherche Pédagogique.

Wentzel, B., Lussi-Borer, V. & Malet, R. (2015) *Professionnalisation de la formation des enseignants. Des fondements aux retraductions nationales.* Nancy: Presses Universitaires de Lorraine.

CHAPTER 3

Between the Philosophy of Self-cultivation and Empirical Research: educational studies in Germany

JÜRGEN SCHRIEWER

SUMMARY Educational studies in Germany is a field characterised by both a long past and a short history. The 'long past' refers to rich and century-old traditions of educational thought and of developing reform-oriented models of educating, teaching, and schooling. The 'short history', by contrast, refers to educational studies' rather late institutionalisation as a university subject in its own right. The chapter, on the one hand, is aimed at analysing the peculiar style of reflective theorising that has emerged out of these contrasting conditions, and which has – in terms of a socially 'involved' philosophical and hermeneutic reasoning –left its marks on the academic field for a long time. On the other hand, it seeks to describe the emergence, expansion, and recent transformation of the field in connection with institutional contexts and successive socio-historical periods of German history. Key periods in this sense include the emergence of the first autonomous chairs of educational study in the tension-filled transition from the Empire to the Weimar Republic; the reconstruction period after World War II; the massive expansion of the entire education system from the mid-1960s onwards; and the challenges represented, for the philosophical style of the tradition, by large-scale international scholastic achievement studies and the attendant rise of empirical educational research, from the mid-1990s onwards. Finally, the resultant diversity of styles of educational knowledge production is interpreted through the lens of a sociology-of-science model and examined with regard to the challenges it represents with regard to teacher training.

A Long Past – but a Short History

'A long past, but a short history' is a description that has occasionally been applied to the field of comparative education – just as to other comparative branches of the social sciences. It holds equally true, however, for educational studies as a whole. It highlights the ambiguities, both of terminology and of theoretical status, attendant on the transition from a field of professional practice to an academic subject, and on the interactions between both conditions. This is all the more so as the practice in question has to be conceived as self-referential, in the sense that it continuously engenders observations, interpretations and considerations of itself, while the academic subject has, in spite of striving for disciplinary status, commonly interacted with, and taken inspiration from, hands-on experience, ideas and models.

Not surprisingly, therefore, the German term *Pädagogik*, embracing a wider meaning than the English *pedagogy*, was – and to some extent continues to be – used used to denote not only well-established patterns of educational practice or elaborate traditions of educational reflection, but also the academic field of educational studies proper. Only from the 1970s onwards was this designation gradually replaced by the more ambitious terms *Erziehungswissenschaft* (the science of education) or even, more recently, *Bildungswissenschaft*. With regard to substance, educational studies in Germany are not comprehensible without paying due attention to the significance that long and rich traditions of educational thought have always had for the field's self-understanding and scholarship. These are traditions which, even setting aside the Graeco-Roman philosophers, range from Humanism and the Protestant Reformation (for instance, Melanchthon and Comenius), over the Enlightenment era (with authors such as Francke, Campe, Pestalozzi and Rousseau) and the philosophers of German Idealism (above all, Kant, Hegel and Schleiermacher), up to nineteenth-century attempts (by Herbart and his followers) at 'scientifying' educational theory as well as to the international Progressive Education Movement and the broad array of varying strands of reform-oriented reflection this movement had encompassed from the late nineteenth century onwards. Even more so, the philosophy of *Bildung* – that is, in Bruford's (1975) terms, of man's individual self-cultivation – has always played, and continues to play, a role of particular prominence for the field (Horlacher, 2016) – with its proponents arguing either through direct reference to the grand programmes developed by the major philosophers of German Romanticism and Neo-Humanism such as Herder, Schiller and Humboldt, or indirectly, through reference to the critics who, in the wake of Nietzsche, emphatically denounced the distortion of *Bildung* as a consequence of its implementation in bureaucratised modern education systems. As one of the leading educationalists of the 1970s and 1980s once held, it is through the idea of *Bildung* that the field of educational studies in Germany has articulated, 'since the days of Herder and Humboldt, its ultimate problem and the very substance of its intentions' (Mollenhauer, 1970, p. 65). In line with these explanations, the broad range of educational thought traditions, and of authors prized as 'classics', were to become central topics of scholarship and discussion once the field had been institutionalised in universities. They thus provided the self-evolutionary potential – or, as a sociologically informed observer once couched it [1], 'pedagogical humus' – for ongoing considerations and theorisations, while at the same time allowing for continuities to be maintained between the 'long past' (of educational reflection) and the 'short history' (of the academic subject).

Continuities of this kind are also reflected in the fact that, as early as the beginning of the nineteenth century, education became the subject of university lectures and seminars. The vast majority of these were held by professors of philosophy. Among the latter were widely known scholars such as Friedrich Paulsen, author of a seminal history of German grammar schools and universities, who acted as an important conveyor of German education and philosophy towards the English-speaking world (see, for instance, Paulsen, 1908), and Wilhelm Dilthey, pioneering thinker of the philosophical-cum-hermeneutic approach to the moral sciences and author of *Pädagogik: Geschichte und Grundlinien des Systems* [Theory of Education: History and Systematic Outline] (1934), which served as a work of reference for several generations. In addition, lectures and seminars on educational topics were also taught in theology faculties and, later on, in faculties of medicine. This ancillary teaching of educational topics was, however, still a long way from the field's academic institutionalisation understood in terms of history-of-science criteria. The traditional practice of teaching education in universities has, in other words, to be clearly differentiated from the fact that there were no dedicated chairs whose incumbents were trusted with representing, and cultivating through ongoing discipline-formation processes, educational studies as an independent field.

Institutionalisation

In German universities, the first institutionalisation of education as a distinct field of academic study emerged only during the second and third decades of the twentieth century. A few isolated chairs for educational studies were created in 1914 in the University of Munich (for Friedrich W. Foerster, a philosopher of moral education and political ethics) and 1916 in the University of Frankfurt on the Main (for Julius Ziehen, a classical philologist and head of the city's schools department). But the crucial deliberations and decisions leading to the permanent establishment of independent education chairs took place towards the end of, and shortly after, the First World War.[2] Moreover, these deliberations and decisions did not follow strictly utilitarian views of educational studies conceived as a means of greater professionalisation of teachers and teacher training. Rather, what was involved – in a political and social context in which ministerial officials and far-sighted politicians were already beginning to brace themselves for a post-war period whose potential difficulties they anticipated – was the institutionalisation of educational theory as a space by reflection on, and, thereby, the legitimation of, the existing educational system. The deliberations accompanying the decision-taking process culminated in a momentous education conference convened by the Prussian Ministry of Public Instruction and Ecclesiastical Affairs, in spring 1917 (Ministerium der geistlichen, 1917). The philosopher Ernst Troeltsch, spokesperson of the powerful faculties of philosophy, who acted as rapporteur of the conference, set the tone for its deliberations:

> What I categorically refuse to do is to construct this discipline [i.e. educational studies] on the basis of psychology; I construct it instead on the basis of the history of the educational system, of institutional analyses as well as of the philosophy of culture. On the basis of psychology, it would be impossible to understand either the given educational system, since it has crystallised as a historical and political fact, or – as you, gentlemen, must admit – the objectives of education (*Bildungsziele*) and the ideals of culture (*Kulturideale*). In cases where people nevertheless proceed in this manner, and where modern psychology is joined with biology and sociology in order to accomplish this task, we can see the development of conceptions of public instruction and its objectives which you would have difficulty applauding, gentlemen. What these conceptions are attempting to do is to put public instruction at the service of a type of progress which is supposed to be justified by sociology and social psychology, and which aspires to bring about educational equality for everyone as well as an essentially utilitarian promotion of the popular masses. Those are the true intentions of a psychology which, in our day, strives for the direction of education, but which, in reality, is nothing but a disguised metaphysics and a doctrine of utilitarian progress. (Ministerium der geistlichen, 1917, p. 24)

While thus specifying the expectations that were to guide the introduction of the new discipline in the Prussian faculties, Troeltsch at the same time pointed to the overt opposition between two contrasting political-cum-ideological camps or – to use a term coined by the sociology of science – 'discourse coalitions' (Wittrock et al, 1991). These were, on the one hand, a coalition between primary school teachers and their unions, the proponents of experimental method in psychology and educational studies, and left-wing parties; and, on the other, a counter-alliance of Prussia's central education authorities, leading *Gymnasium* teacher representatives, and the powerful faculties of philosophy, led by the chairholders of philosophy themselves.

What was at stake for the Ministry was, first and foremost, the preservation of the existing educational system in the face of social upheaval which, in 1917, loomed ahead and in November 1918 eventually brought down the established political order. This concern was all the more pressing because the German educational system at the time was, reflecting the structures of a hierarchical and fragmented society, very socially selective. Its different types of school, which had been defined around 1900, had taken shape in accordance with the reproduction needs of the social strata of pre-war society (Müller et al, 1987). However, this system was increasingly exposed to radical questioning: to political debate by the harbingers of a comprehensive type of schooling, who were strongly supported by the unions of primary school teachers and the Social Democrats; and to scientific scrutiny, as a result of research conducted by specialists in experimental psychology. The former put forward principles of social equity and upward mobility. The latter denounced the character, largely unjustified from the viewpoint of the psychology of aptitude, of a premature distribution of children into hierarchically structured types of schooling leading to very unequal degrees and to differentiated opportunities in life. In view of this constellation, the style of educational theory advocated through the 1917 conference – that is to say, a style of theorising that favoured the historical interpretation of the educational system associated with its reflection in terms of the philosophy of 'culture' – became, in the eyes of the Ministry, an antidote to the attempt of 'modernist' psychologists striving to link positivistic research with political involvement, and experimental method with social and educational reform.

For the teachers' associations, moreover, the debate over the education system and its overall organisation was tightly linked with teacher training and status. Thus, on the one hand, the proponents of comprehensive schooling called for a training programme that was both unified – that is, common to all categories of teachers – and more academic – that is, given in universities. Of course, for the primary school teachers and their unions, such claims went hand in hand with aspirations for increased social recognition, alignment of their status with that of secondary school teachers, and higher salaries. Accordingly, the primary school teachers' associations and the supporters of comprehensive schooling agreed in demanding that the unified training of all teachers be organised within the faculties of philosophy – in other words, in institutions embodying the very core of the Humboldtian university model. These faculties, however, would inevitably see their academic teaching style and their intellectual and moral cohesion jeopardised if they were forced to enrol large numbers of students from more modest social backgrounds, whose intellectual education and life experience differed considerably from that of their traditional clientele. They were naturally disposed, therefore, to reject the idea of organising a training programme relevant to the teaching profession. On the other hand, concerns over social advancement were not unfamiliar to *Gymnasium* teachers either. For decades, they had demanded the alignment of their titles and status with that of higher civil service officials who graduated from the law faculties.

Through a restructuring of the study programme for *Gymnasium* teachers, also agreed in 1917, the Prussian Ministry of Instruction and Ecclesiastical Affairs not only succeeded in defusing attitudes of discontent and frustration widespread among members of this group; it also succeeded in gaining these teachers as allies in its resistance to the social and intellectual ambitions of primary school teachers, and against the threat to the established educational system emanating from these teachers' unions, as well as from the newly emerging group of academics specialising in experimental psychology. For their part, the chairs of philosophy, while proposing an intellectual programme for the new discipline that was responsive to the Ministry's attempts at legitimisation, at the same time defended their own corporate interests. In order to oppose attempts, much in vogue at the turn of the century, to construct the field of educational studies on the model of experimental science, they drew on the epistemological paradigm worked out by Wilhelm Dilthey. They thus advocated the further development of the human and social sciences – in other terms, the *Geisteswissenschaften* – on the basis of philosophical-cum-hermeneutic learning, whereas the experimental science model developed, during the late nineteenth century, by Wilhelm Wundt at the University of Leipzig had come to wield remarkable international influence. From the 1890s onwards, it was systematically adapted to education, notably by Ernst Meumann, a professor of philosophy and education in the University of Zurich and, later, in the predecessor institution of the University of Hamburg. Experimental psychology, while still affiliated with the departments of philosophy, came to epitomise scientific and methodological modernity for the human and social sciences more generally, and therefore succeeded in attracting a considerable number of young researchers. Since, at this time, experimental psychology could barely be distinguished from experimental pedagogy, the extraordinary increase in academic staff specialising in psychology also appeared in educational programmes. In fact, themes dealing with questions of teaching and pedagogy provided psychological researchers with a welcome field of application that also allowed them to combine experimental research with social and educational reform, thus following the example of Meumann himself within the very influential Association for School Reform (*Bund für Schulreform*). According to historical statistics (see especially Drewek, 1996), more than half of the almost 2000 lecture courses and seminars in educational studies given in German universities between 1911 and 1919 had a psycho-experimental approach, whereas courses using philosophical and historical approaches made up only about one third of the total (with the remaining 10-15% from the faculties of theology). Furthermore, the average age of academic staff teaching philosophy was considerably higher than that of psychologists. Given the numerical preponderance of the latter group, as well as the serious crisis in recruitment for positions in philosophy that therefore loomed ahead, well-known philosophers (such as Rudolf Eucken, Edmund Husserl, Paul Natorp, Heinrich Rickert and Wilhelm Windelband) were led, as early as 1913, to publicly denounce the threatening takeover of chairs in philosophy by psychologists, and to demand a clear and clean separation between the two fields. Thus, it was mostly out of concern for the preservation of their own discipline that the chairholders of philosophy, more than any other group, put together every possible means to discard the option, very real at this time, of building the new field of educational studies on the model of experimental psychology.

The significance of the discourse coalition being formed around an intellectual programme defined by Wilhelm Dilthey was therefore threefold. At the political level, this coalition meant counteracting the questioning, advanced with reference to experimental psychology, of the existing educational system and its functioning. At a social and institutional level, it meant safeguarding the social reproduction of philosophy as a distinctive discipline within the eponymous faculties, while, at the same time, channelling aspirations for university training by primary (including non-academic lower-secondary) school teachers into post-secondary, but non-university-level teacher training colleges of a new type – namely, the so-called Education Academies (*Pädagogische Akademien*). At the intellectual level, this discourse coalition succeeded in paving the way for the foundation of the new discipline halfway between history and philosophy – in other words, not as a social science, but as a reflection theory. More than this, by combining the philosophy of *Bildung* (or of *Bildungsideale*) with historical considerations of *Kultur*, understood as 'national culture' – hence, through emphasising the key elements of 'German ideology' (Dumont, 1991) – the new field was entrusted with developing a discourse committing the educational system to a role expected to be instrumental in preserving the unity of the nation beyond the cleavages of class, occupation, religion or region.

Irrespective, therefore, of a broader range of theoretical options that had also been in existence – such as Neo-Kantian philosophy of education, educational research modelled on experimental psychology, or conceptions drawing on social theory and foregrounding the social embeddedness of education – it was the philosophical-cum-hermeneutic paradigm that was successfully implanted, first in Prussian universities, and, subsequently, also in other German territories. Significantly, among the very first scholars to be appointed to the new education chairs were two philosophers who had taken an active part in the 1917 Education Conference: Eduard Spranger, as early as 1919, to the University of Berlin, and Theodor Litt, in 1920, to the University of Leipzig. Spranger was, moreover, a former student of Wilhelm Dilthey, as was Herman Nohl, who was appointed to the University of Göttingen in 1920. In the early 1920s, this group was reinforced by Wilhelm Flitner in the University of Hamburg, by Max Frischeisen-Köhler in the University of Halle, and by Richard Hönigswald in the University of Breslau. Once institutionalised in universities and, at a lower level, in the newly defined Education Academies in Prussia, the field experienced a period of slow, yet steady consolidation. This consolidation was conspicuous in terms of chairs and other teaching positions – up to 1931, the number of academic staff in educational studies had risen to 110 in universities and equivalent institutions (institutes of technology and schools of economics), and to 172 in teacher training colleges. It also became visible in the foundation of

81

professional journals, and in the impact educationalists were able to gain on the educational policy debate and public discourse more generally.

The downfall of the Weimar Republic, however, implied that the consolidation process of the new field also came to an end. The Nazi period from 1933 to 1945 marked a sharp break in its development both in terms of its social composition and with regard to its theoretical orientations. Analyses of academic calendars conclude that – some ambiguities of the categories used notwithstanding – the educationalists active in academia and teacher training were, contrary to the previous consolidation process, reduced in number and, moreover, largely replaced by younger scholars who accepted the ideological orientations of the regime (Tenorth, 1986). Thus, less than half of the academics in education appointed in universities and institutes of technology up to the beginning of the 1930s were still in office in 1940. This proportion was even more modest – scarcely one fifth – for the educationalists appointed to teacher training colleges. Many of them were dismissed, forced to early retirement, or even pushed into exile (Tenorth & Horn, 1996). This all reflects the considerable weight the regime attributed to teacher training and to the role educational studies, redefined as a 'political and ideological foundation discipline' (Tenorth, 1986, p. 304), was thought to play in this training scheme.

During the first ten to fifteen years of the Federal Republic, educational policy was characterised, just as other spheres of public policy were, by the resumption of Weimar institutions and traditions. This also holds true for educational studies. Not more than about 11% of those educationalists who had been appointed in the late 1930s and were recorded in the 1940 academic calendars – and who were therefore likely to be exponents of ideas associated with Nazi conceptions – were able to survive in office up to the 1950s. By contrast, leading representatives of the Weimar tradition of philosophical-cum-hermeneutic learning, as well as their former disciples, were called back onto education chairs. Most conspicuous were, for instance, the cases of Eduard Spranger, who was appointed, after a short interlude as acting rector of the Soviet-controlled University of Berlin, to the University of Tübingen; Theodor Litt, appointed, after an even shorter interlude at the Soviet-controlled University of Leipzig, to the University of Bonn; and Hermann Nohl, reinstalled in his former chair at the University of Göttingen. Central journals were established or re-established by that group, such as the most influential *Zeitschrift für Pädagogik* in 1955. And a first academic society was set up, originally restricted to university-based chairholders, but later on, in 1964, transformed into the more encompassing *Deutsche Gesellschaft für Erziehungswissenschaft* (German Educational Studies Association). The complete dissociation between chairs of philosophy and chairs of educational studies, and the creation of the latter in nearly all German universities, was not achieved, however, until the beginning of the 1960s.

From the 1960s and 1970s onwards, a tremendous expansion of the field, both in terms of staff and students and in terms of areas of study and research interests, began to take place. Several developments fostered this unprecedented growth. To begin with, the general expansion of secondary education and, later on, higher education massively increased the need for teacher training at all levels of the German educational system. This expansion went hand in hand with the enthusiasm, shared by large sectors of society, and heavily supported by both the Liberal Democrats and the Social Democrats, for reforming the whole system, especially in the sense of comprehensive schooling. The slogan, coined by the late Baron Dahrendorf, 'Education is a Civic Right' (Dahrendorf, 1965) clearly pointed at an agenda that entailed the need for considerably increased expertise, information and research. Likewise, new sub-disciplines, such as economics of education, promoted by international organisations such as the Organisation for Economic Co-operation and Development (OECD) and UNESCO's International Institute for Educational Planning (IIEP), strongly suggested more rationalised forms of educational planning, thus reinforcing the emphasis on planning adopted by the federal government led by Willy Brandt, from 1969 onwards. In this reform-friendly context, another discourse coalition, this time a definitely liberal-minded and progressive one supported by leading intellectuals and scholars of the time, was successful in obtaining the establishment of the Berlin-based *Institut für Bildungsforschung* (Institute for Human Development and Education), first, in 1963, under the umbrella of the Max Planck Society, and, from 1971 onwards, as a member institute of this prestigious grouping of large-scale research centres. Originally conceived in clear opposition to the conventional stance of university-based educational studies, the objectives assigned to the new Institute were to link up the field with international standards and developments and to generate social science-based empirical research thought to provide the knowledge needed for educational reform. The German term used for the Institute's designation, apparently coined for the first time in its 1961 founding manifesto – that is, *Bildungsforschung* (educational research) – expressed this mission well. It focused on the integration of different social science disciplines, thus pointing to a form of interdisciplinarity considered as indispensable for an adequate analysis and explanation of complex education processes (Leschinsky, 1996). Nonetheless, in the long run, this Institute – which, from the mid-1990s, was once more to play a pivotal role in conceptualising the German part in international large-scale scholastic achievement studies – took a different path: it turned into an institution placed under the intellectual hegemony of psychology and committed to a research programme focusing on human development in a broad sense, while largely eclipsing education proper. Meanwhile, in accordance with the lines of rationalisation and systematisation formulated during the 1960s, the former teacher training colleges and non-university-level *Pädagogische Akademien* (Education Academies), which had been re-established on the Weimar model after 1945, were promoted to university-level *Pädagogische Hochschulen* from 1962. In a long and stepwise transformation process between the 1960s and the 1980s, most of them were – albeit with considerable variations among the German *Länder* – integrated into universities, thereby forming large departments of educational studies. As a consequence, teacher training programmes, and the place of educational studies in these programmes, also had to be redefined. Finally, and most importantly, during the 1960s new degree courses in education completely distinct from the traditional lecture programmes designed for *Gymnasium* teachers were introduced in most German universities. This concerned, on the one hand, a more academically conceived master's degree course combining educational studies – either as a major or as a minor subject – with two other fields to be chosen by the student from the range of the humanities and social science disciplines. Most influential for the further development of educational studies, however, was a more practice-oriented degree course leading to a certificate (*Diplom*) meant to qualify students for extra-school professional activities, particularly in early childhood education, social education, special education, youth education, adult education and the like.

Taken together, these developments, and the attendant institutional transformations and innovations, entailed considerable consequences for educational studies. These consequences were quantitative, to be sure, with specialised professorships in universities and universities of education rising from 23 in 1960, to over 196 in 1966 and 926 in 1977, up to more than 1000 in the 1980s (Rauschenbach & Christ, 1994). Perhaps even more consequential, however, was the increasing differentiation of the field – hence also of research activities and academic positions – into numerous sub-disciplines. These extend well beyond the traditional core areas of schooling and teacher training and stretch into a multitude of novel areas, thus developing distinctive research traditions, theoretical frameworks, journals and symposia (Macke, 1994). In sum, while in 2014 the total number of teaching and research personnel in education (including special education) in German universities was almost 4900, the present number of professorships in education is 946 (Destatis, 2015, pp. 94-95), and the total membership in the 'German Educational Studies Association' amounts to roughly 3400.

Theory Style(s)

Once established in university chairs, the first generation of academic educationalists, formed around the paradigm of philosophical-cum-hermeneutic scholarship, succeeded, incrementally but enduringly, in ousting their theoretical rivals. These included experimental pedagogy (along the lines of Ernst Meumann and Wilhelm August Lay), sociological conceptualisations (such as developed by the young Ernst Krieck or Hans Weil), and psychoanalytic strands of educational thought (advocated, for instance, by Siegfried Bernfeld), but also the claims of the Churches to have a say in educational matters. In fact, although intellectually close to liberal, secularised Protestantism, the philosophical-cum-hermeneutic paradigm of educational studies nonetheless cultivated a genuine orthodoxy of its own. It did not tolerate either theoretical or disciplinary dissension. It clearly disavowed, couched in its idiosyncratic terms, *empiricism* as much as *psychologism* or *sociologism*. As mentioned above, the dominant discourse was centred, instead, on reiterated explanations and interpretations focusing on the ideas of the great educators past and present, and performed with a view to sifting out some kind of orientation for the ongoing formation of educational practice. Along quite similar lines, this discourse was by and large engaged in delineating and explaining the new field's idiosyncratic concepts, such as, among others, *Bildung* (individual self-cultivation), *Reifung* (maturation), *Subjektivität* (subjectivity), *Selbsttätigkeit* (self-activity), *pädagogischer Takt* (educational tact), *pädagogicher Bezug* (the value-based interpersonal educator/teacher-pupil relation) and *relative Autonomie* (the relative autonomy of education and the educational system from all other social forces or sub-systems of society). Finally, much effort and a good many treatises, journal articles and polemics were devoted to the constantly renewed justification, through intricate epistemological reflections, of the field's theoretical fundamentals and a corresponding ethos (*pädagogischer Grundgedankengang*). These lines of thinking ended up, then, in a largely self-centred and field-specific theoretical orientation, whose historical-cum-reflective style of theorising and overload of epistemological justifications were to be characteristic of the dominant discourse in German educational theory up to the recent past.

Analyses of German educationalists' knowledge production over a period ranging from the mid-1950s to the 1980s – and partially the mid-1990s – have shown the high degree of continuity of this discourse (see Schriewer & Keiner, 1992, 1993; Keiner & Schriewer, 2000). These analyses were based on the quantitative investigation of core journals, especially the *Zeitschrift für Pädagogik*, which clearly correspond to key criteria, such as representativeness of the field, extended coverage of topics, and sustained publication frequency. Moreover, an additional database was included in the form of a major reference work documenting more than two decades of educational study and research, the ten-volume *Enzyklopädie Erziehungswissenschaft* (Lenzen & Schründer, 1983). Informed by concepts coined by the sociology of science, these analyses emphasise in particular the notion of 'communication' and the specific form communications take within the scope of science – that is, 'publication' (Stichweh, 1994). Any publication – these concepts' assumptions run – by incorporating into its own line of reasoning arguments developed in other publications – in other words, by simultaneously making statements of its own and referring to other authors' statements – interacts with preceding ones. By thus combining proposition and quotation, an academic publication displays an array of references which may subsequently be analysed with regard to the theoretical affinities and disciplinary affiliations they give expression to. Taken together, then, the quotations contained in academic journals fan out the reference spaces indicative of the intellectual texture of a disciplinary community such as that of German educationalists.

The findings of these analyses underline the marked intellectual autocentrism of educational studies in Germany. This applies to the journals in which educationalists preferred to publish, and which they in turn quoted in their own publications – in other words, the prevalent pattern of socio-communicative relations. And this applies in particular to the authors whom educationalists most often quoted as sources of theoretical authority and legitimisation – that is, the predominant pattern of cognitive relationships. In conspicuous forms, then, German educationalists' discourse tended to concentrate around a compact central group of prominent authors. Only the first 25 names most often quoted in the field's leading journal up to the mid-1990s account, with relative continuity over time, for three-quarters of the entire array of thousands of quotations included in more than 40 annual volumes. It is these authoritative authors who determined the taken-for-granted centre of the field's communication. Moreover, most of these authors can be attributed either to educational studies proper (including the tradition of educational thought) or to major philosophers who have profoundly shaped educational theory-building and reflection. The prominent scores they reach, not only in the *Zeitschrift für Pädagogik*, but also in the *Enzyklopädie Erziehungswissenschaft*, confirm the theoretical autocentrism of the field. No less conspicuous is the particular weight attributed to those authors who represent the history of educational and philosophical theorising as compared with scholars known for contributing to contemporary knowledge. This tendency towards 'traditionalisation' is illustrated by the high citation scores attained both by the classical authors preceding the field's university institutionalisation (in particular Rousseau, Schleiermacher, Pestalozzi, Humboldt and Herbart) and by the key figures of the Weimar founding generation (such as Flitner, Spranger, Litt, Nohl and Weniger). The high esteem shown for the history of educational thought does not, however, testify to a genuine historical interest. Rather, it gives expression to a specific theory programme that, while being reminiscent of the initial Diltheyan conceptions, met with large consensus among German educationalist of the time. The peculiar forms of reasoning proper to that programme – that is, normative hermeneutics and a mode of arguing thought to distill normative orientation and systematic insight from history (*historisch-systematisch*) – were basically induced by the reflexive style of theorising called *praktische Theorie* (theory committed to practice). This style of theorising – be it in its traditional form of *réflexion engagée*, as the Weimar founding fathers called it, or in the version of 'critical-constructive theorising', as subsequent followers of Critical Theory renamed it – does not aim at the detached historicisation of educational theories and issues. Rather, it is a style of reasoning which is aimed at reiteratively reinterpreting, in the light of changing problem-situations, the normative and conceptual substance purportedly embodied in past educational thought and experience. It is aimed, for instance, at the 'revival of dishonoured promises' (Rang, 1968), at the construction of a consensus committed to Enlightenment norms, or at a historically accredited apology of forms of reflection allegedly commensurate to the field's object domain (Oelkers, 1999). Couched in the words of a most prominent – and most often quoted – educationalist of the 1970s:

> The history of education is therefore not primarily a historical, but
> an educational field of study; in other words, the historical project
> is at the service of the systematic objectives of educational
> theorising. (Blankertz, 1963, p. 131)

This peculiar style of reasoning also illustrates the constant insistence of German educationalists on their field's disciplinary 'autonomy' (*Eigenständigkeit*). This term relates to the claim to cultivate an intellectual approach thought to amalgamate the methodical procedures characteristic of other fields, while at the same time clearly keeping distance from those fields. Thus, educational studies were conceived in terms of a hybrid, being simultaneously 'historical' (but not in the way genuine historians require), 'philosophical' (but not like philosophy proper), and 'norm-interpreting' (but not providing recipes instructing educators how to do). In a significant statement he made during an informal symposium held in the late 1980s, the more than 90 years old Wilhelm Flitner, one of the pivotal Weimar figures, explained it thus:

> What we really wanted [when striving for the institutionalisation
> of educational studies – JS], was a style of theorising close to
> reflection and contemplation (*Besinnung*); the 'science of
> education' was actually imposed on us by the teachers' trade
> unions.[3]

Lastly, reflection theories of this style are not easily compatible with empirical research. Not surprisingly, then, the percentage of publications using statistical evidence was low over the whole period from the mid-1950s to the mid-1980s. No more than 11.4% of the articles published in *Zeitschrift für Pädagogik* included descriptive statistics, while just 2.2% used inferential statistics. A closer look at the evolution over time nevertheless shows that the former percentage rose from 8.1% in the 1950s to almost 14% in the 1980s, whereas the share of inferential statistics rose from an almost non-existent 0.2% to a modest 3.7% (Schriewer & Keiner, 1993, pp. 338f.).

As the latter figures give reason to expect, over the three – let alone the four – decades under consideration, the quotation rankings and, by implication, the theoretical texture of the field expressed by these rankings also underwent some changes. And these were changes likely to modify, to some extent, the portrayal of autocentrism and homogeneity of educational studies in Germany emphasised so far. Thus, while in the first decades Wilhelm Dilthey was still referred to as the leading author in epistemological matters, from the 1970s onwards, this position was increasingly taken over, on the one hand, by Karl Popper, Hans Albert and Wolfgang Stegmüller, and, on the other, by Jürgen Habermas. The opposition which thus became apparent between different philosophical orientations sounds like a distant echo of the so-called positivism dispute in German sociology. This was a far-reaching political-cum-philosophical dispute between the main proponents of Critical Rationalism and of Critical Theory (the Frankfurt School of social philosophy), which was launched in 1961 by Karl Popper and Theodor Adorno and was continued afterwards by Hans Albert (a sociologist who transferred Popperian thought into German social sciences) and Jürgen Habermas. From the late 1960s onwards, it shaped up into an extensive debate within the social sciences in the German-speaking countries more generally. Against the backdrop of this debate, educationalist Wolfgang Brezinka, arguing from the vantage point of the orthodox philosophy of science, came out with a series of incisive critiques of the hybrid status of educational studies' philosophical-cum-hermeneutic paradigm (Brezinka, 1971). Calling into question this paradigm's scientificity, he strongly emphasised the logical necessity to distinguish between *Pädagogik* and *Erziehungswissenschaft* – in other words, between 'practical educational theories' overtly bound to certain moral, religious or ideological assumptions and a strictly analytical 'science of education' committed to elucidating cause–effect relationships likely to be rephrased afterwards into educational technologies. While turning also into a violent critic of the emerging leftist currents of so-called emancipatory education (Brezinka, 1972), Brezinka paid for his iconoclasm by being asked to leave the editorial board of the *Zeitschrift für Pädagogik*.

Not in direct response to these philosophical-cum-political debates, but not completely unconnected with the increased problem awareness engendered by these debates either, obvious tendencies towards the field's theoretical and methodological innovation manifested from the 1970s onwards. The rising quotation scores of authors such as Piaget, Ulich, Roth, Kohlberg, Ingenkamp, Heckhausen, Lukesch and others in the journal – and to an even greater extent in the encyclopaedia – indicated a clear increase both in the import of knowledge from psychology and the social sciences and in corresponding research approaches. While thus attesting to a lasting diversification of the field, the scores attained by these modernisers have, however, never reached the very top of the rankings, the only exception being Jean Piaget. From the 1970s onwards, these top positions were taken by Jürgen Habermas as well as, on a lower level, by Wolfgang Klafki, Herwig Blankertz and Klaus Mollenhauer, who had taken up, and successfully translated into German educationalists' communication process, essential ideas of Habermasian thought. Thus, it was not Popper and Critical Rationalism, but Habermas and the body of theory and critique associated with him who assumed the significance previously assigned to Dilthy. The extraordinary scores Habermas and his supporters attained in the 1970s and

1980s can only be explained against the background of the unique combination of *innovation* – at the level of critical social philosophy – and *continuity* – in terms of the philosophical and hermeneutical style of reasoning – they represented. These scores certainly do not refer to a distinctive theory as such. Rather, they delineate a liberal-progressive zone of understanding, which allowed educationalists to connect their studies with several lines of reasoning alike: with the philosophy of *Bildung* and its critical potential as well as with contemporary socialisation theories; with the normative implications of a field of study committed to its social functions as well as with social science research; and with Enlightenment ideals as well as with expectations on a topical reinterpretation of the 'discourse of modernity'.

It was not, however, the partial modernisation and diversification along multidisciplinary lines of German educational studies, from the 1970s onwards, nor the adoption of certain versions of 'critical theory', but the meteoric rise of *empirische Bildungsforschung* (empirical educational research) from the late 1990s onwards that led to a long-term unsettling of the field's prevailing philosophical traditions and particular style of reasoning. By labelling this approach to educational research as *Bildungsforschung*, its proponents deliberately took up a term that once was coined in connection with the foundation of the eponymous Max Planck Institute, and later on confirmed by recommendations of the *Deutscher Bildungsrat*, a high-level expert council on educational planning and reform that functioned between 1965 and 1975. Adopting this label, the proponents of *Bildungsforschung* not only emphasise the necessarily interdisciplinary character of their approach, drawing on psychology, sociology, economics, education and subject-specific didactics as well as, more recently, the neurosciences; by adding the adjunct *empirisch*, they also insist on the fact that they aim at producing 'evidence-based' – in other words, statistically validated – knowledge according to the standards of Popperian falsificationism (Köller, 2014, p. 103). Furthermore, as a consequence of the interdisciplinarity and multiperspectivism they claim, the advocates of *empirische Bildungsforschung* are no longer inclined to regard their field of investigation as just an extension, or a new sub-field, of educational studies; rather, they see it as a discipline that is, at least partially, distinct from, if not competing with, educational studies proper. Accordingly, in 2012, they established their own scholarly association, the *Gesellschaft für empirische Bildungforschung*, separate from the German Educational Studies Association. They enforced this divorce irrespective of the fact that the spectacular increase in professorships assigned to their field mainly took place at the expense of educational studies altogether – for instance, through the rededication of vacant positions. Thus, by 2012, the share of *empirische Bildungsforschung* positions in the total number of education professorships had risen to as much as 8.61% (Aljets, 2015, pp. 29ff.).

And yet, considering the circumstances at the beginning of the 1990s, nothing gave any reason to expect the extent of the transformation that the whole field underwent in less than two decades. Thus, apart from a few centres and individual researchers placed halfway between education and psychology, the vast majority of research aimed at empirically investigating the conditions, outcomes and consequences of school-based learning and socialisation processes was carried through not by educationalists, but in the framework of educational psychology, the sociology of education, and economics. In addition, over the 1980s and early 1990s, international scholastic achievement studies along the lines of the International Association for the Evaluation of Educational Achievement (IEA) were almost non-existent in Germany. Not least in the wake of a review of the early IEA studies by Dutch mathematics educator Hans Freudenthal (1975) – a biting critique culminating in the translation of the three-letter acronym as *Id est absurdum* – this type of research was thoroughly discredited among German educationalists for almost two decades. Finally, some of the major non-university institutes devoted to educational research were struggling for survival following critical evaluations by the high-level German Council of Science and Humanities (*Wissenschaftsrat*). In this situation, two of the very pioneers of *empirische Bildungsforschung* – Rainer Lehmann and Jürgen Baumert – successfully managed the conceptual transition from former IEA studies to a novel format that facilitated the pursuit of intrinsically academic research interests and issues well beyond the collection of standardised student achievement data. Moreover, they succeeded in negotiating with the education ministries both at the federal and at the *Länder* level the fully-fledged participation of Germany in the Third International Mathematics and Science Study (TIMSS) and its funding, as well as almost complete autonomy in defining the research design and publishing their findings. It was these findings, more than the equally mediocre scores attained by German pupils in the Programme for International Student Assessment (PISA) 2000 study, that caused a serious shock for both the education ministries concerned and the political circles and cultivated public more generally. What emerged, then, out of an outcry of frustration, amplified by the media, regarding the meagre performance of the German school system – previously assumed to be among the world's leading systems – was a hitherto unknown cooperation of politics (involving both the federal and the *Länder* ministries concerned) with academia (the German Research Foundation, numerous universities, non-university institutes for educational research, and the core group of involved specialists of the field), which may well be regarded as another 'discourse coalition' – in fact, a coalition with considerable potential for synergies.

The *Bundesministerium für Bildung und Forschung* (Federal Ministry of Education and Science) (BMBF) had become increasingly concerned, since the early 1990s, about the quality of the German education system as a whole (see Aljets, 2015, pp. 166ff.). This became a topical issue both as a consequence of German reunification and in connection with OECD-launched debates regarding the relationships between investments in education and the competitiveness of national economies under conditions of economic globalisation. By extensively funding large-scale empirical research projects that promised to be academically sophisticated and non-partisan, the BMBF sought to increase its standing with the wider public and, at the same time, to wield influence on the *Länder*, which are, under the German constitution, solely responsible for educational policy. Given these responsibilities, the *Länder*, represented by the consensus-oriented *Ständige Konferenz der Kultusminister der Länder* (Standing Conference of the Ministers of Education and Cultural Affairs of the Länder) (KMK), were plunged into a serious legitimation crisis. They could no longer ignore the public pressure to take action without weakening their own position. Therefore, in a ground-breaking decision taken in 1997, they agreed to engage in the systematic and recurrent evaluation of the performance of the German school systems and to participate in comparative student assessments, not only at OECD level, but also between the sixteen *Länder*. Both the federal and the *Länder* ministries also agreed to fund the large-scale assessment designs presented by the *Bildungsforschung* experts eager to collect not just achievement data but also a broad array of contextual data suited for performing more thoroughgoing analyses of the determinants of varying achievement levels and skills development. In so doing, the political actors expected, in turn, to receive evidence-based social-scientific knowledge that would be conducive to identifying the weak points of the system, improving its workings, and backing relevant policy decisions. The *Deutsche Forschungsgemeinschaft* (German Research Foundation) (DFG), on the other hand, had become concerned, over the years, at the meagre extent of research activities pursued by German educationalists in comparison with other disciplines. The Foundation therefore seized the welcome opportunity offered by the post-TIMSS conjuncture to substantially finance promising research projects and entire research groups that emerged in response to the rising demand for *empirische Bildungsforschung* and, in doing so, sought to strengthen the research profile of the field as a whole. Along similar lines, some of the major non-university research institutes used the changing situation to overcome the structural crisis they were facing as a consequence of negative evaluations. They made strategic appointments to leadership positions, which subsequently enabled them to assume major responsibilities in the emerging field and redefine the institutes' overall scholarly orientation. In addition, by transcending the 'cognitive core' of empirical educational research proper – international large-scale student assessment studies (Aljets, 2015, p. 242) – and by applying the concepts and methods proven by these studies to subject areas and issues that are common to educational studies more generally, such as education processes, schooling and instruction, they contributed to a broader conceptualisation of *empirische Bildungsforschung* and, thus, to its wider acceptance by the educationalists' community. Likewise, a non-negligible number of universities – presidents and department deans alike – took advantage of the rising interest in the new field in order to strengthen their institutions' particular profile: by making strategic appointments, instituting interdisciplinary research centres, integrating subject-specific didactics into *empirische Bildungsforschung*, and, in so doing, restructuring the training of teachers.

The combined endeavours pursued by the aforementioned actors over a period of roughly 15 years have yielded impressive outcomes. Quite apart from the 80 to 90 professorships for empirical educational research that have been instituted and filled up to the present, a wide-ranging and well-funded infrastructure for educational research has emerged. This infrastructure includes, first of all, the establishment, in several universities, of interdisciplinary research groups devoted to *empirische Bildungsforschung* – with 'research groups' constituting, in the German academic context, a highly prestigious research-promotion instrument granted by the DFG on exclusively scholarly criteria and strict evaluation procedures. Moreover, the DFG launched several priority programmes for research on the educational quality of schooling as well as on teaching and learning processes, especially in mathematics, the sciences, and vocational education and training. Several structured doctoral programmes for *empirische Bildungsforschung* have also been set up, one of them even in the framework, and according to the criteria, of the highly competitive 'excellence initiative' launched and largely financed by the federal government. Last but not least, the federal government launched a Framework Programme for Empirical Educational Research meant not only to strengthen the new field on a long-term basis by funding individual projects, but also with a view to generating novel knowledge significant for ongoing educational reform processes. As a complement to this infrastructure for research, the politics-cum-academia discourse coalition has also succeeded in implementing the mid- to long-term institutionalisation of a programme for the systematic monitoring of educational system(s), both at the national and – in connection with the ongoing PISA programme – the international level. This is the mission assigned to the non-university research institutes at Frankfurt-am-Main and Kiel, respectively, which have been completely reorganised for this purpose since the mid-1990s. They share this mission, however, with two more institutes which were set up in the 2000s on the basis of a joint federal government–*Länder* agreement, the Institute for Quality Development in Education established at Humboldt University, Berlin, and the Centre for Cross-national Educational Studies set up at Munich's Technological University. Both centres are generously staffed and well funded, and are dedicated – well beyond their official agenda – to the training of ever more generations of young researchers specialising in empirical educational research. By this is indicated, lastly, that – well beyond the institutionalised educational-system-monitoring scheme – the conceptual and methodological tools developed in this connection have been successfully applied to other, highly significant issues that are in need of being researched. Above all, these are – as Köller (2014, pp. 112ff.) explains – empirical classroom research, inequities in education, methods and tools for educational assessment, and individual development processes (cognitive and motivational) under conditions of institutionalised schooling.

Considering the field of educational studies as a whole, then, the successive conceptions of, and approaches to, the academic study of education that evolved over nearly a century have resulted in the juxtaposition of largely heterogeneous theory styles and methodologies. Highly abstract philosophical reasoning, system-related reflection theories, social science knowledge imports and methodologies, the 'critical turn' inspired by the Frankfurt School of social philosophy, empirical educational research, and, most recently, a gentle 'renaissance' of the philosophy of *Bildung* (Dressler & Sander, 2015) co-exist side by side. They display a scenario that is puzzling not only for the disinterested observer from outside, but also – and particularly so – for any student of education.

Nevertheless, such a scenario is not tantamount to arbitrariness. Rather, it seems to correspond to the structural conditions characteristic of a certain type of academic field, such as educational studies. This, at any rate, is one of the assertions resulting from the sociological conceptualisation based on differentiation and communication theory, which already informed the journal-based analyses of theory styles reported on above. In fact, on the basis of detailed historical evidence, Stichweh (1994, pp. 278ff.) explains how the rise of the modern research university entailed a hitherto unknown, and increasingly clear-cut differentiation between 'disciplines' (oriented towards research and theory-building) and 'professions' (initially meaning only the traditional professions trained in the faculties of law, medicine and theology) as well as, within the latter, a differentiation between the 'core roles of professional practitioners' and 'professional elites' or 'establishments'. Members of these 'elites' or 'establishments' typically did not practise themselves but were in charge of cultivating and imparting profession-related knowledge. Usually placed in academic positions, they, for their part, had to come to terms with divergent commitments, with the commitment to a field of professional activity and its improvement and with the commitment to scientific research and academic values. Imbalances and conflicts therefore did not fail to ensue. These were counterpoised by yet another differentiation, which in turn repeated the differentiation between disciplines and professions within a professional establishment itself. Such is the difference between 'basic research' and 'clinical disciplines', long established in the faculties of medicine. In a similar yet slightly different way, more recent professional establishments, such as the one represented by educationalists, emerged in the form of epistemic hybrids which – in proportions contingent on historical and institutional conditions – allow both scientification and cultivation of profession-related knowledge; social science research and value-based doctrine; and 'scientific theories' and 'reflection theories' (Luhmann & Schorr, 1988). As a rule, therefore, professional establishments of this kind will not reach the intellectual coherence of a 'discipline' *stricto sensu*, such as physics, psychology or history, but constitute, instead, composite areas of study. Inevitably, however, the heterogeneity of theory styles and types of knowledge these areas display raises issues of epistemic integration that are far from being resolved.

Teacher Education

More than ever, the issue of how to reintegrate heterogeneous elements of knowledge with a view to instructing a field of professional practice has become a matter of concern for teacher education. This is linked to the fact that the significance attached to the distinct knowledge components thought to constitute teacher education has considerably altered over the past decades – not to mention the varying status and weight allotted to these components in the training programmes for different categories of teachers. These components not only include the academic disciplines proper that correspond to the curriculum subjects later to be taught; they also encompass the so-called profession-oriented complementary studies in educational theory, philosophy and related disciplines as well as in subject-specific didactics and teaching methodology; finally, they embrace varying periods of internship as student or probationary teacher.

Until recently, these components were defined not in accordance with degree programmes of universities or university departments, but in the framework of the so-called state examination (*Staatsexamen*). This is an institution that emerged in eighteenth-century Prussia, when the modernising state administration, in consideration of the high diversity and unequal validity of the academic degrees awarded by premodern universities, introduced state-defined and state-regulated examinations for those professions whose qualification was to be guaranteed in the public interest. The corresponding process started in 1725 by shifting the authority to grant the licence to practise medicine from the faculties to a state agency. The next step, in 1755, was the introduction of a state examination for the legal professions. And it was Wilhelm von Humboldt in person who in 1810 enforced the *examen pro facultate docendi* for *Gymnasium* teachers, and, in so doing, regulated this 'profession' as such. Over the nineteenth and well into the twentieth century, this examination developed into a demanding final verification of advanced academic studies in two or three disciplines from the sciences or the humanities, but also included a so-called general exam meant to test the candidates' level of liberal education. Over the course of time, the latter assumed the form of a partial exam meant to complete a modest strand of concomitant studies in educational theory and another field – either philosophy or psychology or sociology – supposed to widen the horizon of new *Gymnasium* teachers. As early as 1826, these essentially academic and theoretical studies were complemented by a 'probationary year' completed in the context of a major *Gymnasium*, and under the supervision of its headmaster, with a view to developing the candidates' teaching skills. In a long process, this probationary year was extended to two years (1890), regulated by a second examination (1917), and organised in a particular institution, the *Studienseminar*, under the supervision of the competent educational authorities (1924-1925). Thus, a basic pattern emerged which – quite similar to the patterns pertaining to the medical and the legal professions as well as to the upper-level civil servants more generally – involves two consecutive phases and corresponding examinations. A first phase, normally comprising five to six years of university studies in two to three academic disciplines is completed by the First State Examination. This examination – equivalent to, or even more demanding than, a master's degree – is essentially academic in nature and conducted by university professors, though under the responsibility of the competent educational authorities. By contrast, the second phase consists of a two-year probationary period organised under ministerial supervision. This phase is intended to develop the newly qualified teachers' professional skills and school-related reflexivity, and, in so doing, prepare them for the Second State Examination, comprising demonstration lessons and essays on educational and didactic issues.

Over the twentieth century, this pattern was generalised to some extent, before it was formally extended to all teacher categories through a resolution adopted by the Ministers of Education of the *Länder*, in 1970. This extension concerned, on the one hand, the teachers of vocational schools, who, like *Gymnasium* teachers, have traditionally been trained in technological universities (for the industrial branches) and faculties of economics (for the commercial branches). Their training programmes heavily focused on the academic disciplines corresponding to the curricular subjects later to be taught, whereas complementary studies in educational theory and another social science played only a modest role. On the other hand, the generalisation of the basic format of teacher preparation in two consecutive periods completed by a First and a Second State Examination, respectively, implied an upgrading of the standing of primary and lower-secondary teachers. Previously, these teachers had been trained in non-academic teachers' seminaries since the nineteenth century. During the Weimar Republic, and in accordance with the resolutions adopted by the 1917 Education Conference, their training was elevated to the post-secondary, yet non-university-level, 'Education Academies' (*Pädagogische Akademien*). Accordingly, their programmes continued to give preference not so much to disciplinary studies proper, but to the profession-related fields of educational theory and didactics conceived in the style of philosophical-cum-hermeneutic reflection, thus cultivating future teachers' educational problem-awareness, standpoint and ethos. Over the post–World War II period, the Education Academies were transformed – although in different forms, and at varying points in time, in the various *Länder* – into academically more demanding *Pädagogische Hochschulen*. These in turn successively acquired university-like status and recognition and, between the 1960s and 1980s, were completely integrated into universities in most, if not all, German *Länder*.

Inevitably, the integration of formerly separate teacher training institutions into universities resulted in both the alignment of educational studies along similar lines for all teacher categories and a conscious agenda towards the field's increasing scientification. These developments were further reinforced in connection with the Bologna Process of restructuring university courses of study across Europe, and by the replacement, in most, if not all, of the German *Länder*, of the First State Examination by a Master of Education degree. Not least, the TIMSS and PISA studies and the attendant rise of empirical educational research entailed a far-reaching reconsideration of teacher education programmes, especially in some pioneering institutions such as the Technological University of Munich. At the same time, these studies as well as the promises of *Bildungsforschung* fuelled the considerable strengthening, in most universities, of the weight of subject-specific didactics in these programmes, at the expense of solid knowledge in the subjects proper.

Paradoxically, however, the combined consequences of these transformations do not necessarily represent unambiguous progress. Reports and analyses on the current state of teacher education have in fact adopted a fairly sceptical stance (Herrmann & Prenzel, 2011). The developments that have been taking place under the slogan of the 'scientification' of educational studies – their arguments run – did not lead to a research-based clarifying of valid knowledge nor to the systematisation of such knowledge around an undisputed core of theorising regarding the teaching profession, its role and its demands. 'Scientification', rather, meant the extension of research activities, topics and methodologies on a previously unprecedented scale, a process that was fuelled, moreover, by the massive increase in the number of educationalists active in universities. Moreover, while Critical Theory worked on delegitimising traditional values and attitudes underlying educational ethos, the increased import of social science knowledge implied closely spaced paradigm shifts as well as the rapid obsolescence of theories and insights. And this holds true even more for the subject-specific didactics, which develop their own idiosyncratic theories, sophisticated conceptualisations and research agendas. Taking into account the heterogeneity of theory styles and types of knowledge apparently intrinsic to educational studies (as described above), the 'scientification' of the field was of benefit less to the training of the teaching profession proper than it was to the consolidation of the corresponding professional establishment. There is a certain irony in the fact that an author who, some decades ago, had been one of the harshest critics of the philosophical-cum-hermeneutic paradigm of educational theorising has come to urge, in reflecting on the field's developments since the 1970s, its '*de*-scientification' for the sake of teacher education (Brezinka, 2015).

Notes

[1] Karl-Eberhard Schorr on the occasion of a conference of the German Educational Studies Association, organised in the early 1990s.

[2] See, for the following paragraphs, Drewek (1996, 1998), Tenorth (2011), and, comparing the German case with developments in France from the 1880s onwards, Schriewer (2009).

[3] Personal record of a meeting, held in the University of Tübingen, in the late 1980s, by the Study Group on the History and Sociology of Educational Studies of the German Educational Studies Association.

References

Aljets, B. (2015) *Der Aufstieg der empirischen Bildungsforschung. Ein Beitrag zur institutionalistischen Wissenschaftssoziologie*. Wiesbaden: Springer VS.

Blankertz, H. (1963) *Berufsbildung und Utilitarismus. Problemgeschichtliche Untersuchungen*. Düsseldorf: Schwann.

Brezinka, W. (1971) *Von der Pädagogik zur Erziehungswissenschaft*. Weinheim: Beltz.

Brezinka, W. (1972) *Die Pädagogik der neuen Linken*. Munich: Reinhardt.

Brezinka, W. (2015) Die 'Verwissenschaftlichung' der Pädagogik und ihre Folgen. Rückblick und Ausblick, *Zeitschrift für Pädagogik*, 61(2), 282-294.

Bruford, W.H. (1975) *The German Tradition of Self-cultivation: 'Bildung' from Humboldt to Thomas Mann*. London: Cambridge University Press.

Dahrendorf, R. (1965) *Bildung ist Bürgerrecht. Plädoyer für eine aktive Bildungspolitik*. Hamburg: Nannen.

Destatis (2015) Fachserie 11: Bildung und Kultur, Reihe 4.4: Personal an Hochschulen. Wiesbaden: Statistisches Bundesamt.

Dilthey, Wilhelm (1934) *Pädagogik: Geschichte und Grundlinien des Systems*, Leipzig: Teubner (*Gesammelte Schriften*, vol. 9).

Dressler, J. & Sander, W. (Eds) (2015) Bildung – Renaissance einer Leitidee, *Zeitschrift für Pädagogik*, 61(4), 461-525.

Drewek, P. (1996) Die Herausbildung der 'geisteswissenschaftlichen' Pädagogik vor 1918 aus sozialgeschichtlicher Perspektive, in A. Leschinsky (Ed.) *Die Institutionalisierung von Lehren und Lernen*, pp. 299-316. Weinheim & Basel: Beltz (*Zeitschrift für Pädagogik*, suppl. vol. 34).

Drewek, P. (1998) Educational Studies as an Academic Discipline in Germany at the Beginning of the 20th Century, in P. Drewek, C. Lüth, J. Schriewer & H.-E. Tenorth (Eds) *History of Educational Studies/Geschichte der Erziehungswissenschaft/Histoire des Sciences de l'Éducation*, pp. 175-194. Gent: C.S.H.P.

Dumont, L. (1991) *L'idéologie allemande. France-Allemagne et retour*. Paris: Gallimard.

Freudenthal, H. (1975) Schülerleistungen im internationalen Vergleich, *Zeitschrift für Pädagogik*, 21(6), 889-910.

Herrmann, W.A. & Prenzel, M. (Eds) (2011) *Talente entdecken – Talente fördern: Bildung und Ausbildung an den Hochschulen in Deutschland.* Cologne: Hanns-Martin-Schleyer-Stiftung.

Horlacher, R. (2016) *The Educated Subject and the German Concept of Bildung: a comparative cultural history.* London: Routledge/Taylor & Francis.

Keiner, E. & Schriewer, J. (2000) Erneuerung aus dem Geist der eigenen Tradition? Über Kontinuität und Wandel nationaler Denkstile in der Erziehungswissenschaft, *Schweizerische Zeitschrift für Bildungswissenschaften/Revue suisse des sciences de l'éducation*, 22(1), 27-50.

Köller, O. (2014) Entwicklung und Erträge der jüngeren empirischen Bildungsforschung, in R. Fatke & J. Oelkers (Eds) *Das Selbstverständnis der Erziehungswissenschaft: Geschichte und Gegenwart*, pp. 102-122. Weinheim: Beltz Juventa (*Zeitschrift für Pädagogik*, 60, suppl.).

Lenzen, D. & Schründer, A. (Eds) (1983) *Enzyklopädie Erziehungswissenschaft*, vols 1-10. Stuttgart: Klett-Cotta (several re-editions).

Leschinsky, A. (1996) 'Das Max-Planck-Institut für Bildungsforschung in Berlin', in G. Geißler & U. Wiegmann (Eds) *Außeruniversitäre Erziehungswissenschaft in Deutschland*, pp. 171-190. Cologne: Böhlau.

Luhmann, N. & Schorr, K.-E. (1988) *Reflexionsprobleme im Erziehungssystem.* 2nd enlarged edn. Frankfurt am Main: Suhrkamp.

Macke, G. (1994) Disziplinärer Wandel: Erziehungswissenschaft auf dem Wege zur Verselbständigung ihrer Teildisziplinen, in H.-H. Krüger & T. Rauschenbach (Eds) *Erziehungswissenschaft. Die Disziplin am Beginn einer neuen Epoche*, pp. 49-68. Weinheim: Juventa.

Ministerium der geistlichen und Unterrichts-Angelegenheiten (1917) Pädagogische Konferenz im Ministerium der geistlichen und Unterrichts-Angelegenheiten am 24. und 25. Mai 1917. Theses and Negotiation Report. Berlin.

Mollenhauer, K. (1970) *Erziehung und Emanzipation.* Munich: Juventa.

Müller, D.K., Ringer, F. & Simon, B. (Eds) (1987) *The Rise of the Modern Educational System: structural change and social reproduction 1870-1920.* Cambridge: Cambridge University Press; Paris: Editions de la Maison des Sciences de l'Homme.

Oelkers, J. (1999) Die Geschichte der Pädagogik und ihre Probleme, *Zeitschrift für Pädagogik*, 45, 461-483.

Paulsen, F. (1908) *German Education Past and Present.* London: T. Fisher-Unwin.

Rang, A. (1968) Historische und gesellschaftliche Aspekte der Gesamtschule, *Zeitschrift für Pädagogik*, 14, 1-20.

Rauschenbach, T. & Christ, B. (1994) Abbau, Wandel oder Expansion? Zur disziplinären Entwicklung der Erziehungswissenschaft im Spiegel ihrer Stellenbesetzungen, in H.-H. Krüger & T. Rauschenbach (Eds) *Erziehungswissenschaft. Die Disziplin am Beginn einer neuen Epoche*, pp. 69-92. Weinheim: Juventa.

Schriewer, J. (2009) A Comparative History of Educational Studies: will it ever be possible? In L. Wikander, C. Gustafsson, U. Riis & L. Larson (Eds) *Pedagogik. Som examensämne 100 år*, pp. 119-139. Uppsala: Uppsala University Press.

Schriewer, J. & Keiner, E. (1992) Communication Patterns and Intellectual Traditions in Educational Sciences: France and Germany, *Comparative Education Review*, 36(1), 25-51. https://doi.org/10.1086/447080

Schriewer, J. & Keiner, E. (1993) Kommunikationsnetze und Theoriegestalt: Zur Binnenkonstitution der Erziehungswissenschaft in Frankreich und Deutschland, in J. Schriewer, E. Keiner & C. Charle (Eds) *Sozialer Raum und akademische Kulturen/A la recherche de l'espace universitaire européen*, pp. 277-341. Frankfurt am Main: Peter Lang.

Stichweh, R. (1994) *Wissenschaft, Universität, Professionen. Soziologische Analysen.* Frankfurt am Main: Suhrkamp.

Tenorth, H.-E. (1986) Deutsche Erziehungswissenschaft 1930 bis 1945. Aspekte ihres Strukturwandels, *Zeitschrift für Pädagogik*, 32(3), 299-321.

Tenorth, H.-E. (2011) '*...die praktische Seite der philosophischen Fakultät'. Status und Funktion universitärer Pädagogik.* Berlin: Humboldt-Universität zu Berlin, Public Lecture no. 169.

Tenorth, H.-E. & K.-P. Horn (1996) The Impact of Emigration on German Pedagogy, in M.G. Ash & A. Söllner (Eds) *Forced Migration and Scientific Change. Emigré German-Speaking Scientists and Scholars after 1933*, pp. 156ff. Cambridge: Cambridge University Press. https://doi.org/10.1017/CBO9781139052542.008

Wittrock, B., Wagner, P. & Wollmann, H. (1991) Social Science and the Modern State: policy knowledge and political institutions in Western Europe and the United States, in P. Wagner, C. Hirschon Weiss, B. Wittrock & H. Wollmann (Eds) *Social Sciences and Modern States: national experiences and theoretical crossroads*, pp. 28-85. Cambridge: Cambridge University Press.

CHAPTER 4

Pedagoġija and Educational Sciences: competing traditions in the study of education in Latvia

IRĒNA ŽOGLA

SUMMARY A central part of Latvia's 'redirection' over the last 25 years has been the transforming of the educational system – changing its content and technologies, and joining the European Union with its discussion about the establishment of a 'European space of education'. However, because of differences in interpretation between different educational communities within Latvia, EU documents on education have been interpreted from two fundamentally different perspectives. This has escalated into one of the most influential and long-standing debates on what constitutes the basic approach to the study of education. On the one hand, there is 'Pedagoġija', the long-established intellectual tradition in the study of education in this country; on the other hand, there is the more recently introduced tradition of Educational Sciences – familiar in many parts of the western world. In the light of these different interpretations, the aim of this chapter is twofold. Firstly, it is to explore the relatively unknown Latvian concept of 'Pedagoġija', a concept which involves an understanding of the complex nature of learning that, from a learning-centred perspective, respects the learners' individual needs and seeks to accentuate and energise their capabilities. The second purpose is to explore how, since the political redirection of the early 1990s, Latvia has had to accommodate an alternative perspective, that of Educational Sciences. It should be noted that the approach described in this chapter as 'Educational Sciences' is similar to that termed 'Disciplines of Education'/'Sciences de l'Education' in chapter 1 of this book.

Introduction

A quarter of a century is a short period in a country's life, yet the developments that have taken place in Latvia since the political sea change in the early 1990s are immense. Over the last 25 years the country has jumped into neoliberalism without any significant analysis of what it actually is and of how previously stable cultural values or the economic legacy of the prior system might be undermined. Liberalisation of the economy coupled with the government's concern to destroy everything that came from the previous political system on the way to market-driven policies has in reality reduced the government's power over both the economy and education. At the same time, the global economic recession has led to severe fiscal austerity in ways that have also influenced the choice of priorities. These pressures have forced education policy-makers and practitioners to find quick answers in a major reform process; often those answers have been ill informed and therefore, at best, premature.

Many of the changes in the field of education were and still are focused on democratisation and teachers' acquisition of competences that educators need in order to facilitate and implement changes in a new reality of a global world where there is wide access to sources of information and labour. The leap into the knowledge society, which itself has been only vaguely defined, has involved cajoling those with previous experience into adopting novel approaches to teaching and learning in a comparatively short time.

Townsend (2010) quoted Toffler (1971, p. 10) as saying: 'I coined the term "future shock" to describe the shattering stress and disorientation that we induce in individuals by subjecting them to too much change in too short a time' (pp. 337-338). In Latvia, 'future shock' has been the reality of the education system for many years, a reality that has resulted in many unresolved dilemmas, as well as promising achievements.

A central part of Latvia's 'redirection' was transforming the educational system, changing its content and technologies, and joining the European Union (EU) with its discussion about the establishment a 'European space of education'. However, because of the differences in teacher and educator background knowledge, EU documents on education were interpreted from two fundamentally different perspectives. This has escalated into one of the most influential and long-standing debates on what constitutes the basic approach to the study of education. On the one hand, there is '*Pedagoģija*' [1], the long-established intellectual tradition in the study of education in this country; on the other hand, there is the more recently introduced tradition of *Educational Sciences*.

The aim of this chapter is twofold. First, it is to explore *Pedagoģija* in some detail and highlight the changes in understanding of this notion, which has shifted from an external coercive influence on learners to an understanding of the complicated nature of learning that, from a learning-centred perspective, respects the learners' individual needs and seeks to accentuate and energise their capabilities. *Pedagoģija* will be less familiar to many readers outside of Latvia, though it has much in common with approaches traditionally developed within, for instance, Germany, Poland and Austria, where *Pädagogie, pedagogia, Erziehung* and *Didaktik* are common notions. The second purpose is to outline how, since the political redirection of the early 1990s, Latvia has had to accommodate an alternative perspective,

Educational Sciences. I begin, however, by briefly outlining the current structure of teacher education in Latvia.

The Structure of Teacher Education in Latvia: from undergraduate courses to doctorates

The National Plan for 2014-2020 (MK, 2014), which has the aims of sustainable development (Saeima, 2010), lays out broad goals for re-shaping education based on standards that follow EU and Organisation for Economic Co-operation and Development (OECD) guidance on the development of a high-quality teaching profession (OECD, 2005, 2009). Teacher education programmes run at Latvian universities are of two kinds:

- a three-year bachelor's programme in a specific academic discipline, usually related to school teaching subjects, followed by a one-year professional studies programme for teachers; this comprises about 18 ECTS [2] clusters of *Pedagoģija* and psychology, 6-8 ECTS of subject didactics and 33-36 ECTS of pedagogical practice;
- an integrated four-year programme which usually offers a Bachelor of *Pedagoģija* or Education and a cluster of courses leading to the status of a subject-specific teacher ('Teacher of a particular subject').

The two kinds of programmes differ in the way they organise the content and sequence of courses; however, the clusters of the content and pedagogical practice are in reality quite similar. Moreover, in the main, the content does not differ greatly between universities, except in those circumstances where a specific university has developed expertise in an area that it offers to students, or, if it is involved in particular research (UNESCO/UNITWIN, 2000-2010), being continued as a local project with which students can also become involved (for instance, sustainable development; integrated models of teaching-learning; practices of evaluation). Another peculiarity is marked by the accent being either on *Pedagoģija*, where the programmes accentuate it as a theory and practice of teachers' professionalism, or on *education*, where looser structuring of the content of the programmes is allowed for and there is limited usage of *Pedagoģija*.

The programmes normally meet the requirements for teacher qualifications that have been adopted by the Cabinet of Ministers (MK, 2000, 2014), with the main ones being:

- *The academic component of the studies* consisting of (i) the fundamental sciences for the teaching profession: philosophy, psychology, physiology; (ii) the disciplines which relate to the specific school subjects; (iii) education-related subjects or fundamental theories of *Pedagoģija* (such as general *Pedagoģija*, history of pedagogical thought, pre-school or school *Pedagoģija*, didactics, curriculum theory and practice, content and models of teaching-learning, evaluation, teachers' research). The number of courses in education and/or *Pedagoģija* might reach six to eight and will differ slightly according to the subject specialisation and the level of schooling that teachers are going to teach (pre-school, nine-year basic, secondary or vocational school).

- A cluster of courses that targets the students' *general and contextual knowledge* and usually includes: ethics and aesthetics; the history of culture; the history of Latvia; literature. The actual courses will depend on the university's profile and choices made by the students.
- *Practical and professional studies*, which includes communication, organisational skills, methods of teaching and learning, building mutual relationships in the pedagogical process. These courses usually aim to capture the essence of *Pedagoģija* as a form of 'philosophy-in-use', even if programmes are designed around the central notion of *education*; the students are oriented to capture the mutually dependent nature of the learners' and teachers' actions. By the term 'philosophy-in-use', Latvian educationalists are referring to a complex form of pedagogical thinking, leading to professional judgements that make the teachers' and learners' activities meet and create a dynamic process. Traditionally, *Pedagoģija* firmly follows the historical experience and principle of establishing scientific method through research-based studies so that future teachers can acquire the necessary knowledge through study (Hessens, 1929, p. 124). To accentuate the role of reflection and obtain empirical data, the University of Latvia, for example, has since 2010 delivered a course entitled *Teachers' Research Activities* as a part of its tertiary education programmes.
- *Pedagogical practice* appropriate to the specialisation of the future teachers (even if the programme accentuates the notion of *education*, this practice is called pedagogical). The timetable, targets and content are established for each academic year and special attention is given to students' research, which is undertaken as part of the development of professional competence and also for the graduation paper. The nature of effective practice is one of the most common themes of debate within Latvia.

These programmes lead to either a Bachelor of Education or a Bachelor of *Pedagoģija*, though the differences in the programmes are not marked. This is because in the late 1990s Latvia's universities agreed upon a cluster of pedagogical disciplines to be included in teacher education programmes as the core theory and practice of teacher professionalism. However, more recently, as we will see below, a small number of programmes have been reconceptualised as Educational Sciences, where pedagogy is more narrowly conceived.

Evidence of two distinct existing approaches to the study of education – *Pedagoģija* and Educational Sciences – appears stronger in master's programmes. Four universities offer a Master of Educational Sciences in *Pedagoģija*. Two universities award a Master of Educational Sciences, a Master of Education, and also a Professional Master 'Teacher'. These programmes demonstrate a wide range of different approaches: from those that foreground *Pedagoģija* as the background science of education to those that avoid it and substitute the disciplines of education instead. The degrees in Educational Sciences, however, often do not have any explicit underpinning theory of education. Nevertheless, the diplomas and degrees in Educational Sciences and *Pedagoģija* are equally recognised in Latvia.[3]

The differences in the titles of the degrees do, though, indicate an ongoing discussion of approaches to and terminology in teacher education, and reflect an unfinished period of transition; they keep open discussions on the essence of *Pedagoģija* and Educational Sciences, both of which from time to time are used to justify the eclectic and fragmentary character of teacher education.

The doctoral programmes in *Pedagoģija* follow the classification of sciences adopted by the Latvian Academy of Sciences where *Pedagoģija* with its sub-branches is the only nomination under the heading of Educational Sciences (the degree awarded is the Doctor of *Pedagoģija*). In other words, at this level it is *Pedagoģija* that is strongly identified as the theory and practice of formal education, while philosophy, sociology, economics, etc. are conceptualised as context sciences.

Pedagoģija: a theory and practice of education

Pedagoģija is therefore a central, though sometimes contested, part of teacher education programmes at all levels in Latvia. But what precisely is *Pedagoģija* and how does it differ from western notions of 'pedagogy'? The sections that follow begin by providing an overview and definition of *Pedagoģija*; this is followed by a brief examination of one of the *Pedagoģija*'s most distinctive dimensions – the notion of philosophy-in-use. We then give an overview of the historical development of the concept and conclude with an exploration of how *Pedagoģija* differs from western notions of 'pedagogy'.

Since the University of Latvia was established in 1919, *Pedagoģija* has been among the most important university disciplines in that it follows the principle of establishing scientific method in educational research and developing research-based studies. *Pedagoģija* is grounded in the concept of the nature of human holistic development and implies work with the whole learner (see Appendix Table I). Crucially, the learner, even as a child, is seen as a social being, connected to others and at the same time with his or her own distinctive human and individual features – physical, mental and social. In other words, it is 'a matter of head, hand and heart' (Dauge, 1932; Brühlmeier, 2010) involving a deliberate process of intentional teaching and learning, as well as a process for living (Dewey, 1963). Both formal and non-formal education are seen as mediating the environment that creates the experience and fosters the learner's autonomous learning and development. Therefore a teacher's assistance must comply with the concept that learning is the central activity of a learner's comprehensive development. Knowledge in education, both as an academic discipline and as part of a teacher's professional philosophy is, therefore, a complex matter, requiring knowledge of humanities and social sciences, and including large components of practice.

Teaching is therefore seen as facilitating learning by implementing three mutually integrated aims/objectives of a targeted process (see Appendix Table I) – educational aims (new knowledge, skills, understandings), developmental aims (physical, emotional and intellectual) and educative aims (initiating the learners' self-evaluation by using meaningful criteria and targeting the educational content and organisational settings towards the learners' views, cultural values, attitudes – towards competencies for self-conducted activities). These are integrated within *Pedagoģija*, which provides a firm background system of teaching-learning and leads to the learners' competencies as a complex achievement. From this perspective, simply reducing the concept of *Pedagoģija* to teaching or methods of teaching leads to a loss of integrity in the educative value of deliberate education as both a process and an outcome.

With its assumption that a human being develops all of his or her faculties through different kinds of activities, *Pedagoģija* draws on a wide range of theoretical resources, including twentieth-century research and theory of both action psychology (Leontyev, 1975) and pedagogy (Schukina, 1986), as well as Dewey's 'learning by doing'. The concept highlights the potential of teaching as *assistance to learning* when a learner's development occurs by *changing* his or her learning. The relationship between education, development and the educative nature of *Pedagoģija* as a core of socialisation has become a focus of discussion since the 1950s, especially with reference to formal and non-formal education, when an appreciation of pedagogy's contribution to human development became stronger (Fägerlind & Saha, 1989). Learning and teaching as the central actions/activities in *Pedagoģija* meet and foster the learner's, as well as the teacher's, overall development by using the subject matter as a means or a tool, while the process of the two actions becomes a basis for development, as well as opening new possibilities for value and attitudinal exchange as an educative goal. Teachers, or even parents, can seldom influence learners'/children's views, values, ideals in a direct way; rather, values from the external sphere can be facilitated and fostered through the learner's/child's actions and communication.

Pedagogical action, being based on complex knowledge, ceases when it no longer makes sense to the learner or has no personal importance for reaching a meaningful target; at that point, interaction between the learner and the teacher stops (Hörster, 1998, pp. 35-36). This action consists of the mediation between the proper configuration of subject content and the structured learning activities that the teacher has designed for learners (Jank & Meyer, 1994, p. 81), leaving a space for the learners' self-evaluation.

Overall, there are three levels of *Pedagoģija* that need to be distinguished in order to understand its essence:

The first one – *theoretical level* – constitutes a teacher's professional pedagogical philosophy – well-structured theories and approaches, once acquired, provide deep and strategic understanding and a background for a teacher's pedagogical thinking and professional judgement that is crucial in an ever-changing environment. In a situation where a teacher lacks knowledge of the wider social context or the basics of human development to underpin the chosen tool (content, method, organisation), he or she loses the opportunity to address the learner as a whole and set appropriate goals; more often the educative ones with attitudes in their centre are lost. The tools used then remain just techniques or procedures, limiting the learners' opportunity for ownership and self-evaluation of the process and outcomes, therefore hindering the development of self-regulated learning. Cohran-Smith (2005) describes learning to teach being complex and requiring the acquisition of specialised knowledge and professional skills through formal study to enable teachers to make appropriate adjustments in particular situations. The understanding of this complexity goes even deeper: 'The "knowing-doing" gap is a pervasive, persisting, and important problem because it is driven by deep philosophical thinking' (Ball, 2012, p. 283). Fundamentally, closing the knowing-doing gap is about our holding powerful and generative philosophy-in-use (which we discuss in more detail below).

Methods, technologies and organisational settings that are compliant with the pedagogical theories and approaches, and which, if appropriately used, facilitate the implementation of the pedagogical approach, are the second level. Tools suggested by a teacher are evaluated by the learner and confront personally meaningful criteria. Therefore, the learner's (not the teacher's) choice is decisive for the *methods/models* in *Pedagoġija*, and only those accepted by the learner allow implementation of the aims.

The implementation or putting into practice of the *Pedagoġija*'s philosophy, the ways of knowing how to use the chosen technologies, methods and organisational settings, is no less important, and constitutes the third level. 'Performative realities are *flat realities*, as they focus primarily on the events and their effects, and they are *rich realities* because they let the events come into view' (Wulf & Zirfas, 2007, p. 9) when investigation-based learning is being initiated. This therefore leads us to a discussion of one of *Pedagoġija's* most distinctive features – that of philosophy-in-use.

Pedagoġija as a Philosophy-in-Use

Among the many intellectual influences on *Pedagoġija* has been that of Kant's philosophical views on *pedagogy*, which he characterises as the science of upbringing designed to help a human being develop his or her human qualities. It is seen as a twofold process: first, it is formal, related to the structure of thought embedded in a pedagogical message; second, it is a philosophical generalisation of a holistic phenomenon which relates to all human dimensions and is a guide for practice (as quoted by Fedeli, 2007). In other words, *Pedagoġija* is both an intellectual and a practical framework at the same time: it is a form of 'philosophy-in-use' involving two different dimensions. It involves the teacher's views and understanding of the essence and development of a human being, which leads them to integrate teaching, learning and the subject-matter in order to initiate the appropriate pedagogical process. And the teacher's professional views, integrity and identity manifest themselves in building relationships on a foundation of communication and collaboration with the learner by treating him or her as a whole developing person.

The complicated essence of a teacher's profession, with his or her understanding of human development and ability to select appropriate pedagogical tools, addresses and challenges the learner's diverse and developing needs in concrete situations. This is why *Pedagoġija* is called 'philosophy-in-use' (Hessens, 1929). Interestingly, this double dimension is shared by some western authors writing on pedagogy. For example, Tubbs argues: 'Pedagogy is not just a method. It is first and foremost the judgements made about which methods, given a comprehensive intake, will most effectively fulfil the aim of universal entitlement which underpins the comprehensive system' (Tubbs, 2012, p. 34).

Pedagoġija therefore conceptualises a process involving two people with entirely different actions but both involved in creating a coherent process adjusted to the learner's needs: both of them follow different aims and motives; they use different background knowledge and tools, with the common goal being the learner's achievements (see Appendix Table II).

Because *Pedagoġija* is sensitive towards commonalities and diversity in human development, common methods are adjusted to the current needs of the learner, peculiarities of the situation and new possibilities, like those of information technology (IT); as a result, commonalities become individually different. This is why methods in *Pedagoġija* are personalised due to the teacher's philosophy-in-use and, if compared with other fields of human activities, they cannot be precisely repeated, even in similar situations. This peculiarity leads to the opinion that *Pedagoġija* is an art. *Pedagoġija* is not a fundamental science due to its complex and changeable nature; nevertheless, it is the theory and practice of the teaching profession and therefore a discipline (Meyer, 1997, pp. 10-11). As such, it assists teachers in making a deliberately rationalised process. Teacher's professional thinking, or, as Hessens puts it, 'philosophy-in-use', captures the multi-faceted ongoing changes and learners' needs, investigates the effectiveness of a pedagogical process and chooses pedagogical priorities.

The fundamental humanistic assumptions of *Pedagoġija* in Latvia were further advanced by the introduction of Piaget's and Vygotsky's theories, which became widely known from the 1930s onwards. The theory of the 'zone of proximal development' was especially productive for *Pedagoġija* as a philosophy-in-use: learning always precedes development and 'pulls along' the learner's experience (Vygotsky, 1978). This concept highlighted where the learner's autonomous learning slows down due to his or her limited possibilities and how assistance can speed it up, empowering further learning by addressing his or her experience, preserving its developmental and motivating value, and by doing so creating dynamic links (see Appendix Table II). These 'links' are needed for the personalisation of the process and the self-regulation that leads to personal holistic development.

The Historical Development of *Pedagoģija*

As the foregoing outline makes clear, *Pedagoģija* in Latvia's universities has today developed into a university discipline with specific objectives, problems and goals of research; a system of categorisation, theories and criteria of data analysis; fields of practice; a system of preparation of teachers and educators; history, branches and disciplines – attributes which need not be borrowed from other sciences (Gudjons, 1995, pp. 33-35). However, the theory and practice of *Pedagoģija* in Latvia has a long history; it follows classical European conceptions of *pedagogy* and is founded on a range of different principles and sources.

The first is the nation's values and pedagogical thought as developed through the ages. These are often reflected in folk songs, many of which often have a strong moral component, affective elements and attitudes that are common to the Latvian population and therefore are a component of schooling. Also influential have been diverse visions of and philosophical views on education as they have revealed themselves in long-lasting educational practices in schools (the first school in the Baltic countries was founded in Riga in 1211) and through organised teacher education, which was first established in 1683.

Research related to *Pedagoģija* began in the seventeenth century and has always stressed the importance of empirical investigations (Dauge, 1929, p. 99). This, combined with the rise of anthropology as a science with *Pedagoģija* sitting within it (Kron, 2001, p. 27), has informed research at the University of Latvia since 1919, when it became focused on the holistic essence of the pedagogical process. This involved two distinctive orientations – the humanistic philosophical paradigm, with the learner's mental development and upbringing at the core, and the reflections and empirical approach in research of real situations that followed the paradigm of the natural sciences. Thanks to *Pedagoģija*'s orientation towards philosophy and, as a result, its search for fundamental background assumptions or theories of education, academic components developed to become part of *Pedagoģija* in the nineteenth century (Depaepe, 2002, p. 363).

At the beginning of the twentieth century, leading researchers and educators at the University of Latvia often held both a diploma and an additional specialisation essential for *Pedagoģija* (e.g. in philosophy and psychology, in philosophy and history, in history and literature). Their deep knowledge of European educational practices, along with American progressive education, enabled them to perceive of *Pedagoģija* as a system with its own fundamental elements, separate from other social and humanitarian sciences. Philosophy and history have formed the background of many educationists (Husen, 1979), their understanding of *Pedagoģija* and the teaching profession reaching beyond just teaching techniques or methods when teachers' personal philosophy provides the foundation for their professional behaviours. Between 1919 and 1944, *Pedagoģija* came under the Chair of Philosophy at the University of Latvia and therefore developed under its influence. The scholars, in cooperation with philosophers and experienced teachers, developed the theory and practice of *Pedagoģija* with its traditional perspective focused on an individual's overall development as a person (Dauge, 1932). In 1940 the first doctoral thesis in *Pedagoģija* was defended; in 1944 the first Chair of *Pedagoģija* was established. Later, in the 1970s, social sciences accentuated the humanistic nature of human development and *Pedagoģija* came to be seen as a social science (Kron, 2001, pp. 31-32), transforming regularities from human biological and social development into pedagogical notions and highlighting the integrity of *Pedagoģija*.

Pedagoģija versus Pedagogy: changing definitions

'Education' as a process and an outcome is a very broad concept; without more precise definitions the term 'education' can therefore result in very inconsistent usage. By contrast, *Pedagoģija* aspires towards clarity, by establishing a well-defined scientific core combined with practical implementation and usage. As has already been noted, *Pedagoģija* is seen as a form of 'upbringing' (*audzināšana*), which in general means assisting learners' preparedness for life in a society. It therefore cannot be reduced simply to pedagogy or teaching. *Pedagoģija* requires an understanding of a teacher's educational theories, his/her ways of knowing (instead of what they know) and how s/he conducts interactions with the learner.

For example, Nohl (see Gudjons, 1998, p. 34) argues that the background of upbringing (Erziehung) is based on the emotional attitude of a mature teacher towards developing learners' subjectivities only for their own sake to enable them to build and conduct their lives. Therefore, the 'pedagogical attitude' and upbringing are phenomena only of *Pedagoģija*; they cannot be appropriately defined by any other science such as economics or sociology. Pedagogy (in its broader meaning) therefore develops its own congruent system of notions that reflects the integrity of a targeted process of teaching-learning. *Pedagoģija*, being a well-structured synthesis of teacher's assistance and learner's activities, initiates the learner's self-imposed acceptance and sensitivity towards knowledge, social skills, norms and roles required for integration into a community and supports respect towards the expectations of others.

All this crucially depends on the learner's willingness to accept values that are brought about by the content of teaching-learning, mutual relations, mental and practical activities, and communication within and outside school. In this there are certain similarities between the Latvian approach and other European traditions. These include the German concept of *Erziehung*, the Polish concept of *wychowanie*, the Spanish concept of *crianza* and the Swedish concept of *uppväxt*. In all of these traditions, knowledge is not the aim in itself; it is a means to develop a person's abilities, leading to his/her physical and mental development, attitudes, values, views, judgements and behaviour. This comes close also to the broad notions of *pedagogy*, *pedagogics* and *didactics* as used in continental Europe, especially in Germanic and Nordic countries (Buchberger & Buchberger, 1999).

However, the Latvian conception of *Pedagoģija* is very different from many other western definitions of pedagogy, which focus primarily on teaching (Waring & Evans, 2015). Pollard, for example, sees pedagogy as a 'science, craft and art' of teaching (Pollard, 2010, p. 5); Watkins and Mortimore (1999) talk of 'the science of teaching'; Leach and Moon also see pedagogy as confined to teaching – a 'dynamic process, informed by theories' (Leach & Moon, 2008, p. 6); while Ball and Forzani (2007) talk of 'multiple interactions which we call *instructional dynamics*' (pp. 529-540).

In recent decades, a wider understanding of *pedagogy* has started to emerge in some English texts that have more in common with the Latvian understanding of *Pedagoģija*. Loughran, for example, argues that 'in terms of its European traditions pedagogy entails more than just teaching' – that it 'involves two aspects of learning. The first is associated with what and how students are learning; the second is about the teacher as a learner. Thinking about pedagogy in this way helps to highlight teaching as an educative process for both partners in their relationship rather than a set of technical skills' (Loughran, 2010, pp. 36-37). Equally, the Gordon Commission in the USA affirms this perspective, arguing that 'pedagogy ... the central mechanism operative in education ... is interactively and transformatively inclusive of assessment, teaching, and learning' (Assessment..., 2012, p. 1). Aarhus University uses a similarly wide understanding of *pedagogy*: pedagogics can be defined as the holistic science of education, learning and skill development – that is, of special relationships between teachers and learners, the goal of which is learning, set in a historical, social and philosophical reflection framework (Danish School of Educational Research, 2016). Teachers use the pedagogical content knowledge and, through communication and cooperation, develop their professional competence (synthesis of knowledge, skills and attitudes) in order to assist learners to achieve the complicated targets that support each and every learner's journey towards their own individual successes (Van Driel & Berry, 2012).

In Latvian traditions, *Pedagoģija* creates and investigates *inner dynamic links* between teacher, learner and the content in social, deliberately organised integrative settings, which grow into certain regularities: teachers and learners are mutually dependent in their activities, their orchestrated actions and communication lead to the learner's autonomy; activities are addressed to the same subject-matter, which is a pedagogical tool for teaching to highlight the content for learning. Teacher's and learner's reflection and self-evaluation add to the educative self-imposed value of the process and achievements. Research in *Pedagoģija*, therefore, attempts to detect pedagogical regularities in diverse settings and confront the criteria that confirm a deliberately constructed pedagogical process to be a reality. Research finds not only a synthesis between *Pedagoģija* and the ever-changing disciplines that relate to it, but also transforms the theoretical assumptions of these disciplines into pedagogical constructs where, as Klafki put it, two responsible people, the teacher and learner, analyse, co-construct the pedagogical process and cooperate on a basis of solidarity (Klafki, 1990, p. 95).

The following definition, developed as a result of theoretical analysis followed by a discussion amongst Latvian scholars between 1995 and 2001, reflects the current Latvian understanding of *Pedagoģija*:

> *Pedagoģija* is an integrated humanistic and social science which investigates the combined learner and teacher interactions and communication specifically aimed at achieving an educative goal (*audzināšana*). Realisation of this deliberate goal occurs through internal, dynamic connections activated by targeted, organised, goal-oriented educational processes, which transform mankind's intellectual and cultural values into the meaningful educational, developmental and educative content to facilitate the acquisition of these values by participants of the process and to foster their personal development and self-actualisation.[4]

The Emergence of a Different Perspective: Educational Sciences

The intellectual tradition of *Pedagoģija* in Latvia is therefore both strong and distinctive, and until the early 1990s was well rooted in both the university and the teachers' college system. Its links with German philosophical traditions, with American 'progressive' educational philosophy and with Russian psychological thinking reflect the political history of Latvia over the past century. The result has been the development of an intellectual tradition that is rich and distinctive and potentially has much to contribute to international debate on the nature of educational studies. However, political changes of the past 25 years in the field of education have led to the emergence of a parallel intellectual tradition, that of Educational Sciences.

As Furlong and Whitty argue in this volume (Furlong & Whitty, 2017), Educational Sciences is a long-established intellectual tradition in education internationally. In France, where it is called *Sciences de l'Éducation*, it became a formally recognised area of university study from 1968 onwards, though as Malet (2017) explains, its roots are far older. In the English-speaking world, where it is called the Disciplines of Education, it became established as *the* primary intellectual tradition in the study of education at around the same time, though again, it has older roots going back to the nineteenth century.

Educational Sciences (or the Disciplines of Education) is based on the assumption that educational questions should be addressed by drawing on any one of a range of distinct disciplinary perspectives. Traditionally in the English-speaking world, these have been sociology, psychology, philosophy and history, but many other disciplinary perspectives have at times also been included. Today, for example, economics is a particularly powerful perspective, especially in the USA and the UK. The fact that Educational Sciences is seen as plural (it is Educational Science*s*) is therefore important. No one individual theoretical perspective is seen as sufficient in itself; the study of education necessarily demands multiple different theoretical lenses, each of which offers an interpretation of educational phenomena from its own distinctive theoretical point of view. Indeed, the Educational Sciences model does not purport to provide a unified 'theory' of education. As Tibble (1966) argued in the introduction to his classic book *The Study of Education*, from this perspective there is no such thing as a distinctively 'educational' way of thinking. In studying education, all one can ever do is draw on psychological or historical or sociological or philosophical ways of thinking to throw light on specific educational issues.

It is this perspective that has in recent years emerged as a parallel approach in Latvia, so that Educational Sciences now sits next to *Pedagoģija* in many contexts. The University of Latvia provides an interesting example of these two contemporary approaches, in that it has two separate structural units that have adopted different approaches to deal with education as a field of study today.

On the one hand, the Department of *Pedagoģija* (the former Institute of *Pedagoģija* and Psychology) has since the political redirection focused on the stabilities of the past as a way of facing the future. The most significant of those stabilities is that *Pedagoģija* has been accepted as a commonly understood background for studying formal or institutional processes of education across the country as a whole; its capacity for congruent theories and practices means it is able to reflect paradigm shifts and other changes in a systemic and a systemised way. The department follows the historical traditions and runs well-established master's and doctoral programmes in *Pedagoģija*, and has a number of experienced educators who have been able to function as agents of change – who continue to prepare new generations of researchers and educators. This experience has demonstrated that *Pedagoģija* can credibly continue to act as the foundation for the theory and practice of formal and non-formal education even in these changed times. It is for this reason that in 1999 it was nominated in the revised classification of sciences (LZP, 1999).

At the same time, the university's Faculty of Education, Psychology and Arts, also undergoing considerable change, chose a different conceptual framework – that of Educational Sciences. In that faculty, *Pedagoģija* is conceptualised in its narrowest sense, as a synonym for teaching. The newly introduced approach, which aimed at linking into European terminology, looked innovative and allowed for the introduction of Educational Sciences as a background for teacher education even though it had no unifying theory or definitions. The result has been the use of fragments of *Pedagoģija* combined with disciplinary perspectives (for example, systemology, sociology of culture, and many others) under the title of Educational Sciences, which, as we have noted, in general terms lacks a clear, unifying educational core.

The differences of approach are also evident in different dimensions of government policy, which is defined by using unclear translations. On the one hand, the 1999 Law of Education defines education in a way that is compatible with the perspective of *Pedagoģija*: education is 'a process of systematic acquisition of knowledge and skills, development of attitudes, and the results thereof. The educational process includes teaching and upbringing activities' (Saeima, 1999, p. 4). On the other hand, however, the government's regulations point to the growing dominance of PISA as a powerful tool: (a) to initiate and justify educational developments by participating in projects and comparative studies (OECD, 2011); and (b) through the use of its technical capacity for national indicators to benchmark progress and guide further educational changes. PISA and other similar OECD projects are conducted in Latvia under the title of Educational Sciences; these investigations seldom deal with the background theories of a formal educational process, at least in projects conducted in this country. The failure to recognise the fundamental differences between the two approaches has been criticised by those who follow the framework of *Pedagoģija* as well as by those following Educational Sciences (Blūma, 2016, pp. 76-78).

Multiple strategic areas therefore need clarity, and the universities in Latvia have held a number of discussions on implementing appropriate approaches. The most pressing questions concern how to align with EU concepts of education and what investigations of practices should be supported in order to develop appropriate sciences and sound theoretical underpinnings for study programmes. This also involves the question of whether and how to conduct innovations; whether Latvia should follow the nation's educational tradition of seeing *Pedagoģija* as pivotal due to its core of constantly developing theory and practice, or whether it should adopt the more widely used term 'Educational Sciences'. The debate between these two different ways of conceptualising education is therefore fundamental in that it addresses the very understanding of the theoretical basis of teacher education. It covers the nature and the content of programmes, the balance between theoretical and practical domains, and the social context of the processes of formal education, as well as whether universities should choose academic or fast-track professional education.

Currently, universities, exercising their autonomy, select one or other of the terms: more often *Pedagoģija* is used for the core theory of a process of education, while Educational Sciences is used for studying the context. For example, pre-school teachers need to understand the developmental psychology of early childhood, while those working with adults need andragogy; anyone studying formal and non-formal processes of education needs appropriate background statistics and knowledge of contemporary social developments. All of these different contextual constructs can be called Educational Sciences in the multifaceted sphere of education. At the same time, however, no adequate descriptions have been developed in universities or faculties where Educational Sciences (plural) is used instead of the traditional Latvian *Pedagoģija*. This criticism of the teacher education programme at the Faculty of Education, Psychology and Art at the University of Latvia has recently led to the decision that it must now include a cluster of pedagogical disciplines (currently it covers 18 ECTS).

Meanwhile, the two notions still demonstrate some inconsistency. Usage of the term *Educational Sciences* is still very broad if compared with use of *Pedagoģija*, and educators without appropriate knowledge can get lost between the two terms – this influences programme development, especially for the first-level tertiary teacher education and master's programmes. For example, when the first academic master's programme in Educational Sciences was submitted for accreditation, it represented a compilation of psychology, pedagogy, sociology, and some other areas such as management; this reflected the scope of the problem. Currently this programme has found its focus and is now known as a Master's of Educational Management.

In other attempts to overcome the inconsistencies within the system, universities and the Ministry of Education have initiated a number of research projects examining a wide range of social processes that can affect the quality of education. These investigations, which are mainly concentrated in research institutions and doctoral programmes, might in the future lead to some kind of integration where *Pedagoģija* is more systematically related to social, economic and political disciplines. In other words, a new vision for both *Pedagoģija* and Educational Sciences may be about to appear.

Instead of a Conclusion: the benefit of adopting *Pedagoģija*

As has been argued, *Pedagoģija* in Latvia is practised as a holistic, personalised approach to working with learners in formal and informal educational settings. As such, it provides an overarching system that could bring greater coherence to educational services. It also provides a framework for discussing aims, activities and evaluation of achievements for learners at any age as it deals with general regularities of a pedagogical process.

Education degrees and qualifications are highly popular in Latvia, and graduates report their acceptance across European countries, based on their pedagogical skills that make them a well-equipped, flexible and stable workforce across a wide range of services, including governmental and non-governmental institutions (e.g. mentors for novices or refugees, nurses, trainers, etc.).

Pedagoģija has the potential to act as an inclusive and integrating approach due to its core functions and clear internal system of notions, which allows for coherent, mutually related actions of teaching and learning based on communication and cooperation. Constant inner regularities of the pedagogical process provide a congruency of dynamic links that is a basic criterion for research, and for action-based and process-orientated educational provision. As such, it potentially has much to offer to educationalists in other jurisdictions, perhaps most particularly those in the West.

Acknowledgement

Thanks are due to language consultant Ilona Bruveris of Australia.

Notes

[1] *Pedagoģija* is often translated into English as 'Pedagogy', but as this has particular connotations within English-speaking traditions we have chosen to use the Latvian word instead.

[2] Latvian higher education credits are aligned with the European Credit Transfer System (ECTS) credits. A credit point (CP) in Latvia is defined as one week of full-time study workload. The Latvian credit points are multiplied by 1.5 to be converted to ECTS credits.

[3] In other European countries there are of course many master's programmes in Educational Sciences that do have clear theoretical frameworks and a clear focus; there are also programmes that offer content similar to that of *Pedagoģija*: 'Pedagogy – Science of Education' at the University of Bologna awards the degree MA Pedagogy (http://www.mastersportal.eu/studies/31174/pedagogy-science-of-education.html); 'Pedagogical Sciences' at Radboud University (the Netherlands) awards Master of Sciences, pedagogical sciences (http://www.ru.nl/english/education/masters/pedagogical-sciences/). However, when those models are simply borrowed without appropriate comparative analysis it can give rise to programmes that are flawed in the Latvian context.

[4] Published in *Skolotājs/Teacher* (Žogla, 1995), and in the *News of the Latvian Academy of Sciences* (Čehlova & Špona, 2000; Kopeloviča & Žukovs, 2001; Žogla, 2000); report on pedagogical support of a person's socialisation (Žogla, 2001) at the Department of Humanities and Social Sciences of the Latvian Academy of Sciences (Žogla, 2001).

References

Assessment, Teaching, and Learning: a new vision on pedagogy, in *The Gordon Commission on the Future on Assessment in Education*, vol. 2 (1), 2012.

Ball, A.F. (2012) To Know is Not Enough: knowledge, power, and the zone of generativity, *Educational Researcher*, 41(8), 283-293. https://doi.org/10.3102/0013189X12465334

Ball, D.L. & Forzani, F.M. (2007) Wallace Foundation Distinguished Lecture: what makes education research 'educational'? *Educational Researcher*, 36(9), 529-540.

Blūma, D. (2016) Skolotāju izglītība Latvijā paradigmu maiņas kontekstā (1991-2000) [Teacher Education in the Context of Paradigm Shift in Latvia (1991-2000)]. Riga: University of Latvia.

Brühlmeier, A. (2010) *Head, Heart and Hand: education in the spirit of Pestalozzi.* Cambridge: Sophia Books.

Buchberger, F. & Buchberger, I. (1999) Didaktik/Fachdidaktik as Integrative Transformation Science(-s): a science/sciences of/for the teaching profession? *TNTEE Publications*, 2(1), 67-83.

Čehlova, Z. & Špona, A. (2000) Pedagoģijas zinātnes priekšmeta būtība [The Essence of Pedagoģija's Object], *Latvijas Zinātņu Akadēmijas Vēstis [News of the Latvian Academy of Sciences]*, 54(1-2), 96-98.

Cochran-Smith, M. (2005) Teacher Educators as Researchers: multiple perspectives, *Teaching and Teacher Education*, 21(2), 219-225. https://doi.org/10.1016/j.tate.2004.12.003

Danish School of Educational Research, Aarhus University (2016) What is Pedagogy? edu.au.dk/en/research (accessed on 10 July 2016).

Dauge, A. (1929) Paidagoģija un psīcholoģija [Pedagogy and psychology], *Audzinātājs*, 4, 99.

Dauge, A. (1932) *Vispārīgā paidagoģija: Latvijas Universitātē lasāmo lekciju kurss.* [General pedagogy: notes for the course delivered at the University of Latvia]. *Rokraksta vietā* [manuscript].

Depaepe, M. (2002) The Practical and Professional Relevance of Educational Research and Pedagogical Knowledge from the Perspective of History: reflection on the Belgian case in its international background, *European Educational Research Journal*, 1(2), 363. https://doi.org/10.2304/eerj.2002.1.2.10

Dewey, J. (1963) *Experience and Education.* New York: Collier Books (first published in 1938).

Fägerlind, I. & Saha, L.J. (1989) *Education and National Development: a comparative perspective*, 2nd edn. Oxford: Pergamon Press.

Fedeli, C. (2007) Verso la pedagogia come scienza autonoma, in G. Chiosso (Ed.) *L' educazione nell' Europa moderna. Teorie e istituzioni gall' Umanesimo alprimo Ottocemto.* Milan: Mondadori.

Furlong, J. & Whitty, G. (2017) Educational Knowledge and Academic Traditions, in G. Whitty & J. Furlong (Eds) *Knowledge and the Study of Education: an international exploration.* Oxford: Symposium Books. https://dx.doi.org/10.15730/books.100

Gudjons, H. (1995) *Pädagogisches Grundwissen*, 4th edn. Bad Heilbrunn: Julius Klinkhardt Verlag.

Gudjons, H. (1998) *Pedagoģijas pamatatziņas* [Pedagogical Foundations]. Riga: Zvaigzne ABC.

Hessens, S. (1929) *Paidagoģikas pamati: Ievads lietājamā filozofijā* [Fundamentals of Pedagogy: introduction to philosophy-in-use]. Riga: O.Berga izdevniecība.

Hörster, R. (1998) Paedagogisches Handeln, in H-H. Krüger & W. Helsper (Eds) *Einfürung in Grundbegriffe und Grundfragen der Erziehungswissenschaft*. Opladen: Leske+Budrich.

Husen, T. (1979) General Theories in Education: a twenty-five-year perspective, *International Review of Education*, 25(2-3), 325-345.

Jank, W. & Meyer, H. (1994) *Didaktische Modelle*. Berlin: Cornelsen Verlag Scriptor.

Klafki, W. (1990) Abschied von der Aufklärung? Grundzüge eines Bildungstheoretichen Gegenentwurfs, in H.-H. Krüger (Ed.) *Abshied von der Aufklärung?*, pp. 91-104. Opladen: Leske + Budrich.

Kopeloviča, A. & Žukovs, L. (2001) Pedagoģijas zinātnes priekšmets un apakšnozares [Object of pedagogy as a science and its sub-branches], *Latvijas Zinātņu Akadēmijas Vēstis [News of the Latvian Academy of Sciences]*, 55(1/2), 17-19.

Kron, F.W. (2001) *Grundwissen Pädagogik*. Munich: Ernst Reinhardt Verlag.

Leach, J. & Moon, B. (Eds) (1999) *Learners and Pedagogy*. London: SAGE.

Leach, J. & Moon, B. (Eds) (2008) *Learners and Pedagogy*. London: Paul Chapman Publishing in association with The Open University.

Leontyev, A.N. (1975) *Деятельность. Сознание. Личность* [Action, consciousness, personality], 3rd edn, in Russian. Moscow: Politizdat.

Loughran, J. (2010) *What Expert Teachers Do: enhancing professional knowledge for classroom practice*. London: Routledge.

LR Saeima (Parliament of RL) (1999) *Izgl t bas likums* [Law of Education]. https://likumi.lv/doc.php?id=50759

LZP (1999) *Zinātņu nozares un apakšnozares* [Council of Sciences. Branches and Sub-branches of Sciences). https://www.councilofsciences/branches (accessed on 12 December 2015).

Malet, R (2017) From Science to Sciences de l'Éducation in France: past and present in the construction of a discipline, in G. Whitty & J. Furlong (Eds) *Knowledge and the Study of Education: an international exploration*. Oxford: Symposium Books. https://dx.doi.org/10.15730/books.100

Meyer, H. (1997) *Schulpädagogik. Band II: Für Fortgeschrittene*. Berlin, Cornelsen Verlag Scriptor.

MK (2000) Noteikumi par prasībām pedagogiem nepieciešamajai kvalifikācijai ar un bez iepriekšējas pedagoģiskās izglītības [Cabinet of Ministers on the required pedagogical education for all tertiary educators], no. 347. https://www.google.lv/webhp?ie=utf-8&oe=utf-8&client=firefox-b&gws_rd=cr&ei=AyLyV4fKFMOrsAHu5bbgDw#q=MK+2000+Nr+347 *https://www.google.lv/webhp?ie=utf-8&oe=utf-8&client=firefox-b&gws_rd=cr&ei=AyLyV4fKFMOrsAHu5bbgDw – q=MK+2000+Nr+347*

MK (2014) *Nacionālās attīstības plāns 2014-2020.gadiem* (Cabinet of ministers. National developmental plan for 2014-2020). http://www.varam.gov.lv/lat/pol/ppd/ilgtsp_att/?doc=13858 (accessed on 2 November 2015).

Organisation for Economic Co-operation and Development (OECD) (2005) The Definition and Selection of Key Competencies. http://www.oecd.org/pisa/35070367.pdf (accessed on 2 November 2015).

Organisation for Economic Co-operation and Development (OECD) (2009) 21st Century Skills and Competences for New Millennium Learners in OECD Countries. http://www.oecd.org/officialdocuments/publicdisplaydocumentpdf/?cote=EDU/WKP%282009%2920&doclanguage=en (accessed on 2 November 2015).

Organisation for Economic Co-operation and Development (OECD) (2011) PISA in Focus. www.oecd.org/pisa/48910490.pdf (accessed on 2 November 2015).

Patterson, C. (1973) *Humanistic Education.* New York: Prentice Hall.

Pollard, A. (Ed.) (2010) *Professionalism and Pedagogy: a contemporary opportunity. A Commentary by TLRP and GICE.* London: TLRP. http://www.tlrp.org/pub/documents/TLRPGTCEProf... (accessed on 11 May 2016).

Saeima (2010) *Paziņojums par Latvijas ilgtspējīgas attīstības stratēģijas līdz 2030.gadam apstiprināšanu* [Sustainable development of Latvia until 2030], *Latvijas Vēstnesis,* 101(4293), 29 June 2010 (accessed on 12 December 2015).

Schukina, G.I. (1986) The Role of Action in the Process of Teaching-Learning (published in Russian as: Щукина, Г.И. *Роль деятельности в учебном процессе*). Москва: Просвещение), in Gordon Commission on the Future of Assessment in Education (2012) *Assessment, Teaching, and Learning,* 2(1), 1.

Tibble, J.W. (Ed.) (1966) *The Study of Education.* London: Routledge & Kegan Paul.

Toffler, A. (1971) *Future Shock.* New York: Bantam.

Townsend, T. (2010) Educating School Leaders to Think and Act Both Locally and Globally, *International Journal of Leadership in Education,* 13(3), 335-348. https://doi.org/10.1080/13603124.2010.505300

Tubbs, N. (2012) *The New Teacher: an introduction to teaching in comprehensive education.* London: Routledge.

UNESCO/UNITWIN (2000) *Teacher Education towards the Aim of Sustainable Development 2000-2010.* https://du.lv/fakultates/izglitibas-un-vadibas-fakultate/strukturvienibas/petnieciskie-un-zinatniskie-projekti/

Van Driel, H. & Berry, A. (2012) Teacher Professional Development Focusing on Pedagogical Content Knowledge, *Educational Researcher,* 41(1), 26-28. https://doi.org/10.3102/0013189X11431010

Vygotsky, L.S. (1978) *Mind in Society: the development of higher psychological processes.* Cambridge. MA: Harvard University Press.

Waring, M. & C. Evans (2015) *Understanding Pedagogy: developing a critical approach to teaching and learning.* London: Routledge.

Watkins, C. & Mortimore, P. (1999) Pedagogy: what do we know? In P. Mortimore
(Ed.) *Understanding Pedagogy and its Impact on Learning*, pp. 1-19. London: Paul
Chapman. https://doi.org/10.4135/9781446219454.n1

Wulf, D. & Zirfas, J. (2007) Performative Pädagogik und performative
Bildungtheorien: Ein neues Focus erzhieungswissenschaftlicher Forshung, in
D. Wulf & J. Zirfas (Eds) (2007) *Pädagogik des Performativen. Theorien, Methoden,
Perspektiven.* Weinheim: Beltz.

Žogla, I. (1995) Skolas Pedagoģija [School Pedagogy], *Skolotājs [Teacher]*, 5, 8-10.

Žogla, I. (2000) Didaktikas teorijas un jēdzieni: salīdzinošais aspekts [Theories and
terminology of didactics compared], *Latvijas Zinātņu Akadēmijas Vēstis [News of
the Latvian Academy of Sciences]*, 55(1/2), (612/613), 20-25.

Žogla, I. (2001) *Personības socializācijas pedagoģiskais nodrošinājums* [Pedagogical
support of a person's socialization]. Report at the Department of Humanities and
Social Sciences of the Latvian Academy of Sciences.

Appendix

The structure of human development and basic educational aims	Pedagogical sub-mechanisms related to particular targets of creating dynamic links and verifying pedagogical process as a fact	Pedagogical objectives and strategies which follow the aims and match the mechanisms	Pedagogical regularities, means/tools, settings, dynamic links leading to the learner's success
Upbringing: attitudes, values, motives, viewpoints, responsibility etc. (educative aim)	Learner assessment of knowledge, skills, learning, content of education, cooperation, assistance, achievements etc. by using personally valid and meaningful criteria	Towards the learner's personal/individual, socially justified traits; responsibility and abilities of self-regulated, meaningful and justified choice of activities; outcomes-oriented learning; life-long learning leading to personal development	Meeting the learner's need for personal freedom, freedom to learn and achieving success. Promoting the learner's self-concept, self-regulated activities, criteria for meaningful choice, behaviour. Accent on reflection and self-evaluation skills in compliance with the learner's perspective of individual development
Experience (educational aim)	Integration between the acquired experience and the new information	Towards the skills of autonomous, self-regulated learning and	Modes of learning in pedagogical settings, teacher's targeted support of third-

	through assisted and/or self-regulated learning as the basis of building experience (surface, deep, strategic)	meaningful development of the learner's faculties	generation learning; meeting the learner's abilities and a need for positive emotions; inquiry, discovery, learning etc.
Mental (intellectual, emotional) and physical (posture, strength, agility, health etc.) development (developmental aims)	Education as the exercise of mental abilities and regular training of all physical abilities – always working towards achieving the next improved level; teaching-learning – a field of targeted activities as a basis for development; exercising the learner's mental, physical, social development	Towards creative, divergent and critical thinking, autonomous mind-set and possibly better personal physical qualities	Meeting the learner's mental and physical abilities, experience and developmental needs: content and process; suggested and chosen activities/tasks; learner's experiences and ability-based exercises to 'push' ahead learner's development compliant with their experience and educative achievements

Table AI. Conceptual background for *Pedagoġija*.

Teacher's activities, external component		Learner's activities, internal component
Standards, aims, objectives, incentives	↔	Learning identification, reasoning, motivation
↕		↕
Teacher's experience	↔	Learner's experience and perspective
↕		↕
Suggested process design, teaching structure	↔	Learner's acceptance of process design
↕		↕
Content, subject-matter	↔	Learner's tools, learning structures
↕		↕
Goals (academic outcomes)	↔	Learner's personal achievements
↕		↕
Reflection, evaluation	↔	Self-assessment, self-evaluation
To further aims and objectives		

Table AII. Structure of pedagogical processes.

CHAPTER 5

The Study of Education in Australia: shifting knowledge interests

SUSAN GROUNDWATER-SMITH & NICOLE MOCKLER

SUMMARY This chapter traces the evolution of teacher education policy and practice in Australia and its relationship to the wider discipline of education. It is argued that teacher education has largely been driven by instrumental knowledge interests, particularly in the context of its evolution within teacher training colleges. The case is made for a more transformative stance where teacher education is informed by the foundation disciplines of education, especially the philosophy, psychology, sociology and history of education, which can serve to enable teacher education students to better understand the nature of educational practice. The chapter employs the notion of practice architectures to draw out the argument. It traces out the history of teacher education that informs these assertions. Furthermore, attention is drawn to the role of research in educational practice and the ways in which such research informs not only the development of policy but also of practice.

Education policy governing teacher education in Australia largely reflects the notion that learning how to teach is a 'practical' venture that does not require knowledge of what lies behind teaching practice, its historical roots, its philosophical and social underpinnings and its behavioural manifestations. As initial teacher education becomes increasingly regulated, space within programs of study for the 'foundations' of education (i.e. educational philosophy, psychology, sociology and history) has been seen to give way to a growing explicit focus on literacy and numeracy and content-related curriculum studies. Sjølie (2014, p. 733) distinguishes between theory *for* practice – that is, theory that enables practice – and theory *about* practice – that is, theory that permits a deeper and more profound understanding of the very foundations of practice. She cites Kvernbekk (2005), who argues that theories in teacher education are oriented to the former with a consequence that practice can be regarded as floating free from these important and critical antecedents.

Of course, Australia is not alone in this disposition, and it has not been one that always prevailed in the preparation of teachers. In this chapter, we provide a national case study of the field of Education in Australia, using the conceptual tools of Habermasian knowledge interests and the theory of practice architectures (Kemmis & Grootenboer, 2008) to understand transition over time. We argue that Education Studies in Australia has been the site of struggle between various interest groups, including federal and state governments, universities and other tertiary institutions, statutory authorities and teachers' unions. Some of these struggles are reflective of global policy moves in education studies and teacher education across the anglophone world, while others relate to the particularities of the education field in Australia. We aim to place the current policy settlements that frame education studies within their historical context, and proceed to ask the question 'whose knowledge interests are served in the contemporary field of education in Australia?'

Our account is presented in three parts. In the first, we provide a brief introduction to our conceptual and theoretical tools, and also to the broader context of higher education in Australia. In the second section, we detail the Australian case study, exploring the field of education in Australia via the dual trajectories of teacher education and educational research. In the final section, we reflect on the various knowledge interests as they have played out in Australia, addressing the issue of what counts as 'real' educational knowledge and who gets to say, drawing on these observations to suggest a preferred and alternative vision for teacher education in Australia.

Introduction and Background

Two key and interrelated sets of conceptual and theoretical tools have informed the shaping of this national case study. For this discussion we use both to act as dual lenses. First, the notion of knowledge interests as understood by Jurgen Habermas (1984a, b) is critical, particularly his discussion of the consequences of the persistent colonisation of the *lifeworld* by the *system* in the contemporary age, and the subsequent impacts upon practice. Second, the notions of 'site ontologies' (Schatzki, 2002, 2010) and 'practice architectures' (Kemmis & Grootenboer, 2008; Kemmis et al, 2014) can help us to understand the deeply contextual nature of education studies as a *practice tradition*. Here we understand educational studies as a 'metapractice', defined by Kemmis and Grootenboer (2008) as a practice that frames, shapes and changes other practices.

The broad aim of this discussion is to make a contribution to the development of a stance that is practical, understanding still that it draws upon those matters related to issues *about* practice and *for* practice referred to in our introduction, but that is, nonetheless, a position that should 'not abstract itself from the intended practice', according to Gadotti, but commit itself to:

> educate individuals as a point on the horizon but never a finished
> process because education is really an unending process ...
> Education is at the same time promise and project.
> (Gadotti, 1996, p. 7)

Thus we see that those charged with shaping the provision of Education Studies should imagine the field as a practice-in-making. Not as a template that is reiterative, technical and bureaucratised (Gadotti, 1996, p. xvii), but as a set of principles and procedures whereby we can think our way through the possibilities of where the study of education may take us. Van Manen (1999) has observed that 'Practice' is one of the least theorised concepts that circulate in professional discourse in fields such as health and education, arguing that 'in education the term practice is rarely systematically theorized' (van Manen, 1999, p. 2). Furthermore, 'practice' seldom stands alone – for example: policy and practice; theory and practice; research and practice; structures and practice. The term is often modified: institutional practices; cultural practices; teaching practice; professional practice; place-based practice; communities of practice; evidence-based practice. Is such and such a practice static or is it dynamic? Is it reducible to a complex series of transactions involved in dealing with others or materials? Is it fixed or alterable?

Schwandt (2005) writes of 'practice fields' and argues that a common view of practice is that it is 'a complex set of techniques (for diagnosis; for problem-solving; for treatment; for management; for planning; for assessment; for the administration, organization and delivery of service, etc.) that can be considered, changed, deployed, taught, learned and transferred independently' (p. 316), all within the realm of everyday 'doing' and 'acting'. Bourdieu's theory of practice (1977, 1990) emphasises the 'logics' that shape and frame practice within each field, and the relational constitution of practice, arguing that practice is 'the product of a *practical sense* of a socially constituted "sense of the game"' (Wacquant, 1989, p. 42), born of the interplay between the field itself and the habitus of agents within it.

Practice is inseparable from the knowledge forms and interests on which it is based and the cultural context within which it evolves. This chapter represents a narrative of practice with respect to the study of education in Australia during the twentieth century and into the new millennium. It considers practice as situated in terms of both knowledge and action. Drawing on Nicolini (2013), it sees that practice theory is constituted through a variety of commensurable theoretical approaches that are historically connected and have conceptual similarities. Nicolini contends these to be: the importance of activity, performance and work; embodiment and materiality; being contributed to through agency; being transformative in terms of knowledge, meaning and discourse; and foregrounding 'the centrality of interests in all human matters and therefore [putting] an emphasis on the importance of power, conflict and politics as the constitutive elements of the social reality we experience' (p. 6).

This final constitutive element highlights the way in which the constructs of knowledge interests and practice architectures might be seen as situationally critical in relation to one another. By using the thinking tools related to Habermasian knowledge interests, with their centrality of thinking about power, we are able to address the enabling and constraining conditions that have governed knowledges and beliefs with regard to the study of education as a practice in relation both to skills and understanding and to the ways in which it is informed by contributing disciplines that serve both practical and theoretical purposes.

Two Conceptual Tools:
knowledge interests and practice architectures

Habermas provides us with a form of social explanation that brings together our understanding of knowledge interests and the ways in which they may impact upon each other. It is important, we believe, to acknowledge that while the knowledge interests may each be seen as distinctive in explaining purposes and outcomes, they also impact one upon the other.

Technical knowledge interests serve to predict and control. In today's prevailing neoliberal climate in Australia they have the ascendancy. Thus, under these auspices Education Studies may be evaluated in terms of the ways in which these interests serve an instrumental purpose – engaging in their study will presumably contribute to more improved and efficient educational practices. Technical knowledge interests in education tend to privilege that which can be most easily codified and measured: in the development of teacher or teaching standards, in many of the accreditation processes for initial teacher education, and in moves toward the production of 'classroom ready teachers' (Craven et al, 2015), we see the emergent dominance of technical knowledge interests that will nurture particular forms of practice.

Practical/interpretive knowledge interests are those that lead to informed social understanding, mutual understanding and self-understanding – for instance, around how and why particular practices have arisen and become embedded, or rejected as the case may be. Interestingly, we see much of the contemporary discussion of the necessarily 'practical' nature of teaching to be forged more out of technical knowledge interests than out of practical/interpretive ones, as evidenced by our earlier discussion regarding the evolution of current policies across Australian states and territories. An effacing of the possibilities can arise when those learning to become teachers have insight not only into their own motivations and drivers, contributing to their professional identity, but also into the ways in which the conditions under which they are to practise have been formed by government policies at a variety of levels.

Finally, *critical/emancipatory* knowledge interests are those that aim to actively overcome and resist dogmatism, compulsion and domination, and to support the development of conditions within which others might find opportunities for criticality and emancipation. Education Studies forged out of critical/emancipatory knowledge interests tend to focus on the necessarily contextual nature of 'good' educational practice (as opposed to 'what works' or 'best practice'), and to be concerned with education as a public good, and with the role of education in the creation of just and equitable societies. A teacher education curriculum that has such a focus is difficult to identify in the various programs available in Australian universities.

While the concept of knowledge interests offers a useful framework, it does leave unanswered the question of whether reflecting upon education studies should be interpreted mainly from the standpoint of those who are driven by a marketised, bureaucratic world, steeped in the notion of human capital development as a central aim of school, and indeed university, education, or from the standpoint of those who are driven by an understanding of the importance of the cultural, social and political contexts in which they and their students participate. The first standpoint is represented by the *system* theory of Luhmann (1995), the second by *lifeworld*, as seen in the phenomenological theory of Schutz and Luckman (1973). Habermas deals creatively to overcome this duality (Habermas, 1984b). He developed his theory in an ongoing debate with Schutz's theory of lifeworld and Luhmann's system theory, arguing that each of these are too narrow to understand social phenomena. Habermas is of the view that social situations should be interpreted as a result of the *interplay* of both forces, and this sits in interesting ways when we examine the place of Education Studies in today's Australian university. Is it possible to be creative, daring and subversive in an essentially pragmatic world? Is there a theory of being in the world that can give us some direction?

When we question the extent to which Education Studies are prescribed by the *system*, we need to ask a series of ancillary questions: who actually forms that system, how does the system determine how ends are achieved? What are the roles permitted to academics and their students in that system? What scope do they have to contribute to the structure and construction of education studies and decide upon both means and ends? The work of Schatzki (2002, 2010) and those who have interpreted that work in the form of 'practice architectures' (Kemmis et al, 2014) may give us some purchase here.

Schatzki (2010) sees that practice (in this discussion, the practice of formulating the 'meta practice' of Education Studies) is influenced or 'prefigured' by particular arrangements, specifically the cultural-discursive, material-economic and socio-political influences/arrangements within which

127

practice is enacted. He avers that learning, for example, is not a process, the characteristics of which are independent of the places of its occurrence (Schatzki, 2002); rather, he argues, human lives proceed through practices, and practices form fields, complexes, textures or a 'plenum' where social affairs transpire. Thus, in this example, learning is integral to the context in which that learning occurs. Ontologically, it can be argued that learning in the context of Education Studies is necessarily impelled by the knowledge interests that govern it.

Drawing upon this stance, Kemmis et al (2014) argue that learning is a process of initiation into practice that embraces activities (doings), language (sayings) and relations between people and entities in the world (relatings). Effectively, sayings, doings and relatings 'hang together' in a project of practice – let's say Education Studies. They are both site-based and historically embedded. Understanding each and the interplay between them enables a deep and more profound sense of the conditions for the practice, both those that shape practices and those that prefigure practices to come. Understanding the 'bundling' of sayings and doings and relatings allows for the identification of both enabling and constraining conditions for practice.

By assembling these stances – knowledge interests, *system* and *lifeworld* contrasts, landscapes and architectures of practice – it may be possible to better formulate an understanding and critique of the state of Education Studies today in Australia in the light of their enactment over time and in place. Thus, in this chapter we ask whether we, in Australia, can transcend utilitarian knowledge interests and orientations toward narrow accountability and performative regimes to take up Biesta's challenge to 'give teaching back to education' (Biesta, 2014, p. 44).

The Context of Higher Education in Australia

Before turning to the specifics of teacher education in Australia it is helpful to have access to an overall sketch of higher education as it stands today across the nation. Australia is a federation of six states and two territories. As an accident of history, each has its own procedures for the establishment and governance of its higher education institutions, with currently 43 accredited universities in Australia (including two international universities and one private one). The public funding of universities rests with the Commonwealth, and university fees for local students are currently regulated by the Commonwealth government.

The percentage of Australia's population with a bachelor's degree is high by international standards. In 2013, just over 1.3 million students were enrolled in higher education, and this statistic demonstrates an increase in the share of the population who attend university. The 2011 census data show 36.6% of 20-year-olds attended universities or other tertiary institutions. In 2011, the percentage of the population with a bachelor's degree or higher (18.8%) was over nine times the figure for 1971 (2%)

(Australian Government Department of Education and Training, 2014). This growth was underwritten by the Whitlam government's commitment to making higher education more accessible to middle- and working-class Australians, and with the associated abolition of university fees in 1973. Tertiary education was free for Australian students from 1973 to 1989, when, in response to the increased participation rate, the Hawke/Keating government oversaw the re-introduction of student fees. Despite high admission and completion rates, however, students from lower socio-economic backgrounds and Indigenous students are still under-represented among both students and graduates (Parr, 2015).

Since the large-scale reforms, including restructuring decisions, enacted in the Hawke/Keating years, higher education in Australia has become increasingly subject to market forces. This has had significant consequences for the shaping of courses, with those focused on a liberal education, seen to have value for its own sake, competing for students and funds. This is in comparison with professional education, driven more by notions of human capital investment and development and designed to meet the needs of a range of employers whose demands are themselves shaped increasingly by neo-liberal discourses (Guri-Rosenblit & Sebkova, 2004). This period has seen the burgeoning of such courses at undergraduate level, developed at an increasingly specialised level, along with a corresponding decline in the proportion of undergraduate students engaging in generalist arts, science and economics degree courses. In the public discourse in Australia, higher education is seen either (and sometimes concurrently) as a public investment or as an economic drain. In professional courses, more and more of the university curriculum has been appropriated to meet various state and national standards and accreditation requirements; this will be more widely discussed in relation to studies in education, below.

In common with their international counterparts in many jurisdictions, Australian universities are subject to audits and quality-assurance procedures – for example, the Commonwealth government's Excellence in Research for Australia (ERA) national evaluation, a 'nationwide stock take of discipline strengths and areas for development' (Australian Research Council, 2015b). Such exercises use citation profiles and journal impact factors to decide upon the status of disciplines and universities as a whole (Calver & Beattie, 2015). This has particular consequences for education academics who may wish to predominantly focus on creating, through their work, 'impact' on the professional field, but who are increasingly expected to focus their labours on academic journals with a high impact factor of a different kind, journals which are most usually inaccessible to teachers and other school-based educators. This competitiveness has its effects across the board. Institutions wishing to grow their ERA rankings may even 'buy' whole research groupings in time for the ERA exercise in a given year by taking part in what Ordorika and Lloyd (2015, p. 385) have termed 'an academic arms race'.

These developments have implications for the ways in which teacher education is investigated and researched as a field of practice. Thus the shape of Education Studies in Australia in contemporary times is subject to policy directions around teacher education and educational research, both of which have been 'hot topics' for governments in Australia and elsewhere (Furlong, 2013) over the past two decades.

Mapping the Field of Education in Australia: teacher education and educational research

Teacher Education

Historically, the field of Education Studies in Australia has followed two distinct trajectories: the study of education as a preparation for teaching, and the study of education as what can effectively be seen as a sub-discipline in liberal arts. While distinctive, there has also been seen a crossover between the two where the preparation of teachers in pursuit of a qualification has been informed by disciplinary-based perspectives such as educational psychology, sociology of education, philosophy of education and history of education – a familiar story as told by Lawn and Furlong (2009).

The path that we trace travels from the work of teacher training colleges to the formation of teacher education within colleges of advanced education, and thence to the subsequent creation of a unified national system of higher education and its relation more broadly to higher education policies in Australia today.

The era of the teacher training college. Teacher education across Australia (most commonly referred to as 'teacher training') took a hold following the federation of the various states (former colonies) in 1901 and the establishment of teacher training colleges with varying patterns of interaction with the established universities. As Aspland (2006) has noted, a pronounced binary system emerged between the two world wars. The university system was disconnected from teacher education, 'which in turn, became firmly embedded in training colleges as second tier universities' (p. 146). It should be noted that those attending such teachers' colleges were effectively employees of the Department of Education of the apposite state. They were paid and bonded to teach where and when required. Their lecturers and tutors remained employees of the relevant Department of Education, with their qualifications being based more upon successful practice in schools than upon higher education degrees.

The curriculum of the time was determined by the employing authority and was not noted for critique or reflection; indeed, it was seen as inherently conservative (Hyams, 1979). Expressly, the functions of teachers' training colleges were to develop the techniques and skills of teaching and to become familiar with the requirements of the employing authority (Vick, 2003).

The largely technical knowledge interests of employers thus shaped teacher education in teacher training colleges, contrasting with that which, simultaneously during this period, was developed by university departments of education, usually located within faculties of arts. The academic practice was related to research in the various sub-disciplines and some service teaching to those undertaking postgraduate Diplomas of Education (a common initial teacher education pathway for secondary teachers at the time), and in some cases small 'boutique' Bachelor of Education programs, such as that established by the University of Sydney in the 1970s. On the whole, however, as a metapractice, Education Studies in the days of teacher training colleges was shaped out of a concern for technical knowledge interests, aiming to equip teachers with the technical skills and knowledge required to be effectively initiated into teaching practice.

The introduction of Colleges of Advanced Education. The release of the Martin Report in 1965 [1] led to the establishment of an advanced education sector in the form of Colleges of Advanced Education (CAEs) that developed courses not only in teacher education but also in other professional areas, such as nursing and business studies.

Importantly, the link between the employing authorities and the preparation of teachers was severed and a greater independence achieved.

> In the CAE sector staff provided more praxis, more industry oriented training and education for the professions. They were 'local' and teaching and service oriented, and if they conducted any research, it was applied research. Colleges offered bachelor and master by coursework degrees ... [Whereas] Universities were self-accrediting institutions, established under a state Act of Parliament, institutions in the CAE sector had to have their degree programs accredited by state appointed panels. Both position titles and functions, and salary structure differed in the two sectors. (Moses, n.d., p. 5)

During the later 1970s and 1980s the CAE sector flourished and was the main provider for initial teacher education courses and the main 'home' to Education Studies. The colleges incorporated a number of former teachers' colleges, including those directed to early childhood teaching. They were still state-based and developed to meet the requirements for entry into the teaching profession governed by various state instrumentalities. Education Studies was generally skill-based with an emphasis placed upon learning in the practicum, when students were assigned for periods of time to schools. While not a complete segue from an orientation to those hitherto-mentioned technical knowledge interests, there was a greater focus on satisfying an interpretative approach, particularly in relation to reflection-on-and-in-practice (Boud et al, 1985; Hatton & Smith, 1995; Murray et al, 2008). This development was strongly influenced by the work of Donald Schon (1983), which emphasised concurrent reflection on practice by the practitioner. Even so, there was a concern by some that, paradoxically, reflection can trap a practitioner within 'a New Right ideology of radical interventionism' (Smyth,

1992, p. 267) that required the focusing upon ends that have been determined by others and not an active process of critique. We see here, then, a segue in terms of knowledge interests from the technical encapsulated in earlier models of teacher training to more interpretative/practical knowledge interests, incorporating dimensions of reflective practice, and a broader gaze rather than a narrowly drawn focus on classroom practicalities.

The creation of a unified national system of higher education. In the late 1980s the reforming national government of Hawke and Keating made a decision to dispense with the divide between CAEs and universities, and oversaw a series of amalgamations where 47 CAEs were combined with 19 existing universities to create 38 public universities (Dawkins, 1987, 1988).

In some ways in could be argued that the creation of a unified national system led to greater diversity in forms of teacher education in that the various universities placed an emphasis upon course structures that conformed to their own policies and practices, some of which had existed over a long period of time. It was believed that there would be a more scholarly and theoretical approach to becoming a teacher. Academic staff were encouraged to engage more fully in research and undertake doctoral studies, and other logics of practice of the field of higher education came to shape Education Studies in overt ways during this period. In some quarters programs of study were shaped explicitly out of critical/emancipatory knowledge interests, placing concerns for social justice and the addressing of educational disadvantage at the centre of their design. Furthermore, the role of the foundation disciplines of educational sociology, psychology, philosophy and history expanded in this era in many programs of study, paving the way for a broad focus on education writ large, along with an intention for this broad focus to underpin and frame practical action.

However, the same period also saw the emergence of teaching standards for Australian teachers, and, over the ensuing decades, increasing cries for greater consistency of initial teacher education. At the same time, there was a push to conform to standards in relation to teacher quality and to improve the image of teaching in the community. In the 2000s, teacher education programs began to emerge that were built upon specified professional attributes and national standards tied to teacher accreditation (Ingvarson et al, 2006), a move that could be viewed as having moved teacher education back toward catering for technical over practical/interpretive or critical/emancipatory knowledge interests once again.

Teacher education in an age of compliance: the current field in Australia. In the light of a surge in reviews and investigations into teaching and teacher education, the current policy settlement with regard to the professional field in Australia is a particularly uneasy one. Louden (2008) wrote of the 101 reviews and inquiries into teacher education held at federal and state levels over the years from 1976 to 2006, and the years since then have been no different. Prior to the 2013 federal election, which brought the Liberal government to power, Christopher Pyne, then the Shadow Minister for

Education, responded to a question on ABC Radio National about the first education priority for the prospective new government. He answered:

> The first thing we could do is to make sure that the training of our teachers at university is of world standard... We would immediately instigate a very short term Ministerial advisory group to advise me on the best model for teaching in the world. How to bring out more practical teaching methods, based on more didactic teaching methods or more traditional methods rather than the child centred learning that has dominated the system for the last 20, 30 or 40 years, so teaching quality would be at my highest priority, followed by a robust curriculum, principal autonomy and more traditional pedagogy. So I want to make the education debate, move it on from this almost asinine debate about more money and make it about values because while money is important, what we are teaching our children and how we are teaching them and who is teaching them is all much more important. (Kelly, 2013)

True to his word, the Teacher Education Ministerial Advisory Group (TEMAG) was established shortly after the election, and in February 2015 its report, entitled 'Action Now: classroom ready teachers', was released (Craven et al, 2015). The recommendations of the report focus on the development and use of 'sophisticated approaches' to selection of candidates for teacher education courses, to 'ensure initial teacher education students possess the required academic skills and personal characteristics to become a successful teacher', and the development and implementation of a national literacy and numeracy test to ensure that teaching graduates are in the top 30% of the population for personal literacy and numeracy. The reconstitution of the Australian Institute for Teaching and School Leadership, under the leadership of John Hattie, 'to overhaul and manage the accreditation of initial teacher education programs, and work with the states and territories to ensure rigorous accreditation processes operate effectively with teacher registration', was another recommendation.

As always, the rhetoric is one of 'improvement' and 'quality'. The recommendations from the TEMAG report require tighter and more technical standards for initial teacher education as opposed to processes that encourage critique and diversity, and updated guidelines providing evidence of this were published in December 2015. Interestingly, while the updated guidelines tinker very minimally with the required program structure and content, the previous overarching requirement that 'programs must be sequenced coherently to reflect effective connections between theory and practice' (Australian Institute for Teaching and School Leadership, 2011, p. 13) has been removed in the newest version, and indeed, any mention of 'theory', which was already scant, appears to be both explicitly and implicitly absent in the new guidelines.

The practical implications of the revision to these guidelines remain to be seen; however, a potential shifting or narrowing of the curriculum to allow for more scope for 'impact' to be generated would not be surprising. The established (2011) guidelines might already be seen to be quite narrow and technical in terms of the knowledge interests served. They do, however, leave some room to move for universities wishing to shape teacher education programs to more critical or emancipatory ends, and many, including those at our own institution, aim to do this. Typically, both undergraduate and postgraduate initial teacher education programs include some dedicated study of educational psychology and sociology, with elements of philosophy and history integrated into these 'foundation' elements. The impact of LANTITE, the literacy and numeracy test for initial teacher education students, which began in 2016, in terms of a possible narrowing of the curriculum and increased focus on basic literacy and numeracy, also remains to be seen. All in all, however, the new reforms appear to point to a reclaiming of teacher education on behalf of technical knowledge interests. Much depends on how these moves are engaged with and/or resisted by universities – the extent to which critical/emancipatory knowledge interests in teacher education survive into the next decade certainly does.

What is required is a more nuanced understanding of the variability of place – that is, of the sayings, doings and relatings that are place based and evolve over time, as opposed to an assumption that 'best practice' can be defined once and for all and 'rolled out' to all Australian schools. These assemblages can be seen to be composed of a series of links and interconnections acting as an antidote to the increasingly global forces at work that Apple (2012) argues determine the ways in which key educational practices are increasingly being constructed.

Educational Research in Australia

The burgeoning commercial environment for educational research in a globalised world has had its effect on those who undertake educational research and those who commission it (Harman, 1987, 2003). Harman (2003) has argued that, indeed, in common with other developed nations, Australia has moved rapidly down the path of entrepreneurialism and managerialism in this regard. Citing Marginson and Considine (2000), he indicates that there is a pattern of making universities 'more like business enterprises' (pp. 9-11), with the associated practices of top-down management and a significant decline in the role of academic disciplines.

In their provocative diagnosis of the trajectory of educational research in Australia, McWilliam and Lee (2006) lamented the manner in which research is tied to current policy concerns with little imaginative work directed to what might be possible futures. They document government concerns that current research is too idiosyncratic, employing narrow case-study approaches as opposed to large-scale surveys that could inform policy, reducing concerns to simple solutions provided as clear and unambiguous diagnoses, as opposed to better understanding the contextual nature of educational practices with all of the associated nuanced variations.

The primary research funding body at a national level is the Australian Research Council (ARC), which oversees 'Discovery' and 'Linkage' programs. The Discovery program includes a number of competitive grant schemes, including a range of research fellowships and the 'Discovery Projects' scheme, which aims to:

- support excellent basic and applied research by individuals and teams;
- encourage research and research training in high-quality research environments;
- enhance international collaboration in research;
- expand Australia's knowledge base and research capability; and
- enhance the scale and focus of research in the Science and Research Priorities (Australian Research Council, 2015a).

Recent analysis of ARC funding in education undertaken by Graham and Buckley (2014) indicates that educational researchers were the recipients of 1.33% of the entire funding pool for ARC Discovery Projects (valued at approximately $258 million Australian) in 2014. Additionally, in the Linkage Projects scheme, which funds research conducted in concert with industry partners, research funded in the education field of research (field of research code 13) comprised 1.94% of the total budget for 2015. This is perhaps unsurprising considering the increasingly narrow focus of national research priorities. The Strategic Research Priorities established in 2013 to replace the prior 'National Research Priorities' were organised around 'the five most important challenges facing Australia' – namely: living in a changing environment; promoting population health and well-being; managing our food and water assets; securing Australia's place in a changing world; and lifting productivity and economic growth. In May 2015, their replacement by the new 'Science and Research Priorities' was announced, comprising food, soil and water, transport, cybersecurity, energy, resources, advanced manufacturing, environmental change and health, none of which lend themselves readily to research in education, or indeed the social sciences or humanities more broadly. The priorities themselves each come with a range of 'practical challenges', and the government notes that it 'will ensure that appropriate levels of public funding are allocated to research that addresses the most immediate problems facing the nation' (Commonwealth of Australia, 2015).

Meanwhile, think tanks and consultancies are increasingly generating research to inform education policy and practice. As an example, of the 11 pieces of 'supporting evidence' offered by the Australian Institute for Teaching and School Leadership as constituting the 'evidence base' for the Australian Teacher Performance and Development Framework (Australian Institute for Teaching and School Leadership, 2012), four were generated by consulting firms and think tanks, and a further six by the Organisation for Economic Co-operation and Development (OECD) and its employees. A similar story might be told for many pieces of education policy related to teacher development and professional standards in Australia, despite considerable public outlay on academic research in this area over the past decade, examples of which include the 'Teachers for a Fair Go: exemplary teachers of students in poverty' project, jointly funded by the ARC and the New South Wales Department of Education and Community (Munns et al, 2013), and the 'Effective Implementation of Pedagogical Reform' project (Gore & Bowe, 2015), both of which were large-scale projects funded through the ARC Linkage scheme in the years 2008-2011 and 2009-2012, respectively.

Also key to research informing policy in Australia is the Australian Council for Educational Research (ACER). Initially established in 1930 and supported by a grant from the Carnegie Foundation, the Council is now a non-profit organisation concerned with nine research programs:

- Assessment and Reporting: humanities and social sciences;
- Assessment and Reporting: mathematics and science;
- Higher Education;
- International Surveys;
- National Surveys;
- Policy Analysis and Program Evaluation;
- Psychometrics and Methodology;
- Systemwide Testing; and
- Teaching, Learning and Transitions.

With over 350 full-time employees, ACER produces reports, assessment evaluation and testing tools across the learning lifespan. It works closely with the States and Territories addressing a range of policy and practical issues, and until 2015 led the consortium coordinating the OECD Program for International Student Assessment (PISA), a role recently taken over by Pearson. From 2016 ACER has been responsible for developing and administering the LANTITE.

With respect to educational research, caught up in a world of international comparisons, the field of education found itself receiving a national average rating for research excellence of 2.2 out of 5 in the 2010 ERA, below the 'world standard' of 3 (Harrison & Seddon, 2013). As a result, the Australian Association for Research in Education (AARE) and the Australian Council of Deans of Education (ACDE) established a working party to create a strategic plan for strengthening national research capacity in education, at the same time noting that approximately a third of research entered in the education field of research for the ERA was not conducted by educational researchers, but rather by researchers from other disciplines engaging in scholarship of teaching and learning within their own fields. The ERA 2015 results saw an increase in the national average for education to

2.9, so it could be claimed that this and other capacity-building initiatives have perhaps had some impact. Furthermore, the notion of educational research informing and working alongside the field of practice has not been affirmed by research assessment exercises. The question of 'what impact?' is a salient one for educational researchers who seek to influence school and policy development, which, as noted above, seldom comes through publication in the highest-ranked academic journals (Kemmis et al, 2014), and which may not easily fit the pragmatic imperatives of the national research agenda.

As well as academic research, Australia has, over the years, developed significant funded projects that have encouraged and nurtured shared research that has enabled the field and academy to work together to produce and critique professional knowledge. Such projects as the National Schools Network (Groundwater-Smith, 1998) evolved as a response to what became known as 'the accord' that brought together industrial and professional concerns on the basis that the conditions under which teachers worked were also the conditions under which children learned. Partners included networks of schools, academic associates and teachers' unions. Action research has long been a tradition in Australia (Groundwater-Smith & Irwin, 2011). However, while assisting in providing local solutions to local problems and contributing to an accumulation of professional knowledge, it has rarely been consulted as a body of work that can inform teaching and teacher education, with the majority of reviews being conducted at arm's length from practice.

Conclusion: the state of Education Studies today in Australia – can we imagine possible alternative futures?

Altogether, then, it can be argued that Education Studies in Australian universities and the related field of practice mirror counterparts in English/Welsh institutions, which in turn have been strongly influenced by successive government policies within a broad global policy framework (Lingard et al, 2005). Policy borrowing is extensive and pervasive, but generally, it can be argued, tends to be unidirectional. Australia may lag behind by several years, but seemingly it does not learn the lessons from its counterparts' experiences, but goes on perpetuating the same narrowly informed practices. Furthermore, the study of education is, in Australia as elsewhere, an evolving, complex, multifaceted practice composed of interacting 'sayings', 'doings' and 'relatings' and informed by patterns of power shaped by particular knowledge interests.

As we have demonstrated, those knowledge interests that are currently being served are principally those of the *system world* that embodies the instrumental reasoning and explanatory rationality that satisfies the organisation, management, goals and practices required for the maintenance of large, complex enterprises such as education. Somewhat discounted is the *lifeworld* side of practice that can contribute to the enactment of those goals

137

through a grounding in those education studies that potentially provide a richer and more enhanced understanding of those 'networks of communication' that 'strive towards mutual understanding, intersubjective agreement and unforced consensus about what to do in any given practical situation' (Kemmis, 2005, p. 5).

This tests the argument developed by Groundwater-Smith et al (2013, p. 132) 'that the knowledge that enhances professional learning is produced through four fundamental social processes, these being the capacity to:

- challenge and support each other's perception of a phenomenon;
- create dialogic conditions that allow varying views and beliefs to emerge and be debated in the belief that participants are speaking, as best they can, honestly and openly;
- examine such beliefs in the context of the needs and interests of others, especially those who are vulnerable and have little or no voice; and
- develop authentic critique that gives expression to legitimate action.'

In the immediate future, it remains to be seen how the policy settlements around research and teacher education will impact and shape Education Studies in Australia, and toward what ends. Our preferred future would clearly be one that took up the challenge of critical/emancipatory knowledge interests in a more robust way, understanding the complex interplay of theory and practice and the even more complex role of both in the formation of teachers. The shift, however, towards more pragmatic and quantifiable ends in both educational research and initial teacher education suggests an ever-increasing tilt towards technical knowledge interests and the continued ascendancy of 'what works'. By way of response, we refer to the warning issued by Marilyn Cochran-Smith over a decade ago, arguing that now, more than ever, this call for vigilance is relevant to Australian teacher educators:

> we need to keep in mind how we will be measured by our own
> measures. As researchers, practitioners and policy makers in
> teaching and teacher education, we will not measure up unless we
> preserve a place for critique in the face of consensus, unless we
> keep at the center of teacher education rich and complex
> understandings of teaching and learning that are not easily
> reducible to algorithms ... At this critical juncture in the reform
> and development of teacher education, if we do not take control of
> framing the outcomes in teacher education, then the outcomes
> will surely frame us and undermine our work as teachers, teacher
> educators, researchers, and policy makers committed to a
> democratic vision of society and to the vital role that teachers and
> teacher educators play in that vision. (Cochran-Smith, 2001,
> pp. 543-544)

So how might this be accomplished? Can the ship of state be turned around? Seemingly, the ship of state (with apologies to Plato) is steered less by those who know and understand navigating and are experienced at it, and instead is sailed by politicians with a view to the next election. Is the current reframing of educational policies in Australia with scant reference to the testimony of practitioners and the critical witnessing of practice irreversible? If we take it that underlying the concept of education is a desire to *live well*, avoiding irrationality, contradiction and falsehood, harm, waste and excess, injustice and exclusion (Kemmis, 2010, p. 420), then an appeal to those knowledge interests constructed around interpretive/cultural and emancipatory concepts is essential. What is required is a deep and profound examination of what counts as the kind of educational knowledge that has the possibility to take us forward, rather than being confined in a space bounded by rigid controls.

Kemmis asks 'what is to be done' in this historical moment (2010, p. 424). We would argue for the following desiderata with respect to Education Studies in Australia:

- that teaching is recognised as having a moral as well as a pragmatic purpose;
- that teachers are endowed with a sense of agency in being able to change and vary what is required of them;
- that teachers and their leaders are cognizant of from whence their ideas about practice come and the extent to which they are capable of new and fresh considerations.

Our plea is for policies driving the study of education and in particular teacher education to be infused with a commitment to unmask the shibboleths and truisms too often seen as immutable and sold as ready-made solutions. We argue for the kind of educational policies that result in scholarly, research-informed and research-engaged teachers willing to take warranted risks. We argue for teachers to have an authentic sensibility to the learning needs of those in their charge and occasionally take the hammer to those one-size-fits-all, fool-proof solutions. We ask for those engaged in educational practices and policy formulation to scrutinise such solutions that are offered as proven and continually question whose knowledge interests are being served and to what purpose. Our hope is for educational practitioners, in the context of Australian education, to allow themselves to be irritated by the relentless thrust of a singular discourse that is unremittingly instrumental and instead be prepared to take up the admonition of W.B. Yeats: 'Do not wait to strike until the iron is hot, but make it hot by striking.'

Notes

[1] A committee was established in the 1960s under the chairmanship of Sir Leslie Martin and the direction of the Menzies Liberal (Conservative) government to investigate the future of tertiary education in Australia.

References

Apple, M.W. (2012) *Can Education Change Society?* New York: Routledge.

Aspland, T. (2006) Changing Patterns of Teacher Education in Australia, *Education Research and Perspectives*, 33(2), 140.

Australian Government Department of Education and Training (2014) Higher Education Statistics. https://education.gov.au/student-data

Australian Institute for Teaching and School Leadership (2011) Accreditation of Initial Teacher Education Programs in Australia: standards and procedures. Canberra: Education Services Australia.

Australian Institute for Teaching and School Leadership (2012) Australian Teacher Performance and Development Framework, in Australian Research Council, Discovery Projects. http://www.arc.gov.au/discovery-projects

Australian Research Council (2015a) Discovery Projects. http://www.arc.gov.au/discovery-projects

Australian Research Council (2015b) Excellence in Research Australia. http://www.arc.gov.au/excellence-research-australia

Biesta, G. (2012) Giving Teaching Back to Education: responding to the disappearance of the teacher, *Phenomenology and Practice*, 6(2), 35-49.

Boud, D., Keogh, R. & Walker, D. (1985) *Turning Experience into Learning*. London: Kogan Page.

Bourdieu, P. (1977) *Outline of a Theory of Practice*. Cambridge: Cambridge University Press. https://doi.org/10.1017/CBO9780511812507

Bourdieu, P. (1990) *The Logic of Practice*. Cambridge: Polity Press.

Calver, M. & Beattie, A. (2015) Our Obsession with Metrics Corrupting Science, *The Conversation*, 1 June 2015.

Cochran-Smith, M. (2001) The Outcomes Question in Teacher Education, *Teaching and Teacher Education*, 17(5), 527-546. https://doi.org/10.1016/S0742-051X(01)00012-9

Commonwealth of Australia (2015) Science and Research Priorities. http://science.gov.au/scienceGov/ScienceAndResearchPriorities/Pages/default.aspx

Craven, G., Beswick, K., Fleming, J., et al (2015) *Action Now: classroom ready teachers*. Canberra: Commonwealth Department of Education.

Dawkins, J. (1987) *The Challenge for Higher Education in Australia*. Canberra: Australian Government Printing Service.

Dawkins, J. (1988) *Strengthening Australia's Schools*. Canberra: Australian Government Printing Service.

Furlong, J. (2013) *Education – an Anatomy of the Discipline: rescuing the university project*. London: Routledge.

Gadotti, M. (1996) *Pedagogy of Praxis: a dialectical philosophy of education*. Albany: SUNY Press.

Gore, J. & Bowe, J. (2015) Interrupting Attrition? Re-shaping the Transition from Preservice to Inservice Teaching through Quality Teaching Rounds, *International Journal of Educational Research*, 73, 77-88. https://doi.org/10.1016/j.ijer.2015.05.006

Graham, L. & Buckley, L. (2014) Ghost Hunting with Lollies, Chess and Lego: appreciating the 'messy' complexity (and costs) of doing difficult research in education, *Australian Educational Researcher*, 41(3), 327-347. http://dx.doi.org/10.1007/s13384-013-0137-5

Groundwater-Smith, S. (1998) Putting Teacher Professional Judgement to Work, *Educational Action Research*, 6(1), 21-37. https://doi.org/10.1080/09650799800200051

Groundwater-Smith, S., & Irwin, J. (2011) Action Research in Education and Social Work, in L. Markauskaite, P. Freebody, & J. Irwin (Eds) *Methodological Choice and Design*, pp. 57-70. London: Springer.

Groundwater-Smith, S., Mitchell, J., Mockler, N., Ponte, P. & Ronnerman, K. (2013) *Facilitating Practitioner Research: developing transformational partnerships*. London: Routledge.

Guri-Rosenblit, S. & Sebkova, H. (2004) Diversification of Higher Education Systems: patterns, trends and impacts. UNESCO Forum Occasional Forum Series, Paper No. 6: Diversification of Higher Education and the Changing Role of Knowledge and Research. UNESCO.

Habermas, J. (1984a) *Theory of Communicative Action*, vol. 1. *Reason and Rationalisation of Society*, trans. T. McCarthy. London: Heinemann.

Habermas, J. (1984b) *Theory of Communicative Action*, vol. 2. *System and Lifeworld: the critique of functionalist reason*, trans. T. McCarthy. Boston: Beacon.

Harman, G. (1987) Funding for Education Research in Australia: a note, *Australian Educational Researcher*, 14(3), 57-58. https://doi.org/10.1007/BF03219387

Harman, G. (2003) Australian Academics and Prospective Academics, *Higher Education Management and Policy*, 15(3), 105-122. https://doi.org/10.1787/hemp-v15-art26-en

Harrison, N. & Seddon, T. (2013) Living in a 2.2 World: from mapping to strategic capacity building for Australian educational research, *Australian Educational Researcher*, 40(4), 403-413. https://doi.org/10.1007/s13384-013-0101-4

Hatton, N. & Smith, D. (1995) Reflection in Teacher Education: towards a definition and implementation, *Teaching and Teacher Education*, 11, 33-49. https://doi.org/10.1016/0742-051X(94)00012-U

Hyams, B. (1979) *Teacher Preparation in Australia: a history of its development 1850-1950*. Hawthorn, VIC.: ACER.

Ingvarson, L., Elliott, A., Kleinhenz, E. & McKenzie, J. (2006) *Teacher Education Accreditation*. Canberra: Teaching Australia/ACER.

Kelly, F. (2013) Gonski Education Reforms: Christopher Pyne [Interview]. https://www.pyneonline.com.au/media-centre/transcripts/abc-radio-national-3

Kemmis, S. (2005) Participatory Action Research and the Public Sphere. Paper presented at the Practitioner Research/Action Research (PRAR) 2005 Joint

International Practitioner Research Conference and Collaborative Action Research Network (CARN) Conference, Utrecht.

Kemmis, S. (2010). What is to be Done? The Place of Action Research, *Educational Action Research*, 18(4), 417-427. https://doi.org/10.1080/09650792.2010.524745

Kemmis, S. & Grootenboer, P. (2008) Situating Praxis in Practice: practice architectures and the cultural, social and material conditions for practice, in S. Kemmis & T. Smith (Eds) *Enabling Praxis: challenges for education*, pp. 37-62. Rotterdam: Sense.

Kemmis, S., Wilkinson, J., Edwards-Groves, C., Hardy, I., Grootenboer, P. & Bristol, L. (2014) *Changing Practices, Changing Education*. Dordrecht: Springer. https://doi.org/10.1007/978-981-4560-47-4

Kvernbekk, T. (2005) *Pedagogisk teoridannelse: insidere, teoriformer og praksis [Construction of Pedagogical Theories: insiders, theory forms and practice]*. Bergen: Fagbokforlaget.

Lawn, M. & Furlong, J. (2009) The Disciplines of Education in the UK: between the ghost and the shadow, *Oxford Review of Education*, 35(5), 541-552. https://doi.org/10.1080/03054980903216283

Lingard, B., Rawolle, S. & Taylor, S. (2005) Globalizing Policy Sociology in Education: working with Bourdieu, *Journal of Education Policy*, 20(6), 759-777. https://doi.org/10.1080/02680930500238945

Louden, W. (2008) 101 Damnations: the persistence of criticism and the absence of evidence about teacher education in Australia, *Teachers and Teaching*, 14(4), 357-368. https://doi.org/10.1080/13540600802037777

Luhmann, N. (1995) *Social Systems*. Stanford, CA: Stanford University Press.

Marginson, S. & Considine, M. (2000) *The Enterprise University: power, governance and reinvention in Australia*. Cambridge: Cambridge University Press.

McWilliam, E. & Lee, A. (2006) The Problem of 'the Problem with Educational Research', *Australian Educational Researcher*, 33(2), 43-60. https://doi.org/10.1007/BF03216833

Moses, I. (n.d.) Unified National System or Uniform National System? The Australian Experience. Paper presented at the University of New England, Armidale, NSW.

Munns, G., Sawyer, W. & Cole, B. (Eds) (2013) *Exemplary Teachers of Students in Poverty*. Abingdon: Routledge.

Murray, S., Nuttall, J. & Mitchell, J. (2008) Research into Initial Teacher Education in Australia: a survey of the literature 1995-2004, *Teaching and Teacher Education*, 23, 225-239. https://doi.org/10.1016/j.tate.2007.01.013

Nicolini, D. (2013) *Practice Theory, Work, and Organization: an introduction*. Oxford: Oxford University Press.

Ordorika, I. & Lloyd, M. (2015) International Rankings and the Contest for University Hegemony, *Journal of Education Policy*, 30(3), 385-405. https://doi.org/10.1080/02680939.2014.979247

Parr, G. (2015) Who Goes to University? The Changing Profile of Our Students, *The Conversation*, 25 May 2015.

Schatzki, T. (2002) *The Timespace of Human Activity: on performance, society, and history as indeterminate teleological events*. Lanham, MA: Lexington Books.

Schatzki, T. (2010) *The Site of the Social: a philosophical account of the constitution of social life and change*. University Park, PA: Pennsylvania State University Press.

Schon, D.A. (1983) *The Reflective Practitioner*. New York: Basic Books.

Schutz, A. & Luckman, T. (1973) *The Structure of the Lifeworld*, vol. 2. Evanston, IL: Northwestern University Studies in Phenomenology and Existential Philosophy.

Schwandt, T. (2005) On Modelling Our Understanding of Practice Fields, *Pedagogy, Culture & Society*, 13(3), 313-332. https://doi.org/10.1080/14681360500200231

Sjølie, E. (2014) The Role of Theory in Teacher Education: reconsidered from a student teacher perspective, *Journal of Curriculum Studies*, 46(6), 729-750. https://doi.org/10.1080/00220272.2013.871754

Smyth, J. (1992) Teachers' Work and the Politics of Reflection, *American Educational Research Journal*, 29(2), 267-300. https://doi.org/10.3102/00028312029002268

van Manen, M. (1999) The Practice of Practice, in M. Lange, J. Olson, H. Hansen & W. Bünde (Eds) *Changing Schools/Changing Practices: perspectives on educational reform and teacher professionalism*. Louvain: Garant.

Vick, M. (2003) Building 'Professionalism' and 'Character' in the Single-purpose Teachers' College, *Australian Journal of Teacher Education*, 28, 40-50. https://doi.org/10.14221/ajte.2003v28n1.5

Wacquant, L. (1989) Towards a Reflexive Sociology: a workshop with Pierre Bourdieu, *Sociological Theory*, 7(1), 26-63. https://doi.org/10.2307/202061

CHAPTER 6

The Development and Characteristics of Educational Studies in China

WEN WEN & XIE WEIHE

SUMMARY This chapter provides an overview of the development of educational studies in mainland China since it was imported from the West in the early twentieth century. The chapter examines how educational studies can be understood in the context of its long-term formation. Four periods are identified and the features of educational studies of each period are outlined. It also examines the characteristics of educational studies in relation to knowledge, to find out what type of knowledge tends to be produced by educational studies in China. The discussion about knowledge in this chapter responds to the major debates on educational studies in China and worldwide. It then considers what the future of educational studies in China will be. It concludes that the grammaticality of educational studies needs to be strengthened, and identifies that how to deal with the tension between global/western impact and Chinese legacy in educational studies is one of the most important issues.

Introduction

The common dilemma that educational researchers around the world confront is defining the knowledge base of educational studies and the positioning of education in the hierarchy of disciplines. Contemporary controversies about educational studies include whether education is a discipline or a research field, whether the knowledge of educational studies is theory-oriented or practice-oriented, how to conceptualise the relationships between educational studies and other disciplines, and how to improve the knowledge and standing of educational studies (Bernstein, 1977, 2000; Qu, 1999a; Shi, 2004; Ye, 2004; Xie, 2012).

Amid these debates, Chinese educational researchers have been keen to raise the consciousness of the disciplinary community in China and secure recognition of educational studies as a discipline. The desire to legitimise education as a discipline is driven mainly by the state-led model of research and technology in China. The government plays an important role in steering the development of research by allocating funding and student enrolment on a discipline-by-discipline basis. This top-down approach to the development of research capacity is a defining characteristic of scientific and technological development in China (Wen, 2015).

In recent years, in the context of the challenges posed by globalisation, many Chinese educational scholars have also felt it important to establish an indigenous discipline of educational studies. We have argued elsewhere (Xie & Wen, 2015) that, as work in educational studies provides values and ideas for a nation's educational development, its level of professionalism – the degree of rigour and articulation of the discourse of educational studies – will determine the level of the development of a country's educational system.

This chapter will respond to these debates by providing an overview of the development of educational studies in China since the early twentieth century, when the subject was imported from the West, to see how educational studies can be understood in the context of its long-term formation. We also examine the characteristics of educational studies in China in relation to knowledge, to find out what type of knowledge tends to be produced by educational studies in China, and consider what the future of educational studies in China will be.

The Development of Chinese Educational Studies

China has experienced great changes in its social, cultural, political and economic spheres over the past hundred years. The development of China's educational research was in accordance with, and was influenced by, these macro changes, and can be divided into four stages. The first period was from the beginning of the twentieth century to the 1940s, when the educational theories of Johann Friedrich Herbart and John Dewey were imported into China and education was set up as a formal subject in modern normal schools. The second period was from the establishment of the People's Republic of China (PRC) in 1949 to the end of the Cultural Revolution in 1976, when educational research was greatly influenced by political ideology and was effectively suspended. From 1978, when China's Reform and Opening-up policy was implemented, educational studies was influenced by the accelerating development of the country's educational system, including through marketisation and curricular reform. Stepping into the twenty-first century, particularly in recent years, educational studies in China has been faced with the tension between globalisation and indigenisation – a tension between earning a world-class reputation on the one hand, and an emphasis on constructing an independent Chinese educational research system with its own characteristics on the other hand.

1900-1949: importing from the West

In this period, many western works in educational studies, mainly education theories from the USA and Europe, were translated into Chinese. The introduction of western educational theories resulted in the growth of 'modern' educational research, splitting off from traditional Chinese scholarship in education, which had mainly taken a non-empirical and interpretative approach. Although the ancient Chinese classics such as *The Great Learning, The Doctrine of the Mean* and *The Analects of Confucius* have much to say about education, education was not studied as an independent subject. Compared with other social science subjects, education's lack of indigenous theoretical foundations led to its separation from traditions of Chinese scholarship, and hence the subsequent emergence of a westernised version of educational studies. At the same time, the westernisation of educational studies served other purposes. Chinese officials and scholars held the idea of sustaining traditional Chinese values aided by modern western management and technology. Thus, educational studies, like other social science disciplines introduced from the West, was regarded as an instrument to improve human capital, nurture modern talents and achieve the goal of modernisation (Ye, 2004). In fact, the initial motivation for the engagement with educational studies from the West was to satisfy the needs for training high-quality teachers who could educate 'modern' citizens. In other words, educational studies established itself in China principally to teach pre-service teachers (Hou, 2000).

As a consequence of the belief that 'learning from western education must start from learning their teacher education' (Shu, 1961, pp. 153-154), the government of the Qing dynasty established Nan Yang Normal School [1] as the first Chinese teacher training school in 1897 (Shu, 1961). It is worthwhile noting that there was no course on educational research at that time. Most of the courses focused on teaching practice in primary schools affiliated to those normal schools. In 1902, the Normal College of the Imperial University of Peking (the predecessor of Beijing Normal University) was founded, and education was set up as a four-year formal undergraduate programme. In this period, education was considered as a more effective means than science and engineering to rescue China from invasion and enhance national power (Zhu, 1988). From the end of the nineteenth century to the middle of the twentieth century, education became one of the most popular subjects among Chinese students who studied in the USA. According to the report (1954) of Mei Yiqi and Cheng Qibao, there were 20,906 Chinese students studying in the USA, of whom 943 were majoring in education, occupying 13.9% of humanities and social sciences places, and second only to the number of students majoring in business management and economics.

At the beginning of this period, J.F. Herbart's nineteenth-century theories of teaching and learning were pervasive in Chinese educational studies (Qu, 1998). From 1919, however, other American and European educational scholars' theories became more influential, particularly those of John Dewey. This is partly because many influential educational scholars or practitioners in modern China, such as Hu Shi, Jiang Menglin and Tao Xingzhi, were students of Dewey when studying at Teachers College, Columbia in New York with scholarships from the Boxer Indemnity. After returning to China, many became university presidents, school head teachers, and scholars of education or philosophy, and they all played an important role in spreading Dewey's educational thoughts in China. Dewey himself had visited China in 1919 and delivered lectures on the eve of the May Fourth Movement.[2]

The development of educational studies in China, then, took a short cut by importing the discipline as it had already formed in the West, and this continued for over 40 years. It started with the topics of school hygiene and school management, and then, later on, educational research methods. The legacies of western scholarship, such as emphasising scientific research methods and reasoning, largely reshaped scholarship on education in China, diverging from traditional Chinese studies in the humanities. The tradition of Chinese scholarship advocates 'virtue and the way of learning' and 'the combination of practice and introspection', emphasising the consistency between existentiality and knowledge, and the coherence between mental learning and moral quality. In the tradition of Chinese scholarship, the 'conscience' is prior to theories and interpretations, and researchers can never be bystanders.

1949-1976: the close connection with political ideology

After the foundation of the PRC in 1949, the development of educational studies took a new direction, now learning from the Soviet Union, especially its approach to teacher education (Qu, 1999b; Ye, 2004). In 1954, the Ministry of Education compiled a 'Syllabus of Education for Primary Normal Schools (Draft)', indicating that 'this syllabus is following the general system of the Soviet Union's teacher education'. The 'Syllabus of Teacher Education in Normal Schools (preliminary)' and the 'Syllabus of Teacher Education in Normal Colleges and Junior Colleges' in 1956 both referred to the Soviet Union's syllabus. However, following the disputes between China and the Soviet Union in 1958, the previously pervasive Soviet-style curriculum was criticised and disbanded; Chinese educational studies were forced to look inward. Nevertheless, the influence of the Soviet model could still be seen in China, not least in the close connection between educational studies and the China Communist Party's national education policies, regulations and principles.

The 10-year Cultural Revolution from 1966 to 1976 caused nationwide social and economic disarray. The ideology of 'taking class struggle as the central task' had become all-pervasive in almost every sphere in China's society. Education was considered as the most important superstructure and thus became one of the most ideologically driven sectors. This severely disrupted the development of the Chinese education system. During this period, intellectuals were disregarded; the college entrance examination was abolished; school and college curricula were formulated based on immediate agricultural and industrial needs; classroom-centred schooling was replaced by workplace-study programmes; and schools, factories, farms and military forces shared management duties. The development of educational studies was suspended: universities stopped recruiting education students. Educational studies, like many other social sciences, became the interpretation of quotations from Chairman Mao Zedong.

1977-Early Twenty-first Century: the reconstruction of the educational system and the development of educational research

After the Cultural Revolution, all levels of education experienced comprehensive development. That included higher education and, in the case of educational studies, educational research. In China, the State steers the development of academic research by granting the legislative status of disciplines and allocating funding and student quotas. This is done on the basis of performance targets and capacity-building objectives (Wen, 2005; Marginson, 2011).

Education as a discipline first gained government recognition in the 'Provisional Measures for the Implementation of Academic Degrees of the People's Republic of China', which was promulgated by the State Council in 1983. In the same year, the State Council published 'Categories of Disciplines of Doctoral and Master's Degree Granted by Higher Education Institutions and Research Institutions'. In this document, 34 sub-disciplines under the discipline of education were specified, including higher education, pre-school education, comparative education, and so on. In subsequent modifications, in 1990 and 1997, the sub-disciplines of education were reduced to 33 and 17, respectively. At the same time, educational researchers continued to build the discipline of education. For example, Professor Pan Maoyuan founded the first Institute of Higher Education in Xiamen University and wrote the first theoretical book on higher education.

Another way of formalising a discipline in China is through the government's scientific research project plan. Chinese educational studies are mainly supported by the state – most research projects are funded by the Ministry of Education, other relevant ministries and other institutions affiliated to the ministry (Chen, 2012). In 1979, the Ministry of Education set up a committee of experienced educational scholars and high-level senior administrators to formulate the plan for educational studies. Affiliated to the National Institute of Educational Sciences [3], this committee was in charge of issuing the five-year plan for education research in China, reviewing research proposals, supervising the process of research projects and evaluating project outcomes.

Higher education institutions, especially the research-intensive universities, have become pivotal in shaping educational studies because they have rich resources and inter-disciplinary research foundations. Research universities take more than 80% of national education research projects. Normal universities, such as Beijing Normal University and East China Normal University, and comprehensive universities, such as Tsinghua University and Peking University, have developed their own research activities. For example, normal universities play a leading role in theoretical research and Tsinghua University is renowned for its engineering education research and college student development studies, while economics of education at Peking University has gained nationwide prominence. A large number of primary and middle schools and local research institutions [4], on the front line of educational reform and practice, have also been active in undertaking educational research projects.

At the same time, the dominant paradigms in educational research have continued to evolve. Since reforms of the 1970s to open up and marketise the Chinese economy, the economic returns of education have come to the fore, resulting in the prevalence of performance-based approaches in educational management and educational studies. Empirical studies, with a quantitative approach in particular, began to replace dialectic studies, becoming the dominant paradigm of educational research. In the mid-1990s, Chinese educational researchers also re-examined the concept of essentialism and explored the cultural paradigm in educational studies (Shi, 2004). Subjective and cultural features of educational studies were increasingly emphasised. Indeed, at this time, qualitative research methods such as narrative inquiries became a mainstream paradigm in educational research (Shi, 2004; Zhang, 2010).

Early Twenty-first Century:
tensions between globalisation and indigenisation

Since the dawn of the new millennium, with China's entry into the World Trade Organization, the country has become deeply involved in the process of globalisation. In 1995 and 1998, the government initiated 'Project 211' [5] and 'Project 985' [6] with the aim of creating world-class universities. However, along with the trend of promoting internationalisation in higher education, particularly the strong emphasis on English language publications in academic assessment, there has emerged in educational studies a fierce conflict between 'globalisation' and 'indigenisation.' A long-lasting debate in educational studies over the past decade has been whether China should import educational theories from the West or develop indigenous theories. New concerns have emerged that Chinese educational scholars, the younger generation in particular, have a good mastery of western philosophies and theories, but have neglected the legacy of indigenous philosophies and scholarship – and that there has been a tendency to simply adopt western theories and methods to interpret Chinese educational practices without considering the cultural adaptation needed in introducing these theories into the Chinese context (Ye, 2004; Wen et al, 2016).

Some also argue that as China re-emerged as a great power, it began to take a more active and responsible role in international affairs, such as initiating international institutions like the Asian Infrastructure Investment Bank, as well as the 'One Belt, One Road' strategy. The transition of China's role from a follower to a leader, they argue, also requires it to develop an indigenous academic research system that could provide theoretical resources and research evidence to underpin China's global and regional strategy (Wen et al, 2016).

The Epistemological Characteristics of Contemporary Educational Studies in China

Today, educational studies in China comprise several different elements. There is the study of education through the foundation disciplines of philosophy, history, sociology and psychology (Pan, 2011). Then there is the more all-encompassing perspective of educational studies as a region with an independent discourse system and its own distinctive theories (Wen et al, 2016). There is also a professional/vocational aspect, which involves understanding educational studies in terms of providing the knowledge base for teaching and teacher education. This sometimes means there is a division of educational studies into 'theoretical educational studies' and 'practical educational studies' (Chen, 1998). There are, then, different understandings of the nature of knowledge in educational studies. To explore this, we will now look closely at the characteristics of educational studies in China in the light of Bernstein's theories of knowledge.

Educational Studies as a Region Rather than a Singular

The long-lasting debate on educational studies in China concerns whether it is a discipline or a field. In China, there are three principles for a field of knowledge to be considered a discipline: it must be an 'independent conceptual system', and it must have 'independent research methods' and 'independent research objects' (Chen, 1998). Judging by these criteria, it is not possible for educational studies to become a discipline. According to other classification criteria, educational studies would be considered 'applied' and 'soft' (Becher & Trowler, 1989), or as comprising 'Mode II' knowledge (Gibbons et al, 1994).

Xie (2012) proposed an analytic framework to examine disciplines by adopting Bernstein's concept of 'boundary' (Bernstein, 1999). According to Xie, based on whether the boundary between different knowledges is clear and how strong the connection is, disciplines can be classified into three types. The first type is the pure discipline, such as mathematics, physics, chemistry, literature, history and philosophy, which are constituted by coherent concepts and domains and have a rigorous internal logic and explicit standards of evaluation. The second type is the inter-disciplinary subject where the boundaries are blurred. Biochemistry as an example takes chemistry as the primary resource of knowledge and theories and absorbs other knowledge and theories from biology. The third type is the problem-based discipline which aims at solving problems in particular fields where the boundaries are completely disintegrated. Environmental studies and educational studies are two examples that include a whole set of diversified knowledges (different subjects, academic and practical) which are mixed up (like a mosaic rather than a melting pot) (Clark, 1987).

Drawing more widely on Bernstein's (2000) knowledge theories, which see knowledges as socio-epistemic entities, there are three types of knowledge structures – namely, 'singulars', 'regions' and 'generics'. A singular is 'a specialized discrete discourse with its own intellectual field of texts, practices, rules of entry...', and is 'protected by strong boundaries and hierarchies' (Bernstein, 2000, p. 52). A region is 'constructed by recontextualising singulars into larger units which operate both in the intellectual field of disciplines and in the field of external practice' (Bernstein, 2000, 52). Regions need to 'face both ways' (Barnett, 2000, p. 153) – namely, towards the 'intellectual field of disciplines' and the contexts of 'external practice' (Bernstein, 2000, p. 52). Generics are constructed with no connection to disciplinary sources and with little regard to the broader 'culture and practices' of an occupation, but draw extensively on 'local', 'organizational' or 'workplace' horizontal discourses. The varying or even contrasting structures, purposes, practices and grammaticality across the different disciplines within educational studies make it difficult to present educational studies as a coherent field. For example, economics and sociology are markedly different in their methodological process and epistemological considerations (Lauder et al, 2009), and little agreement is offered on what aspects of education it may be of value to study, let alone what counts as a worthwhile research design.

The older generations of Chinese educational scholars have made great efforts to integrate the foundation disciplines (sociology, philosophy, history and psychology) of educational studies and form a unified and coherent body of knowledge for educational studies. This helped education to gain legitimacy in the early 1980s: listed by the government as one of 10 formal disciplines, it received funding from the government on an annual basis, and was assigned a student quota. However, under the state-supervised system of academia and science in China, the efforts to form educational studies as a singular were mainly externally driven rather than internally/intrinsically driven. The resulting lack of a unified and explicit identity or of shared concerns and practice among this academic community makes it harder to see educational studies as a genuine singular. For example, scholars of the economics of education tend to adhere to the intellectual community of economics; psychology of education appears to be housed primarily in psychology departments rather than education; sociology of education is thought to have taken on a life of its own (Lauder et al, 2009); scholars of higher education are trying to distinguish themselves from other educational scholars, who draw more on history, sociology and policy analysis (Wen, 2005).

Contrasting Tendencies of Grammaticality:
practice-oriented and policy-oriented

Like most of its foundation disciplines, educational studies could be considered as 'horizontal knowledge structures' comprising a series of specialised languages with different and often opposing assumptions and criteria for legitimate texts (Bernstein, 2000, p. 161). Among horizontal knowledge structures, 'strong grammar' indicates those whose languages have an explicit conceptual syntax capable of relatively precise empirical descriptions and/or of generating formal modelling of empirical relations, while 'weak grammar' means those powers are much weaker (Bernstein, 2000, p. 162). For educational studies, its grammaticality – its level of abstracting and formalising conceptual languages and its capability of representing the objects' experiences in educational activities – determines the boundary between theories in education studies and theories in other disciplines and also affects the identification and legitimacy of education studies as an individual discipline in its own right.

According to Bernstein, grammaticality is constituted in the relationship between the internal language of description (ILOD) and the external language of description (ELOD) (Bernstein, 2000; Moore & Muller, 2002; Horden, 2016), with the ILOD comprising 'the syntax whereby a conceptual language is created' and the ELOD 'the syntax whereby the internal language can describe something other than itself' (Bernstein, 2000, p. 132). For ILOD and ELOD, the weakening of one aspect will result in the weakening of the other. However, influenced by the existing theoretical standings or dominant 'specialized languages', the weak form of ILOD is likely to be the one that will keep weakening (Horden, 2016). As such, it is of fundamental importance to strengthen the ILOD of grammar. The weak form of ILOD is one of the most significant features of Chinese educational studies.

First, educational studies lack a consistent and logical system as well as widely recognised core concepts and theoretical fundamentals; it only has orientations, condensed intimations, metaphors that point to relevancies (Bernstein, 2000, p. 134). Second, the progress of theory constructing in educational studies is falling behind educational practices and reforms in China and is thus unable to guide practice. In the new century, with ongoing reforms and transforming economic and social structures in Chinese society, a huge gap between the past and present has emerged in the content, forms and purposes of education development (Xie et al, 2008). As such, the weak grammaticality of educational studies, especially that of the internal language of description, becomes a significant issue in this transitioning period of Chinese society.

Take the nationwide 'new curriculum' reform that commenced in the late 1990s as an example. This reform has in and of itself encouraged the trend of practice-oriented educational studies in China. Although research universities have played a major role in undertaking educational research, primary and secondary school teachers and head teachers have been encouraged to conduct research projects to solve practical problems in everyday teaching, learning and school management when implementing the curriculum reform. Taking naturalism and realism as their stance, those educational practitioners and some educational researchers have developed the type of educational studies that is based on reflections on and insights into educational issues and which venerates individual experience in practice as a source of valuable knowledge. For example, Dou Guimei, the head teacher of a primary school in Beijing, developed a series of integrated courses (called '1+X' courses) to promote students' all-round development in her school; Li Xigui, the head teacher of a senior middle school in Beijing, developed the 'selective class system' in his school to promote individualised learning. The '1+X' courses and 'selective class system' were proved to be effective and successful models, and have risen in prominence and prevalence across the country. However, as these discourses developed in educational practice remain 'local', as horizontal discourse, and are not absorbed within the vertical knowledge base in China, there are concerns that this practice-orientated educational studies will inhibit the development of the discipline, restricting the grammaticality of educational studies to a 'lower' (more localized) level.

As noted, the other characteristic of educational studies in China is its close connection with the state and government. Chinese academic scholarship, in the social sciences in particular, has a legacy of emphasising the influence of scholars and their research upon state policy. As a Confucian slogan says, 'he who excels in study can follow an official career'. Taking the highest level of educational research projects as an example, from 2001 to 2011, there were only 29 projects related to education theory, with the other 72 projects all being policy-related research. This policy orientation forces educational studies to form a stronger grammar and greater verticality, as government and policy actors are looking for explicit and quantitative answers and solutions to educational problems, and tend to fund research that demonstrates strong grammars.

In particular, in transitional Chinese society, the government urgently needs an 'internal language of description' (Bernstein, 2000, p. 132) which possesses specific concepts and theories that are able to describe empirical evidence in the abstract in order to provide theoretical support for policy making and equip educational reforms with theoretical tools and fundamental concepts. This is why economic and comparative approaches to educational studies (with a quantitative emphasis) have seen greater growth than other foundation disciplines in recent years. However, this tendency has the risk of valuing 'routinized method' and 'atheoretical empiricism' (Furlong & Lawn, 2011, cited in Thomas, 2012), making the grammar look 'strong', while doing little to advance theoretical understanding at a broader level.

The Future of Chinese Educational Studies: appeals for indigenous theories

Many Chinese scholars in educational studies think the current approach of the discipline is too globally oriented rather than locally oriented. From the emergence of educational studies in China, the major subjects were 'imported' from abroad and based on foreign templates. The admiration of foreign ways has meant that the development of educational studies in China has not been built on its own roots (Ye, 2004). Without borrowing education theories from the West, we seem not to have a system to explain the educational reality of our own. Ye Qizheng, a contemporary Chinese sociologist, thinks the direction of globalisation is from the developed countries to developing countries.[7] He argues that the current standard of academic research that globalisation embodies is the core-periphery theoretical framework, and that the standards of developing and developed countries should be different. Influenced by such a framework, developing countries are dedicated to strengthening their military power and adapting technology from developed countries, the tendency of which should be a choice regarding world views rather than a fixed acknowledgement of the lesser development of developing countries. Globalisation under these circumstances is an unequal process that was generated by historical roots and continues to be strengthened by biased conceptual judgements.

A growing number of Chinese scholars have come to share these concerns regarding educational studies and are appealing for more indigenous research. The construction of indigenised theories is to be built on three foundations. First is the recognition of the differences between Chinese and western traditions in education and teaching. Rather than regarding the differences as distinctive disjunctures, we should regard them as specific characteristics. Chinese educational traditions integrate intellectual training and moral education as a whole system. In other words, compared with the western way of recognising higher learning as intellectual cultivation, the Chinese tradition in education and teaching is to treat the cultivation of character as the primary goal – this is what the ancient Chinese quotation 'learning for one's self' means. Second, despite Chinese ancient ideologies such as Mo Zi and Song Ming Neo-Confucianism sharing some similarities with western logical reasoning, traditional Chinese studies primarily utilise the hermeneutic approach. Scholars usually analyse the authorised contexts with great respect and utilise the way of 'The Six Classics Annotate Me and I Annotate the Six Classics' (I try to grasp the essence of the six classics, and then use the original texts in them to explain my ideas, even if I abuse them deliberately) to describe classics rather than studying them in an original way. Third, Chinese philosophy has its own historical and experiential traits that differ from Aristotle's philosophy of logic; Chinese philosophy emphasises integrity and harmony.

There is a related sense among Chinese scholars that the community should nurture a healthy scholarly culture that is based on confidence, openness and integrity. Confidence comes from the outstanding performance of China's educational reforms and development in recent decades as well as from the contributions that China's educational development could make with its indigenous experience and ideas. Openness is the open-minded attitude towards educational studies that has been achieved as a consensus in educational academia: as a diverse body of knowledge aggregates the contemporary discipline, the specific problems and practices in education studies should not be barriers between educational studies and other disciplines. In other words, not being viewed in isolation, educational studies are opened to the scholars in every other discipline as well as to educational practitioners. Academic integrity is reflected by meritocratic values, free enquiry and competition. This is not only a prerequisite for strengthening grammaticality in education, but is also a basis for dealing with the relationship between western and Chinese academic traditions. Yang (2016) refers to lack of integrity and ethics, together with misconduct, as the toxic academic culture, and he points out that corruption is eroding East Asia academia, and that academic misconduct is particularly serious in China. We think that the toxic academic culture also reflects China's greatest challenge: universities and scholarly communities have not yet figured out how to combine the 'standard norms' of western higher education with traditional values.

Conclusion

China does not have its own educational scholarship in a modern sense. Educational studies was imported from the West as an instrument to enhance human capital and national power. Between the 1950s and the 1970s the development of educational studies was largely shaped by ideology and politics, and then driven by economic development. From the 1980s, Chinese educational scholars began to emphasise the independence of educational studies in an academic sense rather than an ideological or economic sense and have made every effort to enhance the grammaticality of educational studies. There was much academic debate about the conceptual system, methodology and theory of educational studies. An open attitude and a multi-disciplinary approach have been taken during the process of grammar construction.

Many Chinese educational scholars have argued that the level of grammaticality of educational studies reflects and can support the level of educational development and the intrinsic logic of educational practice and institutional arrangement in an education system (Wen et al, 2016). However, one of the biggest challenges Chinese educational scholars have encountered on their way to strengthening the grammaticality of educational studies is the tension between globalisation and indigenisation. Globalisation has exerted pressure for western criteria and standards to be adopted in Chinese academic practice, and Chinese academia has taken for granted that they are more scientific and advanced. Many scholars have a good grasp of western concepts, systems and theories, but have abandoned the traditional Chinese legacy in scholarship. Wen et al (2016) argue that only when rooted in its own independent and mature scholarly tradition can Chinese educational studies make a unique and valuable contribution to the world. As 'to be confident with our culture' and 'to be confident with our theories' were formally proposed by the Chinese Party Secretary-General Xi Jinping recently, it is anticipated that the Chinese legacy will be taken into consideration in the process of enhancing grammaticality in educational studies in the near future.

Notes

[1] 'Normal school' refers to a teacher training school at the senior middle school level. Its purpose is to train teachers for primary schools and kindergartens. After the adjustment of colleges and departments in 1952, China established a normal education system comprising normal schools (training primary school teachers), normal colleges (training middle school teachers), and normal universities (training senior middle school teachers). With the aim to promote pre-service teachers' academic development, the government cancelled normal schools and integrated a few of them into normal colleges or normal universities. Almost all primary and secondary teachers are now trained in normal universities, except for some regions in western China where teacher training schools still remain. Since the 1990s, with the government's initiative of building world-class universities, most Chinese normal universities have transformed from typical teacher training colleges to comprehensive universities, and their function of training school teachers has declined. Normal universities integrated teacher education with undergraduate education in order to maintain a high standard for teacher preparation. Normal universities have also built their research status by promoting other disciplines.

[2] The May Fourth Movement was a cultural and political movement that primarily grew out of student participants in Beijing on 4 May 1919. The movement protested against the then Chinese government's response to the Paris Peace Conference after World War I that gave German rights over Shandong to imperial Japan. During the movement, many social intellectuals initiated the New Culture Movement, which promoted the development of anti-imperialist ideas in Chinese society. The values of 'democracy' and 'science' publicised by leaders of the New Culture Movement had an impact on the intellectual enlightenment of the Chinese public.

[3] The National Institute of Educational Sciences is a research institute of the Ministry of Education whose work is often related to current policies. Its relationship with universities is very weak and sometimes competitive in terms of accessing research grants.

[4] Such as Beijing Institute of Educational Scientific Research (BIESR) and Beijing Institute of Education (BIE), both of which are funded by the municipality. The main focus of BIE is teacher training, especially in-service training. BIESR is focused on primary and secondary school education. Typically, they undertake research commissioned by local government. There are several differences between these research institutions and normal universities. In terms of teacher training, normal universities do pre-service training, while BIE pays attention to in-service training targeted on teachers in position. Normal universities mainly focus on theoretical research, while the research institutions are often policy- and practice-oriented. Occasionally, research institutions and normal universities work together on specific projects.

[5] A project of National Key Universities and colleges initiated in 1995 by the Ministry of Education, with the intention of raising the research standards of high-level universities and cultivating strategies for socio-economic development.

[6] This project was first announced by CPC General Secretary and Chinese President Jiang Zemin at the 100th anniversary of Peking University on 4 May 1998, to promote the development and reputation of the Chinese higher education system by founding world-class universities. It was named after the date of the announcement, May 1998, or 98/5, according to the Chinese date format.

[7] From the lecture 'Internationalization and Indigenization: reflections on Chinese higher education' given by Professor Ye Qizheng at Peking University, 4 April 2016.

References

Bernstein, B. (1997) *Class, Codes and Control*, vol.3. *Towards a Theory of Educational Transition*. London: Routledge.

Bernstein, B. (1999) Vertical and Horizontal Discourse: an essay, *British Journal of Sociology of Education*, 20(2), 157-173. https://doi.org/10.1080/01425699995380

Bernstein, B. (2000) *Pedagogy, Symbolic Control and Identity*, 2nd edn. New York: Rowman & Littlefield.

Chen, G. (1998) *The Construction of Educational Studies*. Shanghai: East China Normal University Publication.

Chen, Y. (2012) *Analysis and Research of the Ongoing Status and Trend of the Established Projects in Chinese Education Science Development since the 21st Century.* Shanghai: East China Normal University.

Clark, B. (Ed.) (1987) *Perspectives on Higher Education: eight disciplinary and comparative views.* Berkeley: University of California Press.

Gibbons, M., Limoges, C., Nowotny, H. et al (1994) *The New Production of Knowledge: the dynamics of science and research in contemporary societies.* London: SAGE.

Hordern, J. (2016) Grammaticality and Educational Research, *British Journal of Educational Studies*, 2016, 1-17. https://doi.org/10.1080/00071005.2016.1228824

Hou, H. (2000) *The Rethinking of the Development of Pedagogy in China in the First Half of the 20th Century.* Huazhong: Huazhong Normal University.

Lauder, H., Brown, P. & Halsey, A.H. (2009) Sociology of Education: a critical history and prospects for the future, *Oxford Review of Education*, 35(5), 569-585. https://doi.org/10.1080/03054980903216309

Marginson, S. (2011) Higher Education in East Asia and Singapore: rise of the Confucian model, *Higher Education*, 61(5), 587-611. https://doi.org/10.1007/s10734-010-9384-9

Moore, R. & Muller, J. (2002) The Growth of Knowledge and the Discursive Gap, *British Journal of Sociology of Education*, 23(4), 627-637. https://doi.org/10.1080/0142569022000038477

Pan, M. (2001) *Higher Education Studies from a Multi-disciplinary Perspective.* Shanghai: Shanghai Education Press.

Qu, B. (1998) A Hundred Years of China's Educational Studies, *Educational Research*, 12, 3-12.

Qu, B. (1999a) Development of Pedagogy in China during the Past 100 Years (II), *Educational Studies*, 1, 7-30.

Qu, B. (1999b) Development of Pedagogy in China during the Past 100 Years (III), *Educational Studies*, 2, 23-30.

Shi, Z. (2004) Essentialism, Anti-essentialism and Pedagogic Study in China, *Educational Studies*, 1, 11-20.

Shu, X. (1961) *Historical Documents on Modern Education in China.* Beijing: People's Education Press.

Thomas, J. (2012) Disciplinarity and the Organization of Scholarly Writing in Educational Studies in the UK 1970-2010, *British Journal of Educational Studies*, 60(4), 357-386. https://doi.org/10.1080/00071005.2012.741219

Wen, W. (2005) A Review of the Development of Higher Education Studies in China, *Higher Educational Studies*, 26(6), 54-59.

Wen, W., Xie, W. & Xu, T. (2016) From Social Constructivism to Social Realism: the implication of Michael Young's curriculum theory, *Educational studies*, 3, 155-159.

Xie, W. (2012) Analysis of the Principles of Disciplines, *Chinese College Teaching*, 7, 4-16.

Xie, W., Li, L., Sun, F. & Wen, W. (2008) Educational Equity and Educational Development in China (1990-2005). Beijing: Educational Science Publishing.

Xie, W. & Wen, W. (2015) The Independence of Chinese Higher Education: the implication of constructing a discourse system of higher education research with Chinese characteristics, *Chinese Higher Educational Studies*, 8, 1-9.

Yang, R. (2016) Corruption Undermines Rise of East Asian Universities, *University World News*.
http://www.universityworldnews.com/article.php?story=20160126130528586

Ye, L. (2004) Development of Pedagogy in China: a review of century-long issues, *Educational Studies*, 7, 3-17.

Zhang, Y. (2010) Paradigm of Educational Research and Paradigm Transformation in China: concurrently on culturology paradigm of educational research, *Educational Research*, 10, 3-10.

Zhu, Y. (Ed.) (1988) *Documents on Educational System in Modern China*. 2nd edn. Huazhong: Huazhong Normal University Press.

CHAPTER 7

Framing Education: cautionary tales from the USA of the relationship between education studies and teacher education

LYNN PAINE

SUMMARY This chapter explores the shifting terrain of education as a field of study and research in the USA and examines parallel shifts in the relation of education to practice. Based on a review of what is highlighted, accorded most authoritative space, and awarded most funding in education, the it is argued that in recent decades the contours of education as a field of scholarly inquiry have become more sharply drawn and less fluid. There is increasing emphasis on 'scientific research' in education and heightened attention to outcomes and impact. Neoliberal transformations within US higher education also contribute to these shifts. Similarly, education as a field of practice has been under intense pressures. Questions about the value of teacher preparation, its location, and its knowledge foundations have been prominent. These have implications for the role and nature of research, as well as the involvement of new actors. The chapter uses selected examples of illustrative events to examine the confluence of pressures in these debates. The chapter considers the problematic consequences of the redefinition of the field of education and its relation to the profession in US education and US teacher education.

Introduction

A number of top universities, including Yale and Johns Hopkins, have dropped schools or departments of education over the years, partly over financing and partly because they did not fit in with classic models of academic research. While Chicago held on, the department found itself increasingly unable to get money for new appointments since education research often appeared to lack rigor in the eyes of the university administrators who controlled the money:

> Dean Saller said that when he took over the social sciences division, he was troubled by the frequent lack of peer review for publication in education and the way in which government agencies or foundations sometimes set the research agenda by financing their own pet projects rather than the ideas generated by scholars themselves. He noted that some 20 percent of the PhDs earned in America are in education, yet the field has failed to live up to its promise. (Bronner, 1997)

Such was the 1997 *New York Times'* description of the case for closing the University of Chicago Education School. Only a few years earlier, in the book *The University and the Teachers*, Harry Judge (Judge et al 1994) had described US education as a field that was challenged, and for which its academic and institutional home – schools, colleges or departments of education – reflected divided loyalty. Equilibrium involved a tension between competing visions, definitions and purposes: 'Because they serve several functions, they become the centre of tensions between theory and practice, between detached academic study and pragmatic professional answers to the work which has to be carried out in classrooms' (Judge et al, 1994, p. 138). Twenty years on, we see continued and intensified challenge to what education as a field is and how it speaks to and relates to the profession.

In this chapter, I briefly explore the shifting terrain of education as a field of study and research in the USA and then examine the related and parallel shift in the relation of education to practice. In particular, I consider the implications of these shifts for teacher education. I close with brief thoughts about the consequences for what get considered as questions today in US education and US teacher education. I attempt to outline these not in a comprehensive way, but through selected examples of illustrative events and policies that speak to the confluence of pressures and reflect the redefinition of the field of education and its relation to the profession (in this case, as I discuss it, teacher preparation).

Shifting Contours and Terrain of Education as a Field in the USA

Since the *University and the Teachers* work in the early 2000s, what constitutes education as a field, as viewed by various indicators, has, if anything, expanded. In the USA, what Judge et al (1994) called the 'academic study' of education historically comprised a broad set of perspectives and was informed by a large range of social science and humanities disciplines. But that breadth, from some vantage points, appears to have grown. In the past 15 years the leading association of educational researchers, the American Educational Research Association (AERA), has grown from over 19,000 members in 2002 to over 25,000 by 2016 (Council Minutes, 2002, p. 43; American Educational Research Association, 2016a). Many would claim that as a group, educational researchers, and the field they represent, are more diverse and fragmented than in earlier eras. A review of AERA-member scholarship, of the increase and growth of special interest groups (SIGs) and of other measures suggests a growing diversity in what counts as education research. Just over the past 10 years, for example, the SIGs in AERA have grown from 107 to 150; one could see this in particular as an indication of both increasing specialization and broadening scope within the field of educational research (American Educational Research Association, 1996; Special Interest Group Directory 2016-2017 (2017). More voices are included in educational journals, there is a greater diversity of methods, and one could argue that research occurs in, or is conducted in, more sites (as, for example, social media becomes a subject and method for research).

But another view of the past 15 years would suggest that what has occurred is less an expansion than a reorganizing of the topography of educational research. What gets highlighted, what is most visible and prominent, what is accorded more authoritative space (in the lead journals) and provided official funding reflects less diversity, perhaps, than the AERA patterns listed above might suggest. The textures or contours of education as a field seem more sharply drawn and less fluid.

Reshaping Education Research

Indeed, looking at other indicators besides article topics, location of author, or SIGs, one notes an increasingly narrow vision of education research, one that has worked to clearly define itself in ways that emphasize the scientific basis of education research and stress the importance of experimental designs, randomized controlled trials (RCTs) and causal links as keys to generating new knowledge of and in education. For instance, in the federally funded 'What Works Clearinghouse' (WWC) [1], which can be seen as a window on visible and highly disseminated research, 903 studies are listed as meeting WWC standards 'with or without reservations'. Of these, over half (504) were categorized as RCTs and another 180 were quasi-experimental in design, while only 11 were single case design studies (Institute of Education Sciences, 2017b).

The commissioned report by the National Research Council (National Research Council [NRC], 2002) [2] significantly and explicitly engaged the discussion about definitional boundaries of educational research. That report originated in part from an assumption that the quality of educational research is weak. While the final report did not definitively arrive at that conclusion, it did assess the field as 'uneven' in its quality and found evidence that it is widely 'perceived to be of low quality', saying that many, even some members of the education research community itself, lament weak or absent theory, accumulations of anecdote masquerading as evidence, studies with little obvious policy relevance, seemingly endless disputes over the desired outcomes of schooling, low levels of replicability, large error margins, opaqueness of data and sources, unwillingness or inability to agree on a common set of metrics, and the inevitable intrusion of ideology at the ground level. (Feuer et al, 2002, p. 5)

In the debate accompanying the NRC report, its lead authors argued that their view of education was not restricting the importance of foundational scholarship outside traditions of 'scientific' research:

Our final caveat concerns an important and subtle distinction between education scholarship generally and scientific educational research specifically. We focus on the latter. Though we assume unapologetically that scientific research is an endeavor that can uniquely contribute to greater understanding and improvement of education, we do not intend to minimize the significance of humanistic, historic, philosophical, and other nonscientific forms of study in education. (Feuer et al, 2002, p. 5)

Yet others suggested that the highly discussed report buried any suggestions of the power of humanities and other 'non-scientific' scholarship to inform education (Graham, cited in Tobin, 2007, p. 329). Michael Feuer, lead author of the report, has joked that others had claimed that any report on 'scientific research in education' would be short, but some argue that the report pushed towards a community stance that favors 'the strength of science over other forms of scholarship' (Tobin, 2007, p. 330).[3] While historically the field of education in the USA has drawn on a wide range of disciplines and an 'eclectic mix' of scholars (Feurer et al, 2002, p. 7), in the 2000s, many would claim there has been a shift towards a narrower vision of educational research.

One example of this was the establishment of the Society for Research on Educational Effectiveness (SREE) in 2005. Seen as a challenge to the dominant education research community (AERA) and its increasing diversification of what counts as research, SREE argued for 'forming a research organization that would be recognized by its commitment to applying procedural norms of science to the study of educational problems' (SREE, 2015), with financial support from the US Department of Education's Institute for Education Sciences (IES). There the focus is on causal explanation and a concern for outcomes, more than educational processes, as the object of study.

But others argue that the rise of this particular definition of education research brings with it several problematic assumptions: the assumption of the relevance of a medical metaphor to describe educational research; 'an equating of 'scientific' with 'empirical' or 'rigorous'; the problem of a 'linear' view of educational research; conflating 'research quality with utility'; and 'parochialism' (Tobin, 2007, p. 325).

The debate over the importance and definitions of 'scientific research in education' focused in part on methodological issues. Berliner (2002) takes issue with what he describes as an 'orthodox view of science' that underappreciates the complexity of education and the centrality of context, as well as how these require different methodological approaches from those favoured by government-endorsed definitions of science:

> Our science forces us to deal with particular problems, where local
> knowledge is needed. Therefore, ethnographic research is crucial,
> as are case studies, survey research, time series, design
> experiments, action research, and other means to collect reliable
> evidence for engaging in unfettered argument about education
> issues. A single method is not what the government should be
> promoting for educational researchers. It would do better by
> promoting argument, discourse, and discussion.
> (Berliner, 2002, p. 20)

Tobin (2007) argues that the move of privileging 'scientific research in education' 'positions education practitioners as downstream, as receivers but not producers of knowledge about teaching or worse, as functionaries who should be given scripted lessons to deliver, rather than trusted to follow their own professional judgment instincts' (p. 334).

Hordern (2015), in drawing on Bernstein, suggests that we might examine education as a field that could be viewed as a singular, a region, or a generic. The heightened attention in the US scholarly community to education's ability or need to be 'scientific' suggests that there has been, in the field of educational research as seen in the USA in the past decade, an emulation or striving to see that knowledge as a singular, or more as a collection of singulars and more disciplinary knowledge-based. Using a different theorist, Tobin also points to the growing tendency in US mainstream scholarly discourse and its authoritative center (such as the NRC) to articulate a vision of educational research that emphasizes rules (and goals) for the field. That is, the newer directions in defining what constitutes education as a field (and the norms of educational research) reflect 'privileging what Bruno Latour describes as forms of science that seek to be universal over forms that are highly contextual' (Tobin, 2007, p. 334).

Latour suggests that these 'spread more successfully not just because they are pushed by more powerful forces but also because they are less dependent on context and therefore more able to travel' (Tobin, 2007, p. 334). Funding from national educationally relevant organizations (e.g. the National Science Foundation) has privileged methodological approaches that, for example, meet criteria related to 'pure disciplines' (Hordern, 2015) and 'scientific' valuing of the importance of sampling, replicability, and so on.[4] Randomized controlled trials (RCTs) are deemed the gold standard.

'This means, for example, that ethnographic, "situated cognition" and "cultural historical activity theory" approaches to studies of learning in particular communities ... are less likely to be seen as valuable or as deserving of major funding as studies featuring randomized assignment design, which are considered to be the educational research "ideal" (in the language of SRE [scientific research in education]) or "gold standard" (in the language of IES) because such experimental designs are believed to be the best suited to identify "what works"' (Tobin, 2007, p. 334).

The rise of RCTs [5] reflects an increasing attention to framing the important questions of education as ones about outcomes and impact (see e.g. the IES website 'user friendly' discussion on why RCTs are 'critical' [IES, 2003]). In fact, the creation of the 'what works' mantra in US discussions of education as a field is ultimately about that; the 2002 creation of the 'What Works Clearinghouse' in the US Department of Education's IES is itself an illustration of the weight given to notions of education as a science and particular definitions, practices and boundaries associated with the notion of science. And in consolidating federal research dollars, review panel criteria, and other mechanisms around these notions, the framing of other questions – what a phenomenon is in education, how it is experienced, what its meaning might be in a particular context or for particular actors, all questions that could be seen as foundational for education research – gets crowded out. Within the collection of disciplines that historically have comprised the field of education in the USA (sociology, psychology, history, philosophy, anthropology and so on), as Tobin's critique suggests, certain disciplinary traditions – perhaps particularly psychology – benefited from the newer framing of what counts as educational research and rigor, while others (e.g. anthropology) were overshadowed and seen as less significant.

Berliner (2002) criticizes the tendency to move towards a singular notion of education as a field and argues for the need for heterogeneity. He proposes funding would be well spent:

> sponsoring panels to debate the evidence we have collected from serious scholars using diverse methods. Helping us to do our damndest with our minds by promoting rational debate is likely to improve education more than funding randomized studies with their necessary tradeoff of clarity of findings for completeness of understanding. We should never lose sight of the fact that children and teachers in classrooms are conscious, sentient, and purposive human beings, so no scientific explanation of human behavior could ever be complete. In fact, no unpoetic description of the human condition can ever be complete. When stated this way, we have an argument for heterogeneity in educational scholarship and for convening panels of diverse scholars to help decide what findings are and are not worthy of promoting in our schools.
> (p. 20)

Aware of shifts in funding, Berliner cautions against 'limiting who is funded' as it diminishes the power of educational scholarship to inform practice (2002, p. 20).[6]

Not only has the notion of what counts as the academic study of education narrowed in the eyes of powerful stakeholders, but the emphasis within this field also appears to have shifted. The early expansionist days of US educational research saw psychology as the dominant discipline. The latter decades of the twentieth century and the early twenty-first century, as the AERA SIG growth reflects, found a widening set of frameworks, methodologies and disciplines shaping the academic study of education. While developments in the early 2000s began with the increasing efforts to define education as a science, more recently one witnesses the ascendance of economics and quantitative measures within much of the most influential educational research. The dominance of notions of 'value' and 'value added' are visible examples today of the rise of economic lenses for educational questions.

We see this in both research focus and institutional emphasis. *Educational Researcher*, the AERA's flagship journal and the only one of its many publications that is directed to the entire AERA membership, highlighted these ideas by having a special issue on value-added methods. The concept of and approaches to 'value added' occasioned 'intense interest and concern within the educational community', explained the issue's editors (Harris & Herrington, 2015, p. 71). As another reflection of the growing interest in the importance of economics to education as a field, consider how Michigan State University's College of Education, for example, created a new doctoral specialization in economics of education and hired additional faculty to strengthen its work in this area. At the same time, new faculty searches in the Department of Teacher Education were focused on 'teacher quality'. This term, which by its vagueness could mean many things and be associated with very different intellectual traditions (Kennedy, 2008), has often, as in the case of the faculty search, come to stand for an economics-oriented approach to defining quality.

Interestingly, a content analysis of the range of topics and disciplinary backgrounds in education research (as seen in AERA publications, for example) might suggest the field's widening scope. While the rise of interest in humanistic research, education for social justice, and postmodern perspectives is clearly evident in the larger conversations around education – as understood in terms of professional organizations and scholarly debate – the terms of the discourse in many ways now are dominated by causal, outcomes-focused notions of education scholarship. (The ways in which funding flows is a powerful example of this.) Other voices are present, but often reflecting a frustration with the ways in which much education research is bounded by dominant discourses. The responses of Erickson and Gutierrez (2002) to the NRC report on scientific research in education and of Darling-Hammond (2015) to the *Educational Researcher* special issue on value-added are just two examples of this. In both cases, the scholars critique how the dominant framing positions discussion in ways that make it difficult to pose what they see as fundamental questions in education; the narrow focus on scientific rigor obscures the importance of context.

Transformations within Higher Education and Their Influence on Education

The closing of the University of Chicago's School of Education may be a symbol of the larger challenge to the field of education's place in the academy and its relation to education as a profession. Labaree's work (2004) argues persuasively that in the USA the 'trouble with ed schools' has a long history and, in part, is closely connected to the tenuous status of education as a field within higher education institutions. The pressure that has made education vulnerable within a discipline-based institution of a university has, if anything, grown as higher education itself has been under attack, with, at the same time, the education research community dealing with shifting external pressures from funders and policy, and the general public having an ever more critical view of education as a professional practice.

In the midst of this challenge to education as an academic field (and to its positioning within the university) there have been two noteworthy shifts in the past couple of decades. One is the rise of neoliberalism and associated market frames and accountability pressures (Levin & Aliyeva, 2015). For higher education within the USA, the rise of rankings systems and criteria used to measure university quality (and units within the university) has reinforced the drive of education towards a self-definition that rewards 'rigor', evidence-based work and discipline-based research. US higher education faces what Geiger (2004) calls the 'paradox of the marketplace'. Thelin (2011) explains:

> Market forces have profoundly affected the contemporary research university's fundamental task of creating, processing, and disseminating knowledge. They arguably have provided American universities access to greater wealth, stronger students, and stronger links with the economy. Yet they also have exaggerated inequalities, diminished the university's control over its own activities, and weakened the university's mission of serving the public. (p. 381)

These tendencies now reach far beyond just the major research universities (Bok, 2013). The reduction of public funding for higher education institutions and the greater reliance on external, competitive funding push faculty in schools and colleges of education to seek out the grants that flow from the large federal agencies that see a 'gold standard' in a particular version of education research. 'Federal funding is concentrated heavily on *scientific* research' (Bok, 2013, p. 389, emphasis added), a fact that affects faculty members in schools of education as notions of 'scientific' in education are under debate. For a faculty member in education today, despite whatever personal definitions and motivations for what counts as education as a field, institutional norms of the academy increase the attraction towards certain topics (e.g. impact of educational interventions), certain areas (e.g. science, technology, engineering, and mathematics, or STEM) and certain methods (e.g. RCT). While this of course does not capture all educational research, the support for the researcher working outside 'hot' topics (a colloquial term that even the National Science Foundation (NSF) uses in identifying important areas) is more restricted.

Related to this first trend of the growing role of neoliberal pressures within the academy is the pressure of the external referent (Schriewer & Martinez, 2004; Marginson & van der Wende, 2007; Shahjahan & Morgan, 2016). While the *Times Higher Education*, QS, Shanghai World Ranking, and US News and World Report rankings all use somewhat different metrics, their power is nonetheless increasingly felt within US universities. These new ranking systems bring universities, and fields or departments within them, into direct comparison with counterpart units. External references become more important in this context. Rankings highlight certain dimensions of a university's mission and emphasize particular measures of academic success. 'By privileging particular disciplines and fields of investigation, outputs and achievements, rankings – like similar research assessment exercises – help to reaffirm a traditional understanding of knowledge production and research' (Hazelkorn, 2009, p. 1). In this way, the increasing role of rankings in the discourse of higher education exacerbates pressure on the field of education because it is located within the university, and it is positioned as a field that produces scientific research.

However, it is interesting how the references that animate US educational research are nevertheless significantly circumscribed, typically to US literature. The landmark report *Scientific Research in Education* (National Research Council, 2002) justifies its claims with research that is chiefly from the USA and works from the assumption that the research should address US education problems, in that sense acting as a field that is defined by its utility:

> In the contemporary USA, during an era of increased calls for more and better education research, there is decreasing interest in (and funding for) international/comparative education. In SRE, there is very little mention of research done in other countries (other than mentions of the US lagging on TIMMS and other international measures of educational achievement and a description of Robert Putnam's study of civic engagement in Italy). In the reference sections, of the approximately 300 works cited, it is difficult to find any not done by US based researchers, on US populations, published in a US based book or journal. As in the Sputnik era, the argument of SRE is couched in national and even patriotic tones: what can the USA do to improve the

quality of educational research in the USA and thereby improve the quality of education in the USA. Similarly, the science being called for and funded by the Institute of Education Sciences is a science that focuses on the question of what works in the context of education in the USA. (Tobin, 2007, p. 336)

More recently, in a review of literature on US research on education related to teachers and teaching, my colleagues and I were struck by how, even more than 10 years after the NRC report and in the context of greater attention to globalization, the research tended to be heavily parochial and as a field appeared to have national boundaries (Paine et al, 2016). The leading journal of teacher education (*Journal of Teacher Education*) similarly reflected recently on how much it had come to be seen as parochial (Knight et al, 2015).

When international research is incorporated into US education scholarship, most often it is in a league-tables-mentality process of comparison or externalization. When comparative and international perspectives are present, they frequently are 'methodologically reductionist, elevating simple statistical correlation over the exploration of culture' (Alexander, 2010, p. 801). Even the titles of books that bring research education outside the USA into consideration of US education convey the referent in some comparative, even competitive, way (such as in *Surpassing Shanghai* (Tucker, 2011) or *Catching Up or Leading the Way: American education in the age of globalization* (Zhao, 2009). In the end, these two tendencies – to emphasize accountability frames and external reference – further reinforce the narrowing of dominant notions of education as an academic field.

Shifting Topology in Education as a Profession: how education as a field shifts in the ways it speaks to teaching and teacher preparation

What education is understood to be and study as an academic area is undergoing real shifts. How education is studied is also, as discussed above, shifting. At very much the same time, what research is validated and how research informs the profession of education is also undergoing transformation in the USA in recent years. The University of Chicago story offers us one example of the threat to notions of what counts as education as an *academic* field. We can turn to the case of another US university – Arizona State University (ASU) – as an illustration of patterns of challenge, shift and tension within the notion of education as a *professional* field.

In fact, changes at ASU reflect the longstanding tension between education as an academic field and education as professional practice. In 2009, ASU undertook a dramatic reorganization that merged what had been separate programs in education, including a graduate program with strong research faculty, into the Mary Lou Fulton College of Education. The university's administrators justified it as responding to a familiar US challenge in 'bridging the traditional status divide between professors who specialize in producing research and clinical faculty members' (Sawchuk, 2011, p. 1):

> Though spurred in part by budget pressures, the university leaders intentionally merged a research oriented school focused on the preparation of scholars with one that had focused mostly on undergraduate preparation. (A newer, third school focusing on undergraduate and master's level preparation was also folded in.) 'Research universities tend to focus on graduate education, and teacher preparation is often separate, and I actually think that is quite detrimental,' Ms. Capaldi said. 'We saw an opportunity to bridge that divide. Putting [all the programs] into the teacher prep college was a statement that producing high quality teachers is our priority.' President Crow said the investments in improving teacher education were also spurred by a drive to do something to improve lackluster state K12 academic performance.
> (Sawchuk, 2011, p. 1)

The *Education Week* article that described this move treats it as one response to a common problem. Yet the tenor of the shift and the language used to explain it reflect the dramatic change involved, as well as a rejection of much of what had conventionally been seen as the ways university education spaces might include education both as an academic field and as a professional field. In all, the plans for reorganization, included the following:

> Disestablishing the Mary Lou Fulton College of Education.
> Disestablishing the Division of Curriculum and Instruction.
> Disestablishing the Division of Educational Leadership and Policy Studies.
> Disestablishing the Division of Psychology in Education.
> (Robbins, 2009)

Thus, creating the new Teachers College meant 'disestablishing' much of what was traditionally seen as the foundations of education and the centrality of curriculum (and the study of it) as professional knowledge. Many education scholars, as well as officials at AERA, in fact criticized the move, 'fearing it would affect scholarship' (Sawchuk, 2011, p. 1). Yet ASU has not only hailed its reorganization as the new direction for education but had also been very successful in getting federal funding. That fact is significant when current funding related to teacher education has, if anything, favored teacher education providers outside of higher education (Zeichner 2014).[7]

Michael Crow, ASU's president, explained: 'What we have done is to reorganize and restructure ourselves to focus on our two separate tasks related to K-12 education. One task is related to policy ideas, concepts and philosophy; the other focuses specifically on teacher production. We think that will tighten up our teacher production, allow us to focus our attention on teacher production, and enable us to take responsibility for teacher production' (ASU, 2009).

It is important here to note Crow's use of 'teacher production'. Some could see it as indicative of the philosophy of this shift, as the university moves to scale up teacher preparation. (Indeed, President Crow argues that the university should increase its teacher 'production' by 25% every year, and the program uses what some would call an industrial approach of observation and measurement in the process.[8] The echoes of neoliberal models of market efficiencies and accountability are threaded throughout the story of ASU's reform; these themes also characterize much of the shift in direction in teacher education more generally.

Defenders of ASU's restructuring emphasize ideas of effectiveness and acknowledge the ways in which this reorganization has meant a significant redefinition of what counts as education and what education is necessary for teachers:

> The goal of the project, according to its leaders, is to graduate
> teachers who, in their first year on the job, match the effectiveness
> of second year teachers. Getting there has meant no less than an
> entire shift in philosophy, according to Mari Koerner, the dean of
> ASU's Mary Lou Fulton Teachers College. 'The idea was to have
> a college of education that was part of the solution, as opposed to
> one that was only defining problems,' Ms. Koerner said. 'For a
> research level one college, it's a different perspective.'
> (Sawchuk, 2011, p. 1)

But Arizona State's reconfiguration of education's relationship to the profession is not a unique example. Most recently, and certainly as a more extreme version, we see the creation of Relay Graduate School of Education which has grown out of charter schools in New York. Lauded by the US Department of Education as an example of innovative leadership in moving teacher education to a new orientation, Relay:

> measures and holds itself accountable for both program graduate
> and employer satisfaction, as well as requires that teachers meet
> high goals for student learning growth before they can complete
> their degrees. Students of Relay teachers grew 1.3 years in reading
> performance in one year. (US Department of Education, 2014)

The relationship of education to the profession is shifting at rapid speed. University-based teacher education faculties, always vulnerable to criticisms from within and outside the university (Labaree, 2004), are increasingly under attack, morphing into new forms, looking for transformation and hybrid spaces/approaches (Wilson, 2014). ASU's reorganization and the creation of Relay Graduate School of Education exemplify some of this effort at innovation that both includes and affects what has historically been the institutional base of education as a field of study – the college or school of education.

The education school in the USA, home to teacher preparation and hence the link to the profession, has long been seen as weak. In the early 2000s, that chorus of criticism grew. In an influential critique of teacher preparation in the USA, Levine (2006) referred to it as the 'wild west'. Others have lodged similarly negative accounts. 'By almost any standard, many, if not most, of the nation's 1,450 schools, colleges, and departments of education are doing a mediocre job of preparing teachers,' wrote Duncan (2009), then secretary of education. Knowles (2013) claimed that 'America has a broken teacher preparation system' (p. 7). The lines of criticism most often centered around a set of problems typically described in terms of quality, efficiency and effectiveness.

Challenge to Traditions of Education as Educational Foundations and Curriculum

The reorganization of teacher education raises the question of 'whose knowledge counts?' (Zeichner et al, 2015). At Arizona State and elsewhere, what had been the traditional content of teacher education is undergoing significant change. In particular, the domains of educational foundations have been marginalized, criticized for being too distant from the needs of the profession.

In teacher education programs more generally there has been a growing tendency to minimize 'the importance of professional education coursework that is not seen as directly connected to daily teaching practice' (Zeichner et al, 2015, p. 123). ASU, for example, reduced its pedagogy coursework by 25% and doubled the amount of time in schools (Leger, 2013). As for Relay:

> Gone are the courses on education theory and history with no practical bearing ... Professors are not lofty academics, they are accomplished practitioners in the field ... RELAY provost Brent Maddin said 'the key is not to weed out theory, but rather ... to distill it down to essential points for the busy teacher.'
> (Caperton & Whitmire, 2012, pp. 77, 83, quoted in Zeichner et al, 2015, p. 123)

Traditionally, university-based teacher education programs have included courses in general education, subject matter, educational foundations and curriculum, teaching methods and practicum. How these have been distributed have varied by program. With the critiques of the 'relevance' of teacher preparation in preparing intending teachers for practice, the most common changes have been, then, shifts in the amount of, and approach to, coursework taught at the university, especially courses in foundations, curriculum and teaching methods. In some teacher education programs, this de-emphasis on curriculum, foundations and pedagogy is coupled with a redoubling of attention to subject matter. ASU, for example, decided to reduce pedagogy coursework and to increase content area work. Interestingly, in terms of scholarship on education, one notes a contemporaneous effort to invest in discipline-based education research (DBER), focusing on learning in specific disciplinary subjects (Shepard, 2016).

As states have ratcheted up the push for focus (course time) on subject knowledge, there is less time for foundations, and time spent on the direct connection to daily teaching crowds out seeing the study of curriculum as a field. This leads to social foundations being seen as 'non-essential' (Walsh & Jacobs, 2007).

The attacks from outside teacher education suggest that schools of education are out of touch with and ineffective in addressing the needs of schools.[9] Leading voices within teacher education, while not wholly agreeing with the external critique, have nonetheless also called for substantive reform. They argue that there is a 'consensus' about what 'we' know about what supports good teacher education (Darling-Hammond, 2006). Broadly categorized, reformers from within schools of education have been working to develop teacher preparation programs that have greater coherence and a closer integration of university and school-based learning. They recognize that lay people assume teaching does not require complex knowledge of both theory and practice (Labaree, 2004; Darling-Hammond, 2006; Cohen, 2011) but argue vigorously that indeed the practice of teaching requires professional judgment and knowledge. And they claim that this depends not only on time in classrooms (practical experience) but also on well-placed and connected theoretical understanding that allows future teachers to learn beyond recipes and trial and error. They also suggest that today's increasingly diverse student population, growing up in a 'knowledge economy', makes new demands on teacher education (Darling-Hammond, 2006).

Such discussions have led to and been supported by research on new approaches to teacher preparation that help the preservice teacher learn through analyzing and then developing core practices of teaching (McDonald et al, 2013). Through structured activities that sequence learning, preservice teachers engage in learning to 'notice' students and curriculum (and students interacting with content) (Barnhart & Van Es, 2015) [10] or to undertake 'rehearsal' of core practices (Lampert et al, 2013). These lines of reform, aimed at addressing the gaps and weaknesses teacher educators see, have produced new pedagogies of teacher education. Such pedagogies also reposition the teacher preparation program in relation to teachers and the school. For instance, whether it is through internship programs that extend opportunities for field-based learning or through traditional length programs that rely on rehearsal-oriented pedagogy, reformers are not calling (simply) for more time in schools or more time studying content. Rather, they make the case for engaging the opportunities that universities and schools, brought together, can make possible.[11] As such, teacher educators have been articulating a response to critics. This response not only argues for changes that they suggest are necessary for teacher education; it also serves to make a case for its location within the university (Wilson, 2014; Zeichner, 2014).

In this sense, the education of US teachers today could be seen as profoundly shaped by alternatives to imagining the preparation of teachers as appropriately a university-based practice. Fast-track, early-entry alternatives to teacher education now account for a significant portion of the new teachers entering schools. In 2010, over 30% of new teachers were coming via alternative routes rather than via traditional higher education-based teacher preparation (US Department of Education, 2013).[12] This proportion reflects a significant rise over time: in 1985-86 only '275 teachers were certified through alternative routes'; by 1990 'the numbers increased steadily'; and by the first decade of the twenty-first century, between 50,000 and 62,000 teachers annually were certified through alternative pathways (Wilson, 2014, p. 186).

These paths are varied: in California alone in 2009 there were 63 alternative routes, and Texas claimed 75. Yet, despite real variation within the broad category of alternative approaches, they reflect a topographical shift in the field of education. As a group these alternative programs define themselves, typically, in opposition to what they describe as the ineffectiveness and inefficiencies of traditional teacher preparation. Just as significant, however, is the way that even university-based programs are now framed by these debates (Lakoff, 2004). The description of reforms in teacher education above suggest that much of the discourse of change coming from teacher educators themselves takes up the frames of the critics.

Part of the argument in teacher education and how it is positioned hinges on the state of research in and about teacher education. Critics outside the enterprise suggest that research shows teacher education based in universities makes no significant contribution; they claim that fast-track programs produce teachers of comparable quality with less cost (Walsh 2001; Hess 2002; Kane et al, 2006). Others point to the 'thin' body of solid research that speaks to the quality, the effects and ultimately the value of teacher education (Floden, 2105, p. 282). Within the research community, including the teacher education research community, many call for rigorous research, scientifically based, that can shed light on the challenges of the practice (National Research Council, 2010; Feuer et al, 2013). Threaded through all these discussions of teacher education research is evidence of the profound shifts in the terrain of the practice and of the field as a research field. In both landscapes, concerns about accountability, efficiencies and effectiveness resonate.

Redefining Research in and for Teacher Education

The discussions and debates of the boundaries and qualities of educational scholarship reflect the shifting terrain of the field of education as an academic field. Similarly, investigation of the growing discussion of research in teacher education illuminates the fault lines that are altering the landscape of education as a practice.

Teacher education has, within the field of education, been a relatively under-researched topic. By the standards of the NRC report on the scientific basis of education, within the body of scholarship on teacher education there has been a much smaller portion that meets the standards of rigor now frequently held up as a measure of educational research quality (Wilson et al, 2001). Analysis of the position of teacher education within the academy helps explain this: traditionally schools and colleges of education have organized their staff to divide research and teaching responsibilities in ways that lead teacher educators to have less 'time and encouragement' for research than other university-based faculty (Floden, 2015, p. 282).

The growing pressures on all sectors of higher education, however, have raised the importance of research, and these pressures are felt within teacher education as well. At the same time, pressures on K-12 schools to respond to demands for evidence of accountability frame the larger discourse of education as one that privileges 'evidence-based' decisions and practices. Given these two trends, it should not be surprising that there is increased attention to research in teacher education, particularly research that responds to calls for evidence of outcomes and provides warrants about the value of investment. The third trend – the increasing competition from non-university/alternative programs certifying teachers – further presses schools and colleges of education to produce support for the effectiveness of their work (Arbaugh et al, 2015).

Today the accountability threads that are woven into notions of education as a field are similarly present in the idea of knowledge for and in teacher education (Cochran-Smith & Villegas, 2015). One can look to the flagship scholarly journal of teacher education in the United States, the *Journal of Teacher Education (JTE)*, to see the presence of articles written in response to value-added models and alternate routes to teaching, both phenomena typically presented in tropes of value, efficiency and effectiveness. Even when the *JTE* articles are offering critiques of these phenomena, or urging caution (Floden, 2012), the discussion is nonetheless framed by these larger discourses, not ones emerging from the teacher education community.

New Actors in the Landscape:
intermediating institutions and entrepreneurs

In the midst of these redefinitions of education, new pressures on education as an academic field, and parallel pressures and shifts on the profession, new actors enter the field, serving as brokers, intermediaries and entrepreneurs. McPherson (2004) reported on the view from the Spencer Foundation's former president, Tom James:

> James criticized the 'linear model' in which research makes discoveries which are transmitted to practitioners who apply them. Among the defects James pointed out is that this linear model makes the practitioner a 'consumer [who] is excluded from active participation in the development of new solutions to fundamental problems'. James thought that this and other problems could be helped by the development of intermediary 'brokerage' institutions that 'encourage interaction between practitioners and scholars'. And indeed many such intermediary institutions, including, as James noted, 'the independent research firms, the consulting firms and ... the research and development centers', among others, have grown up into increasingly important roles.
> (McPherson, 2004, p. 8)

There are multiple examples of the ways in which the repositioning of university-based teacher education and the debates over definitions of scholarship in education lead to new actors on the scene. I briefly mention three: assessment providers and systems such as the Teacher Advancement Program (TAP) and the edTPA; the accreditation organization Council for the Accreditation of Educator Preparation (CAEP); and the National Council on Teacher Quality (NCTQ) and the rankings system it created.

The first example involves the ways that new mechanisms for monitoring teacher education create new actors and reposition where knowledge is held. The TAP has become widely used as a performance assessment tool for teacher educators to use in their work with preservice teachers, yet its script-like approach, requiring training of teacher educators, removes teacher educators of agency and, some would argue, disregards the knowledge they bring (Wegwert & Foley, 2016).

The story of edTPA and the ways its scoring has been outsourced suggest another aspect to the nature of actors in the work of education/teacher preparation. As a performance assessment of preservice teachers, edTPA is organized on a national corporate model. It is already in seven states. It has been criticized as another instance of standardization:

> First, some of the most vocal criticisms of the edTPA have centered on the outsourcing of the scoring process from higher education to a corporate entity that has the business infrastructure to build an electronic platform to house and protect thousands of teacher candidate performance assessments each year and hire and pay teachers and teacher educators as external scorers on a year-round basis. These critics argue that engaging a corporate entity risks making teacher education a big business enterprise that is driven by profit and a production mind-set. (Sato, 2014, p. 423)

Performance assessment mechanisms are part of a large accountability press within teacher education that directs energy and labor towards topics, values particular measures and methods, and concentrates on what counts as education for the profession. The CAEP has come on the scene as a relatively new player in teacher education. In 2013 it became 'fully operational' as the sole provider of accreditation of teacher education programs, dealing directly with universities in ways that represent an extension and shift from past accountability arrangements (Council for the Accreditation of Educator Preparation, 2017). Its goal is to help support a 'more evidence-based system of teacher education' (Allen et al, 2014, p. ii). CAEP's standards focus on outcomes, and attention to measures signal a significant diversion from earlier iterations of accreditation processes, which focused on inputs or processes. As teacher educators contend with the detailed documentation and reporting required of the CAEP process, the significant time demand means not doing something else. In some cases, new staff positions have been created to engage in (teacher preparation program) data management and/or analysis. In the zero-sum game of departmental staffing budgets, this means personnel devoted to crunching numbers rather than working with schools.

While CAEP signals a shift in accountability mechanisms, the rise of rankings, rather than ratings, reflects a deeper change in how the profession is positioned (and by whom). The NCTQ, a non-governmental organization established in 2000, has become a vocal participant in debates about teacher education. It has been a prominent critic of what it regards as the low quality of teacher preparation:

> Ever so slowly, the United States is taking a harder look at how its teacher preparation schools are improving the quality of the teachers they produce. The signs are everywhere – from proposed federal action to state legislatures and school boards passing new oversight laws and regulations, to a newly marshaled push for stronger accreditation by the institutions themselves. The country is finally waking up to the critical importance of improving teacher preparation quality to produce more classroom-ready teachers. But as *NCTQ Teacher Prep Review 2014* shows, far more needs to be done to expand the pool of teachers properly prepared to meet the challenges of the contemporary American classroom. (NCTQ, 2015, p. 1)

In the process, it has brought new levels of measuring, rating and even the ranking of programs. It explained in a recent report that:

> we have discarded our system of ratings for a system of rankings to make it easier for users of our results to assess the relative performance of programs in a crowded market. There are now both national rankings and regional rankings out of consideration for aspiring teachers' tendency to attend teacher preparation programs relatively close to home. (NCTQ, 2015, p. 2)

Not surprisingly, NCTQ has met resistance from colleges of education (Fuller 2014). The response to NCTQ from teacher education argues that NCTQ missed the mark in what to look at in understanding teacher education:

> Many of the criteria and elements used in the NCTQ ratings lack a sufficient research base to warrant their use without additional exploration. For example, student-selectivity criteria, including grade point averages and SAT or ACT scores, were chosen despite serious questions about whether these thresholds are ultimately related to the quality of teaching; how the relationships between GPA (or test scores) and quality teaching might be mediated by learning experiences provided in the teacher-preparation program; or how setting specific selectivity criteria based on grades and test scores might not account for other equally or more important criteria and experiences for prospective teachers. (Heller et al, 2013)

Teacher educators fault the NCTQ challenge for having insufficient and inappropriate data. It is nonetheless important to recognize that even in this high-stakes debate about the work and future of teacher education, the discourse is still framed by the dominant metaphors of science, evidence-based practice, and rigor. The back and forth between critics and defenders reminds us of the weak evidentiary basis used in teacher education and of the contentiousness of defining what 'research' in education is.

Viewing Shifting Landscapes, Imagining the Future

What does this mean for the relationship between education and the profession? All seem to agree that we are at a critical juncture. What is not agreed on is what that juncture suggests about the future.

It appears that the shifts in the terrain of education as an academic field of study can be viewed in multiple ways, depending on where one stands. From one perspective, there is a multiplicity of voices, questions and approaches to the study of education; it is not a single field, but multiple streams, each flowing almost independently. Yet, housed institutionally within universities, with budgets and resources (both financial and symbolic) to be procured and dispensed, and hence vulnerable to resource pressures, education appears to have sharpened its focus on particular topics, with favored approaches. While US schools of education still have faculty who reflect a broad range of disciplinary backgrounds, theirs is not a level playing field. From this view, the rise of accountability and market frames powerfully explains much of what is occurring in the academic spaces of education.

Within education as a field of practice, US schools and teachers are themselves increasingly vulnerable to similar pressures. In a nation known internationally for having a decentralized education system and an absence of national curriculum or high-stakes testing, policy changes in the past 15 years have dramatically introduced external processes of monitoring and evaluation and increased efforts at standardization.

For the corner of education that connects both university and schools – the teacher education program – the parallel shifts, from university transformation and school and curriculum reform, have pushed teacher education into a moment of real challenge. Across the landscapes of education as a field and as a practice, there appears to be significant fracture. As Wilson summarized:

> Teachers matter. Preparing teachers to teach matters. That the current national education rhetoric aligns with that reality should be heartening. However, the busyness of the teacher preparation marketplace – with new and old actors, shifting values, intensifying cries for data and accountability – leaves several questions yet unanswered. (Wilson, 2014, pp. 190-191)

The University of Chicago closed its School of Education in the face of concern about definitions of education as a field of study and in defense of a vision of academic quality. ASU reorganized its school of education in an effort to make a case for the value of practice. To what extent are the shifts in both the study of education and the practice of education likely to mean that the two worlds become increasingly separate? Can they co-exist? The stories of these two universities' decisions would, at the very least, raise concerns.

The nature of education generally is one that has historically proven problematic to how it is constituted as a field in the USA. With knowledge that is seen as soft, a focus on children (themselves low-status members of the broader community) and a tendency to engage in the production of applied knowledge, education has long been vulnerable (Labaree, 2004; Cohen, 2011). What is important to watch for the future is how the current pressures on education – both in the academic field and in its university-based home of practice (teacher education) – shift the gaze not only to outcomes but also to a focus on the individual. Such a direction would lead to atomization in the nature of questions examined in research and policy issues considered. Yet historically – and very much fundamental to the earliest days of the field of education in the USA – educational questions are not only about the individual, they are also about the social. The popularity of certain frames in education today encourages a gaze towards the individual (and outcomes related to them) and away from broader questions. Should that happen in the long run, we lose the opportunity to think about the organizational and social aspects of education.

The direction of change in education also risks decoupling knowledge from where it should be taught. What is the role of the school of education? As alternative providers of teacher preparation challenge the work of schools of education in that area, is it likely that schools of education will forego their historical roles as preparers of teachers? From a resource and institutional perspective, it seems unlikely. But it also appears likely that teacher education, like the larger field of which it is a part, bends to the pressures of a narrowed view of scholarship. The privileging of the universal – in notions of scientific value – poses a threat to possibilities of knowing and doing that teacher education in the USA, at least at present, is only beginning to try to articulate in its defense.

Acknowledgements

I would like to thank Elena Aydarova, Brian DeLany, Aaron Pallas, Iwan Syahril and Kris Windorski for their valuable effort to help me as I developed this chapter, and John Furlong and Geoff Whitty for their very generous and insightful editorial support. I have benefited from the help of many. Errors and shortcomings are all mine.

Notes

[1] Established in 2002 within the US Department of Education's Institute for Education Sciences (IES), the WWC is, according to its website, 'a central and trusted source of scientific evidence on education programs, products, practices, and policies. We review the research, determine which studies meet rigorous standards, and summarize the findings. We focus on high-quality research to answer the question "what works in education?"' (Institute of Education Sciences, 2017c).

[2] The NRC was created in the nineteenth century to advise the government with balanced and informed expertise.

[3] See, for example, Berliner's (2002) and Erickson and Gutierrez's (2002) critiques of how the report can be read as endorsing an overly narrow or limited view of science.

[4] It is, as Michael Feuer suggested, perhaps a reflection of a US approach that privileges the power of science: 'there is a longstanding, historical traditional [*sic*] in American society to turn to science, technology, and rational thinking as a way to address very fundamental complex problems' (Feuer, quoted in Tobin, 2007, p. 329). But this framing of the importance of science in setting a bar for educational research in the early twenty-first century operationalizes science in particular (and hence new) ways.

[5] Even the use of the acronym RCT indicates how powerful the concept has become within education circles. Once a particular set of epistemological assumptions and methodological approaches has become widely enough promoted it can be reduced to a familiar set of letters. One might think of IQ, SAT and other examples in earlier times.

[6] Making a different but related argument, Snow (2016) worries about the emphasis on 'relevance' in research that is too narrowly drawn and misses the opportunity to inform important conversations and practices. She advocates for the value, for example, of 'practice-embedded research' and the need for

'researcher-practitioner partnerships'. She suggests that funding has gone to 'traditional' research in ways that reduce the chance for important work, that is practice-based, to be undertaken. 'Funding priorities and criteria also need to be revised if practice-based research is to thrive' (p. 68).

[7] For example, in the 2010 'Innovation in Education' competition funded by the US Department of Education, none of the proposals submitted by university-based teacher preparation programs received awards. The only teacher education programs to receive funding were those outside the university: Teach for America, the New Teacher Project and the Boston Teacher Residency Program (Zeichner, 2014, p. 555).

[8] ASU relies on TAP (the Teacher Advancement Program), as do an increasing number of teacher education programs (Cavazos, 2016). TAP has many features, but underlying its observations and evaluations of teachers is what some would see as an emphasis on a technicist orientation geared towards treating teaching and teacher development in 'scientific' ways.

[9] Going further, some critics also challenge university-based teacher education for being hamstrung by 'a rigid, liberally progressive ideology' (Wilson, 2014, p. 185).

[10] The literature on 'noticing' argues that a central task of teaching is being able to recognize what to pay attention to. Classrooms are busy places, and teachers 'need to decide to what to pay attention, and they need to reason about what they see to make decisions about how to proceed with the lesson' (van Es, 2011, p. 134). In teacher preparation, novices need to understand the importance of this work and develop the skills and knowledge to engage in it.

[11] Many would argue that some of the current approaches to 'new' teacher education are informed by 'old' ideas about teacher learning, particularly those developed by Dewey (Carroll et al, 2007).

[12] In parts of the country, the presence of alternative route teachers is far greater. Zeichner (2014) notes that in some areas traditionally certified and alternative certified teachers are nearly equal in number, and that in Texas the two largest producers of teachers, of all programs (traditional and other), are online for-profit programs (p. 553). There are many ways and program types that are considered alternatives to traditional (university-based) teacher education. For the purposes of this chapter, I consider all such fast-track programs that bypass traditional degree programs based in higher education as alternative programs.

References

Alexander, R.J. (2010) 'World Class Schools': noble aspiration or globalised hokum? *Compare*, 40(6), 801-817. https://doi.org/10.1080/03057925.2010.523252

Allen, M., Coble, C. & Crowe, E. (2014) Report Highlights: building an evidence-based system for teacher preparation by teacher preparation analytics. Council for the Accreditation of Educator Preparation (CAEP) and Pearson Higher Education.

American Educational Research Association (1996) 1996-1997 Special Interest Group Annual Directory, *Educational Researcher*, 25, 38-42. https://doi.org/10.3102/0013189X025005038

American Educational Research Association (2016a) About AERA, fact sheet. http://www.aera.net/About-AERA/Who-We-Are

Arbaugh, F., Ball, D.L., Grossman, P., Heller, D.E. & Monk, D. (2015) Deans' Corner: views on the state of teacher education in 2015, *Journal of Teacher Education*, 66(5), 435-445. https://doi.org/10.1177/0022487115602314

Arizona State University (2009) Restructured Colleges, Grant Target K-12 School Performance. https://asunews.asu.edu/20091007_educationcolleges

Barnhart, T. & van Es, E. (2015) Studying Teacher Noticing: examining the relationship among pre-service science teachers' ability to attend, analyze, and respond to students' thinking, *Teaching and Teacher Education*, 45, 83-93. https://doi.org/10.1016/j.tate.2014.09.005

Berliner, D. (2002) Comment: Educational Research: the hardest science of all, *Educational Researcher*, 31(8), 18-20. http://www.jstor.org/stable/3594389

Bok, D. (2013) *Higher Education in America*, Kindle edn. Princeton, NJ: Princeton University Press.

Bronner, E. (1997) End of Chicago's Education School Stirs Debate, *New York Times*. http://www.nytimes.com/1997/09/17/us/end-of-chicago-s-education-school-stirs-debate.html

Carroll, D., Featherstone, H., Featherstone, J., Feiman-Nemser, S. & Roosevelt, D. (2007) *Transforming Teacher Education: reflections from the field*. Cambridge, MA: Harvard Educational Press.

Cavazos, S. (2016) Seasoned Teachers Mentor Colleagues through 'TAP' Evaluation Program. 7 April. http://www.chalkbeat.org/posts/in/2016/04/07

Cochran-Smith, M. & Villegas, A.M. (2015) Framing Teacher Preparation Research: an overview of the field, Part I, *Journal of Teacher Education*, 66(1), 7-20. https://doi.org/10.1177/0022487114549072

Cohen, D.K. (2011) *Teaching and its Predicaments*. Cambridge, MA: Harvard University Press. https://doi.org/10.4159/harvard.9780674062788

Council for the Accreditation of Educator Preparation (2017) History of CAEP. http://www.caepnet.org/about/history

Council Minutes (2002) *Educational Researcher*, 31(9), 42-48. http://www.jstor.org/stable/3594497

Darling-Hammond, L. (2006) Constructing 21st-century Teacher Education, *Journal of Teacher Education*, 57(3) (May/June), 300-314.

Darling-Hammond, L. (2015) Can Value Added Add Value to Teacher Evaluation?, *Educational Researcher*, 44(2), 132-137. https://doi.org/10.3102/0013189X15575346

Duncan, A. (2009) Teacher Preparation: reforming the uncertain profession. Speech given at Teachers College, Columbia University, New York, 22 October. https://www.ed.gov/news/speeches/teacher-preparation-reforming-uncertain-profession

Erickson, F. & Gutierrez, K. (2002) Comment: culture, rigor, and science in educational research, *Educational Researcher*, 31(8), 21-24. http://www.jstor.org/stable/3594390

Feuer, M., Towne, L. & Shavelson, R. (2002) Scientific Culture and Educational Research, *Educational Researcher*, 31(8), 4-14. http://www.jstor.org/stable/3594387

Feuer, M.J., Floden, R.E., Chudowsky, N. & Ahn, J. (2013) *Evaluation of Teacher Preparation Programs: purposes, methods, and policy options*. Washington, DC: National Academy of Education.

Floden, R.E. (2012) Teacher Value Added as a Measure of Program Quality: interpret with caution, *Journal of Teacher Education*, 63(5), 356-360. https://doi.org/10.1177/0022487112454175

Floden, R.E. (2015) Learning What Research Says About Teacher Preparation, in M.J. Feuer, A.I. Berman & R.C. Atkinson (Eds) *Past as Prologue: the National Academy of Education at 50. Members Reflect*, pp. 279-284. Washington, DC: National Academy of Education.

Geiger, R.L. (2004). *Knowledge and Money: research universities and the paradox of the marketplace*. Stanford, CA: Stanford University Press.

Harris, D. & Herrington, C. (2015) Editors' Introduction: the use of teacher value-added measures in schools: new evidence, unanswered questions, and future prospects, *Educational Researcher*, 44(2), 71-76. https://doi.org/10.3102/0013189X15576142

Hazelkorn, E. (2009) Impact of Global Rankings on Higher Education Research and the Production of Knowledge. UNESCO Forum on Higher Education, Research and Knowledge, Occasional Paper No. 18. http://unesdoc.unesco.org/images/0018/001816/181653e.pdf

Heller, D., Segall, A. & Drake, C. (2013) An Open Letter to NCTQ on Teacher Prep, *Education Week*, December. http://www.edweek.org/ew/articles/2013/12/11/14heller.h33.html

Hess, F.H. (2002) Break the Link, *Education Next*, 2(1), 22-28.

Hordern, J. (2015) Bernstein's Sociology of Knowledge and Education(al) Studies. Paper presented to the *Educational Studies – The University Project in Different Jurisdictions* conference, Oxford, 15-16 July.

Institute of Education Sciences (2017b) Reviews of Individual Studies. https://ies.ed.gov/ncee/wwc/ReviewedStudies

Institute of Education Sciences (2017c) Who We Are. https://ies.ed.gov/ncee/wwc/WhoWeAre

Judge, H., Lemosse, M., Paine, L. & Sedlak, M. (1994) *The University and the Teachers: France, the United States, England*. Oxford: Symposium Books. https://doi.org/10.15730/books.31

Kane, T.J., Rockoff, J.E. & Staiger, D.O. (2006) What Does Certification Tell Us About Teacher Effectiveness? Evidence from New York City. NBER Working Paper No. 12155. https://doi.org/10.3386/w12155

Kennedy, M.M. (2008) Sorting Out Teacher Quality, *Phi Delta Kappan*, 90(1), 59-63. https://doi.org/10.1177/003172170809000115

Knight, S.L., Lloyd, G.M., Arbaugh, F., Gamson, D., McDonald, S.P., Nolan Jr., J. & Whitney, A.E. (2015) Contextualizing versus Internationalizing Research on Teacher Education: competing or complementary goals? *Journal of Teacher Education*, 66(3), 197-200. https://doi.org/10.1177/0022487115580422

Knowles, T. (2013) New Pathways for Teachers, New Promises for Students: a vision for developing excellent teachers. Special Report 3. Washington, DC: American Enterprise Institute.

Labaree, D. (2004) *The Trouble with Ed Schools*. New Haven, CT: Yale University Press.

Lakoff, G. (2004) *Don't Think of an Elephant: progressive values and the framing wars – a progressive guide to action*. White River Junction, VT: Chelsea Green Publishing.

Lampert, M., Franke, M.L., Kazemi, E., Ghousseini, H., Turrou, A.C., Beasley, H. & Crowe, K. (2013) Keeping it Complex: using rehearsals to support novice teacher learning of ambitious teaching, *Journal of Teacher Education*, 64(3), 226-243. https://doi.org/10.1177/0022487112473837

Leger, R. (2013) How to Get More Quality in Arizona Classrooms, *Arizona Republic*, 12 December. http://archive.azcentral.com/opinions/articles/20131215new-arizona-education-teachers.html

Levin, J.S. & Aliyeva, A. (2015) Embedded Neoliberalism within Faculty Behaviors, *Review of Higher Education*, 38(4), 537-563. https://doi.org/10.1353/rhe.2015.0030

Levine, A.E. (2006) *Educating School Teachers*. Washington DC: Education Schools Project.

Marginson, S. & van der Wende, M. (2007) To Rank or to be Ranked: the impact of global rankings in higher education, *Journal of Studies in International Education*, 11(3/4), 306-329. https://doi.org/10.1177/1028315307303544

McDonald, M., Kazemi, E. & Kavanagh, S. (2013) Core Practices and Pedagogies of Teacher Education: a call for a common language and collective activity, *Journal of Teacher Education*, 64(5), 378-386. https://doi.org/10.1177/0022487113493807

McPherson, M. (2004) President's Comments, in *The Spencer Foundation Annual Report*, 1 April 2003-31 March 2004. http://www.spencer.org/foundation-reports

National Center for Teacher Quality (NCTQ) (2015) 2014 Teacher Prep Review: a review of the nation's teacher preparation programs. Washington, DC. www.nctq.org/teacherPrep/review2014

National Research Council (2002) *Scientific Research in Education*, ed. R.J. Shavelson & L. Towne. Committee on Scientific Principles for Education Research, Center for Education, Division of Behavioral and Social Sciences and Education. Washington, DC: National Academies Press.

National Research Council (2010) *Preparing Teachers: building evidence for sound policy*. Committee on the Study of Teacher Preparation Programs in the United States, Center for Education, Division of Behavioral and Social Sciences and Education. Washington, DC: National Academies Press.

Paine, L., Bloemeke, S. & Aydarova, O. (2016) Teachers and Teaching in the Context of Globalization, in D. Gitomer & C. Bell (Eds) *Handbook of Research on*

Teaching, 5th edn. Washington, DC: AERA.
https://doi.org/10.3102/978-0-935302-48-6_11

Robbins, L. (2009) ASU Announces Academic Reorganization.
https://asunews.asu.edu/20090121_reorg

Sato, M. (2014) What is the Underlying Conception of Teaching of the edTPA?,
Journal of Teacher Education, 65(5), 421-434.
https://doi.org/10.1177/0022487114542518

Sawchuk, S. (2011) Nation's Biggest Teacher-prep School Revamps Training,
Education Week, 31(12) (16 November), 1.

Schriewer, J. & Martinez, C. (2004) Constructions of Internationality in Education,
in G. Steiner-Khamsi (Ed.) *The Global Politics of Educational Borrowing and
Lending*, pp. 29-53. New York: Teachers College Press.

Shahjahan, R.A. & Morgan, C. (2016) Global Competition, Coloniality, and the
Geopolitics of Knowledge in Higher Education, *British Journal of Sociology of
Education*, 37(1), 92-109. https://doi.org/10.1080/01425692.2015.1095635

Shepard, L. (2016) Testing and Assessment for the Good of Education: contributions
of AERA presidents, 1915-2015, *Educational Researcher*, 45(2), 112-121.
https://doi.org/10.3102/0013189X16639599

Snow, C. (2016) The Role of Relevance in Education Research, as Viewed by Former
Presidents, *Educational Researcher*, 45(2), 64-68.

Society for Research on Educational Effectiveness (2015) History.
https://www.sree.org/pages/history.php

Special Interest Group Directory 2016-2017 (2017) Online Directory.
http://www.aera.net/About-AERA/Member-Constituents/SIGs/SIG-Directory

Thelin, J.R. (2011) *A History of American Higher Education*, Kindle edn. Baltimore,
MD: Johns Hopkins University Press.

Tobin, J. (2007) An Anthropologist's Reflections on Defining Quality in Education
Research, *International Journal of Research & Method in Education*, 30(3),
325-338. https://doi.org/10.1080/17437270701614816

Tucker, M.S. (2011) *Surpassing Shanghai: an agenda for American education built on the
world's leading systems*. Cambridge, MA: Harvard Education Press.

US Department of Education (2013) Preparing and Credentialing the Nation's
Teachers: the secretary's 9th report on teacher quality. Office of Postsecondary
Education, Washington, DC.

US Department of Education (2014) US Department of Education Proposes Plan to
Strengthen Teacher Preparation. https://www.ed.gov/news/press-releases/us-
department-education-proposes-plan-strengthen-teacher-preparation

van Es, E. (2011) A Framework for Learning to Notice, in M.G. Sherin, V.R. Jacobs
& R. Phillips (Eds) *Mathematics Teacher Noticing: Seeing through teachers' eyes*,
pp. 134-151. New York: Routledge.

Walsh, K. (2001) *Teacher Certification Reconsidered: stumbling for quality*. Baltimore,
MD: Abell Foundation.

Walsh, K. & Jacobs, S. (2007) *Alternative Certification Isn't Alternative*. Washington,
DC: National Council on Teacher Quality.

Wegwert, J.C. & Foley, J.A. (2016) Colleges of Education and the Making of the Neoliberal University. Paper presented at the Annual Meeting of the American Educational Research Association, Washington, DC, April.

Wilson, Suzanne (2014) Evolving Systems of US Teacher Preparation, *Theory into Practice*, 53, 183-195. https://doi.org/10.1080/00405841.2014.916569

Wilson, S.M., Floden, R.E. & Ferrini-Mundy, J. (2001) *Teacher Preparation Research: current knowledge, gaps, and recommendations.* Seattle: Center for the Study of Teaching and Policy.

Zeichner, K. (2014) The Struggle for the Soul of Teaching and Teacher Education in the USA, *Journal of Education for Teaching*, 40(5), 551-568. https://doi.org/10.1080/02607476.2014.956544

Zeichner, K., Payne, K.A. & Brayko, K. (2015) Democratizing Teacher Education, *Journal of Teacher Education*, 66(2), 122-135. https://doi.org/10.1177/0022487114560908

Zhao, Y. (2009) *Catching Up or Leading the Way: American education in the age of globalization.* Alexandria, VA: ASCD.

Part 3. Conceptualising and Realizing Education as a Field of Study

CHAPTER 8

Bernstein's Sociology of Knowledge and Education(al) Studies

JIM HORDERN

SUMMARY This chapter provides an overview of some key concepts in Basil Bernstein's sociology of knowledge and their development and use by other authors working in related traditions. These concepts are then used to discuss disciplinary structures and the organisation of education(al) studies, with particular reference to the UK context. Bernstein's work allows for a nuanced characterisation of education(al) studies in its varied forms, while acknowledging the influence of other disciplines, of prevalent notions of professionalism, and of conceptions of educational practice.

Introduction

This chapter outlines various 'Bernsteinian' concepts that may be useful in thinking through how elements of 'academic knowledge about education' and 'professional knowledge in education' may be brought together to constitute the discipline of 'education studies'. By 'Bernsteinian' I mean concepts developed originally by Basil Bernstein, particularly in his later work (Bernstein, 1999, 2000), and then iterated, applied and 'recontextualised' by others (i.e. Muller, 2009; Young & Muller, 2014), in particular to discuss knowledge constitution, production and differentiation in 'academic' and 'professional' disciplines. Conceptualising the notion of a 'professionally orientated' discipline may be important for a discussion of the nature of education(al) studies, given the close relationship in some countries between the study of education and the education of teachers (Furlong, 2013).

This cannot be an entirely 'purist' exercise – a good deal of Bernstein's work in this area, while insightful, is somewhat fragmented, and there is little that is focused explicitly on the problematics of conceptualising professional or practice knowledge in a professionally (or practice-) orientated discipline. Thus, the work of Muller (2009), Barnett (2006), Young (2008), Young & Muller (2014) and others working within a broadly 'social realist' tradition is particularly important here in fleshing out an analytical approach that can cover those questions that relate to professional knowledge. There are important links too with the work of Winch (2010, 2013) on differing aspects of knowledge and expertise. I will also attempt to sketch some questions that I think arise from the work of the social realist thinkers for the conceptualisation of professional practice and its relation to professional education. While this skeletal coverage represents just a fraction of the work in this area, it is hoped that it will provide some food for thought. Having introduced these concepts in the first part of the chapter, the second part briefly conjectures on what this might illuminate about the discipline of education studies, drawing on examples from the UK context. The notion of 'discipline' is used here, rather than 'field', primarily because this chapter seeks to demonstrate the use of one set of conceptual tools to approach the social organisation of knowledge without entering into debates about definitions of, and differences that may exist between, those particular terms, important as these are.

Part 1: Bernstein and Social Realist Work on Knowledge: some key concepts

Vertical and Horizontal Discourses

The delineation between vertical discourse and horizontal discourse, within which different 'forms of knowledge' are 'realised' (Bernstein, 1999, p. 158), underpins Bernsteinian sociology of knowledge. Vertical discourses are described as 'specialised symbolic structures' which are 'systemically principled' (Bernstein, 1999, p. 161), while horizontal discourse is 'local, context-dependent', 'everyday' and 'common sense' (p. 159) knowledge. This is knowledge differentiation, rooted in Durkheim's distinction between the sacred and profane, with similar delineations also suggested by Bourdieu, Habermas and Giddens (Bernstein, 1999, p. 158). Bernstein (1999, 2000) asserts that there are substantive differences in both the social conditions of production and the epistemic structure of these two knowledge/discourse types. While vertical discourse is context-independent knowledge conserved through intricate social formations, horizontal discourse is always 'contextually specific' (Bernstein 1999, p. 161), 'consumed by that context' (Wheelahan, 2010, p. 20), and circulated and exchanged through fluid and unsystematic social processes (Bernstein, 1999, pp. 159-160). Vertical discourse consists of 'explicit' propositional knowledge, but it could also be said to consist of aspects of procedural and inferential 'know how' (Muller, 2014 drawing on Winch, 2010, 2013) which are constituent elements of disciplinary knowledge structures. For Young (2008) and Muller (2009) this vertical 'specialised' discourse bears the 'imprint' of specific forms of 'sociality' that conserve and iterate its intrinsic value. This value lies in the capacity of this knowledge to enable abstract conceptualisation, conjecture and hypothesis-building, taking the thinker beyond her immediate experience (Young & Muller, 2013). This 'sociality' is husbanded within disciplinary communities and represented in forms of critique and scrutiny which tease out the validity of truth claims, and for Young and Muller (2007) must demonstrate a commitment both to 'truthfulness' and to the possibility of truth. Specialised 'vertical' knowledge is seen as 'systematically revisable', 'emergent', 'real', 'material and social', an approach to knowledge that is contrasted with relativism and social constructivism (Young & Muller, 2013, pp. 236-238; Moore, 2007). These forms of insight are not available, however, through horizontal discourse, a form that offers no basis for thinking beyond immediate experience (Bernstein, 1999).

Within vertical discourse Bernstein identifies two types of knowledge structure. The first is 'hierarchical', characterised by 'integrating propositions' (Bernstein, 1999, p. 162) that drive the development of a coherent and relatively unified structure of knowledge that is established through hypotheses that are advanced and refuted through empirical correlates, based upon certain shared methodological and epistemological assumptions. The archetypal hierarchical knowledge structure is represented by the physical sciences (Bernstein, 1999, p. 164; Muller, 2009; Wheelahan, 2010, p. 21). The second is (slightly confusingly) the 'horizontal' or 'segmented' knowledge structure, which consists of a series of different 'languages' or theoretical perspectives which together comprise the discipline but each have a distinct perspective, methodological tradition and epistemological position (Bernstein, 1999, pp. 162-163). The 'languages' may not agree on a great deal – and this, some might argue, might pose an obstacle to attempts at 'progression' in the discipline. Bernstein suggests sociology as an archetypal horizontal or segmented knowledge structure (1999, p. 162).

Bernstein also discusses the notion of 'grammaticality', which is used to distinguish between the character of different languages within horizontal knowledge structures (1999, pp. 163-164). Languages that have an 'explicit conceptual syntax capable of "relatively" precise empirical descriptions' have 'strong grammars', whereas those which have 'weaker' relations between concepts and empirical description are 'weak grammars' (1999, pp. 163-164). Maths, economics and linguistics are all offered as examples of horizontal structures which contain languages with 'strong grammars', and 'sociology' and 'cultural studies' have language with weak grammars (1999, p. 164), although Bernstein's formulation allows for the possibility of a knowledge structure containing languages with very different grammatical strengths. The point of a strong grammar is also important – Bernstein relates more 'precise' analytical and empirical description to theoretical disciplinary development. The strong relationship between the 'external' and 'internal', the empirical and the theoretical, leads to greater 'explanatory/descriptive powers' (1999, p. 164).

Table I attempts to summarise key features of the two discourses, and the knowledge structures in vertical discourse.

Vertical discourse		Horizontal discourse
'context independent', 'explicit', 'specialised'		'oral', 'local' , 'context dependent'
Hierarchical structures	*Horizontal or 'segmented' structures*	'learning to dress' 'using a telephone' (Bernstein, 1999, p. 161)
Physical sciences (physics, chemistry)	*'Strong grammar'* maths, economics, linguistics	'informal experience'; 'personal experience' (Breier, 2004)
	'Weak grammar' sociology, cultural studies	And also, perhaps, – 'local practices', organisational and workplace-specific knowledge (Hordern, 2014a)

Table I. Vertical and horizontal discourses compared.

Singulars, Regions and Generics

'Singulars',' regions' and 'generics' are the names Bernstein (2000, p. 52) offers for 'performance modes' or socio-epistemic entities that represent types of knowledge structure. The 'singular' represents an academic discipline, 'a specialised discrete discourse with its own intellectual field of texts, practices, rules of entry', and is 'protected by strong boundaries and hierarchies' (2000, p. 52). Bernstein mentions 'physics, chemistry, history, economics, psychology' (2000, p. 52) as examples of singulars, encompassing all forms of knowledge structure within vertical discourse. However, given the discussion in the previous section, it seems that singulars will be differentiated in terms of the type of vertical discourse (hierarchical/horizontal), the degree of 'grammaticality' and the social relations that characterise them. One might suggest that a hierarchical structure, such as physics, has more universal and explicit 'rules of entry' and 'practices' as a discipline than sociology, where practices may differ by 'language'/theoretical perspective, and 'rules of entry' to the discipline are less stringent.

A region, meanwhile, is 'constructed by recontextualising singulars into larger units which operate both in the intellectual field of disciplines and in the field of external practice' (Bernstein 2000, p. 52). Regions are 'the interface between singulars and the technologies they make possible' (2000, p. 52) – 'engineering, medicine, architecture' are regions, with 'contemporary regions' including 'cognitive science, management, business studies, communication and media' (2000, p. 52). Thus regions may represent the traditional professions, newer professions, or new areas of knowledge that somehow relate to an (often 'industrial') purpose or area of practice (Beck & Young, 2005; Muller, 2009). What Muller calls a 'supervening purpose' (2009, p. 213) orientates the 'recontextualisation' of singulars towards the objectives of the occupational field or practice. The need to 'face both ways' (Barnett, 2006, p. 152), to the 'intellectual field of disciplines' and to 'external practice' (Bernstein, 2000, p. 52), suggests complex processes in which multiple stakeholders may be involved in 'selecting', 'appropriating' and 'transforming' knowledge from disciplines for the needs of the regional (i.e. professional, occupational, industrial, practice-orientated) knowledge base (Barnett, 2006; Hordern, 2014a).

However, it is likely that not all 'regional' knowledge is recontextualised directly from disciplines. In certain sectoral or professional fields, 'cognate' regions within those fields may be recontextualising knowledge from other regions within the field – that is, those of the built environment (architecture, surveying, construction) or the health professions (medicine, nursing, pharmacy) (Hordern, 2014e). What may be emphasised, or neglected, in the 'recontextualisation' process may depend on how the epistemic structure of the knowledge is construed, and on the social relations between the various stakeholders in the region and the wider sectoral or professional field. One can also theorise that certain regions may be particularly 'proximate' to certain singulars, drawing knowledge and practices from them (Hordern, 2014e). Thus engineering may draw on advances in the physical sciences or medicine on the physical and biological sciences, or education (if it is a region – to be discussed below) on various social sciences. The knowledge structures of the singulars will impact on the how and what of recontextualisation – multiple languages in a segmented knowledge structure may lead to some languages being selected and recontextualised to a region to the exclusion of others (Hordern, 2014a, e). Broader debates and contests in sociology and psychology, for example, may be lost in the social work or education regions if certain sociological or psychological 'languages' are preferred within those regions.

Drawing more widely on Bernstein's (1971, 2000) theoretical work we might suggest that some regions are more strongly insulated (or 'bounded') than others, capable of developing a stronger identity and capacity to 'recontextualise' knowledge on their own terms (Hordern, 2014e). Such regions may also develop greater independence in the production of knowledge for their profession or practice – thus medicine, a region with its own defined knowledge base, established professional bodies (recontextualisation agents) and disciplinary practices (Beck & Young, 2005), may start to impact on the purposes of the singulars which have traditionally provided it with a knowledge base (at least in the modern era [Foray & Hargreaves, 2003]), perhaps particularly if key stakeholders (i.e. government) encourage such a development. Nursing, on the other hand, may be concerned to maintain connections with medicine and other health profession regions, relying as much on the recontextualisation processes of these regions as its own to build its knowledge base (McNamara & Fealy, 2014). Less strongly insulated regions may be prone to dominance by external stakeholders who seek to orientate the work of an occupation towards particular policy objectives. It could be argued that 'distance' from singulars, and reliance on other regions, could result in the neglect of the forms of inference and claim validation that are hallmarks of disciplinary development in vertical discourse (Muller, 2014 – drawing on Winch, 2010, 2013; Hordern, 2014e). Thus, it can be argued that regions must demonstrate the 'capability' to recontextualise knowledge in accordance with the underpinning structure of that knowledge (Hordern, 2014e).

Singulars	Regions	Generics
'Pure disciplines'	'Applied' or 'professionally orientated' disciplines	Constructed with no connection to disciplinary sources and with little regard to the 'culture and practices' of an occupation (Bernstein, 2000, p. 53)
May be 'narcissistic' and self-referential (Bernstein, 2000, p. 52)		
	Have a relation to singulars, to practice and perhaps to other regions	
Develop specific 'rules of entry' and 'practices' which may then be recontextualised to related regions		
	Degree of 'boundedness' variable	Driven by logics that seek the maximisation of labour productivity (Taylorism, Functional Analysis)
Generally strongly 'bounded'/'insulated'	May acquire considerable strength and defined identity or may be prone to policy objectives of stakeholders	
		May draw extensively on 'local', 'organisational' or 'workplace' horizontal discourses

Table II. Key characteristics of singulars, regions and generics.

Generics, or 'generic modes', are 'constructed and distributed outside, and independently of, pedagogic recontextualising fields' (Bernstein, 2000, p. 53), and thus by external agents who may have little interest in disciplinary knowledge production (perhaps governments or employers). Examples of generic modes are 'the distinctive "competences" methodology' that emerged in the 1970s and 1990s through the Manpower Services Commission and the development of NVQs (National Vocational Qualifications) (Bernstein, 2000, p. 53). They are 'produced by a functional analysis of what is taken to be the underlying features necessary to the performance of a skill, task, practice or even area of work' (2000, p. 53). Generics can thus be seen to sit directly in opposition to the disciplinary and professional cultures and practices of both singulars and regions, which may be deemed as anachronistic or irrelevant, standing in the way of the fundamentals of completing a task or undertaking an occupation efficiently and effectively.

Recontextualisation

A little more should also be said here about the notion of recontextualisation. Bernstein describes recontextualisation as involving a 'principle that selectively appropriates, relocates, refocuses and relates other discourses to constitute its own order' (2000, p. 53). It is undertaken by 'recontextualisation agents' with 'recontextualising functions' who operate within 'recontextualising fields' (2000, p. 53). These fields are located between the fields of the 'production' and 'reproduction' of discourse, within the broader structure of the 'pedagogic device' (2000, p. 37). Recontextualisation is the process by which knowledge is 'relocated' from singulars to regions, from a discipline to a professional knowledge base, and then into curricula. The identification of both 'agents' and 'principle' suggests that the level of control of the 'agents' depends on that afforded them by a macro-structure that is socio-historically and politically constituted (Hordern, 2014a, e). Thus, recontextualisation is 'social', but also 'epistemic' as the existence of definitive (hierarchical and horizontal) knowledge structures suggests that knowledge should be recontextualised in accordance with the structure of its underpinning conceptual system. Put another way, concepts gain their meaning in relation to other concepts (Winch, 2010), and to compromise the structure that holds these relations in place undermines the value of those concepts. It is only vertical discourses that provide the 'rules' that guide how disciplinary concepts can be combined with, and relate to, other disciplinary concepts (Bernstein, 1999; Young, 2008; Muller, 2009), and thus structure a recontextualisation process. Only vertical discourses show how differing forms of propositional knowledge relate to one another and provide the basis for the development of procedural and inferential know-how (Winch, 2010; Muller, 2014). In other words, the underpinning structure of knowledge suggests how knowledge should be structured in its new 'location', and intentional or unintentional 'errors of recontextualisation' (Hordern, 2014a) may result from lack of acknowledgement or lack of awareness of this structure.

Barnett (2006) provides a useful analysis of how recontextualisation works to develop a knowledge base in professional and vocational occupations. He points to how the 'technological or organisational problems' (Barnett, 2006, p. 147) of an occupation provide a stimulus for the selection, appropriation and transformation of knowledge from disciplines for the needs of the occupation. This process of 'reclassificatory recontextualisation' leads to a 'toolbox of applicable knowledge' (p. 147), that then undergoes a further process of 'pedagogic recontextualisation' (p. 147) within classrooms and workplaces. The definition of these 'problems of practice' may be highly contested, involving various agencies and actors (e.g. government, professional associations, employers and educational institutions), each with their own perspective on what constitutes a valid 'problem' (or practice purpose [Muller, 2009]) and therefore which kinds of disciplinary (or practice) knowledge should be recontextualised into the 'toolbox'. Hordern (2014b) has tried to show how this happens within early years education by drawing attention to how the weakness of professional bodies and the fragmented nature of the employment structure in England are enabling government to take the lead in defining the problems and purpose of early years practice, in contradistinction to some other European countries, with implications for knowledge selection and transformation. A similar phenomenon could be said to be occurring with school teaching in England (i.e. we might surmise this from Whitty [2014] or Hulme & Menter [2011]). While Barnett's (2006) overall formulation might be usefully reconfigured to focus more clearly on the formulation of a form of professional/vocational subject (i.e. in Winch's [2010] terms), rather than on a 'toolbox of applicable knowledge', the processes he maps are helpful for thinking about the development of a knowledge base for a professionally orientated discipline.

It is important also to mention the work of some authors who have used the concept of recontextualisation but locate it within a different tradition. For Evans et al (2010), recontextualisation occurs in 'content', 'pedagogy', 'workplaces' and by learners, thereby extending the domains and contexts in which the process takes place. For Guile (2014), recontextualisation is a 'continuous, iterative and multifaceted process' (p. 91) that can illuminate the theory–practice relationship. This work draws on theories of workplace learning (and in Guile's case, cultural historical activity theory and philosophical sources) to focus on how knowledge is transformed through the interrelation between education and work. It focuses primarily on curricula and pedagogic processes in workplaces and on (inter-) professional learning, rather than on the construction of disciplines as such. Nevertheless, there may be important insights from this work relating to how professional and workplace practices support or neglect specialised forms of knowledge, which may also have bearing on how a discipline is constituted.

How 'Practice' May Contribute to Valuable Knowledge

The Bernsteinian theory outlined above has not as yet settled on a conceptualisation of 'practice', and specifically how forms of practice contribute to valuable knowledge for an occupation or professionally orientated discipline. Young and Muller (2014) in their recent book *Knowledge Expertise and the Professions* assert that what they term 'practice-based' theories of expertise are flawed in that (in discussing Schon) they tend towards an 'experientialism without content or history' (p. 12), venerating individual experience 'in practice' as a source of valuable knowledge. However, this does not fully explain how forms of practice may differentially influence the recontextualisation of knowledge and decisions about knowledge value. Medical practice, for example, could be described as 'knowledge-rich', in that forms of recontextualised disciplinary knowledge form the basis for judgement and action. The 'workplace curriculum' (Billett, 2006) differentially encountered by novice medical practitioners may (to a greater or lesser extent) support the development of medical expertise, and this, in turn, may be shaped by the 'expansiveness' or 'restrictiveness' of that learning environment and the 'productive systems' in which it sits (Fuller & Unwin, 2004; Felstead et al, 2009; Hordern, 2014d).

Other professions or vocational occupations may not have the institutional conditions that encourage organisational and workplace practice to support the development of expertise. Muller (2014) discusses how 'rules of thumb', or procedures developed in occupational practice, may remain 'local' as horizontal discourse, whereas in other cases these procedures and forms of knowledge may be absorbed within the established 'vertical' knowledge base, through relation to a disciplinary conceptual system and by meeting the criteria or 'rules of entry' specified within the discipline. However, in certain less developed or 'weaker' regions, we can also surmise that 'rules' are less rigorously enforced and practice-based knowledge may be more easily, and with less scrutiny, incorporated within a knowledge base. Occupational practices thus vary in their capacity to contribute to the development of individual and collective expertise, and in their capacity to contribute to a knowledge base.

Part 2: Application to Education(al) Studies

Education(al) studies is a discipline with multiple potential personalities, at least in the UK. There is the study of education through the 'foundation disciplines' of philosophy, history, sociology and psychology of education (McCulloch, 2002; Furlong, 2013). There is the more all-encompassing activity of educational research, which may draw on the above disciplines or see them as potentially restrictive in their particular concerns – tensions expressed in debates about the role of the British Educational Research Association itself (McCulloch, 2002; James, 2012). There is also a 'professional' or 'occupational' discipline of education that is specifically designed to provide a knowledge base for teaching and teacher education, although this is considerably compromised currently in England (Furlong, 2013), but perhaps less so in Scotland (Hulme & Menter, 2011). There is also perhaps a 'professionally orientated' (or practice-orientated) discipline of education, which more directly provides a knowledge base of and for educational practice, broadly defined.

To proceed now with the application of the Bernsteinian concepts, a number of questions are suggested. I will concentrate most of the discussion of the first two of these, drawing on some aspects of the situation in England and sometimes the wider UK.

- Is education studies a vertical or horizontal discourse? And, if a vertical discourse, then are the knowledge structures 'hierarchical' or 'horizontal' in nature? Is there a 'strong grammar' in the study of education? What is the relation between the 'vertical' and the 'horizontal'?
- Can education studies be considered a 'singular'? A 'region'? A 'generic'? How 'insulated' or 'bounded' is it as a discipline? What factors might determine this?
- What is the nature of 'recontextualisation' in education studies?
- To what extent is how 'educational practice' is conceived relevant to this discussion?

Verticality, Horizontality and Grammaticality in Education Studies

The 'disciplines' identified as the foundations of education studies (sociology, philosophy, history and psychology of education), in addition to other contributors (economics and geography of education) (Lawn & Furlong, 2009), could generally be considered vertical discourses with 'horizontal knowledge structures', albeit with contrasting 'grammars' and 'practices'. For Bernstein, 'economics' and 'parts of psychology' have 'strong grammars', demonstrating 'explicit conceptual syntax capable of "relatively" precise empirical descriptions' (1999, p. 164). Bernstein also suggests that structures with strong grammars often impose 'rigorous restrictions on the phenomena they address' (1999, p. 164), a type of 'boundedness' that insulates and reinforces the jurisdiction of the discipline. This is contrasted with a very horizontal knowledge structure with a mostly weak grammar such as sociology (1999, p. 164), which has a wide variety of conceptual traditions and a wide spectrum of potential phenomena. Indeed, for sociology, it is a particular form of 'imagination' or 'reflexivity' that could be considered most fundamental to its practice (Wright Mills, 1959; Lauder et al, 2009), notwithstanding (for example) the 'political arithmetic' tradition that maintains a key role in studies of social mobility (Lauder et al, 2009).

It could be suggested that the nature of the 'foundation disciplines' poses problems for any more unified conceptualisation of education(al) studies. The varying practices and 'grammaticalities' of these disciplines may not lend themselves to easy reconciliation in a coherent form. Economics and sociology, for example, are markedly different in their methodological process and epistemological considerations (Lauder et al, 2009), and thus it may be difficult to agree on what aspects of education it may be of value to study, let alone agree on any form of worthwhile research design. Sociological 'languages' abound, and contestation of dominance is inherent to the disciplinary culture, whereas in economics a 'neo-classical' paradigm is strongly embedded. On the other hand, philosophy of education appears to have a distinct, relatively bounded identity, rooted in the 'historical tradition' and 'contemporary expression' of 'philosophical writing', and yet anxious about its influence and engagement with the wider educational research community (Oancea & Bridges, 2009, pp. 555, 564-565). Its objects of inquiry and methodologies have been systematically deliberated (Oancea & Bridges, 2009) – its 'conceptual syntax' suggests a 'strong grammar' (Bernstein, 1999), although it is forms of reasoning rather than empirical description that provide precision. History of education has tended to reflect the practices of the wider historical discipline (McCulloch, 2002; Goodman & Grosvenor, 2009), with its characteristic processes and procedures for establishing authenticity and validity. It appears to have experienced some marginalisation within the family of foundation disciplines over recent time (Thomas, 2012), but maintains a strong core internal community of researchers (Goodman & Grosvenor, 2009). Psychology of education appears to be housed primarily in psychology departments rather than education, partly due to the strength of psychology as a discipline in the UK (Crozier, 2009), and appears to demonstrate publication practices that are separate and distinct from the other foundation disciplines (Crozier, 2009; Thomas, 2012), restricting opportunities for interdisciplinary engagement. Crozier (2009) indicates that 'theoretical developments and methodological originality and refinement' (p. 588) are the core concern of psychology departments, with 'applications' (which, it may be inferred, are the domain of the psychology of education) less highly valued. The implication is that the psychology of education is, organisationally, primarily part of psychology rather than education studies, and is pressured towards meeting the 'strong grammar' expectations of the broader psychology discipline rather than seeking greater coherence with sociology, history and philosophy.

So do the ongoing contrasts in structure, purposes, practices and grammaticality across these foundation disciplines inhibit any form of coherence in education studies, whatever the benefits of the diverse disciplinary perspectives this engenders? If disciplines need to demonstrate their 'singularity' and develop distinct identities and 'boundedness' to gain recognition in the academy (Bernstein, 2000; Foray & Hargreaves, 2003; Muller, 2009), then what hope is there if the foundation disciplines 'face' either inwards towards themselves or outwards towards their broader disciplinary roots, rather than towards the other foundation disciplines with the aim of greater reconciliation? Can education studies grow in strength if there is not a more concerted effort towards coherence? Studies of the foundation disciplines indicate that in some cases there may be not only detachment from others within this foundational group, but also the risk of an increasingly arm's-length relationship with the broader disciplinary structures from which they emerged – thus, sociology of education is thought to have taken on a life of its own (Lauder et al, 2009). Advocates of the disciplines argue for the advantages that their various perspectives bring to bear (McCulloch, 2002), but the resultant lack of 'boundedness' that would stem from a more unified 'education' disciplinary community and identity built around a degree of agreement on shared concerns could make it easier for government and other interested parties to dismiss the discipline as fragmented and incoherent. Thomas (2012) does detect, however, the emergence of a potential 'core discourse' (p. 378) and 'integrated conversation' (p. 380) that revolves around four journals, three that might be described as 'generalist' and one (*British Journal of Sociology of Education*) disciplinary, and this may extend to other prominent journals too (i.e. *Journal of Education Policy*, for example [Thomas, 2012, p. 367]). However, the 'disciplinarity' of this discourse remains unclear – is it predominantly informed by a particularly 'permeable' set of disciplinary 'languages' (i.e. primarily from sociology) that have resonated more widely? Why do philosophical and historical traditions, however vibrant in their own way, remain comparatively marginalised from this 'core discourse' (Thomas, 2012)?

However, it is policy-related, practice-related, economic and some comparative forms of educational research that have in recent time shown as much growth as, if not greater growth than, the foundation disciplines (Lawn & Furlong 2009). In some cases, this research may draw on the foundation disciplines, although economics research clearly has its own disciplinary referents. Policy studies in education often draw on sociological theory and practice, as is suggested by analysis of publications (Thomas, 2012), and comparative methodology draws on sociological and historical traditions, in addition to economics and politics (Crossley & Watson, 2009). Certainly, there seem to be few restrictions on the phenomena deemed acceptable as subjects of research study by prominent journals in these areas (e.g. see aims and scope of *Journal of Education Policy* and *Compare*), suggesting a weak grammar and the importance of certain forms of 'imagination' and 'reflexivity', although one should also mention here the significance of quantitative studies, particularly in comparative research. Thomas (2012) has also suggested that studies of curriculum and pedagogy are only marginally integrated with the concerns of the foundation disciplines, as demonstrated by the relative isolation of the *Journal of Curriculum Studies* from generalist and disciplinary journals 'in terms of citation behaviour', 'topics', 'leading lights' and 'authorship' (p. 379).

It is important to emphasise that there are considerable pressures for forms of 'stronger' grammar and greater 'verticality' in educational research stemming from government and policy actors with interests in education who are looking for 'answers' to educational problems that establish a degree of certainty and 'move the debate forward'. In the UK educational research funding is increasingly directed towards forms of research that demonstrate these particular grammars (Lawn & Furlong, 2009, pp. 548-549; James, 2012), while policymakers, and some educationalists (e.g. Hargreaves 1999), maintain that much educational knowledge is irrelevant or impenetrable (James, 2012; Furlong, 2013). However, this 'stronger' form of grammar often tends to value 'routinized method' and 'atheoretical empiricism' (Furlong & Lawn, 2011, cited in Thomas, 2012) based on a 'naïve technocratic positivism' (Oancea & Bridges, 2009, p. 564), over and above any internal theoretical coherence. Thus the grammar, while appearing 'strong', may do little to advance theoretical understanding at the general level – it may not contribute to the establishment of a 'discipline'. It may become progressively more difficult to relate these pieces of research to one another, and build a coherent body of knowledge that can be drawn upon to aid future analysis. The non-academic research infrastructure, already responsible for a significant percentage of research activity (Lawn & Furlong, 2007), may be better placed to illustrate (or manufacture) forms of this (apparently strong) grammaticality (James, 2012), with consequences for the role of the disciplines and academic research in education.

While discussion of knowledge structures may help illuminate tensions in education(al) disciplines and research, it is also worth briefly considering how we might relate vertical and horizontal discourses to teaching, as this may have implications for how certain forms of education(al) studies are conceptualised. Subject teachers in UK schools at the secondary level (ages 11-18) could be considered to draw on two vertical discourses – first, on that of the subject they teach (maths, English, history or chemistry, for example), but also on that of the discipline of education (or pedagogy) (Hordern, 2015). These vertical discourses may consist of rather different hierarchical or horizontal knowledge structures, and different strengths of grammaticality. Indeed, there may be something of a resistance to the educational, pedagogical discourse if it exhibits rather different practices and grammatical expectations than the subject discourse. If teaching is conceived of primarily as a 'craft', it may be that the subject teacher is encouraged to rely on only one vertical discourse, that of their subject, with 'local' and 'functional' horizontal discourses filling the vacuum left by the absent pedagogical/educational discourse (Hordern, 2015). On the other hand, primary generalists, teaching children from ages 5 to 11, may draw to a greater extent on one educational/pedagogical vertical discourse (Hordern, 2015) rather than on a particular subject discourse, and that pedagogical discourse may, to a greater or lesser extent, correspond to the pedagogical discourse used by secondary-level practitioners.

Education Studies as a Singular, Region and Generic

Given the discussion above, it is possible to conjecture that education studies has the potential to become a more coherent 'singular' if it moves forward from being comprised of different singulars (or fragments of singulars sometimes semi-detached from parent singulars and semi-detached from each other) towards greater intellectual 'integration'. If this integration was deemed desirable, considerable efforts would be needed! Aspects of historical, philosophical, psychological, sociological, economic and geographical traditions could be 'recontextualised' to form a new singular. However, the self-referential nature of a 'singular' pure discipline suggests that these developments are most likely to succeed if internally driven and organic (Muller, 2009). An 'artificially constructed' singular is likely to fail as it would lack the form of emergence that has characterised the development of disciplinary forms of knowledge (Muller, 2009). To impose a 'pure' and 'coherent' education studies discipline would seem inadvisable without a critical mass of adherents to the cause with an agreed set of practices and methodologies. Could that 'core discourse' (Thomas, 2012, p. 378) provide a starting point for a disciplinary identity? And what of the richness of the current foundation disciplines that might be lost in the process? Perhaps forms of 'interdisciplinarity' provide a more promising conceptualisation (McCulloch, 2012, and 2017, in this volume)?

If conceptualising education studies as a pure and unified singular seems problematic, what of the region? There are at least two potential models here. The first 'region' has education studies as a professional discipline, of a similar genus to that of medicine and engineering, and therefore the 'supervening purpose' (Muller, 2009, p. 213) of the region is the provision of knowledge for educators, and perhaps specifically schoolteachers. This model therefore sees education studies and teacher education as inextricable, with knowledge selected, appropriated and transformed from disciplinary sources with the 'problems' and 'contexts' of teaching in mind. In a classical 'professional region', similar to that of medicine, the key 'recontextualisation agents' would be professional bodies or even 'royal colleges', responsible for stipulating the curricula offered to novice professionals and the processes by which these professionals are accredited, and consisting of stakeholders with mutual and co-dependent roles in professional formation (Beck & Young, 2005; Hordern, 2014d, e). Thus, a college of medical practitioners brings together institutions, employers and senior practitioners to specify the knowledge requirements of the profession. A form of 'professional logic' is preserved in the ideal 'classical' professional region, ensuring that forms of knowledge are recontextualised to provide a disciplinary knowledge base in accordance with the perceived needs of the profession, notwithstanding pressures from 'bureaucratic' and 'market' logics for accountability and efficiency (Freidson, 2001; Beck & Young, 2005).

For teacher education in England, however, the conditions for this 'classical' professional region seem remote, given the lack of a professional body performing the functions identified above and the fragmentation of the provision of schooling, with academicisation and the rise of new forms of 'branded' or 'organisational' professionalisms (Hordern, 2014c; Whitty, 2014). Recontextualisation of knowledge for teacher education is heavily influenced by government prescription in England, although system fragmentation may see more local forms of teacher education curricula emerging (Whitty, 2014). The use of a set of standards or competences to shape a teacher education curriculum suggests increasing aspects of 'genericism' (Bernstein, 2000; Beck, 2009). Meanwhile, the growth of these 'local professionalisms' at the expense of a 'national' professionalism (Whitty, 2014) suggests the potential for increasing inclusion of forms of horizontal discourse representing local, organisational and workplace knowledges that have no explicit link to disciplinary knowledge (Beech & Bagley, 2013; Hordern, 2015). In contrast, the differing institutional relations and policy context in Scotland may underpin a more classically 'professional region' (Hulme & Menter, 2011; Hordern 2014c).

While the 'classical' or 'professional region' may prove unachievable due to governmental or systemic influences undermining professional autonomy, it is also possible to conceptualise education studies as orientated towards, and seeking to illuminate, a broad conception of 'educational practice', encompassing informal, vocational, higher, early childhood and workplace education and learning as much as 'schooling', as suggested above. The 'technological and organisational problems' (Barnett, 2006, p. 147) of educational practice could be defined by a wider range of 'practitioners', while debates on the purpose of education could assume a central role in defining where knowledge would need to be recontextualised from to sustain this debate. In such a conception, 'education studies' is inextricable from educational activities or 'education in practice', and clarity might be needed over who is a practitioner and what constitutes the practice of education (Noddings, 2003). However, the wide range of practice contexts that education studies would be seeking to illuminate is likely to suggest a relatively unbounded 'region' with difficulties in establishing greater 'grammaticality' in the 'languages' within the knowledge structure. The wide variety of objects of study is likely to lead to knowledge being appropriated and transformed from various singulars, and possibly other regions underpinned by knowledge recontextualised from social science. While this 'practice-orientated' discipline might arouse curiosity among some students, it is possible to see it dismissed by government and professional groups as irrelevant, and by disciplinary communities as insufficiently intellectually rigorous. Such a region would be challenged to demonstrate its *raison d'être* and to clearly communicate its jurisdiction and object of study. One possible way out of this may be to develop a conception of partially 'bounded' specialised practice underpinned by recontextualised disciplinary knowledge (Hordern, 2015), in which becoming an 'educator', broadly defined, or 'educationally literate', is the objective.

Lastly, detachment from disciplinary thought and practice and a focus on reductive models of skills and competence leads to the model of education studies as a 'generic', where the objective is 'trainability' (Bernstein, 2000, p. 53) and where professional logic is replaced by that of the market and/or bureaucracy (Freidson, 2001; Beck & Young, 2005). Generics place full control in the hands of stakeholders such as governments and employers rather than educational institutions, enabling the evacuation of any form of disciplinary-based knowledge from qualifications (Beck & Young, 2005), and also from what is considered valid research. Various 'techniques' and atheoretical research inquiry derived from practice or from enterprising 'edu-preneurs' may become the substance of education studies, a model that may appeal to certain ambitious educational organisations. What Beck and Young (2005) describe as a belief in the 'inevitable obsolescence of accumulated knowledge' (p. 191) takes hold, leaving students and researchers in education studies ambivalent towards knowledge claims and unaware of disciplinary practices that establish their validity. The generic model can be seen as where education studies merges with instrumental and 'competence-based' (of the Anglo-Australian rather than the continental European variety [Wheelahan, 2010; Winch, 2010]) or 'standards-based' forms of teacher education. Beach and Bagley's (2013) warnings about reforms to teacher education in Sweden and England, with the increasing growth of horizontal discourse, thus provide a scenario for the development of a 'generic' education studies. Similarly, the drive towards forms of research with superficially strong grammars that are not located within disciplinary forms or practices can be seen as a facet of genericism.

Some Potential Scenarios for the Organisation of Education Studies

In the light of the discussion above, some possible suggestions for how education studies might be organised are very briefly summarised below. There is no suggestion here that this is an exhaustive list. It is possible, and may even be likely, that more than one model exists at any one time in a particular national context. It is also possible that certain forms of singular and region may be co-dependent, relying on mutual contribution to meet the varying demands on education studies.

1. Education studies as *a set of fragments of singulars* based around the 'foundation disciplines'. These fragments may have differing

relations with the singulars of which they are a part, and varying degrees of common ground. This suggests different horizontal knowledge structures, practices, grammaticality and foci of inquiry, but a potentially rich variety of perspectives.

2. Education studies *as a singular*. Education is seen as a 'pure' discipline within the social sciences. It suggests a horizontal knowledge structure that could have a strong grammar (i.e. like psychology) or a weaker grammar (i.e. like sociology). This does not appear to have emerged in the UK.

3. Education studies as a *professionally orientated region*. The purpose of education studies is providing a knowledge base for the profession of teaching. Knowledge may be recontextualised from various disciplines and 'reclassified' taking account of the 'problems' or 'contexts' of the profession. The region may develop forms of knowledge production modelled on the practices of related singulars, but this could be complicated by the multiple singulars involved.

4. Education studies as a *practice-orientated region*. The purpose of the region is to provide knowledge for and about educational practice, which may be broadly or more specifically defined. How practice is defined is likely to have an impact on which disciplinary sources are recontextualised, and on whether a form of knowledge production emerges within the region.

5. Education studies as a *generic*. Education studies is defined narrowly in terms of observable behaviours, 'skills', 'standards', techniques or competencies, and local practices. There is no necessary connection with disciplinary knowledge and 'local' or organisationally specific horizontal discourses are increasingly seen as valid knowledge for research and practice. This arrangement may suit those governments or employers that seek de-professionalisation of teaching (or a remodelled craft or technical model of the teacher), and to take control of what is considered valid educational research.

References

Barnett, M. (2006) Vocational Knowledge and Vocational Pedagogy, in M. Young & J. Gamble (Eds) *Knowledge, Qualifications and the Curriculum for South African Further Education*, pp. 143-157. Pretoria: Human Sciences Research Council.

Beach, D. & Bagley, C. (2013) Changing Professional Discourses in Teacher Education Policy Back Towards a Training Paradigm: a comparative study, *European Journal of Teacher Education*, 34(4), 379-392. https://doi.org/10.1080/02619768.2013.815162

Beck, J. (2009) Appropriating Professionalism: restructuring the official knowledge base of England's 'modernised' teaching profession, *British Journal of Sociology of Education*, 30(1), 3-14. https://doi.org/10.1080/01425690802514268

Beck, J. & Young, M. (2005) The Assault on the Professions and the Restructuring of Academic and Professional Identities: a Bernsteinian analysis, *British Journal of Sociology of Education*, 26(2), 183-197.
https://doi.org/10.1080/0142569042000294165

Bernstein, B. (1971) On the Classification and Framing of Educational Knowledge, in M. Young (Ed.) *Knowledge and Control: new directions for the sociology of education*, pp. 47-69. London: Collier Macmillan.

Bernstein, B. (1999) Vertical and Horizontal Discourse: an essay, *British Journal of Sociology of Education*, 20(2), 157-173.
https://doi.org/10.1080/01425699995380

Bernstein, B. (2000) *Pedagogy, Symbolic Control and Identity*, rev edn. New York: Rowman and Littlefield.

Billett, S. (2006) Constituting the Workplace Curriculum, *Journal of Curriculum Studies*, 38(1), 31-48. https://doi.org/10.1080/00220270500153781

Breier, M. (2004) Horizontal Discourse in Law and Labour Law, in J. Muller, B. Davies & A. Morais (Eds) *Reading Bernstein: researching Bernstein*, pp. 204-217. London: RoutledgeFalmer.

Crossley, M. & Watson, K. (2009) Comparative and International Education: policy transfer, context sensitivity and professional development, *Oxford Review of Education*, 35(5), 633-649.
https://doi.org/10.1080/03054980903216341

Crozier, W.R. (2009) The Psychology of Education: achievements and challenges, *Oxford Review of Education*, 35(5), 587-600.
https://doi.org/10.1080/03054980903216317

Evans, K., Guile, D., Harris, J. & Allan, H. (2010) Putting Knowledge to Work, *Nurse Education Today*, 30(3), 245-251.
https://doi.org/10.1016/j.nedt.2009.10.014

Felstead, A., Fuller, A., Jewson, N. & Unwin, L. (2009) *Improving Working as Learning*. London: Routledge.

Foray, D. & Hargreaves, D. (2003) The Production of Knowledge in Different Sectors, *London Review of Education*, 1(1), 7-19.
https://doi.org/10.1080/14748460306689

Freidson, E. (2001) *Professionalism: the third logic*. Cambridge: Polity Press.

Fuller, A. & Unwin, L. (2004) Expansive Learning Environments: integrating organizational and personal development, in H. Rainbird, A. Fuller & A. Munro (Eds) *Workplace Learning in Context*. London: Routledge.

Furlong, J. (2013) *Education – an Anatomy of the Discipline: rescuing the university project*. London: Routledge.

Goodman, J. & Grosvenor, I. (2009) Educational Research – History of Education a Curious Case?', *Oxford Review of Education*, 35(5), 601-616.
https://doi.org/10.1080/03054980903216325

Guile, D. (2014) Professional Knowledge and Professional Practice as Continuous Recontextualisation, in M. Young & J. Muller (Eds) *Knowledge, Expertise and the Professions*, pp. 78-92. Abingdon: Routledge.

Hargreaves, D.H. (1999) Revitalising Educational Research: lessons from the past and proposals for the future, *Cambridge Journal of Education*, 29(2), 239-249. https://doi.org/10.1080/0305764990290207

Hordern, J. (2014a) How is Vocational Knowledge Recontextualised?, *Journal of Vocational Education and Training*, 66(1), 22-38. https://doi.org/10.1080/13636820.2013.867524

Hordern, J. (2014b) Knowledge, Practice and the Shaping of Early Childhood Professionalism, *European Early Childhood Education Research Journal*, 24(4), 508-520. https://doi.org/10.1080/1350293X.2014.975939

Hordern, J. (2014c) The Logic and Implications of School-based Teacher Formation, *British Journal of Educational Studies*, 62(3), 231-248. https://doi.org/10.1080/00071005.2014.955079

Hordern, J. (2014d) Productive Systems of Professional Formation, in S. Billett, C. Harteis & H. Gruber (Eds) *International Handbook of Research in Professional and Practice-based Learning*. Dordrecht: Springer. https://doi.org/10.1007/978-94-017-8902-8_7

Hordern, J. (2014e) Regions and their Relations: sustaining authoritative professional knowledge, *Journal of Education and Work*, 29(4), 427-449. https://doi.org/10.1080/13639080.2014.958653

Hordern, J. (2015) Teaching, Teacher Formation, and Specialised Professional Practice, *European Journal of Teacher Education*, 38(4), 431-444. https://doi.org/10.1080/02619768.2015.1056910

Hulme, M. & Menter, I. (2011) South and North – Teacher Education Policy in England and Scotland: a comparative textual analysis, *Scottish Educational Review*, 43(2), 70-90.

James, M. (2012) Growing Confidence in Educational Research: threats and opportunities, *British Educational Research Journal*, 38(2), 181-201. https://doi.org/10.1080/01411926.2011.650681

Lauder, H., Brown, P. & Halsey, A.H. (2009) Sociology of Education: a critical history and prospects for the future, *Oxford Review of Education*, 35(5), 569-585. https://doi.org/10.1080/03054980903216309

Lawn, M. & Furlong, J. (2007) The Social Organisation of Education Research in England, *European Educational Research Journal*, 6(1), 55-70. https://doi.org/10.2304/eerj.2007.6.1.55

Lawn, M. & Furlong, J. (2009) The Disciplines of Education in the UK: between the ghost and the shadow, *Oxford Review of Education*, 35(5), 541-552. https://doi.org/10.1080/03054980903216283

McCulloch, G. (2002) Disciplines Contributing to Education? Educational Studies and the Disciplines, *British Journal of Educational Studies*, 50(1), 100-119. https://doi.org/10.1111/1467-8527.t01-1-00193

McCulloch, G. (2012) Introduction: disciplinarity, interdisciplinarity and educational studies – past, present and future, *British Journal of Educational Studies*, 60(4), 295-300. https://doi.org/10.1080/00071005.2012.744185

McNamara, M. & Fealy, G. (2014) Knowledge Matters in Nursing, in M. Young & J. Muller (Eds) *Knowledge, Expertise and the Professions*, 157-170. Abingdon: Routledge.

Moore R. (2007) *The Sociology of Knowledge and Education.* London: Continuum.

Muller, J. (2009) Forms of Knowledge and Curriculum Coherence, *Journal of Education and Work*, 22(3), 205-226. https://doi.org/10.1080/13639080902957905

Muller, J. (2014) Every Picture Tells a Story: epistemological access and knowledge, *Education as Change*, 18(2), 255-269. https://doi.org/10.1080/16823206.2014.932256

Noddings, N. (2003) Is Teaching a Practice?, *Journal of Philosophy of Education*, 37(2), 241-251. https://doi.org/10.1111/1467-9752.00323

Oancea, A. & Bridges, D. (2009) Philosophy of Education in the UK: the historical and contemporary tradition, *Oxford Review of Education*, 35(5), 553-568. https://doi.org/10.1080/03054980903216291

Thomas, J. (2012) Disciplinarity and the Organisation of Scholarly Writing in Educational Studies in the UK 1970-2010, *British Journal of Educational Studies*, 60(4), 357-386. https://doi.org/10.1080/00071005.2012.741219

Wheelahan, L. (2010) *Why Knowledge Matters in Curriculum: a social realist argument.* Routledge, New York.

Whitty, G. (2014) Recent Developments in Teacher Training and their Consequences for the 'University Project' in Education, *Oxford Review of Education*, 40(4), 466-481. https://doi.org/10.1080/03054985.2014.933007

Winch, C. (2010) *Dimensions of Expertise: a conceptual exploration of vocational knowledge.* London: Continuum.

Winch, C. (2013) Curriculum Design and Epistemic Ascent, *Journal of Philosophy of Education*, 47(1), 128-146. https://doi.org/10.1111/1467-9752.12006

Wright Mills, C. (1959) *The Sociological Imagination.* Oxford: Oxford University Press.

Young, M. (2008) *Bringing Knowledge Back In: from social constructivism to social realism in the sociology of education.* London: Routledge.

Young, M. & Muller, J. (2007) Truth and Truthfulness in the Sociology of Educational Knowledge, *Theory & Research in Education*, 5(2), 173-201. https://doi.org/10.1177/1477878507077732

Young, M. & Muller, J. (2013) On the Powers of Powerful Knowledge, *Review of Education*, 1(3), 229-250. https://doi.org/10.1002/rev3.3017

Young, M. & Muller, J. (2014) Towards the Sociology of Professional Knowledge, in M. Young & J. Muller (Eds) *Knowledge, Expertise and the Professions*, pp. 3-17. Abingdon: Routledge.

CHAPTER 9

Education: an applied multidisciplinary field? The English Experience

GARY McCULLOCH

SUMMARY The case of educational studies and research in England, and elsewhere in the United Kingdom, provides an interesting example of the character of fields and disciplines and the idea of practice of interdisciplinarity. Rather than a discipline, this may be described as an applied multidisciplinary field. Key disciplines have helped to shape this field through an extended university project, involving academic conferences, societies, journals and centres, as well as university education departments. There have been interdisciplinary visions and initiatives, including key organisational developments such as the Standing Conference on Studies in Education and the British Educational Research Association, and leading institutions like the Institute of Education London and the University of Leicester.

The historian of literacy Harvey J. Graff has demonstrated the importance of a historical perspective in tracing interdisciplinarity in the USA through the twentieth century and across several case studies in the university curriculum (Graff, 2015). Graff argues that disciplinarity and interdisciplinarity have been closely linked and dependent on each other in a symbiotic and dynamic relationship over time, and should be understood in relation to each other. According to Graff, the tension between them has been played out in different ways from one discipline to another, often resulting in what he calls 'interdisciplines'. Both disciplines and interdisciplines, he suggests, are products of the modern research university, with their origins in the nineteenth century. He points out also that interdisciplinarity is possible within disciplines – for example, in the new social history and social science history that developed from the 1960s onwards (Graff, 2015, chapter 4).

This chapter will investigate the character of disciplines as they emerged and developed, and also the idea of interdisciplinarity, in the case of educational studies and research in the UK. There has been increasing international interest in the history of educational studies and research over the past decade. In the USA, the most important work has no doubt been Ellen Condliffe Lagemann's *An Elusive Science*, which traced the 'troubling history' of education research through the twentieth century, highlighting its variety and range, and defining itself as a 'discipline history' in the sense that it sought to investigate 'the changing ecology of knowledge and the politics that has been part of that' (Lagemann, 2001, p. xiv; see also Lagemann, 1997). David Labaree, also in the USA, has valuably examined the low status of schools and departments of education within the academy, commenting: 'The ed school is the butt of jokes in the university, where professors portray it as an intellectual wasteland; it is the object of scorn in schools, where teachers decry its programs as impractical and its research as irrelevant; and it is a convenient scapegoat in the world of educational policy, where policymakers portray it as a root cause of bad teaching and inadequate learning' (Labaree, 2006, pp. 2-3). Labaree explains this poor reputation in terms of the historical association of schools of education with teacher education.

In western Europe, Hofstetter and Schneuwly have analysed the institutionalisation of educational science in terms of the number of academic chairs, textbooks, institutions and posts that supported educational research, publications in specialised journals, and public discourses in education (Hofstetter & Schneuwly, 2004). Other recent European work has begun to chart the development of the educational sciences in different European countries since the Second World War (Laot & Rogers, 2015). In the Baltic states, too, there has been a growth of interest in this theme – for example, with the publication of two edited collections on the development of the educational sciences in Baltic countries during the twentieth century (Baltic Association of Historians of Pedagogy, 2009, 2010). In Western Australia, a comparative history of five different departments of education in universities across the state has also been produced (Gardiner et al, 2011).

There has until recently been relatively little written on the history of educational studies and research in the UK as a whole (see McCulloch & Cowan [2017] for a detailed social history of educational studies and research in the UK). A number of studies have considered the development of particular disciplines applied to education – for example, a collection edited by Furlong and Lawn on the 'disciplines of education' (Furlong & Lawn, 2011). This focused on the state of the key disciplines of sociology, psychology, philosophy, history, economics, comparative and international education, and geography in relation to educational research, and argued that although they were all confident about their own roles and importance, they were becoming increasingly small and isolated. This view differed markedly from that of J.W. Tibble forty years before, who in 1966 had edited a widely noted work, *The Study of Education*, which framed the study of education fundamentally around the 'foundation disciplines' of philosophy, history, psychology and sociology (Tibble, 1966b; see also McCulloch, 2002). Another significant recent work is John Furlong's 'anatomy of the discipline' of education (Furlong, 2013). Furlong's work seeks first to consider the history of the study of education in UK universities, and then to understand the current situation of education in relation to teaching and research.

Certainly, this is an interesting and distinctive example of an academic field of study that has been powerfully shaped by the disciplines, but which has also sought to present itself in different ways over the longer term. Rather than a discipline, it may be most helpful to label this as an applied multidisciplinary field: applied rather than pure; multidisciplinary rather than unidisciplinary, interdisciplinary or indeed transdisciplinary; and a field rather than a discipline. Key disciplines have exerted a vital role in this field, and continue to do so – despite predictions of their death or demise – through what we might call the extended university project, involving academic conferences, societies, journals and centres, as well as education departments. At the same time, there have been interdisciplinary visions and initiatives at regular intervals over the past eighty years, episodes that have punctuated and also helped to shape the making of the field during this time. These have included key organisational developments in the field – the Standing Conference on Studies in Education (SCSE) (founded in 1951 and renamed the Society for Educational Studies [SES] in 2001), and the British Educational Research Association (BERA), established in 1974. At an institutional level, also, there have been significant initiatives in interdisciplinarity, with the UCL Institute of Education London and the University of Leicester providing useful examples of these. Leading individuals in the field have also embraced interdisciplinary ideals in different forms. All of these initiatives and ideals have had a strong disciplinary base, while the power of the disciplines exerted itself to shape the character of the initiatives themselves. Disciplinarity was the other side of the coin of interdisciplinarity, with the outcome of their symbiotic relationship often being a multidisciplinary formation of the field.

Theories of Interdisciplinarity

Theoretical debates over the role of the disciplines and the nature of interdisciplinarity have been current since at least the 1970s. Differentiating between multidisciplinarity and interdisciplinarity has occupied much of this activity. In the 1970s, Hugh Petrie defined the key difference between these approaches:

> The line is not hard and fast, but roughly it is that
> multidisciplinary projects simply require everyone to do his or her
> own thing with little or no necessity for any one participant to be
> aware of any other participant's work. Perhaps a project director

or manager is needed to glue the final product together, but the pieces are fairly clearly of disciplinary size and shape. Interdisciplinary efforts, on the other hand, require more or less integration and even modification of the disciplinary subcontributions while the inquiry is proceeding. Different participants need to take into account the contributions of their colleagues in order to make their own contribution.
(Petrie, 1976, p. 9)

More recent analyses have largely maintained this basic distinction. For example, one of the leading theorists in this area is the American scholar Julie Thompson Klein, whose 1990 volume *Interdisciplinarity: history, theory, and practice* (Klein, 1990) set the tone for much detailed work. According to Klein, a subtle restructuring of knowledge has produced new divisions of intellectual labour, collaborative research, team teaching, hybrid fields, comparative studies, increased borrowing across disciplines, and new pressures on the traditional divisions of knowledge. All of these trends, she argues, have encouraged a trend towards unity, synthesis and convergence, and the growth of 'interdisciplinarity'.

Klein has also produced a general model or taxonomy of interdisciplinarity that serves to highlight the key distinctions between multidisciplinarity, interdisciplinarity and transdisciplinarity (Klein, 2010). In this model, multidisciplinarity is about juxtaposing, sequencing or coordinating different disciplines, in which they complement each other in a common endeavour leading to a partial integration of work. Interdisciplinarity is a more radical shared enterprise in which the disciplines integrate, interact, link, focus and ultimately blend together. Transdisciplinarity is more radical still, conceived as an activity conceived with the university but moving beyond the academy with the aim of transcending, transgressing and transforming boundaries in society as a whole (Klein, 2010, p. 16). While 'conventional taxonomies' should not be jettisoned, she affirmed, 'they need to develop open, dynamic, and transactional approaches capable of depicting research in a network representation that is more aligned with changing configurations of knowledge and education' (Klein, 2010, p. 28).

Beyond these fairly abstract distinctions, Klein also identifies the traits that she associates with what she terms the 'interdisciplinary individual'. She argues that in terms of career patterns it is usually well-established and senior academics who have the confidence and experience to be able to step out of line and engage in interdisciplinary activities (Klein, 1990, p. 182). On the other hand, according to Klein, the enthusiasm and creativity of many new scholars may lead them in such a direction, regardless of the conventional obstacles and restraints of the modern university. She also proposes a number of character traits of the interdisciplinary individual, including reliability, flexibility, patience, resilience, sensitivity to others, risk-taking, a thick skin, and a preference for diversity and new social roles (Klein, 1990,

p. 183). There are also certain abilities that might be linked with such individuals, including a capacity to look at issues from different perspectives, and also skills such as differentiating, comparing, contrasting, relating, clarifying, reconciling and synthesising (Klein 1990, p. 183). Appraising the work of such individuals through their career and biography, she suggests, might be an effective means of highlighting their contributions to interdisciplinarity.

An idealised theorisation of a trend towards new forms of knowledge production was Gibbons et al's *The New Production of Knowledge* (1994). According to Gibbons et al, 'a new form of knowledge production is emerging alongside the traditional, familiar one' (Gibbons et al, 1994, p. vii). The older form, they proposed, could be characterised as 'Mode 1': disciplinary, hierarchical, institutionalised. The new knowledge production, Mode 2 knowledge, was by contrast transdisciplinary, non-hierarchical and non-institutional. It would be diffused more evenly and efficiently throughout society to help guide problem-solving efforts. This work attributed the structural shift towards Mode 2 knowledge to the expansion of higher education since the 1940s, the increasing number of institutions, a vast expansion in the supply of knowledge, and increasing internationalisation and globalisation that encouraged both collaboration and competition across nations. Overall, they contended:

> In transdisciplinary contexts, disciplinary boundaries, distinctions between pure and applied research, and institutional differences between, say, universities and industry, seem to be less and less relevant. Instead, attention is focused primarily on the problem area, or the hot topic, preference given to collaborative rather than individual performance and excellence judged by the ability of individuals to make a sustained contribution in open, flexible types of organisation in which they may only work temporarily.
> (Gibbons et al, 1994, p. 30)

This was a confident vision of the future that emphasised social benefits and improvements rather than the potential problems and complexities of new forms of knowledge production.

The British political scientist Wyn Grant has also analysed this general development. He explores the intellectual and practical challenges involved in working across disciplines, especially in teams and in 'thick' interdisciplinary work across the social and natural sciences, but points out the potential rewards in terms of understanding and responding to the large urgent problems of today such as the environment and climate change (Greaves & Grant, 2010). Both Klein and Grant emphasise, moreover, that interdisciplinarity does not necessarily replace the disciplines but indeed depends on disciplinary knowledge for its further development. This is also a key point for Peter Weingart, who insists that disciplines and their derivatives, specialities and research fields remain 'the principal organisational unity for the production and diffusion of knowledge'. At the same time, Weingart comments, boundaries between the disciplines are softened, and new interdisciplinary fields emerge, allowing cross-boundary research activities. Even if social and political interests were to promote interdisciplinary approaches, according to Weingart, this would be unlikely to lead to a system based exclusively on interdisciplinarity, and therefore he concludes that 'traditional disciplines and inter-, multi-, and transdisciplinary research fields will exist side by side' (Weingart, 2010, p. 13).

Further discussions have assessed the nature of boundary work around and across the disciplines. Klein has suggested that impermeable boundaries are associated with tightly knit, convergent communities, indicating the stability and coherence of intellectual fields such as the physical sciences and economics, while permeable boundaries are more characteristic of loosely knit, divergent academic groups, signalling a more fragmented, less stable, comparatively open-ended structure like sociology. She also points out that some fields of knowledge are hybrid in nature, including child development, cognitive science, women's studies, biopolitics and criminology (Klein, 1993). The potential for interaction between and among the disciplines is frequently emphasised. For example, Jan Parker suggests that higher education curricula in the humanities need to build on both core disciplinary and supra-disciplinary texts, as well as on 'texts which both inculcate and question interdisciplinarity, preparing students to work in interdisciplinary collaborations' (Parker, 2008, p. 264). The sociologist Neil Smelser insists, moreover, that '[t]he boundaries of most disciplines have become so permeable and indistinct, and so much exportation and importation has occurred that if one ranges widely in his or her discipline, one is being in effect interdisciplinary' (Smelser, 2003, p. 653). These ideas are taken further in new work by Richard Thaler on the making of behavioural economics, a combination of psychology and economics, over the past half-century, highlighting the vagaries of individual decision making (Mullainathan & Thaler, 2000; Thaler, 2015).

The Case of Education

There have been a number of attempts to define the nature of education as an academic study, with the question of its relationship to academic disciplines always to the fore. In the 1960s, the philosopher of education Richard Peters claimed that education was not a distinct discipline, but a field where a group of disciplines had application, as with politics. All questions of educational policy and practice, according to Peters, were hybrid questions that should be broken down into their various components: 'In brief, we must make an end of the undifferentiated mush that is often perpetrated under the heading of educational theory before the different types of question have been distinguished; but we must make sure that the research and training carried out under the aegis of the different disciplines is brought together again in an integrated conversation on matters of common concern' (Peters, 1965, p. 3). This view itself stemmed from the major role of the so-called foundation disciplines of psychology, sociology, history and philosophy in the development of educational studies. In the 1960s in particular, these disciplines were at the heart of the study of education, treated separately and independently in a number of key texts of the time such as J.W. Tibble's *The Study of Education* (Tibble, 1966b; see also McCulloch, 2002; Biesta, 2011).

More recently, many formulations have been offered. Alan Blyth in the early 1980s described the study of education as 'a new form of synthesis..., an autonomous but interrelated field of study' that would be able increasingly to collaborate with other disciplines (Blyth, 1982, pp. 13, 16). The historian Brian Simon regarded it as an 'interdisciplinary field' (Simon, 1990, p. 138). In the 1990s, Keith Hoskin reflected on his own experience in an education department to dismiss claims that education should be regarded as a discipline. Hoskin was especially conscious that the historical roots of educational studies and research, at least in England, lay in teacher training, which left it in a position of low status in the academy. He noted that it was widely regarded as 'a melting-pot for the "real" disciplines, best disregarded in serious academic company' (Hoskin, 1993, p. 271). Moreover, as Hoskin recalled, 'In my first post, in an Education Department, the then-professor went out of his way to define Education in this subdisciplinary way: as a field made up in some way never quite specified (and certainly never achieved) of a combination of the real disciplines, psychology, philosophy, sociology and history, each rendered appropriate to our concerns (and thus inevitably inferior to the disciplinary models) by the addition of the prefix *Educational*' (Hoskin, 1993, p. 272).

The study of education has its own distinctive history as far as the tensions between the disciplines and interdisciplinarity are concerned. Until the Second World War, except in Scotland, it struggled to develop as a recognisable university subject (see, for example, Lawn et al, 2010). As J.W. Tibble noted, its position had always been 'ambiguous and peripheral' (Tibble, 1966a, p. 1). Very little time was allowed for future teachers to study broad educational issues, and so the courses were regarded as being superficial. The schools, for their part, tended to regard them as being irrelevant to their practical needs, and too remote from the classroom (Tibble, 1966a, p. 1). Overall, they suffered from very low status and esteem within universities.

As early as 1877, Alexander Bain's famous essay 'Education as a Science' insisted that the scope of the study of education should be confined to its psychological dimensions – that is, 'the means of building up the acquired powers of human beings' (Bain, 1877, p. 6) – thus leaving its environmental aspects for other departments to pursue. An emphasis on psychology over other potential approaches to the study of education continued well into the twentieth century. 'Educational psychology' was an established subject of study by the 1920s, fostered, for example, by Cyril Burt, appointed to the London County Council in 1913 as the first educational psychologist (Tibble, 1966a, p. 10).

Day training colleges for the training of elementary school teachers in connection with local universities or university colleges were established in the 1890s under the Education Department's Code for 1890, following the recommendations of the Cross Report of 1888. The first day training colleges were set up at King's College London, Manchester, Durham, Sheffield, Birmingham, Nottingham and Cardiff, and the first Chair of Education in England, Mark Robinson Wright, at Durham in 1895 (Gordon, 1980, pp. xi-xii). Their courses included study of the theory, history and psychology of education, and they increasingly catered for the training of secondary school teachers. Nevertheless, they were designed on the whole for teacher training purposes rather than for the academic study of education.

The separate disciplines of education, in particular psychology, history, sociology and philosophy, emerged at different times and have had their own trajectories and institutional traces. As noted, educational psychology developed strongly in the 1920s, especially through the work of Cyril Burt, but also Charles Spearman in London and Godfrey Thomson in Edinburgh (Tibble, 1966a, b). This growth was supported further by the British Psychological Society (founded in 1901), the psychology of education section of the BPS from 1919, and the *British Journal of Educational Psychology*, edited by C.W. Valentine, from 1931. The institutionalisation of the philosophy of education began strongly from the 1940s, with the analytical approach developed through Hirst and Peters at the University of London Institute of Education, and the introduction of the Philosophy of Education Society of Great Britain in 1964 and the *Journal of Philosophy of Education* in 1967. The history of education also became well established after the Second World War, although the defining work of Brian Simon and the establishment of key texts and a society and journal took place in the 1960s and early 1970s with Simon's *Studies in the History of Education* (Simon, 1960), the History of Education Society (1967), and the journal *History of Education* from 1972 (McCulloch, 2010, 2011). The sociology of education became increasingly prominent from the 1950s, dominated initially by the London School of Economics and the British Sociological Association (itself established only in 1951), but increasingly influenced by the Institute of Education in London, especially through Basil Bernstein, the inaugural Karl Mannheim Professor of the Sociology of Education from 1977 to 1991. Other developments included the establishment of the *British Journal of Sociology of Education* in 1980 and the sociology of education conferences held initially at Westhill College, Birmingham (see also e.g. Barton & Walker, 1978; Szreter, 1980; Banks, 1982; Whitty, 2012).

The diversity of subdisciplines and approaches to educational studies generally thwarted attempts to develop it either as a discipline in its own right or as a fully interdisciplinary subject. Other factors included the continued low status of educational studies in the academy, and its applied nature related to educational practice in the schools and other educational institutions. Nevertheless, there were a number of interesting and significant initiatives to redefine it in an interdisciplinary direction. As mentioned earlier, two key developments that were interdisciplinary in nature from within the field were SCSE in the 1940s and 1950s and BERA in the 1970s.

The SCSE originated from the activities of Section L, 'Educational Sciences', of the British Association for the Advancement of Science (BAAS), led by Fred Clarke, director of the Institute of Education. Clarke's short book *The Study of Education in England* (Clarke, 1943) highlighted the lack of esteem of this area of study, and emphasised that greater planning and purpose would be essential in the postwar society. In 1949, Clarke became the president of Section L of BAAS (founded in 1901), and in this capacity he championed what he described as 'the widening scope of the study of education'. This emphasised the idea of an 'educative society' as was envisaged in the Education Act of 1944, which would include an enlarged vision of the study of education, embracing sociology, social psychology, the social history of education, comparative education and philosophy (Clarke, 1949).

It was this potentially interdisciplinary vision that underpinned the creation of the SCSE as an elite professorial body in 1951, and the *British Journal of Educational Studies* the following year. However, both the new society and the journal that it gave birth to revealed the tensions that existed within educational studies, especially between the specialisation of the core disciplines and their more generalised contribution to the study of education. There was an increasing emphasis on the separate roles of the disciplines which, by the 1960s, had become uppermost and distinct to an unprecedented degree (McCulloch, 2012).

The establishment of BERA was also motivated at least partly by the allure of interdisciplinarity and an awareness that the separate disciplines had tended to cultivate supposed respectability at the expense of practical applications in the improvement of schools and teaching. As K.B. Start of the National Foundation for Educational Research emphasised in private correspondence with other key figures in the formation of the new Association – namely, Brian Dockrell of the Scottish Council for Research in Education, John Nisbet in Aberdeen, Noel Entwistle in Lancaster and Gordon Miller in London – 'The lack of a central association and forum in which the interdisciplinary study of education can be promulgated has exercised the minds of most of us in the last few years' (Start, 1973). According to Start, 'The idea of a British Educational Research Association to which can be brought all those with interests in education as an area and with skills involved in other disciplines has obvious attractions' (Start, 1973).

A meeting was held in Birmingham in October 1973 that agreed on open membership (unlike the elite basis of the SCSE) and 'interdisciplinary commitment, so that whatever disciplines seem relevant to educational research in the widest sense shall be included' (Whitfield, 1973). At the inaugural conference of the new body, held at the University of Birmingham in April 1974, the presidential address of the first president, John Nisbet of the University of Aberdeen, confirmed this approach (Nisbet, 1974). Nisbet suggested that the large increase in educational research over the previous ten years, accompanied by greater funding and a widening range of approaches, had encouraged the growth of specialisms that had now to be contained within a national professional organisation. BERA's inaugural meeting took place at the University of Birmingham on 4-5 April 1974, chaired by Edgar Stones. It agreed to establish informal relationships with kindred organisations 'to avoid conflict and reduce duplication of activities'. It was hoped that this would both strengthen the achievements of BERA itself and promote the representation of other bodies (BERA, 1974, minute 4). It was agreed also to avoid a duplication of dates with those of other conferences. The first annual conference of BERA would be held in September 1975, with the aim also of maintaining a principle of interdisciplinary approaches to educational research (BERA 1974, minute 5). Yet it soon became, as Alec Ross of Lancaster University anticipated, a 'jamboree' of many different groups (Ross, 1974) that was essentially multidisciplinary rather than interdisciplinary in nature.

Nisbet's aforementioned inaugural address to BERA at its first meeting reviewed the state of the art of educational research. He emphasised the growth of the field over the previous thirty years, which he suggested had carried with it the danger that the study of education might 'split up into less and less meaningful sub-divisions' (Nisbet, 1974, p. 2). His own department at Aberdeen, although still relatively small, held special meetings to ensure that there was some link between the various aspects of educational research, and every member of staff was required to carry out some tutorial work across all the boundaries. Nisbet's research, conducted with Noel Entwistle at Edinburgh, included theoretical issues, a historical section, a chapter on comparative studies, an empirical study, and a small piece of action research. Overall, Nisbet took the opportunity that his presidential address at BERA afforded him to 'argue strongly against the fissiparous trend in current educational research' (Nisbet, 1974, p. 2). Yet there was within his own design of the field more than a hint of multidisciplinary rather than interdisciplinary features, and it was these former aspects that tended to assert themselves in the field as a whole.

Departments and Disciplinarity

These tensions between disciplinarity and interdisciplinarity were also experienced at a departmental level. This tendency was exemplified in two leading university education departments of the postwar era, in London and Leicester. The London Institute of Education was a specialist institution that since the 1930s under Fred Clarke had established itself as a dominant institution in the field (Aldrich, 2002; McCulloch, 2014b). The Leicester department was new, and based in a new university, but quickly became regarded as one of the most important departments in the country.

In the 1960s and 1970s, the discipline-based approach of the Institute was at its most rigid and influential. This was the intellectual home and heartland of Richard Peters, the successor to Louis Arnaud Reid as the Professor of the Philosophy of Education. Intellectual depth in a particular disciplinary area was prized above breadth or range of studies. As the Institute grew rapidly in size, it was also most convenient to compartmentalise studies in different areas rather than attempt to embrace educational issues in general terms. From this point of view, a typical exchange took place in November 1965 between Peters and a comparative educationalist, Brian Holmes. The latter agreed with Peters that teacher training courses should be based mainly on specialist teaching by philosophers, psychologists, sociologists and comparative educationists, rather than through seminars conducted by every member of staff. He emphasised that '[t]here are too many areas of special study to make it possible for teaching to be undertaken in every area by non-specialists' (Holmes, 1965).

Yet it was still possible to challenge or at least mitigate this dominant regime. For example, a new initiative designed to lessen the Institute's dependence on a discipline-based approach was the creation in 1972 of the Department of Curriculum Studies (DCS). This reflected both the prominence of curriculum change as a national issue in which teachers and local education authorities (LEAs) had key roles, and the significance of the Schools Council for the Curriculum and Examinations, introduced in 1964, as both an initiator of curriculum innovation and a provider of funding. Within the Institute, this trend was led by Denis Lawton, appointed initially as a researcher in a sociological project in 1963 and then as a senior lecturer in curriculum studies from 1967 before being promoted to a professorship in 1974 and later Director (Aldrich, 2002, pp. 150, 172). Richard Pring, a philosopher and lecturer in the department and later a professor at Exeter and then Oxford, has recalled that the Institute was 'a rather feudal society, ruled by the strong, "autonomous barons" of the "foundation disciplines" and chaired by a director with limited power over his baronial subjects' (Pring, 2005, pp. 195-196). The DCS was intended to provide a means of bringing these disciplines together in the study of the school curriculum, as well as being a way of linking theory to practice. However, it largely failed to bring into existence a distinctively interdisciplinary approach to educational studies and research.

According to Lawton himself, the rationale for the DCS was that, as he put it, 'there is a need in the highly specialised Institute for one department which would (a) be concerned with the development of educational theory generally and curriculum theory in particular, and (b) be concerned with interdisciplinary courses and encourage other departments to contribute to the work' (Lawton, 1974). He suggested that the DCS should be relatively small and avoid becoming a 'mini-Institute', and that it would be helpful to establish a formal structure to 'make decisions about proposals of an interdisciplinary kind' (Lawton, 1974). It was committed from the beginning to bringing the different disciplines together to study the curriculum as a whole, an endeavour that was reflected in its staff members who had experience of one or more of the foundation disciplines (DCS, 1981). In practice, it retained an emphasis on the separate disciplines working together more than being a fully integrated approach.

This emphasis on the disciplines was reflected in Lawton's own publications. For example, Lawton's *Social Change, Educational Theory and Curriculum Planning*, published in 1973 (Lawton, 1973), was organised first in terms of the principles of curriculum planning, including separate chapters on social factors and psychological theories, then a socio-historical study of the school curriculum in the UK, and finally an examination of how theory was implemented in practice to become what he called the 'common culture individualised curriculum'. By the time of his inaugural professorial lecture in 1978, Lawton recognised the increasingly active role of the state in the school curriculum by also stressing the importance of politics in shaping the curriculum, but he retained a fundamentally disciplinary model (Lawton, 1978/1980). Nor was this approach unusual among curriculum theorists. John Kerr, Professor of Education at Leicester and a specialist in the science curriculum, edited a volume entitled *Changing the Curriculum* (Kerr, 1968), with chapters on the contributions of philosophy (by Paul Hirst), history (by Kenneth Charlton), psychology (by Philip Taylor) and sociology (by Frank Musgrove). Such texts, and the intellectual frameworks on which they were based, served to structure courses in curriculum studies.

By the early 1980s, with Malcolm Skilbeck having succeeded Lawton as the head of the CSD, the disciplinary model of curriculum studies was under review but with little consensus as to what should replace it. According to Skilbeck's summation at a staff conference held in July 1982, 'There was general agreement that curriculum studies had developed beyond the discipline based model that the department originally embodied (according to DL [Denis Lawton] more for pragmatic than ideological reasons) but less clarity as to what it had developed into' (Skilbeck, 1982). Skilbeck went on to propose three potential models for course and research in curriculum studies that the department might adopt. In the first, curriculum studies would be treated as a picture of the field of curriculum studies itself, its history, literature, methodology and current position. In the second, it would focus on current issues or problems. In the third, it would become an orientation to action, and it was argued that courses should be framed more clearly around this overall approach rather than around one of understanding and reflection. Staff discussion around the relationship between the core courses and the disciplines, according to Skilbeck, 'generated the most discussion and the least agreement!' Indeed, the contribution of the disciplines remained unresolved (Skilbeck, 1982).

At Leicester, there was an impressive grouping of educationists, including Tibble and Simon, as well as Robin Pedley, John Kerr, Geoffrey Bantock and others. Simon had emerged in the early 1960s as the leader of the 'new' history of education, his approach taking its cue from Fred Clarke's ideas about a social history of education but interpreting this innovation on Marxist lines (see, for example, McCulloch, 2010; McCulloch, 2011, chapter 4). His discipline-based contribution to Tibble's iconic collection emphasised the importance of the history of education in terms of understanding education as a social function, or 'a vital contribution to social history' (Simon, 1966, p. 95). He thus rejected what he characterised as its traditional production of 'a somewhat indigestible mass of dates and facts, orders and Acts' (Simon, 1966, p. 91), and elsewhere as 'a flat record of acts and ordinances, punctuated by accounts of the theories of great educators who entertained ideas "in advance of their time"' (Simon 1966, p. 95). It was much more important, according to Simon, to consider the social origins of such ideas, which would in turn illuminate 'the elements in society ready for change at different times..., why changes of a particular kind were needed, what assisted or prevented their realisation, what compromises were made, break-throughs achieved, and with what effect' (Simon, 1966, pp. 95-96). This was an approach to the history of education that resonated with contemporary political tensions over the direction of educational policies – for example, on comprehensive schools designed for all abilities and aptitudes – and especially with controversies over social class and education. In many ways, then, Simon's contribution to educational studies and research was based squarely in his key role as the national leader of the history of education as a subdiscipline.

At the same time, however, Simon also harboured strong interdisciplinary ideals of education as a field of study. Simon's inaugural lecture as the Professor of Education at Leicester University, also in 1966, reiterated his disciplinary approach but also attempted to explain his perspective on education in general, and emphasised the interdependence of the disciplines. He aspired towards a 'fruitful cooperation' between the disciplines in education, 'in which no one lays down all the laws but everyone rubs off corners' (Simon, 1966/1980, p. 91). Indeed, he insisted, 'There cannot be a permanent leasing out of concessions in the field of education to other disciplines which then operate exactly as they would at home' (Simon, 1966/1980, p. 91). Simon therefore argued in favour of a conscious cultivation of interrelations. As befitted a historian, he chose an arresting historical analogy to make this point, proposing that what might be hoped for was 'something like that settlement whereby an Anglo-Saxon country, invaded in turn by Danes and Normans, triumphantly emerged from the process as English' (Simon, 1966/1980, p. 91). This notion of 'interdisciplinary cross-fertilisation' (Simon, 1966/1980, p. 92) is interesting as it marks Simon out as a leader and champion of his own discipline who also promoted interdisciplinary ideals.

The head of department at Leicester was J.W. Tibble, who supported the disciplinary approach at Leicester also. Tibble had graduated in English at the University of Leeds in 1922 before going on to teach and then being appointed as a lecturer in education at the University College of the South West (later Exeter University) in 1929, where he stayed for thirteen years. In 1946 he was appointed to a professorship of education at what was then Leicester University College and built the department up over the next twenty years. In the 1960s, the disciplines of education were offered in the context of a general education course outside a subject-method course component, with Simon teaching the history of education, Geoffrey Bantock taking educational philosophy in the form of a historical study of educational theorists, Tibble himself teaching sociology, and other colleagues taking psychology (Jones, 2001). Simon himself had joined the Leicester department as a lecturer in 1950 and, when Tibble retired in 1966, he, Bantock and the science educator J.F. Kerr were all given professorships. While generally sympathetic to the 'four disciplines' approach, which he later argued had 'promoted a higher level of educational studies generally than had existed before', and had given many of its students 'a wider, more informed, view of the nature of education as a social process', Simon was nevertheless critical of some of its more adverse effects. For example, as he recalled, each student was asked to follow courses on any two of the disciplines according to their choice, and a split developed between the 'method' tutor on the one hand and the 'basic course' tutor on the other that betokened a tension between theory and practice (Simon n.d./1990s).

Nevertheless, in his role as head of the Leicester department in the 1970s, Simon continued to support a fundamentally disciplinary approach. In a formal note to the university's vice-chancellor in February 1974 to recommend future developments in the school of education, he requested that strength should be built up in the relevant specialisms in order to support the further development of work for higher degrees and diplomas. The original 'four disciplines' approach now required modification, and cooperation with the education service and schools demanded greater expertise in research design and statistics. In terms of the disciplines, he argued that the school was best known for its work in his own area, the history of education, which had also developed links with other areas of the university such as urban history and the history of science, although he pleaded that it needed more cover in pre-nineteenth-century history of education. He explained that his own wife, Joan, who was well known as an author of academic studies in Tudor history of education (Simon, 1965), was only 'called in unofficially' (Simon, 1974). Simon noted that staffing in the philosophy of education appeared adequate, while the sociology of education was tending to publish in sociology journals rather than supporting interdisciplinary work in educational studies. There was meanwhile, he proposed, a 'crying need for a good educational psychologist with experience in teaching in ways relevant to the intending teacher, who could also participate in research' (Simon, 1974).

Simon's contribution to the debate about the future direction of BERA was also notable. As president of BERA in 1977, he argued in his presidential address that BERA represented 'a coming together from various disciplines' (Simon, 1978, p. 2), which would in his view encourage 'submerging the undesirable aspects of contributory disciplines while extracting the most from them from the educational point of view' (Simon, 1978, p. 4). Simon, indeed, was emphatic in his belief that '[t]he study of education has manifestly suffered from subordination to disparate modes of approach and methodologies deriving from fields quite other than education which have simply been transferred to the educational sphere, and which, once there, have tended to maintain their own distinctive languages and approaches, to pursue their own ends' (Simon, 1978, p. 4). At the same time, he also warned against a growing tendency to 'let a hundred flowers bloom', which might encourage a tendency to 'pull in different directions' rather than focusing on the conceptual and practical problems of education as a whole (Simon, 1978, p. 4). Here were the competing yet complementary pressures of disciplinarity and interdisciplinarity expressed at their most explicit. Simon, one of the leading disciplinary exponents of his generation, was also one of the most prominent advocates of an interdisciplinary approach.

Conclusions

This chapter has highlighted the changing and contested set of relationships involving educational studies and interdisciplinarity through a brief historical review. It has proposed and attempted to demonstrate that the extended university project embracing a wide range of institutional spaces has been the locus for this continuing debate, and also that a critical historical approach is well suited to such an examination. These tensions seem likely to continue into the future, albeit in a broader context that is continuing to change rapidly.

There is scope for a great deal of further research to deepen our understanding of educational studies as an applied multidisciplinary field. The social and historical experiences of the journals, societies, centres, conferences, projects and other spaces and places in this field still await detailed treatment. The role of what Klein has described as 'interdisciplinary individuals' in pursuing an interdisciplinary agenda within a broadly multidisciplinary context is a further key issue for detailed analysis (Klein, 1990; see also McCulloch, 2014a). And finally, increased comparative, international, transnational and cross-cultural awareness is likely to extend still further our collective engagement with educational studies as an applied multidisciplinary field.

Acknowledgements

I am pleased to acknowledge the Society for Educational Studies for its generous support for the National Award 'The social organisation of educational studies', and also my collaborators in this project, Gemma Moss, James Thomas and Steven Cowan.

References

Aldrich, R. (2002) *The Institute of Education 1902-2002.* London: Institute of Education.

Bain, A. (1877) Education as a Science, *Mind: A Quarterly Review of Psychology and Philosophy*, 2(5), 1-21.

Baltic Association of Historians of Pedagogy (Ed.) (2009) *History of Education and Pedagogical Thought in the Baltic Countries up to 1990: an overview.* Riga, Latvia: RaKa.

Baltic Association of Historians of Pedagogy (Ed.) (2010) *History of Pedagogy and Educational Sciences in the Baltic Countries from 1940 to 1990: an overview.* Riga, Latvia: RaKa.

Banks, O. (1982) The Sociology of Education, 1952-1982, *British Journal of Educational Studies*, 30(1), 18-31. https://doi.org/10.1080/00071005.1982.9973610

Barton, L. & Walker, S. (1978) Sociology of Education at the Crossroads, *Educational Review*, 30(3), 269-283. https://doi.org/10.1080/0013191780300310

BERA (1974) Inaugural meeting, 6 April (BERA papers, Modern Records Centre, University of Warwick, 368/10/4).

Biesta, G. (2011) Disciplines and Theory in the Academic Study of Education: a comparative analysis of the Anglo-American and Continental construction of the field, *Pedagogy, Culture and Society*, 19(2), 175-192. https://doi.org/10.1080/14681366.2011.582255

Blyth, A. (1982) Response and Autonomy in the Study of Education: a personal account of three decades, *British Journal of Educational Studies*, 30(1), 7-17. https://doi.org/10.1080/00071005.1982.9973609

Clarke, F. (1943) *The Study of Education in England.* Oxford: Oxford University Press.

Clarke, F. (1949) The Widening Scope of the Study of Education, *The Schoolmaster*, 8 (September).

Department of Curriculum Studies (DCS) (1981) Note on Departmental Visitation, February. DCS papers, IOE.

Furlong, J. (2013) *Education – an Anatomy of the Discipline: rescuing the university project?* London: Routledge.

Furlong, J. & Lawn, M. (Ed.) (2011) *Disciplines of Education: their role in the future of education research.* London: Routledge.

Gardiner, D., O'Donoghue, T. & O'Neill, M. (2011) *Constructing the Field of Education as a Liberal Art and Teacher Preparation at Five Western Australian Universities: an historical analysis.* New York: Edwin Mellen Press.

Gibbons, M., Limoges, C., Nowotny, H., Schwartzman, S., Scott, F. & Trow, M. (1994) *The New Production of Knowledge: the dynamics of science and research in contemporary societies.* London: SAGE.

Gordon, P. (1980) Introduction, in P. Gordon (Ed.), *The Study of Education: a collection of inaugural lectures*, vol. 1. *Early and Modern*, pp. ix-xxiii. London: Woburn Press.

Graff, H.J. (2015) *Undisciplining Knowledge: interdisciplinarity in the twentieth century.* Baltimore, MD: Johns Hopkins University Press.

Greaves, J. & Grant, W. (2010) Crossing the Interdisciplinary Divide: political science and biological science, *Political Studies*, 58, 320-339. https://doi.org/10.1111/j.1467-9248.2009.00828.x

Hofstetter, R. & Schneuwly, B. (2004) Introduction: educational sciences in dynamic and hybrid institutionalisation, *Paedagogica Historica*, 40(5), 569-589. https://doi.org/10.1080/0030923042000293661

Holmes, B. (1965) Letter to Richard Peters, 16 November. R.S. Peters papers, IOE.

Hoskin, K. (1993) Education and the Genesis of Disciplinarity: the unexpected reversal, in E. Messer-Davidow, D.R. Shurrway & D.J. Sylvan (Eds) *Knowledges: historical and critical studies in disciplinarity*, pp. 271-304. Charlottesville: University Press of Virginia.

Jones, D. (2001) *School of Education 1946-1996.* Leicester: University of Leicester.

Kerr, J. (Ed.) (1968) *Changing the Curriculum.* London: University of London Press.

Klein, J.T. (1990) *Interdisciplinarity: history, theory, and practice.* Detroit: Wayne State University Press.

Klein, J.T. (1993) Blurring, Cracking, and Crossing: permeation and the fracturing of discipline, in E. Messer-Davidson, D.R. Shumway & D.J. Sylvan (Eds) *Knowledges: historical and critical studies in disciplinarity*, pp. 185-211. Charlottesville: University Press of Virginia.

Klein, J.T. (2010) A Taxonomy of Interdisciplinarity, in R. Frodeman (Ed.) *Oxford Handbook of Interdisciplinarity*, pp. 15-30. Oxford: Oxford University Press.

Labaree, D. (2006) *The Trouble with Ed Schools.* New Haven, CT: Yale University Press.

Lagemann, E. (1997) Contested Terrain: a history of education research in the United States, 1890-1990, *Educational Researcher*, 26(9), 5-17. https://doi.org/10.2307/1176271

Lagemann, E. (2001) *An Elusive Science: the troubling history of education research.* Chicago: University of Chicago Press.

Laot, F. & Rogers, R. (Eds) (2015) *Les Sciences de l'Education: Emergence d'un Champ de Recherche dans l'Apres-Guerre.* Rennes: Presses Universitaires de Rennes.

Lawn, M., Deary, I., Bartholomew, D. & Brett, C. (2010) Embedding the New Science of Research: the organised culture of Scottish educational research in the mid-twentieth century, *Paedagogica Historica*, 46(3), 357-381. https://doi.org/10.1080/00309230903396480

Lawton, D. (1973) *Social Change, Educational Theory and Curriculum Planning.* London: University of London Press.

Lawton, D. (1974) Curriculum Studies Department and Interdepartmental Cooperation. Memorandum, February. Department of Curriculum Studies (DCS) papers, IOE.

Lawton, D. (1978/1980) The End of the Secret Garden? In P. Gordon (Ed.), *The Study of Education*, vol. 2, pp. 305-325. London: Woburn Press.

McCulloch, G. (2002) 'Disciplines Contributing to Education'? Educational Studies and the Disciplines, *British Journal of Educational Studies*, 50(1), 100-119. https://doi.org/10.1111/1467-8527.t01-1-00193

McCulloch, G. (2010) A People's History of Education: Brian Simon, the British Communist Party and *Studies in the History of Education, 1780-1870*, *History of Education*, 39(4), 437-457. https://doi.org/10.1080/00467601003687580

McCulloch, G. (2011) *The Struggle for the History of Education*. London: Routledge.

McCulloch, G. (2012) The Standing Conference on Studies in Education: sixty years on, *British Journal of Educational Studies*, 60(4), 301-316. https://doi.org/10.1080/00071005.2012.691958

McCulloch, G. (2014a) Birth of a Field: George Baron, educational administration and the social sciences in England, 1946-1978, *Journal of Educational Administration and History*, 46(3), 270-287. https://doi.org/10.1080/00220620.2014.919902

McCulloch, G. (2014b) Fred Clarke and the Internationalisation of Educational Studies and Research, *Paedagogica Historica*, 50(1-2), 123-137.

McCulloch, G. & Cowan, S. (2017) *A Social History of Educational Studies and Research*. London: Routledge.

Mullainathan, S. & Thaler, R. (2000) Behavioural Economics. Working paper 7948, National Bureau of Economic Research, Cambridge. http://www.nber.org/papers/w7948 (accessed on 13 February 2016).

Nisbet, J. (1974) Educational Research: the state of the art. BERA presidential address.

Parker, J. (2008) Beyond Disciplinarity: humanities and supercomplexity, *London Review of Education*, 6(3), 255-266. https://doi.org/10.1080/14748460802489389

Peters, R. (1965) The Place of Philosophy in the Training of Teachers, in Department of Education and Science, *Conference on the Course in Education in the Education of Teachers, 16th to 21st March, 1964*, pp. 1-9, DES, London.

Petrie, H. (1976) Do You See What I See? The Epistemology of Interdisciplinary Inquiry, *Educational Researcher*, 5(2), 9-14. https://doi.org/10.3102/0013189X005002009

Pring, R. (2005) The Development of Curriculum Studies at the Institute of Education, in D. Halpin & P. Walsh (Eds) *Educational Commonplaces: essays to honour Denis Lawton*, pp. 195-208. London: IOE.

Ross, A. (1974) Letter to E. Stones, 21 January. BERA papers, 268/10/3, University of Warwick.

Simon, B. (1960) *Studies in the History of Education, 1780-1870*. London: Lawrence & Wishart.

Simon, B. (1966) The History of Education, in J.W. Tibble (Ed.) *The Study of Education*, pp. 91-131. London: Routledge & Kegan Paul.

Simon, B. (1966/1980) Education: the new perspective, in P. Gordon (Ed.) *The Study of Education*, vol. 2, pp. 71-94. London: Woburn Press.

Simon, B. (1974) Some Reflections on the School of Education. Memorandum to Vice-chancellor, Leicester University, 24 February. Simon papers, DC/SIM/5/3/2, IOE.

Simon, B. (1978) Educational Research: which way?, *Research Intelligence*, 4(1), 2-7. https://doi.org/10.1080/0141192780040101

Simon, B. (1990) The Study of Education as a University Subject, in J.B. Thomas (Ed.) *British Universities and Teacher Education: a century of change*, pp. 125-142. London: Falmer Press.

Simon, B. (n.d./1990s) University and the School of Education, 1950-1980. Note. Simon papers, DC/SIM/4/5/2/30, IOE.

Simon, J. (1965) *Education and Society in Tudor England*. Cambridge: Cambridge University Press.

Smelser, N. (2003) On Comparative Analysis, Interdisciplinarity and Internationalisation in Sociology, *International Sociology*, 18(4), 643-657. https://doi.org/10.1177/0268580903184001

Start, K.B. (1973) Letter to W.B. Dockrell, N.J. Entwistle, J. Nisbet & G. Miller, 19 April. BERA papers, 268/10/1.

Szreter, F.R. (1980) Landmarks in the Institutionalisation of Sociology of Education in Britain, *Educational Review*, 32(3), 292-300. https://doi.org/10.1080/0013191800320306

Thaler, R. (2015) *Misbehaving: the making of behavioural economics*. London: Allen Lane.

Tibble, J.W. (1966a) The Development of the Study of Education, in J.W. Tibble (Ed), *The Study of Education*, pp. 1-28. London: Routledge & Kegan Paul.

Tibble, J.W. (Ed.) (1966b) *The Study of Education*. London: Routledge & Kegan Paul.

Weingart, P. (2010) A Short History of Knowledge Formations, in R. Frodeman (ed), *Oxford Handbook of Interdisciplinarity*, pp. 3-14. Oxford: Oxford University Press.

Whitfield, R.C. (1973) Letter to W. Taylor, 19 October. BERA papers, 268/10/1, University of Warwick.

Whitty, G. (2012) A Life with the Sociology of Education, *British Journal of Educational Studies*, 60(1), 65-75. https://doi.org/10.1080/00071005.2011.650945

CHAPTER 10

Teachers' Knowledge in England and Germany: the conceptual background

DINA KUHLEE & CHRISTOPHER WINCH

SUMMARY This chapter looks at three 'ideal types' in a typology of teachers' knowledge and the ways in which it is linked to their know-how: the craftworker, the executive technician and the professional technician. These categories are applied to an examination of the ways in which teaching is conceptualised in England and Germany. The current English policy landscape is examined and it is maintained that the craftworker conception is the dominant one. When the German policy landscape is examined, by contrast, it can be seen that the craftworker and the executive technician conceptions have rather little influence and that the professional technician conception has been consistently dominant. Reflections on differences in the policymaking process in the two jurisdictions are also made in order to discuss relations between political reform intentions and effects of reform.

In this chapter we examine the differences in the way in which teacher education is organised in England and Germany in order to reveal the differences in how the two countries view the professional knowledge of teachers.

Three Different Conceptions of Teaching:
craftworker, executive technician, professional technician

In order to understand the ways in which teachers' knowledge is understood in different jurisdictions, it will be helpful to set up three 'archetypes' of the teacher (and hence of teaching) that correspond more or less to dominant conceptions of the teacher in different regions. We will call these conceptions the craftworker, the executive technician and the professional technician, respectively.[1]

The craftworker teacher's day-to-day activity is closely aligned with that of the traditional craftworker. If we consider the analogy of the potter, the wheelwright or the baker, working in a pre-industrial context, then the following features of their work are drawn on by proponents of the teacher-craftworker analogy:

- Know-how is based on manual skill and situational judgement.
- Relevant knowledge is situated and context specific, not theory-based (Sturt, 1923/1976).
- Learning the occupation takes place through apprenticeship conditions – for example, through legitimate peripheral participation (Lave & Wenger, 1991).

The skills of the teacher are based on the ability to handle people and to communicate effectively. Furthermore, teachers have to draw on subject knowledge and render it into a form suitable for their students, so the analogy with the traditional craftworker is not perfect. However, the claim that teaching is skill-based, that it does not depend on a theory of teaching and learning and that it is best learned 'on the job' is dominant in the rhetoric of proponents of the craft-based teacher. Perhaps the craft most associated with teaching is midwifery, with the analogy of bringing forth knowledge in the student being the dominant image, as in Plato's dialogue *Meno* (Plato, 1970).

The executive technician by contrast is a worker whose operations are controlled by protocols derived from a theoretical basis by a technologist in order to achieve an aim determined by someone else.[2] Like the craftworker, know-how is skill-based; unlike the craftworker, knowledge is theory-based; unlike the learning of the craftworker, learning to be an executive technician involves training and practice in the relevant protocols. Situational judgement is at a minimum. A programme like the National Literacy Strategy, implemented in England from 1997, is a good example of a teaching programme designed to be run by executive technicians.

The professional technician draws on a body of systematic knowledge in order to make appropriate judgement *in situ* in the workplace (e.g. in the church, the courtroom, the operating theatre, the classroom or the design studio).[3] Although professional technicians need skills, they also need higher-order abilities to plan, coordinate, communicate and evaluate. These abilities are explicitly recognised in the German context within the national standards for teacher education (e.g. KMK, 2000, 2004/2014). Professional formation is usually prolonged and involves a mixture of professionally relevant theory, controlled practice and reflection on practice. The regular and systematic analysis of and reflection on teachers' knowledge and teaching practice involving relevant theory is seen as central to developing the necessary professional expertise. In the German context this results in an overall professional capacity known as *professionelle Handlungskompetenz*, or 'capacity for professional action' (see the discussion below). We can see this model dominant in Germany, but also, to a lesser extent, within the UK, in Scotland and, up to a point, Wales (for Scotland, see Donaldson, 2010; General Teaching Council for Scotland, 2012).

The Elements of Teacher Knowledge: conceptual framework, pedagogical content knowledge, empirical research, self-knowledge

Of these three conceptions of teaching, the professional-technician conception is the most expansive, so will serve to illustrate the dimensions of teacher knowledge which can be found in practice and in the literature, although obviously not in all conceptions of teaching. Subject knowledge (knowledge of the material to be taught) is considered important for the craftworker and for professional conceptions of the teacher, less so for the executive technician. Understanding of the conceptual field of education – for example, the link between assessment and pedagogy or between aims and curriculum, together with the fact that these links are contestable – is an important component of the knowledge of a professional technician. Pedagogic content knowledge (PCK) (Shulman, 1986) is subject knowledge recontextualised into a form suitable for pedagogic purposes. Whether it is knowledge or a form of know-how is debatable, but the ability to recontextualise subject knowledge is considered to be a vital tool in the armoury of both the craftworker teacher and the professional teacher. They would disagree about how it should be developed. For the craftworker teacher it is a matter of intuition mediated by experience; for the professional it is a matter of theory mediated by experience. The executive technician's PCK is produced by an educational technologist who renders the subject matter to be taught into a series of scripts, materials and textbooks to be applied by the teacher with little discretion.

Each conception of teaching sees the role of empirical knowledge in enabling teachers to work effectively in a different way. The craftworker teacher relies strongly on his/her own experience and, vicariously, on the experience of seasoned practitioners. Local knowledge of students, the school and the community are all considered to be important ingredients of the knowledge needed to teach successfully. For the executive technician, empirical research is important, but only to the extent that its relevant findings are distilled into classroom protocols by an educational technologist. The executive technician does not need to understand the research or its implications, only the teaching protocols that issue from it. The professional technician, on the other hand, is expected to be able to understand empirical research and what its implications might be for his/her practice, and to adopt a critical stance towards it.

The English Conception of Teaching as Craft

We can now consider what the dominant conception of teaching in England is and how it is supported (if it is supported) by government policy. It has long been established that the dominant English conception of the teacher, largely accepted both by teachers and by policymakers, is the craftworker conception, although, as we shall presently see, the actual policy picture has become quite complex. Hoyle (1974) established that the dominant conception held amongst teachers was that of the 'restricted professional', corresponding with our craftworker classification. Despite attempts from the 1960s to the 1980s to strengthen the academic content of teacher education programmes, the craftworker conception remained dominant. Partly this was because neither the PGCE nor the BEd routes into teaching were capable of fully supplying the intellectually rigorous content that would have allowed for the development of professional technicians. In the case of the PGCE, the time allocated would have precluded this. In the case of the BEd the programmes were, in most cases, simply not ambitious enough and did not tackle difficult topics either with the seriousness which they demanded or with the close alignment with practical experience which would have made the theoretical content sufficiently relevant to the intending teacher.

From the late 1980s onwards, these programmes became the target of attacks from a lobby intent on removing higher education's role in teacher education (O'Hear, 1988; Lawlor, 1990). This lobby, which strongly advocated the craftworker conception, was politically influential up until 1997 and has become so again since 2010. It is worth examining why the craftworker conception has become so dominant. In order to do this, it is helpful to look at professional education in England more generally. In the case of the traditional professions like medicine, engineering and law, the transition into preparation through higher education was relatively uncontroversial and has remained so. Few dispute the relevance of academic knowledge to successful professional practice, and the idea that surgeons could learn to practise successfully solely through trial and error in the operating room would be regarded as a macabre joke.

The English Conception of Teaching as Craft Informed by Research: is this coherent?

However, the position for the non-professions (trades) is somewhat different. These would be roughly equivalent to the governmentally recognised German *Berufe*. England has always been ambivalent about the degree and quality of preparation needed to practise these. From the time of Adam Smith's *Wealth of Nations* (1776/1981) onwards, a dismissive tone has been adopted towards the trades and we can see in certain occupations how the educational requirements have been progressively lowered over the last twenty years, often under pressure from employers who wish to cut costs. The knowledge requirement in particular has come under pressure, with an increasing emphasis being placed on effective practice in operational conditions. There are partial exceptions in areas of engineering and the electrical industry, but here as well, the tendency towards simplification and the downgrading of theory has been evident. Thus, the move towards an executive-technician model has become quite pronounced in the trades, those occupations which do not have professional or semi-professional status (see below).

Then there are the semi-professions, which occupy a place within a continuum between the trades and the traditional professions (Etzioni, 1969). Usually, these occupations require a higher education qualification for entry, but do not possess either the prestige or the high academic entry qualifications of the traditional professions. Typically, they do not control their own membership and, in some cases, the qualifications needed for ability to practise are fluid. Teaching in England is such an occupation and some of the professional characteristics, such as the rigour of the demand for qualifications required to practise, have been weakened in recent years and may be weakened further in the near future. The government White Paper of 2010 observed that '[t]oo little teacher training takes place on the job, and too much professional development involves compliance with bureaucratic initiatives rather than working with other teachers to develop effective practice' (Department for Education [DfE], 2010, p. 19). The then Secretary of State for Education observed in 2010 that '[t]eaching is a craft and it is best learnt as an apprentice observing a master craftsman or woman. Watching others, and being rigorously observed yourself as you develop, is the best route to acquiring mastery in the classroom' (Gove, 2010). These are by no means eccentric views in the English context and command the agreement of a large proportion of teachers and the public, as well as of a significant number of academic commentators. It appears fair to say that the dominant conception of teaching is of a craft-based semi-profession, the formation of whose cadres should be conducted through a kind of apprenticeship in the workplace and for whom educational theory disseminated at universities is at best an irrelevance and at worst a distraction.

Despite this apparent unambiguity, however, the official position on teaching is not quite that simple. The Education Endowment Foundation, set up and funded by the government in 2011, aims to disseminate relevant research and to commission research of relevance to classroom practice and school improvement. When we look at the Teachers' Standards, promulgated in 2013, we find that in Standard 5 teachers must:

> have a secure understanding of how a range of factors can inhibit pupils' ability to learn, and how best to overcome these.

> demonstrate an awareness of the physical, social and intellectual development of children, and know how to adapt teaching to

support pupils' education at different stages of development.
(HMSO, 2013, p. 11)

It is hard to see how these standards can be realised without knowledge of the empirical research underlying pupil learning and development. The Carter Review of 2015 also emphasised the role of research in teacher effectiveness, in its section on evidence-based teaching:

> XVI. We believe it is critical that ITT should teach trainees why engaging with research is important and build an expectation and enthusiasm for teaching as an evidence-based profession. International evidence, including the RSA-BERA inquiry ... shows us that high-performing systems induct their teachers in the use, assessment and application of research findings.
>
> XVII. Our findings suggest that sometimes ITT focuses on trainees conducting their own research, without necessarily teaching trainees the core skills of how to access, interpret and use research to inform classroom practice. It is important that trainees understand how to interpret educational theory and research in a critical way, so they are able to deal with contested issues.
> (DfE, 2015, p. 8)

It is natural to suppose that these statements suggest a move towards the professional model. However, the Carter Review also recommends that '[a] central portal of synthesised executive summaries, providing practical advice on research findings about effective teaching in different subjects and phases, should be developed' (DfE, 2015, p. 8), which suggests that the review may actually have in mind an executive-technician model to resolve the 'contested issues' referred to above.

Finally, we need to look at the latest official treatment of this area in the 2016 White Paper *Educational Excellence Everywhere* (DfE, 2016), where the importance of research in developing good teaching is given some prominence. Thus, concerning the teacher education curriculum:

> We will strengthen ITT content, focusing on helping new teachers enter the classroom with sufficient subject knowledge, practical behaviour management skills, understanding of special educational needs, and a greater understanding of the most up-to-date research on how pupils learn. We'll ensure discredited ideas unsupported by firm evidence are not promoted to new teachers.
> (DfE, 2016, p. 12)

The White Paper adds that a new independent College of Teaching will assist in carrying out these objectives (DfE, 2016, p. 16)
As to the role of universities:

> There will continue to be an important place for high quality universities in ITT with a strong track record in attracting well-qualified graduates. We want the best universities to establish 'centres of excellence' in ITT, drawing on their world-leading subject knowledge and research. (DfE, 2016, p. 34)

An explicit reference to the research findings on the use of synthetic phonics in the teaching of reading is found on p. 41 (DfE, 2016).

There will also be a British education research journal that will publish research findings relevant to teaching in an accessible way:

> We will also support the establishment of a new, peer-reviewed British education journal by the new College of Teaching, helping to spread cutting edge national and international research in an accessible and relevant format so that teachers can use it to improve their teaching. We hope that, in time, this will play a similar role in teaching as the British Medical Journal has in the medical profession – helping to raise standards and spread evidence-based practice. (DfE, 2016, p. 42)

We can see, therefore, that although much of the official rhetoric surrounding teachers' know-how develops traditional thinking about teaching as a craft, nevertheless the role of research in official publications has become stronger. It may be concluded that one can extract elements of all three teacher archetypes – craftworker, executive technician and professional technician – from the documents of the last six years.

Where does this leave us in understanding the conceptual underpinnings of teaching in England? Since all three archetypes are appealed to, we need to set these alongside what is actually happening in policy. The 2016 White Paper establishes that schools, not universities, will be the awarding bodies for teaching qualifications. No school that is not under local authority control will be obliged to employ qualified teachers. The 'high quality universities' are probably those Russell Group universities with a successful REF (Research Excellence Framework assessment) performance together with an 'Outstanding' grade from their most recent Ofsted (Office for Standards in Education, Children's Services and Skills) inspection of teacher education – no more than 12 of the 50 or so universities currently offering teacher education courses in England. The implication is that the vast majority of universities currently offering teacher education in England will cease to do so. Thus, apart from a small elite group of student teachers, most will learn 'on the job' with little higher education contribution to their professional formation, which will itself not be strictly necessary to entry to the profession or possibly even to progression within it.

Despite the Carter recommendations that intending teachers adopt an informed and critical stance towards educational research, it is difficult to see how they will be equipped to do this on their own. Perhaps it is the view of those who drafted the 2016 White Paper that having a good bachelor's degree in the subject that one is going to teach is sufficient preparation for understanding and adopting a critical approach to educational research. The remark about a new journal on p. 42 (DfE, 2016) hints that there is a difficulty here: the research will have to be both accessible and useful in the improvement of teaching. Carter's reference to the contestability of research and the need to adopt a critical attitude has got lost, suggesting that there is a tilt towards the executive-technician model within the White Paper. The problem is that the ability to understand and interpret educational research needs preparation through professional education just as much as doctors' ability to make constructive use of the *British Medical Journal* does – that is, after at least five years of the study of medicine. One gets a strong sense that the government wants to have its cake and eat it. Teachers need to learn on the job as a craft occupation, they need 'digestible' research to act on and they should be sufficiently well educated to adopt a suitably critical and interpretive attitude towards educational research. It is far from obvious that, jointly, these constitute a coherent and consistent set of aspirations.

Towards a Coherent Conception of a Research-informed Profession

We have had reason to doubt whether the emerging conception of the teacher in the English policy framework can actually work. In this section we will suggest ways in which England could develop a workable conception of teaching as a research-informed profession. The first point to make is that to have a substantial number of the teaching force unqualified is not only to damage teaching's status as a semi-profession, but also to make it almost impossible that it could be, apart from a small elite, a research-informed profession. The White Paper does argue that full qualification to teach should only be awarded against rigorous criteria and after a number of years of classroom practice. However, this aspiration is undercut by the non-mandatory nature of the qualification and a refusal to involve universities in the formation of teachers.

What, then, would need to be done in order to develop teaching as a research-informed profession? First, the government would have to accept that a qualification would be necessary for entry. This could be without prejudice to a further qualification that guarantees full licensure. Such a qualification – for example, the PGCE – is necessary to enable new teachers to operate with a reasonable degree of confidence and efficiency, while still falling far short of expert status. We will see that Germany has a system of this kind. The final qualification, which could be obtained while employed as a teacher, would be at master's level and would involve demonstrable ability to understand, interpret and use academic research in practice. Only on achievement of such a master's-level qualification could a teacher be said to be fully licensed to practise (Orchard & Winch, 2015). Thus, a professional type of teacher could emerge out of the current system of teacher education.

Whether there is a will for such a development in England may, however, be doubted.

Teaching as Profession: the German discussion

Different from this English view of teaching as a craft, teaching in Germany is understood as a profession. This is evident in political debates and policy making on teaching, teacher education and the teaching profession. It is also noticeable in the academic treatment of the subject and the wider perception of teaching in society.

Despite this perception of teaching as a profession in general terms, a critical and ambivalent discussion emerged during the last decades in the academic discourse in Germany. Three different theoretical perspectives for the analysis of teaching as a profession can be distinguished, related to the terms *profession*, *professionalism* and *professionalisation* (e.g. Nittel, 2004, 2011; Helsper & Tippelt, 2011; Terhart, 2011), which will be reviewed in the following.

Profession

The term *profession* reflects an analytical perspective at societal macro-level that focuses on institutional and structural aspects of teaching. With reference to the Anglo-American sociology of professions of the 1950s and 1960s, the term profession refers to 'free professions' such as physicians and lawyers. Here, a profession features certain key characteristics (e.g. Nittel, 2004, 2011) such as an exclusive social mandate to fulfil specific tasks highly relevant for the society as seen in medicine and law. Professionals in this sense develop a specific working relation with their clientele, based on trust and not (primarily) on commercial aspects. These professions are tightly linked to a specific academic discipline that provides relevant academic knowledge and professional training. In addition, professions develop an exclusive professional culture and identity connected to a specific professional ethos. A further and central concept here is that of professional autonomy – professionals fulfil their work with a very high degree of autonomous decision-making and responsibility.

Over the years it has been debated whether the teaching profession in Germany falls under the definition of a profession, given that teaching does not meet all the criteria listed above. For example, teaching did not develop a close connection with a specific academic discipline as seen in medicine or law. In addition, it is embedded in a state-regulated school system as teachers in Germany traditionally hold civil servant status. And compulsory education forces students to participate without having much choice in their teachers. This has led to the teaching profession being referred to as 'semi-professional' (e.g. Nittel, 2004; Terhart, 2011).

The ideal model of a free profession, however, has also come under criticism. It does not account for the fundamental changes of the last decades, which impacted on traditionally free professions (Helsper & Tippelt, 2011). Facing increasing regulation and organisational control, free professions lost autonomy (e.g. Bonnet & Hericks, 2014). Trust in these professions and in the unique competence of professionals to fulfil specific tasks is eroding in a post-modern knowledge society (Nittel, 2004). In addition, new professional groups have developed that do not fit the traditional model. Therefore, as Stichweh (1996) argues, professions in the traditional sense could be described as an obsolete model with their central role in society fading. Main arguments for the differentiation between professions and non-academic occupations are losing ground and the term profession is relinquishing its central position in the German debate (e.g. Terhart, 2011).

As a result, analytical perspectives have shifted to operational tasks and requirements demanded of teaching professionals. Teaching processes and professional actions of teachers became the focus of research and academic debate. Professional decision-making and the preconditions for successful teaching moved into the centre of interest and, hence, the debate moved to the *professionalism* of teachers. This resulted in questions such as: what are the specific professional approaches of teachers? How can they be described? What are their preconditions? How can professional approaches be developed?

Professionalism

Debates around *professionalism* focus on teaching as a process. Topics include professionalism as the 'reconstruction' of the demands of teaching and specific professional patterns of behaviour and expertise required (Bauer, 1998; Helsper & Tippelt, 2011). Professionalism considers the quality of service provision at the point of action. In other words, professionalism focuses on the necessary professional expertise of teachers. As such, professionalism does not necessarily require institutional structures that form part of the traditional socio-professional theory (Nittel, 2004). As profession and professionalism separated, professionalism can exist without profession (Helsper & Tippelt, 2011).

A number of different approaches have been developed to describe and analyse the specific features of professionalism in teaching. The two most influential are:

(1) *Strukturtheoretischer Ansatz* (see Oevermann, 1996, Helsper, 2004). This approach focuses on the tasks and demands of teaching from a structural perspective and describes them as contradictory in themselves. Teachers are confronted with a variety of highly complex tasks. Individual aspects of these tasks, however, may have inconsistent structures. Two examples: (1) while teachers have to consider the individual characteristics of

each learner and their capabilities, they have to enforce predetermined learning outcomes; (2) teachers have to provide equal treatment for all students but must take into account their individual differences (Terhart, 2011, p. 206). Professionalism in this context means the ability to cope with these tensions. It requires a competent and reflective management of the uncertainty of everyday teaching. Self-critical and reflective analyses of one's own teaching practice are seen as central features in developing the necessary professional expertise (Terhart, 2011, p. 206).

(2) *Kompetenztheoretischer Ansatz* (Baumert & Kunter, 2006). Here, professionalism in teaching is described as professional competence or expertise in action (*professionelle Handlungskompetenz*). Baumert and Kunter (2006) differentiate areas of competence and dimensions of knowledge and skills based on the detailed description of the actual tasks of teaching. The central question is: what kind of professional competences and their preconditions lead to successful teaching processes? 'Successful' in this case refers especially to students' learning outcomes, defined as learners' achievements. The term professionalism focuses on the skills and attitudes needed to meet the different teaching requirements. Different areas of teaching requirements are, for example, teaching as such, diagnostics, assessment and advice, individual and collective professional development, self-regulation and coping with work-related pressures (Terhart, 2011, p. 207). In this context, knowledge and proficiency include declarative, procedural and strategic knowledge that form the centre of professionalism (Baumert & Kunter, 2006, p. 481). In reference to Shulman (1986), general pedagogical knowledge, subject knowledge and subject-specific pedagogical knowledge/pedagogical content knowledge (PCK) are essential typologies of knowledge in teaching processes. Teaching relevant attitudes and values, motivational and self-regulation capabilities contribute significantly to professional expertise in this approach. Even so, available empirical data on the impact and effectiveness of these different types of knowledge and attitudes are still insufficient. Professional expertise also comprises the ability to cope with the general uncertainty in terms of the success of teaching and the fact that teaching approaches and processes cannot be standardised. With regard to the development of professional expertise, the discussion refers to the theory of expertise (Baumert & Kunter, 2006, pp. 505-506; Bromme, 2014; Krauss & Bruckmaier, 2014). Professional expertise in teaching is seen as 'gradable' and has to be developed over time (Terhart, 2011, p. 207), with a key role played by the regular and systematic analysis of and reflection on teachers' knowledge and their teaching approaches and practices.

A third perspective should be mentioned. It follows a biographic approach and explains the development of professional expertise in teaching over the professional lifetime connected to the individual development of a person (Terhart, 2011, pp. 208-209). While this perspective on professionalism is compatible with the competence-oriented approach by

Baumert and Kunter (2006), it is closely associated with the debate around *professionalisation* (e.g. Helsper & Tippelt, 2011, p. 275).

Professionalisation

Professionalisation gained attention in the context of debates on teacher professionalism. Two dimensions are differentiated: the first looks at the individual development of professionalism in teaching; the second looks at the formation of a profession and its position within the hierarchy of professions and occupations over time (e.g. Nittel, 2004; Helsper & Tippelt, 2011). The debate on professionalisation focuses therefore on both – on the *individual* and the *collective* processes of professional learning and development (Nittel, 2004, p. 347).

Having moved from profession to professionalism, the current debate focuses on questions of teachers' professional competence or expertise and their development. Moving outside the academic sphere, it has influenced political reform initiatives in teacher education in Germany, particularly the introduction of teacher education standards in 2004 (KMK 2004/2014). In this context, models of professional expertise and development of teachers influenced political initiatives, despite their theoretical variation (Terhart, 2002; Baumert & Kunter, 2006). The standards in teacher education, for example, show that teachers are seen as experts who require a variety of academically based knowledge and know-how (KMK, 2000, 2004/2014). Teaching practice and its systematic analysis and reflection allows this knowledge to be further developed into pedagogical proficiency (KMK, 2004/2014, see below). In the following, the recent political reform processes in teacher education are discussed further.

Initial Teacher Education in Germany: political reform initiatives in structure and content

During the past 15 years, teacher education has been subjected to intense political scrutiny. Influenced by international developments such as the early PISA studies in 2000/2001 and the Bologna Declaration in 1999, teacher education reforms took place in the traditionally reform-resistant German system (for more details, see e.g. Kuhlee, 2017). Two initiatives have been central in this development: a structural reform process that focused on the implementation of the two-track bachelor's and master's system in initial teacher education (ITE); and a competence-based reform initiative that introduced teacher education standards. While these two complementary strands of reform initiatives are discussed separately in the following sections, their interconnectivity will become apparent.

The Structure of ITE: the Bologna reform process

As part of the Bologna reform process, the Standing Conference of the Ministers of Cultural Affairs of the German States (*Kultusministerkonferenz*, KMK) [4] agreed on the general legal terms and conditions for the introduction of a two-track system of university-based ITE in 2002. In 2005, the KMK approved structural features of the new ITE study programmes to be implemented by the states (KMK, 2005). Despite general agreement on main reform features, specifications remained rather sketchy, and not all states introduced the new structures. For those that did, the vagueness of specifications meant that states and especially stakeholders at universities implemented their interpretation of requirements in line with existing practice (Maeße 2010; Bauer et al, 2012). As a result, university-based ITE programmes differ throughout Germany. This is particularly evident in the amount of content allocated to subject-specific topics and pedagogical content. As Bauer et al (2012, p. 115) indicate in their study on ITE programmes for upper-secondary teachers in different states, the amount of subject-specific pedagogical content, for example, differs by a factor of 4.2. Students in ITE programmes with a strong focus on this content have to invest up to 4.2 times more time than students in programmes with a lower focus. As a result, the Bologna Process enhanced and furthered visibility of the already existing heterogeneity of university-based ITE programmes (Keuffer, 2010; Bauer et al, 2012).

Despite these reform initiatives with their enhanced heterogeneity of programmes, the very central core of German ITE remained stable, offering only one pathway into teaching, via university studies followed by a practical teaching phase (*Vorbereitungsdienst*). This applies to teachers of all school phases and includes primary as well as lower and higher secondary teacher education. In addition to providing essential academic knowledge and teaching skills, the aim of university studies is:

> to develop the skills and capabilities to handle the tasks and requirements of the profession in an autonomous and critical manner, not only to pass on one's own experiences, but to see alternative ways to act, e.g. to train the eye for the variety against the dogmatism of practice, to reflect the limits of schemata, to recognise the capacities of the organisation while being reserved against activist exuberance – in short, to experience the usefulness of theory and research. (Tenorth, 2004, p. 21, translated)

Student teachers are to be equipped to focus on teaching in a reflexive manner, not just implementing given schemata and scripts. A university education is seen as 'essential' for this kind of learning (Tenorth, 2004, p. 22, translated). The executive-technician model of teaching is thus firmly rejected, while certain craft elements in professional practice receive recognition.

This particular emphasis on an academic orientation of all teacher education programmes has its roots in the 1960s and 1970s. The 'then deep and unbroken belief in the strength of the sciences and scientific rationality to ensure progress and innovation in society as well as in education and schooling' (Terhart, 2016, p. 71, translated) was crucial for the overall academic conceptual underpinning of teacher education in Germany. It was also a main step in the status alignment of teacher education for primary and lower secondary teachers with that of *Gymnasium* teachers, which has always been academically oriented (for more details, see Terhart, 2016).

The explicit recourse to academic studies is reflected in ITE structures throughout Germany after the reform initiative too, although there is a tendency to connect these more intensely with practical learning phases.

Teacher trainees [5] for upper-secondary schools in the two-track system, for example, enrol in a three-year bachelor's course with two academic subjects of their choice, which correspond to their later teaching subjects. During their course, they acquire knowledge in these subjects, in subject-specific pedagogy (didactics) and general pedagogy. While the bachelor's programme is geared towards the acquisition of subject knowledge, the following two-year master's degree focuses on education and teaching-specific content, although students continue to study their chosen subjects in parallel. Both courses include practical teaching phases; some states have already introduced, or are currently in the process of doing so, an entire semester of practice. Following the successful completion of those study programmes, student teachers enter a programme of practical teaching (*Vorbereitungsdienst*) of 1.5 to 2 years, depending on the state. Here, they acquire practical teaching skills in their subjects under the supervision of a senior teacher (mentor) and take further school-based courses in general pedagogy and subject-specific pedagogy. This practical training ends with the 'second state examination', which awards the licence to teach. Similarly, primary teacher training comprises a three-year bachelor's course in German, mathematics and a third subject relevant for primary education (e.g. social studies, sports). Teacher trainees acquire knowledge in these subjects and in subject-specific pedagogy (didactics) and general pedagogy. Unlike ITE programmes for upper-secondary teachers, academic subject knowledge and subject-specific pedagogy are strongly interconnected and integrated. At the same time, the bachelor's programme has a more intense focus on education and teaching-specific content. The subsequent master's degree covers – depending on the state – one or up to two years of study and focuses on subject knowledge, subject-specific pedagogy and general pedagogy. In recent years, more and more states introduced the two-year master's degree. This has been linked to the introduction of a whole semester of practice in these programmes in different states. After successful completion of their academic programmes, primary teacher students enter a period of practical teaching (*Vorbereitungsdienst*) too, which again culminates in the 'second state examination'.

Alongside these new two-track structures, the design of the study programmes changed too, driven by the introduction of a credit point system based on the European Credit and Accreditation Transfer System (ECTS). Within the ECTS, student workload is seen as the central measure for both the award of credits (for a critical account, see Kuhlee, 2012) and the modularisation of programmes. Each module requires the description of the expected professional competences to be acquired, which should be defined by teacher education standards (see below). The modularisation of programmes led to a more structured examination system that increased the amount of performance tests and exams for students significantly.

With the introduction of this two-track modularised system in university-based ITE programmes, the German Academic Council (*Wissenschaftsrat*) explicitly recommended the application of specific didactic approaches and teaching methods to these programmes. The council particularly focused on the use of research-led learning, which indicated its intention to enhance the research orientation in teacher education (*Wissenschaftsrat*, 2001, e.g. pp. 41 & 68ff.). The aim is to enable future teachers to apply their theoretical knowledge to their professional action, to analyse and shape their professional area based on academically validated knowledge. A research-oriented approach is seen a key characteristic of a forward-looking teacher education (*Wissenschaftsrat*, 2001, p. 41).

Overall, the implementation both of the two-track modularised ITE programmes and of teacher education standards as discussed in the following reflect the growing interest in organising university-based ITE more according to the demands of the profession (e.g. Bauer et al, 2012, p. 104).

The Content of ITE:
the introduction of teacher education standards

The implementation of teacher education standards came in the wake of more extensive school reforms of the early 2000s. The 'PISA-shock' (e.g. Gruber, 2006), triggered by the poor performance of German students in the achievement tests, resulted in an intensive public debate on the performance of the German education system. Central to reform initiatives was a new strategy of school governance implemented by the KMK. It aimed at enhancing transparency of outcomes, leading, for example, to the introduction of standards, achievements tests, quality management and educational monitoring systems (Baumert & Füssel, 2012, p. 260).

The intensive discussion on the performance of students and the increasing criticisms of the quality of the education system eventually focused on the teaching profession and teacher education. This discussion was further fuelled by the 2003 OECD teacher study and its analysis of the deficiencies of German teacher education (Döbrich et al, 2003; Halász et al, 2004; Oelkers, 2009). In its wake, teacher education became a focal point for educational policy making and for the improvement of the quality of the education system.

Surveys and experts' reports, especially from within academia, were used by political stakeholders to develop concepts and strategies. Terhart (2014, p. 303, translated) noticed: 'We never had so much advice on teacher education!' The *Bremer Erklärung* of the KMK (KMK, 2000), a statement on the teaching profession by ministers of cultural affairs and the teacher trade unions, and the report, 'Perspectives of Teacher Education in Germany' (Terhart, 2000), by the specifically established commission of academic and administrative experts in teacher education, proved to be especially influential (Terhart, 2014). A working group, established in 2003, eventually developed teacher education standards on general pedagogy and education (*Bildungswissenschaften*) as one main part in the ITE programmes, which were introduced in 2004 (KMK, 2004/2014). Subject-specific standards followed in 2008 (KMK 2008/2015, Oelkers, 2009). Traditionally, ITE curricula were exclusively regulated by each of the German states on their own, mainly by setting regulations regarding study programmes and examinations (Oelkers 2009, p. 16). Therefore, for the first time the KMK intervened in the teacher education curricula of German states.

The KMK resolution on teacher education standards on general pedagogy and education (*Bildungswissenschaften*) (KMK 2004/2014) described standards explicitly in terms of competences which are needed to fulfil the requirements of professional practice in German schools, and which have to be reached by student teachers in the university-based and school-based ITE parts. The KMK (2004/2014, p. 4, translated) indicates that the relation between the university-based and school-based parts of ITE has to be coordinated in a way 'that overall a systematic, cumulative development of professional expertise is realised'. General pedagogy, education and connected academic disciplines are seen as crucial for the development of expertise in the professional field 'school'. This holds true despite the fact that teaching and educating in schools take place in subject-specific contents (KMK, 2004/2014, p. 4).

Key curricular areas in general pedagogy and education are: education in institutional processes; teaching as a profession and the role of teachers; didactic approaches and methodology of teaching; learning processes, child development and sociology; learning and performance motivation; heterogeneity, diversity, integration and individual support; diagnostics, assessment and guidance; communication; media literacy; school development and educational research (KMK, 2004/2014, p. 5).

Taking this curricular context into account, four areas of competence – 'Teaching', 'Educating', 'Assessing' and 'Innovating' – are differentiated and broken down into eleven key competences. For each key competence, detailed standards are assigned for each of the two ITE components. The standards therefore only reflect key areas for each ITE part; they do not have to be understood as being delimiting (KMK, 2004/2014, p. 7).

For example, key competence [6] 10 in the area 'Innovating' is defined as: 'Teachers understand their profession as a mission of continuing learning' (KMK, 2004/2014, p. 13, translated). Expected standards for both parts of ITE training are described as shown in Table I (KMK, 2004/2014, p. 13, translated).

Standards for the university-based training part	Standards for the practical training part
Graduates ...	Graduates ...
– know methods of internal and external evaluation in context of school development and quality assurance – receive and evaluate findings of educational research – know the organisational conditions of schools and the structures of cooperation within schools and their environment – reflect the professional requirements regarding the handling of diversity and heterogeneity	– reflect their professional attitudes, experiences and competences and their developments. They reach conclusions based on that and adapt their approaches respectively – use results of educational research for their own professional approaches – document their work and its results – give feedback and use the feedback of others to optimise their work – participate in the broader professional and school community – know and use systems of support for teachers – use different opportunities for further and continuing training

Table I. KMK teacher education standards on general pedagogy and education, key competence 10 in the area 'Innovating' (KMK, 2004/2014, p. 13, translated).

The KMK interprets teacher education standards as the definition of main targets in teacher education. It therefore sees the opportunity for a systematic evaluation of the achievement of targets. With the approval of standards, the German states agreed not only to implement but also to evaluate their teacher education programmes along defined standards (KMK, 2004/2014, p. 2).

These reform initiatives on standards reflect an understanding of teaching as a professional-technician occupation in our classification, where practice is informed by research evidence. Germany recognises the craft element in teaching, but as described above, this is integrated into the overall professional-technician schema.

Although the KMK stated that these standards were introduced by the states in the training year 2005/06 (KMK, 2016; also Terhart, 2014), the question arises of whether they were reflected in the study and course programmes, and in the individual teaching and learning processes. Empirical evidence for this is hard to find. The few empirical studies on the reproduction of the standards in ITE study and course programmes indicate the following (Terhart et al, 2010; Hohenstein et al, 2014): curricular design in university-based ITE shows considerable differences between different universities and states. Ten years after the introduction of the standards, the adaption of the course curricula is still not (fully) implemented. Hohenstein et al (2014, p. 505) summarise: 'A consistent base of knowledge or comparable competences at the end of university-based ITE cannot be assumed.' Terhart (2014, pp. 311-313) identifies, however, a somewhat better degree of implementation in the school-based ITE part. Therefore, the curricular design of the ITE programmes in different universities and states seems to be still rather fragmented.

Governance of ITE in Germany

This implementation issue leads to the matter of governance in German teacher education, which has to be taken into account to understand teacher education in its current form. This indicates another highly relevant difference from ITE in England. It is not only the teaching profession that seems to be differently understood in the two countries, with consequences for the ITE programme design – there are also significant differences in the governance of teacher education. As has been indicated, the introduction of teacher education standards in Germany did not lead to a technocratic and fundamental revision of the system. Institutions and stakeholders interpreted guidelines in a rather idiosyncratic manner, adapted them to their own practice, or managed to circumvent them. Thus, reform in the German education system and, hence, in teacher education has to be seen as a process of cultural change influenced by different factors where the introduction of standards is only one aspect. It is an incremental change by innovation rather than a technocratic revision (Terhart, 2014, p. 304). Two characteristics of the teacher education reforms and of governing in the education system are central to this. First, the recent educational reforms are generally not linked to a rigid system of incentives to generate some form of 'coercive compliance' (Wilkins, 2015, p. 225) by stakeholders, such as universities as ITE providers. Unlike in England, in cases of non-compliance stakeholders in Germany are so far not confronted with profound consequences such as the loss of the licence to offer ITE or of the financial support by the state government for their ITE programmes. Universities seem to consider the political recommendations on the content of their programmes less intensely than, for example, English ITE providers do. And they orient their ITE programmes more strongly in alignment with their individual perspectives and academic judgement. Second, the specific institutional structure regarding political decision-making in education is crucial for the enforcement of educational reforms. The individual responsibility of the states for education and the consensual-oriented negotiation process of the KMK regarding joint characteristics of the 16 German educational systems seem to work against one-sided party political reforms and rigorous structural changes in teacher education. Unlike the situation in the Westminster system, this hinders the implementation of fast and profound structural changes in the German system (Kuhlee et al, 2015).

This specific cultural embeddedness and the institutional characteristics of the education system lead overall to the result that even under the current reform enthusiasm, notably influenced by the so-called Global Educational Reform Movement (GERM) (see Sahlberg, 2012), the professional concept of teaching remains the central feature of teaching and teacher training in Germany, with its central path into teaching via university studies.

Joint Summary: does the German teaching profession have a better claim to be a research-led profession than the envisaged English one?

What conclusions can we draw from this brief comparison of recent developments of teacher education in England and Germany? England has historically exhibited a preference for a craft-based conception of the teacher, which became increasingly significant in government policy from the 1980s onwards. This has to be somewhat qualified, as we have seen at various times a partial emergence of the executive-technician model as well as at least some gestures towards a research-informed, professional conception of teaching, in particular in some of the most recent government documents (e.g. DfE, 2016). It remains to be seen whether these prove to be anything more than gestures, however, within the overall architecture of reform proposed in *Educational Excellence Everywhere*, which placed multi-academy trusts firmly in the driving seat of teacher education. The dominant conception of the teacher as a craftworker has been reinforced both by a long-standing cultural suspicion of theory and by an increasingly centralised and non-consensual approach to teacher education policy.

By contrast, Germany, in alignment with its own cultural dispositions, has been more sympathetic to an approach to professional formation that emphasises the relevance of theory and its application to practice. Like England, Germany has not been immune to performance anxiety in relation to international comparative studies of educational performance. As in England, this has resulted in political pressure on the education system and increased scrutiny of teacher education, albeit in the context of a federal, somewhat loosely coupled national education system. However, the work of the KMK has, if anything, reinforced and systematised the professional conception of education while at the same time (as in England) encouraging universities to work more closely with schools in the professional formation of teachers (e.g. KMK, 2005). German universities, unlike English ones, seem to have considerable scope for interpreting and implementing these initiatives in their own preferred ways. In Germany, therefore, the professional conception of teaching remains dominant while in England the craftworker conception, if it has not won the intellectual battle, looks as if it has won the political battle for the time being.

Notes

[1] In English, to call a white-collar worker a 'technician' is disparaging; we use the term to indicate someone who employs a body of theoretical knowledge within their practice (see Freidson, 1986). There is thus a divergence between the sociological understanding of the term and its everyday use in English.

[2] The *locus classicus* is Adam Smith's (1776 [1981]) discussion of what he misleadingly calls the 'division of labour' – in reality the progressive fragmentation of the labour process (Williams, 2000). For other educational examples, see Mackay, 2006; Miskin & Archbold, 2007.

[3] See note 1 above. The 'professional technician' is someone who can apply theoretical knowledge to their professional judgement and practice, in contrast to the 'executive technician'.

[4] The responsibility for cultural affairs and, hence, education lies in the Federal Republic of Germany with the individual states (Article 30 and Article 70ff. of the German Basic Law, *Kulturföderalismus*). Therefore there exist in Germany 16 educational systems. The KMK is an institution to ensure certain coherence between the different states in terms of structure, design and content of the educational systems. Here, the different states negotiate and agree on education policy and reform initiatives based on the principle of consensus.

[5] The following descriptions focus on those states that have introduced the two-track structure.

[6] In Germany, competences are seen as overarching capacities rather than as behaviourally based skills, although their components can be analysed, as in Table I.

References

Bauer, J., Dierecks, U., Rösler, L. Möller, J. & Prenzel, M. (2012) Lehramtsstudium in Deutschland: Wie groß ist die strukturelle Vielfalt?, *Unterrichtswissenschaft*, 40(2), 101-120.

Bauer, K.-O. (1998) Pädagogisches Handlungsrepertoire und professionalles Selbst von Lehrerinnen und Lehrern, *Zeitschrift für Pädagogik*, 44(3), 343-359.

Baumert, J. & Füssel, H.-P. (2012) § 62 Kooperation im föderalen Bildungssystem – zwischen Wettbewerb und Qualitätssicherung, in Härtel, I. (Ed.) *Handbuch Föderalismus – Föderalismus als demokratische Rechtsordnung in Deutschland, Europa und der Welt*, pp. 247-273. Berlin: Springer.

Baumert, J. & Kunter, M. (2006) Stichwort: Professionelle Kompetenz von Lehrkräften, *Zeitschrift für Erziehungswissenschaften*, 9(4), 469-520. https://doi.org/10.1007/s11618-006-0165-2

Bonnet, A. & Hericks, U. (2014) Professionalisierung und Deprofessionalisierung im Lehrer/innenberuf. Ansätze und Befunde aktueller empirischer Forschung, *Zeitschrift für Interpretative Schul- und Unterrichtsforschung*, 3(1), 3-8.

Bromme, R. (2014) *Der Lehrer als Experte. Zur Psychologie des professionellen Wissens.* Münster: Waxmann.

Department for Education (DfE) (2010) *The Importance of Teaching*. London: HMSO.

Department for Education (DfE) (2015) *The Carter Review of Initial Teacher Training*. London: HMSO.

Department for Education (DfE) (2016) *Educational Excellence Everywhere*. London: HMSO.

Döbrich, P., Klemm, K., Knauss, G. & Lange, H. (2003) Ausbildung, Einstellung und Förderung von Lehrerinnen und Lehrern (OECD-Lehrerstudie). Ergänzende Hinweise zu dem Nationalen Hintergrundbericht (CBR) für die Bundesrepublik Deutschland. https://www.oecd.org/edu/school/suplement.pdf (accessed on 1 June 2016).

Donaldson, G. (2010) *Teaching Scotland's Future: report of a review of teacher education in Scotland*. Edinburgh: Scottish Government.

Etzioni, A. (Ed.) (1969) *The Semi-Professions and their Organization: teachers, nurses and social workers*. London: Collier Macmillan.

Freidson, E. (1986) *Professional Powers: a study of the institutionalization of formal knowledge*. Chicago: University of Chicago Press.

General Teaching Council for Scotland (2012) The Standards for Registration: mandatory requirements for registration with the General Teaching Council for Scotland. Edinburgh: General Teaching Council for Scotland.

Gove, M. (2010) Address to the National College Annual Conference, Birmingham. https://www.gov.uk/government/speeches/michael-gove-to-the-national-college-annual-conference-birmingham (accessed on 6 June 2016).

Gruber, K.-H. (2006) The German 'PISA-shock': some aspects of the extraordinary impact of the OECD's PISA study on the German education system, in H. Ertl (Ed.) *Cross-national Attraction in Education: accounts from England and Germany*, pp. 195-208. Oxford: Symposium Books. https://dx.doi.org/10.15730/books.21

Halász, G., Santiago, P., Ekholm, M., Matthews, P. & McKenzie, P. (2004) *Attracting, Developing and Retaining Effective Teachers. Country Note: Germany*. Paris: OECD.

Helsper, W. (2004) Antinomien, Widersprüche, Paradoxien: Lehrerarbeit – ein unmögliches Geschäft? Eine strukturtheoretisch-rekonstruktive Perspektive auf das Lehrerhandeln, in B. Koch-Priewe, F.-U. Kolbe & J. Wildt (Eds) Grundlagenforschung und mikrodidaktische Reformansätze zur Lehrerbildung, pp.49-98. Bad Heilbrunn: Klinkhardt Verlag.

Helsper, W. & Tippelt, R. (2011) Ende der Profession und Professionalisierung ohne Ende? Zwischenbilanz einer unabgeschlossenen Diskussion, in W. Helsper & R. Tippelt (Eds) *Pädagogische Professionalität, Zeitschrift für Pädagogik*, Supplement 57, 268-288. Weinheim: Beltz.

HMSO (2013) Teachers' Standards. https://www.gov.uk/government/uploads/system/uploads/attachment_data/file/301107/Teachers__Standards.pdf (accessed 6 June 2016).

Hohenstein, F., Zimmermann, F., Kleickmann, T., Köller, O. & Möller, J. (2014) Sind die bildungswissenschaftlichen Standards für die Lehramtsausbildung in den Curricula der Hochschulen angekommen? *Zeitschrift für*

Erziehungswissenschaften, 17(3), 497-507.
https://doi.org/10.1007/s11618-014-0563-9

Hoyle, E. (1974) Professionality, Professionalism and Control in Teaching, London Education Review, 3(2), 15-17.

Keuffer, J. (2010) Reform der Lehrerbildung und kein Ende? Eine Standortbestimmung, Erziehungswissenschaft, 21(40), 51-67.

Krauss, S. & Bruckmaier, G. (2014) Das Experten-Paradigma in der Forschung zum Lehrerberuf, in E. Terhart, H. Bennewitz & M. Rothland (Eds) Handbuch zur Forschung zum Lehrerberuf, pp. 241-261. Münster: Waxmann.

Kuhlee, D. (2012) Brauchen wir eine Workload-Diskussion? Zur Rolle formaler Studienworkloads für das Lern- und Studierhandeln. Eine empirische Studie bei Lehramtsstudierenden des Master of Education, Das Hochschulwesen, 60(4), 79-87.

Kuhlee, D. (2017) Lehrerbildung in England und Deutschland – vergleichende Betrachtungen zu Reformen neoliberaler Provenienz in der Lehrerbildung und deren Effekte, in C. Allemann-Ghionda, G. Kula & L. Mignon (Eds) Diversität im europäischen Bildungssystem und in der LehrerInnenbildung in Europa. Frankfurt am Main: Lang.

Kuhlee, D., Buer, J. van & Winch, C. (2015) Zusammenfassende Einordnungen: Rechtsstruktur, Lehrprofession und Governance in der Lehrerbildung, in D. Kuhlee, J. van Buer & C. Winch (Eds) Governance in der Lehrerbildung: Analysen aus England und Deutschland, pp. 305-328. Wiesbaden: Springer.

Kultusministerkonferenz (KMK) (2000) Aufgaben von Lehrerinnen und Lehrern heute – Fachleute für das Lernen. Gemeinsame Erklärung des Präsidenten der Kultusministerkonferenz und der Vorsitzenden der Bildungs- und Lehrergewerkschaften sowie ihrer Spitzenorganisationen Deutscher Gewerkschaftsbund DGB und DBB – Beamtenbund und Tarifunion. http://www.kmk.org/fileadmin/Dateien/veroeffentlichungen_beschluesse/2000/20 00_10_05-Bremer-Erkl-Lehrerbildung.pdf (accessed on 1 June 2016).

Kultusministerkonferenz (KMK) (2004/2014) Standards für die Lehrerbildung: Bildungswissenschaften. http://www.akkreditierungsrat.de/fileadmin/Seiteninhalte/KMK/Vorgaben/KMK_ Lehrerbildung_Standards_Bildungswissenschaften_aktuell.pdf (accessed on 1 June 2016).

Kultusministerkonferenz (KMK) (2005) Eckpunkte für die gegenseitige Anerkennung von Bachelor- und Masterabschlüssen in Studiengängen, mit denen die Bildungsvoraussetzungen für ein Lehramt vermittelt werden. Beschluss vom 02.06.2005. http://www.kmk.org/fileadmin/Dateien/veroeffentlichungen_beschluesse/2005/20 05_06_02-gegenseitige-Anerkennung-Bachelor-Master.pdf (accessed on 1 June 2016).

Kultusministerkonferenz (KMK) (2008/2016) Ländergemeinsame inhaltliche Anforderungen für die Fachwissenschaften und Fachdidaktiken in der Lehrerbildung. http://www.kmk.org/fileadmin/Dateien/veroeffentlichungen_beschluesse/2008/20 08_10_16-Fachprofile-Lehrerbildung.pdf (accessed on 1 December 2016).

Kultusministerkonferenz (KMK) (2016) Lehrerbildung in den Ländern. https://www.kmk.org/themen/allgemeinbildende-schulen/lehrkraefte/lehrerbildung.html (accessed on 1 June 2016).

Lave, J. & Wenger, E. (1991) *Situated Learning: legitimate peripheral participation.* Cambridge: Cambridge University Press. https://doi.org/10.1017/CBO9780511815355

Lawlor, S. (1990) *Teachers Mistaught: training in theories or education in subjects?* London: Centre for Policy Studies.

Mackay, J. (2006) The West Dunbartonshire Literacy Initiative. West Dunbartonshire County Council.

Maeße, J. (2010) *Die vielen Stimmen des Bologna-Prozesses. Zur diskursiven Logik eines bildungspolitischen Programms.* Bielefeld: transcript.

Miskin, R. & Archbold, T. (2007) *Read Write Inc. Phonics: parent handbook – help your child read with phonics.* Oxford: Oxford University Press.

Nittel, D. (2004) Die 'Veralltäglichung' pädagogischen Wissens – im Horizont von Profession, Professionalisierung und Professionalität, *Zeitschrift für Pädagogik,* 50(3), 342-357.

Nittel, D. (2011) Von der Profession zur sozialen Welt pädagogisch Tätiger? Vorarbeiten zu einer komparativ angelegten Empirie pädagogischer Arbeit, in W. Helsper & R. Tippelt (Eds) *Pädagogische Professionalität, Zeitschrift für Pädagogik,* Supplement 57, 40-59. Weinheim: Beltz.

Oelkers, J. (2009) *I Wanted to be a Good Teacher…: Zur Ausbildung von Lehrkräften in Deutschland.* Berlin: Friedrich Ebert Stiftung.

Oevermann, U. (1996) Theoretische Skizze einer revidierten Theorie professionalisierten Handelns, in A. Combe & W. Helsper (Eds) *Pädagogische Professionalität. Untersuchungen zum Typus pädagogischen Handelns,* pp. 70-182. Frankfurt am Main: Suhrkamp.

O'Hear, A. (1988) *Who Teaches the Teachers?* London: Social Affairs Unit.

Orchard, J. & Winch, C. (2015) *What Kind of Training do Teachers Need?* London: Philosophy of Education Society of Great Britain.

Plato (1970) Meno, in B. Jowett, *The Dialogues of Plato.* London: Sphere Books.

Sahlberg, P. (2012) How GERM is Infecting Schools Around the World, 2012. http://www.washingtonpost.com/blogs/answer-sheet/post/how-germ-is-infecting-schools-around-the-world/2012/06/29/gJQAVELZAW_blog.html. (accessed on 1 June 2016.

Shulman, L. (1986) Those Who Understand: Knowledge Growth in Teaching, *Educational Researcher,* 15(4), 4-14. https://doi.org/10.3102/0013189X015002004

Smith, A. (1776/1981) *The Wealth of Nations.* Indianapolis: Liberty Fund.

Stichweh, R. (1996) Professionen in einer funktional differenzierten Gesellschaft, in A. Combe & W. Helsper (Eds) *Pädagogische Professionalität. Untersuchungen zum Typus pädagogischen Handelns,* pp. 49-69. Frankfurt am Main: Suhrkamp.

Sturt, G. (1923/1976) *The Wheelwright's Shop.* Cambridge: Cambridge University Press.

Tenorth, H.-E. (2004) Lehrerarbeit – Strukturprobleme und Wandel der Anforderungen, in U. Beckmann, H. Brandt & H. Wagner (Eds) *Ein neues Bild vom Lehrerberuf. Pädagogische Professionalität nach PISA*, pp. 14-25. Weinheim: Beltz.

Terhart, E. (2000) *Perspektiven der Lehrerbildung in Deutschland*. Weinheim: Beltz.

Terhart, E. (2002) *Standards für die Lehrerbildung. Eine Expertise für die Kultusministerkonferenz*. Münster: Institut für Schulpädagogik und Allgemeine Didaktik.

Terhart, E. (2011) Lehrerberuf und Professionalität: Gewandeltes Begriffsverständnis – neue Herausforderungen, in W. Helsper & R. Tippelt (Eds) *Pädagogische Professionalität, Zeitschrift für Pädagogik*, Supplement 57, 202-224. Weinheim: Beltz.

Terhart, E. (2014) Standards für die Lehrerbildung: Bildungswissenschaften – nach zehn Jahren, *Die Deutsche Schule*, 106(4), 300-323.

Terhart, E. (2016) Wandel der Schulstruktur – Wandel der Lehramtsstruktur: Langfristige Entwicklungsmuster und aktuelle Problemlagen, in T.-S. Idel, F. Dietrich, K. Kunze, K. Rabenstein & A. Schütz (Eds) *Professionsentwicklung und Schulstrukturreform. Zwischen Gymnasium und neue Schulformen in der Sekundarstufe*, pp. 64-79. Bad Heilbrunn: Klinkhart.

Terhart, E., Lohmann, V. & Seidel, V. (2010) Die bildungswissenschaftlichen Studien in der universitären Lehrerbildung. Eine Analyse aktueller Studienordnungen und Modulhandbücher an den Universitäten in Nordrhein-Westfalen. University of Münster: Institute of Education Science.

Williams, M. (2000) *Wealth without Nations*. London: Athol Books.

Wilkins, C. (2015) The Impact of the Inspectorate System on Initial Teacher Education in England, in D. Kuhlee, J. van Buer & C. Winch (Eds) *Governance in der Lehrerausbildung: Analysen aus England und Deutschland*, pp. 225-244. Springer: Wiesbaden.

Wissenschaftsrat (2001) Empfehlungen zur zukünftigen Struktur der Lehrerausbildung. Berlin.

CHAPTER 11

The Configuration of Teacher Education as a Professional Field of Practice: a comparative study of mathematics education

MARIA TERESA TATTO & JIM HORDERN

SUMMARY Using a comparative approach, the authors analyse the role of educational studies in the secondary teacher education curriculum in Germany, Poland, Singapore and the USA. The data come from an analysis of syllabi from cross-national representative samples of pre-service programmes. The analysis focused on the emphasis given by programmes to five domains typically considered as essential elements of teacher education: the knowledge of the discipline, the knowledge of the school curriculum for the discipline, the pedagogy of the discipline, the general pedagogy (or education studies), and the practicum. The discipline of interest in this case is mathematics because it has a relatively 'uniform' grammar across nations. Using Bernstein's sociology of knowledge, the authors discuss the differential emphases given to these domains within and across countries as an expression of the re-contextualisation of knowledge from singulars to regions – for instance how the educational foundation disciplines and elements of mathematical knowledge are recontextualised to address a particular problem of practice: how to prepare knowledgeable secondary teachers of mathematics. These results are considered in light of national and global accountability discourses that prioritise some 'knowledges' over others and the implications for the future of 'education(al)' studies.

Introduction

Views on the knowledge and expertise needed for teaching are varied. Some see a central role for the systematic disciplinary educational knowledge produced and iterated in higher education, on the grounds that future teachers require forms of conceptual knowledge upon which they can reliably

255

build their professional judgements. This is often coupled with the suggestion that teachers should be 'reflective professionals' capable of making their own autonomous judgements on claims to knowledge, suggesting models of teacher education that are concerned more extensively with foundational debates in educational studies, and with consideration of the contested 'purposes' of education (Winch, 2012; Winch et al, 2015). Importantly, Winch et al (2015) suggest that engagement with this systematic knowledge enhances teachers' technical and situated knowledge and capability, and thus supports the development of teaching expertise.

Putting aside the issue of whether education studies represents a coherent discipline (see, for example, McCulloch, 2002), the contrasting perspective is that teachers do not need to engage directly with this knowledge. This position would argue that curricula and associated materials can be developed that can reduce any potential 'human error' on the part of the teacher in conveying subject knowledge systematically to pupils (see Winch et al, 2015). 'Teacher-proof' teacher education for such future teachers can thus focus more on issues of curriculum implementation than on consideration of curriculum alternatives. The research that informs such teacher education may sit apart from the teaching community, disregarding the role of teacher as researcher. Instead, new 'expert' findings are translated into curricula and pedagogic 'scripts', 'technique' or 'routine' for teachers to follow and share within their learning communities (Cochran-Smith & Lytle, 1999, p. 266). Such a vision posits teaching as purely a narrow technical activity, in which individual discretion and judgement are to be minimised in favour of effective technical performance.

Sitting seemingly in opposition both to the 'reflective professional' and the 'technical' model of teaching outlined by Winch et al (2015) is the argument that forms of systematically organised knowledge are largely irrelevant for teachers, as expertise can only be acquired through participation in teaching practice, thus rendering systematically organised theory redundant (see Carr, 2006). For those who advocate such a position, knowledge for teaching is situated and embodied: one can learn from expert teachers, but primarily it is immersion in the practical activity of teaching which is important (where so-called expert teachers gained their knowledge is not a concern of this perspective).

The different perspectives on teacher knowledge and professionalism imply different institutional arrangements for the design and delivery of teacher education. If the teacher is seen as a 'reflective professional', in the terms of Winch et al (2015), and therefore requiring the capacity to make autonomous professional judgements based on research, then higher education institutions are likely to assume an important position. The development of teacher education programmes may still involve schools and government agencies, but forms of disciplinary-based educational knowledge will be central to the programme, and thus the involvement of higher education. If the teacher is seen narrowly as a 'technician' then government agencies and or employers may play a stronger role in specifying the content of teacher education. As well as reducing universities' role in preparing teachers, this may also significantly influence the nature of educational research and knowledge production (Stuart & Tatto, 2000; Furlong, 2013). Similarly, if teacher education foregrounds teaching as a 'craft' and teaching expertise is always seen as formed in practical action then schools and colleges – the educational institutions in which teaching practice takes place – are likely to assume particular importance, probably at the expense of the higher education institutions (Whitty, 2014).

In this chapter we use Bernstein's (1990, 2000) notion of recontextualisation to examine the mathematics teacher education curriculum and its relationship with institutional arrangements in a selection of countries. Bernstein discusses how a 'recontextualisation principle ... selectively appropriates, relocates, refocuses and relates' forms of discourse, including knowledge, 'to constitute its own order' (2000, p. 33). This encapsulates processes by which knowledge is selected and transformed between different contexts, from disciplinary knowledge to curriculum knowledge (Bernstein, 2000; Muller, 2009), and potentially from the 'intended' to the 'implemented' and 'received' curriculum via pedagogic processes (Evans et al, 2010; Hordern, 2014). Recontextualisation can be a highly contested process, occurring within 'recontextualisation fields' that can be both 'official' (i.e. the 'official recontextualisation field', or ORF) and 'pedagogic'(PRF) (Bernstein, 2000, p. 33). The ORF represents governments and their agencies, while the PRF represents teachers and educationalists. Debates around how teachers are best educated can be seen through the lens of the struggle between the ORF and the PRF. This struggle is accentuated if there is a significant divergence of opinion between the ORF and the PRF, and may be further complicated by differences between groupings within the PRF (e.g. between university-based teacher educators and those based in schools).

In our analysis we draw extensively on data collected as part of the TEDS-M study, a 'cross-national study of primary and secondary mathematics teacher education (TEDS-M) sponsored by the International Association for the Evaluation of Educational Achievement (IEA) and the US National Science Foundation' and which 'focuses on how teachers are prepared to teach mathematics in primary and lower secondary school' and on 'the variation in the nature and impact of teacher education programs within and across countries' (Tatto et al, 2008, p. 13).

The TEDS-M study is the first international and comparative study of the outcomes of mathematics teacher education carried out with representative national samples of preservice teacher education programmes and their future teachers in 17 countries, and involved assessing future teachers' knowledge as well as surveying course content. The study was carried out via the collaborative agreement of a range of recontextualisation agents seeking to answer together the question of teacher education effectiveness (much in the way Winch [2004, p. 191] suggests). In the TEDS-M study a range of these agents were invited to collaborate in the design and development of the study. This collaboration ultimately led to agreement on terms, such as the meaning of a programme, of a curriculum, of pedagogical content knowledge, and so on. Understanding the recontextualisation of national mandates for teacher education involved the study of the official K-12 curriculum in each country and the standards set by teacher education programmes.

For explanatory value we decided to focus for this chapter on four of the 17 countries, selecting those that have two types of secondary programmes (most other countries in the study have only one). One type of programme addresses the needs of teachers teaching the 'lower or middle' grades of secondary teaching, and the other addresses the needs of those who will teach the 'higher or upper' grades of secondary school. These include Germany, Poland, Singapore and the USA. The examination of these four countries and their dual programmes to prepare secondary teachers adds nuance to the exploration of what it means to teach secondary school mathematics and whether there is a unified conception of mathematics education for secondary teachers. Table I shows the number of participating programmes offering secondary teaching credentials in the sample, the number of future secondary teachers within countries participating in the study, and demographic information.

Country	Number of Participating Programmes Offering Preparation to Teach at the Secondary Level (National Sample)	Future Secondary Teachers Sample size/Valid n	Future Secondary Teachers Demographics Means (Standard Deviation)			
			SES	Age	Proportion Female	Prior Attainment*
Germany	28	771/620	.41 (.94)	28.98 (4.91)	0.62 (0.48)	3.32 (0.88)
Poland	35	298/247	-0.11 (.86)	23.13 (2.00)	0.81 (0.48)	3.28 (0.95)
Singapore	4[a]	393/371	-.55 (.79)	26.73 (4.00)	0.48 (0.50)	3.52 (0.95)
USA (public institutions only)	72	607/461	0.46 (0.84)	25.26 (6.45)	0.69 (0.28)	3.88 (1.00)

* 1=below average for year level; 5=always at top of year level.
[a] Census data.

Table I. Number of participating programmes offering secondary teaching credentials, future secondary teachers within countries, and demographics.
Source: Tatto, 2013, pp. 241-251.

Recontextualisation and the Comparative Analysis of Mathematics Teacher Education

Why Mathematics?

Mathematics is a useful subject to focus on for cross-country comparative studies because it has a relatively uniform grammar across countries – thus minimising one possible point of difference between national systems. Bernstein's (1999) work is useful here in distinguishing between different types of disciplinary knowledge structure.

Bernstein (1999) first differentiates between 'vertical discourse', described as 'coherent', 'explicit' and 'systematically principled', and 'horizontal discourse', which is 'local', 'context dependent and specific'. Essentially, vertical discourse is the specialised knowledge and practice of disciplines, while horizontal discourse is non-specialised and unregulated. Within vertical discourse there are 'hierarchical knowledge structures' that 'appear ... to be motivated towards greater and greater integrating propositions' (e.g. the physical sciences) and 'horizontal knowledge structures' that are characterised by 'specialised languages' that each produce distinctive perspectives on a particular disciplinary problematic (e.g. sociology, philosophy) (Bernstein, 1999, p. 162). Horizontal knowledge structures can, in turn, be differentiated from each other by the strength of their 'grammar', meaning the extent to which they can provide 'an explicit conceptual syntax capable of relatively precise empirical descriptions' (Bernstein, 1999, p. 164). Mathematics is described as a horizontal knowledge structure with one of the strongest grammars, consisting of a set of discrete languages, for particular problems that generally do not have empirical referents, nor are they designed to satisfy empirical criteria (Bernstein, 1999, p. 164).

As per Shulman's (1987) typology, in (mathematics) teacher education programmes we can differentiate between (mathematical) content knowledge ([M]CK) and general pedagogical knowledge (GPK). MCK is selected from the mathematics discipline, but may be ordered, sequenced and categorised in particular ways in the curriculum. For GPK, knowledge may be recontextualised from 'pure' disciplines, or 'singulars' (Bernstein, 2000), such as philosophy, sociology or psychology, to form a set of education 'fundamentals' or 'foundations' that may be considered important for future teachers – that which we often define as the 'education studies' component of teacher education. This knowledge may be selected specifically for the insights it provides into the nature of education, or it may be selected because it is thought useful in illuminating some aspects of educational practice. This GPK may then serve to shape what is considered as pedagogical content knowledge (PCK) in that (subject) curriculum context. Mathematics pedagogical content knowledge (MPCK) involves multiple forms of knowledge recontextualisation, including knowledge of the discipline, the curriculum and instruction, and of students' thinking. In the TEDS-M study the MPCK assessment framework included three sub-domains with sub-themes that illustrate the complexity of learning to teach mathematics and the key role of teacher education in this process (Tatto et al, 2012, p. 131): *mathematics curricular knowledge* (e.g. knowing the school mathematics curriculum; establishing appropriate learning goals; identifying key ideas in learning programmes; selecting possible pathways and seeing connections within the curriculum; knowing different assessment formats and purposes); *knowledge for planning for mathematics teaching and learning* (e.g. selecting appropriate activities; predicting typical students' responses, including misconceptions; planning appropriate methods for representing mathematical ideas; linking didactic methods and instructional designs; identifying different approaches for solving mathematical problems; choosing assessment formats and items); and *enacting mathematics for teaching and learning* (e.g. explaining or representing mathematical concepts or procedures; generating fruitful questions; diagnosing students' responses, including misconceptions; analysing or evaluating students' mathematical solutions or arguments; analysing the content of students' questions; responding to unexpected mathematical issues; providing appropriate feedback). Thus, future mathematics teachers must not only have a high level of mathematics knowledge but should be able to recontextualise it in a way that responds to curricular demands and to students' learning needs.

As an aside, there may be some notable distinctions here between primary generalist teachers and secondary 'specialists' – with the identities of this latter group as teachers being particularly bound up with the subjects they teach (Hordern, 2015). While the distinction between these teacher types is by no means pertinent to every education system, it is influential across many countries (Le Métais, 2003; Zulijan & Vogrinc, 2011). While a generalist teacher is likely to rely substantially on the nature of the educational knowledge relayed in their teacher education, a specialist teacher is shaped both by discourse of the subject they teach and by the aforementioned educational knowledge (Hordern, 2015), and indeed by how these are effectively combined in teacher education.

The very strong grammar of mathematics leads to considerable agreement around the forms of the mathematics discipline across countries, as can be seen by the TEDS-M study. Thus, participants in the study were able to arrive at agreed definitions of what constituted (mathematics) content knowledge and, to a great extent, (mathematics) pedagogical content knowledge (Tatto et al, 2008). The structure of mathematical knowledge, in terms of what is considered important for the mathematics curriculum, is a reflection of mathematical universality.

This does not necessary imply, however, that there is cross-national agreement on how mathematics should be taught or how mathematics teachers should be educated. For this there is more substantive variation. As outlined, the configuration of recontextualisation agents varies by country and can involve governments, universities, other teacher education institutions, schools, as well as teacher educators in a complex and contested dynamic over the teacher education curriculum. The TEDS-M researchers also explored additional layers of pedagogical recontextualisation that occurred as future teachers 'received' their preparation and applied that learning. In this chapter, however, we will predominantly concentrate on a comparative analysis of the structure of the teacher education syllabi, and the recontextualisation relationship between the mathematics curriculum standards and these syllabi. Figure 1 shows the process of recontextualisation assumed by the study.

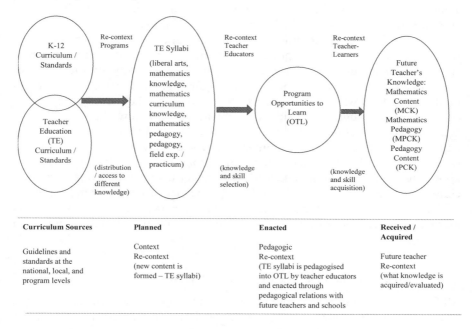

Figure 1. Recontextualisation of the teacher education secondary curriculum for secondary teachers in TEDS-M as a case of the configuration of teacher education as a professional field of practice.

Analysis of the Official School Curriculum and Standards

The preparation of new mathematics secondary teachers is deeply influenced (if not regulated) by the construction of the school curriculum. Thus, before describing the results of the teacher education syllabi analysis, it is important to take a look at how these different countries have fashioned their secondary curriculum. The school curriculum and standards-in-use at the time of the study were analysed according to the framework for the mathematics content knowledge domains including number, geometry, algebra and data, constituting all together 65 sub-topics (Tatto et al, 2012, p. 130).

The topics that receive most attention across countries and grade levels are numbers and fractions, followed by geometry. There is alignment across the four countries in the coverage of 'number and operations' topics (such as percentages, exponents, roots, and radicals, estimating computations, mental arithmetic and reasoning); 'geometry and measurement' topics (such as measurement, computations and properties of length, perimeter, area and volume; 1-D and 2-D coordinate geometry; topics of axiomatic geometry, including angles, parallelism, triangles and polygons; and circles and 3-D geometric figures); and 'data and chance' topics (such as representation and analysis – including statistics – and uncertainty and probability). Less emphasis was found in the 'algebra and functions' topics.

In theory, the strong grammar of mathematics as a discipline could be seen to suggest not only the potential for uniformity of curriculum structure across national contexts, but also a potential uniformity of mathematics teacher education programmes. The requirement for specific forms of mathematical knowledge to demonstrate a level of mathematical competence could therefore suggest considerable constraints on how the 'professional competence' of mathematics teachers is conceived. This could be contrasted with subjects with 'weaker grammars' (e.g. sociology and cultural studies) (see Bernstein, 1999), where fewer limitations on what counts as subject knowledge might be thought to lead to a greater diversity in terms of teacher competence. However, as indicated, and as is clear from the data presented in Tables II to VI, there remains some substantive variation in how mathematics teacher education programmes are constructed across and even within nations.

Analysis of the Teacher Education Syllabi

All TEDS-M countries that completed the syllabi analysis tasks undertook a census of the syllabi for required and relevant elective courses in the areas of academic mathematics, mathematics, pedagogy, general pedagogy, and the field experience and practicum in all teacher education institutions that participated in the TEDS-M sample. The syllabi analysis resulted in counts of the different topics covered in the areas addressed in teacher education programmes. Tables II to VI show the percentage of programmes that cover a topic across the programmes for lower- and upper-secondary mathematics. (Please note that the numbers 5 and 6 next to each country assignation correspond to programmes that prepare future teachers to teach 'middle grades' and 'upper grades' of secondary school, respectively.)

Mathematics Topics

In Tables II and III, Singapore programmes stand out in that they do not cover any of the mathematics or school mathematics topics; in other countries the same topics receive various degrees of attention. This is because the Singapore programmes are offered at the postgraduate level and programme selection standards require mathematics degrees or qualifications. Thus, strong knowledge of mathematics is assumed (the same applies for Germany). In the other countries, as far as mathematics is concerned, and in accordance with the emphasis we observed when we examined the school curriculum standards, a large majority of the programmes cover axiomatic geometry, which, as we saw, is one of the topics that has strong alignment across the school curriculum in all countries. The same can be said of analytic geometry, and to a lesser degree – and only among those preparing to teach upper-level secondary grades – linear algebra, calculus and probability. Other topics receiving attention mostly in Poland are functional analysis, discrete mathematics and mathematical logic.

Mathematics	GER		POL		SGP		USA	
	DEU5	DEU6	POL5	POL6	SGP5	SGP6	USA5	USA6
	$n = 22$	$n = 16$	$n = 20$	$n = 31$	$n = 2$	$n = 2$	$n = 19$	$n = 59$
Axiomatic geometry (including Euclidean axioms)	76	36	70	84	0	0	37	54
Analytic/coordinate geometry	41	64	95	95	0	0	47	54
Non-Euclidean geometry (e.g. geometry on a sphere)	0	9	40	53	0	0	37	44
Differential geometry	0	9	25	47	0	0	5	5
Topology	0	9	85	89	0	0	0	3
Linear algebra	65	91	100	95	0	0	37	78
Set theory	18	18	80	74	0	0	21	12
Abstract algebra (e.g. group theory, field theory, ring theory, ideals)	6	64	100	89	0	0	16	69
Number theory	65	45	70	89	0	0	37	51
Beginning calculus topics (e.g. limits, series, sequences)	47	73	95	79	0	0	42	76
Calculus (e.g., derivatives and integrals)	53	91	95	89	0	0	47	81
Multivariate calculus (e.g. partial derivatives, multiple integrals)	0	45	90	84	0	0	16	69
Advanced calculus or real analysis or measure theory	0	27	60	89	0	0	0	36
Differential equations	6	64	65	89	0	0	5	34
Functional analysis, theory of complex functions	0	9	40	100	0	0	16	37
Discrete mathematics, graph theory, game theory, combinatorics	18	9	65	79	0	0	42	58
Probability	29	45	85	100	0	0	58	75
Theoretical or applied statistics	29	45	60	68	0	0	53	69
Mathematical logic	12	9	95	89	0	0	32	47
Other mathematics topics	18	9	75	89	0	0	47	66

Table II. Percentage of teacher education institutions that cover mathematics topics in each country according to the TEDS-M analysis of the teacher education syllabi.

Singapore also stands out in the extent to which programmes are standardised. This suggests limited discretion for teacher educators as recontextualisation agents in comparison with the other national contexts, where institutions and teacher educators are able to have greater control over the syllabus, albeit often within parameters. The standardised model in Singapore suggests a central authority with a specific vision of the relationship between mathematical knowledge and mathematical pedagogy, reflecting reforms started 20 years ago in that country (Hogan & Gopinathan, 2008). In such a model future teachers are required to have strong mathematical competence as a prerequisite for teacher education programmes, but there may be difficulties in bridging the gap between an initial qualification in mathematics and the teaching qualification if there is minimal attention to how mathematical knowledge is presented in the curriculum. The Singaporean model could be seen to imply that mathematical pedagogy and school experience/practicum are considered very important, and that the relationship between 'pure' mathematical knowledge and mathematics in the curriculum is unproblematic. Attention is focused on the pedagogisation of mathematics rather than on its recontextualisation into a curriculum. Such a pattern may also be commonplace in consecutive models of teacher education.

School Mathematics	GER*		POL		SGP		USA	
	DEU5	DEU6	POL5	POL6	SGP5	SGP6	USA5	USA6
	$n = 22$	$n = 16$	$n = 20$	$n = 31$	$n = 2$	$n = 2$	$n = 19$	$n = 59$
Whole numbers	29	0	20	26	0	0	42	10
Fractions & decimals	29	0	15	26	0	0	47	15
Integer, rational & real numbers	29	0	30	32	0	0	42	19
Other numbers & number concepts & number theory	29	0	25	26	0	0	32	20
Estimation & number sense concepts	29	0	10	21	0	0	32	12
Ratio and proportionality	29	0	0	11	0	0	37	5
Measurement units	29	0	5	0	0	0	16	3
Computations & properties of length, perimeter, area & volume	29	0	0	0	0	0	0	0
Estimation & error in measurement	29	0	5	5	0	0	16	8
1-D & 2-D coordinate geometry	29	0	35	42	0	0	16	8
Euclidean geometry	29	0	55	47	0	0	32	22
Transformational geometry	29	0	50	42	0	0	37	19
Congruence and similarity	29	0	30	32	0	0	32	19
Constructions with straightedge and compass	29	0	40	32	0	0	32	15
3-D geometry	29	0	40	42	0	0	32	8
Vector geometry	29	0	20	26	0	0	5	5
Simple topology	29	0	15	0	0	0	0	0
Patterns, relations & functions	29	0	15	0	0	0	26	17
Equations & formulas	29	0	10	0	0	0	21	10
Trigonometry & analytic geometry	29	0	55	68	0	0	16	20
Data representation & analysis	29	0	15	26	0	0	32	20
Uncertainty & probability	29	0	30	37	0	0	53	29
Elementary analysis	29	0	15	32	0	0	16	19
Validation & structure	29	0	40	42	0	0	11	20
Other school mathematics topics	29	0	20	21	0	0	16	14

*In Germany, 'school mathematics' is considered with the 'mathematics' domain. This is because the institutions are from the second phase of the consecutive route. For purposes of comparison we include it here.

Table III. Percentage of teacher education institutions that cover school mathematics topics in each country according to the TEDS-M analysis of the teacher education syllabi.

By contrast, in the other countries studied, forms of mathematical knowledge or 'school mathematics' are a constituent element of the teacher education programmes, signifying a differentiation between mathematics as 'pure' knowledge and mathematics in its curriculum form, and acknowledging the importance of including this in a teacher education programme. As far as the mathematics of the school curriculum is concerned, given that these are programmes that are preparing secondary teachers, a lower proportion of programmes cover basic mathematics topics and a larger proportion cover more complex topics such as geometry. The exception is the USA, where almost 50% of the programmes cover basic topics of the mathematics school curriculum, such as fractions and decimals, and numbers.

Mathematics Pedagogical Content Knowledge and General Pedagogy Topics

With regard to mathematics pedagogical content knowledge, the coverage of the teacher education programmes looks quite different. There is full coverage in Singapore for most topics, with the exception of discussion of affective issues, instructional materials, the context of mathematics education, and the development of mathematical ability. In other countries the provision seems to concentrate on such areas as mathematics instruction, developing mathematics teaching plans, analysing/observing/reflecting on mathematics teaching, and methods of presenting mathematics concepts. In Poland and the USA there is also reasonably widespread coverage of the context of mathematics education and the selection of instructional materials, suggesting a broad conception of the role of the mathematics teacher (see Table IV).

In the area of 'general pedagogy' (which also includes such topics as history, psychology, philosophy and sociology) (see Table V), all countries saw the majority of topics as important, with the exception of research methods, and counselling and pastoral care. Singaporean programmes appear very comprehensive in general pedagogic areas, but educational research and counselling are absent. This could reflect a very strong version of the technician model (Winch et al, 2015) in which teacher innovation and teachers' pastoral roles are marginal. Teachers are therefore perhaps not seen themselves as recontextualisers of knowledge, but rather as highly skilled subject specialists who are involved in implementing a national mandated curriculum in the context of a tightly controlled uniform programme of teacher education. Professional competence is, in effect, not in the hands of teachers or teacher educators to shape, but rather is driven by a centrally established norm.

In Poland, general pedagogy seems relatively weak in the more technical aspects of teaching (e.g. classroom management, instructional media) and also in some disciplines (history, psychology), while retaining a widespread commitment to covering philosophy of education.

German teacher education programmes have a relatively limited coverage of philosophy, and educational research methods are marginal, but there is more on psychology and 'theories of schools'. On this it is worth bearing in mind long-standing traditions of educational theory and pedagogy in Germany, and the 'distinctive style of philosophical and hermeneutic reasoning' (Schriewer & Keiner, 1992, p. 29) that continues as a dominant strand in German educational thought (Ertl et al, 2015). This tradition may obviate the separate identification of 'philosophy of education' in syllabi, as philosophical and theoretical tenets may be highly absorbed within other key parts of the syllabi. This in particular may feed into what are termed in the survey 'Principles of Instruction' and 'Practical Knowledge of Teaching' (the latter has 100% coverage in German teacher education). Across many of the German teacher education programmes there is also a strong commitment to including coverage of counselling and to the more pastoral dimensions of the teaching role. This may reflect the persistence of more 'social pedagogic' notions in the German context, conceptualising the teacher role beyond that of 'subject specialist', 'highly skilled technician' or 'instructor'.

The US programmes seem to be the most comprehensive, with notably high levels of coverage of educational psychology, sociology of education and theories of schools. However, there is limited coverage of counselling and pastoral care.

Mathematics Pedagogy	GER		POL		SGP		USA	
	DEU5 $n = 22$	DEU6 $n = 16$	POL5 $n = 20$	POL6 $n = 31$	SGP5 $n = 2$	SGP6 $n = 2$	USA5 $n = 19$	USA6 $n = 59$
Theories/models of mathematics ability and thinking	24	36	40	16	100	100	21	8
Nature and development of mathematics ability and thinking	24	27	40	21	0	0	37	27
Aspects of mathematical ability and thinking	41	45	70	68	100	100	68	64
Mathematical problems and solutions	29	45	55	58	100	100	74	61
Mathematics instruction	88	91	95	68	100	100	84	78
Developing of mathematics teaching plans	88	100	85	89	100	100	58	56
Analysing/observing/reflecting on mathematics teaching	88	100	65	89	100	100	53	54
Knowledge of mathematics standards and curriculum	29	36	85	63	100	100	63	69
Studying and selecting textbooks and instructional materials	18	27	85	63	0	0	42	19
Methods of presenting main mathematics concepts	47	73	55	53	100	100	79	53
Foundations of mathematics	18	18	70	58	0	0	32	61
Context of mathematics education	18	18	55	26	0	0	47	36
Affective issues (beliefs, attitudes, anxiety, etc.)	0	9	50	37	0	0	5	8

Table IV. Percentage of teacher education institutions that cover mathematics pedagogy topics in each country according to the TEDS-M analysis of the teacher education syllabi.

In terms of differences within (as opposed to between) countries in the sample, the relative diversity of teacher education programmes in Germany and Poland in particular suggests a strong role for teacher education institutions in recontextualising knowledge, certainly for the general pedagogy element of the curriculum. Norms of 'general pedagogy' are, in those contexts, inflected by the preferences and expertise of those involved in teacher education, and also therefore may provide a greater degree of choice and opportunity to future teachers, but also less consistency in terms of teacher knowledge.

General Pedagogy	GER		POL		SGP		USA	
	DEU5 $n = 22$	DEU6 $n = 16$	POL5 $n = 20$	POL6 $n = 31$	SGP5 $n = 2$	SGP6 $n = 2$	USA5 $n = 19$	USA6 $n = 59$
History of education and ed. systems	47	55	35	21	100	100	74	69
Educational psychology	71	91	50	26	100	100	100	90
Philosophy of education	12	27	80	58	100	100	74	78
Sociology of education	53	64	65	58	100	100	100	93
Intro. to education /theories of schools	71	82	80	47	100	100	95	93
Principles of instruction	94	91	90	89	100	100	95	86
Methods of educational research	18	0	35	16	0	0	32	42
Classroom management	53	45	35	21	100	100	95	85
Assessment and measurement theory	65	64	55	63	100	100	63	58
Counselling, advising, and pastoral care	71	55	0	0	0	0	16	12
Instructional media and operation	88	64	50	47	100	100	74	81
Practical knowledge of teaching	100	100	80	74	100	100	100	92

Table V. Percentage of teacher education institutions that cover general pedagogy topics in each country according to the TEDS-M analysis of the teacher education syllabi.

Field Experience and Practicum Topics

In terms of the emphasis placed across countries and programmes on connecting theory with practice, the diversity found in our analysis is somewhat surprising (see Table VI). The school or practicum experience is constituted by a wide array of experiences, not all internally coherent. Yet most of the topics are covered in programmes in Poland, Singapore and the USA, with the exception of experiences such as 'serving as teachers', 'attending conferences', 'engaging in research projects', and being involved with the community through, for example, 'organising social activities and working with parents'. Singapore in particular is notable for the complete absence of these research and community activities as part of the teacher education programme, with no exposure at all to working with parents or supervising or organising social activities; this sits in contrast to their inclusion within between a third and a half of programmes in the USA and

Poland. The strongest levels of coverage across Poland, Singapore and the USA were in observing teachers, reporting on observations and discussing experiences with peers. Singapore demonstrates a uniform approach to the practicum with a much higher level of coverage of most topics than in Poland and the USA. Singaporean school experience involves responsibility for student assessment and for design and delivery of instruction, delivering and supervising non-mathematics instruction, and participating in formal school meetings. Germany did not collect data on the practicum experience.

School Experience/Practicum	POL		SGP		USA	
	POL5 $n = 20$	POL6 $n = 31$	SGP5 $n = 2$	SGP6 $n = 2$	USA5 $n = 19$	USA6 $n = 59$
Observe a teacher	75	81	100	100	47	66
Serve as a teacher	5	0	0	0	11	14
Design instruction in mathematics	0	3	100	100	19	37
Design instruction in other than mathematics	50	16	100	100	32	15
Deliver mathematics instruction	0	0	75	75	18	31
Deliver instruction in other than mathematics	55	23	100	100	32	19
Supervise non-mathematics instruction	50	26	100	100	16	14
Assess students (full responsibility)	45	32	100	100	32	36
Supervise or organise social activities	45	26	0	0	0	19
Work with parents	35	48	0	0	26	37
Participate in formal school teacher meetings	35	45	100	100	21	37
Participate in school-level administration	45	32	100	100	0	2
Design and carry out an action research project	10	6	0	0	5	19
Discuss practicum experience with peers	65	71	100	100	26	44
Write report of observing teaching	50	32	100	100	47	56
Meet with supervisor to discuss practicum	30	13	100	100	47	56
Attend professional conferences	5	0	0	0	11	15
Other	10	23	100	100	5	3

Table VI. Percentage of teacher education institutions that cover school experience activities and topics in each country according to the TEDS-M analysis of the teacher education syllabi (Germany omitted as it did not collect syllabi for field experience).

Institutional Arrangements: hours dedicated to teacher education areas or knowledge domains

To explore institutional arrangements, we looked at programmes' areas of emphasis as indicated by the amount of teaching contact hours (including lectures, class meetings, tutorial classes and any other required meetings that bring future teachers together to meet as a group with staff of the teacher preparation programme) allocated to the different areas. The data, presented in Table VII, show that across programmes the study of liberal arts is given emphasis in Poland and the USA. In Poland the amount of hours programmes dedicate to academic mathematics for the lower and upper secondary levels is very high in contrast with those allocated by programmes in the USA. The study of the school curriculum received relatively low emphasis across the countries. For Singapore the allocation of time to these three areas – liberal arts, academic mathematics, and school mathematics – is zero.

Programme group	Country	Overall number of programmes reporting	Mean number of teaching contact hours allocated to:					
			Liberal arts courses[a]	Academic math.	School math.	Mathematics pedagogy	Foundations	General pedagogy
Lower	Germany*							
secondary	Poland†	20	184	666	54	108	64	66
(Grade 10	Singapore	2	0	0	0	108	72	48
maximum)	USA†	14	272	125	61	52	96	166
Lower &	Germany							
upper	Poland	15	149	1310	41	124	84	60
secondary	Singapore	2	0	0	0	108	72	48
(to Grade 11	USA	46	499	442	87	72	144	145
& above)								

† Some or all future teachers in these countries are being prepared to teach primary and lower-secondary students. The programme groups preparing future primary teachers and the programme groups preparing lower-secondary teachers are therefore partly or fully overlapping.
[a] Excludes mathematics.
*Germany did not report these data.

Table VII. Mean number of teaching contact hours in liberal arts, academic mathematics, school mathematics, mathematics pedagogy, foundations and general pedagogy that future secondary teachers attend during their programmes.
Source: Tatto et al, 2012 Exhibits A4.2 & A4.2., pp. 216 and 218.

Mathematics pedagogy is allocated more than 100 contact hours in the three countries with the exception of the lower-secondary programmes in the USA. Foundations and general pedagogy receive emphasis in Poland and Singapore but not as much as in the US programmes. Overall, the US programmes appear the most comprehensive across the differing elements, albeit with some slightly lower coverage of mathematics pedagogy. Poland has a high concentration of academic mathematics content and mathematics pedagogy, while Singapore is notable for the absence of liberal arts and the lowest general pedagogy time commitment.

Abridged Analysis of Knowledge Acquisition and the Curriculum

The TEDS-M assessments uncovered a moderate correlation between future teachers' mathematics knowledge and their mathematics pedagogical knowledge as defined by their mathematical curricular knowledge, their knowledge of planning for mathematics teaching and learning, and their ability to enact mathematics for teaching and learning (see Tatto et al, 2012, pp. 130-131 for the MPCK and PCK frameworks). For instance, future teachers in Singapore did very well in both the MPCK and PCK assessments. However, the MPCK assessment results are of particular importance across countries because the MPCK curriculum and its implementation is within the domain of teacher education programmes. The assessment was developed according to a constructivist approach to teaching and had a higher level of difficulty as it required the recontextualisation of mathematics knowledge as applied to teaching, to classroom situations and to interaction with learners. With the exception of future teachers in lower secondary in the USA, all other future teachers scored above the international mean of 500, with lower secondary future teachers in Singapore obtaining the highest scores (539), followed by those in Poland (520); however, the size of the standard deviations within and across countries revealed wide variability in knowledge, which may reflect the variable nature of the teacher education curriculum and of the opportunities to learn provided to future mathematics teachers (see Tatto et al, 2012, pp. 142-150). Future teachers preparing to teach the upper grades of secondary school demonstrated higher levels of knowledge in all countries (with almost a half standard deviation above the international mean), with upper secondary future teachers in Germany and Singapore reaching the highest scores (586 and 562 respectively). The connections across the K-12 curriculum, the teacher education curriculum, opportunities to learn as experienced by future teachers, and future teachers' attained knowledge are areas for further exploration and highlight the complex and delicate architecture in the design of effective teacher education.

Concluding Remarks

The analysis above highlights a series of points regarding the configuration of mathematics teacher education in different national contexts.

1. The disciplinary knowledge structure of mathematics, with its high levels of 'grammaticality' (Bernstein, 1999, 2000) and universality across countries, suggests that it is possible to conduct a rigorous comparative analysis of teacher education syllabi across national contexts. This analysis has shown that the uniformity of mathematical knowledge structures and general levels of agreement about the mathematics curriculum do not necessarily lead to a uniformity of mathematics teacher education – across or within countries.

2. The countries studied here (Germany, Poland, Singapore and the USA) have configurations of mathematics teacher education that are variably influenced by the decisions of different recontextualisation agents (i.e. governments, curriculum authorities, teacher education institutions, teacher

educators). Some nations are dominated by what might be termed an 'official recontextualisation field' (ORF) (Bernstein, 2000), and therefore experience a standardisation of teacher education curriculum mandated by a central authority and strong constraints on diversity across institutions (e.g. Singapore). The Singapore case may also reflect the extent to which smaller nations with a centralised concentration of administrative power may seek to organise teacher education. Other nations demonstrate greater influence in the 'pedagogic recontextualisation field' (PRF), involving teacher education institutions and teacher educators to a greater extent in shaping the content of teacher education programmes, with greater independence from a central authority (i.e. Germany, Poland and the USA in this study). This leads to greater diversity in terms of coverage of mathematics content, mathematics pedagogical content and general pedagogy – for both the lower- and upper-secondary stages.

3. Singapore provides a clear example of a context in which notions of mathematics teachers' professional competence are controlled centrally. In that context, there is also a strong preference for the development of what might be termed the advanced technical aspects of teaching practice, while not entirely neglecting aspects derived from a more disciplinary-based education studies. However, this may also be seen alongside requirements for high levels of subject expertise in mathematics, acquired prior to the teacher education programme. Singaporean programmes demonstrated universal coverage of topics such as classroom management, assessment and measurement, and instructional media coupled with a very comprehensive approach to mathematics pedagogy and the practicum (including high levels of responsibility for instructional design and delivery). As such programmes assume a high level of previous mathematical competence, they gain space to rigorously develop technical pedagogic competence relevant to the discipline. However, more 'holistic' elements (e.g. working with parents, pastoral duties or social activities), and therefore what might be termed a broader pedagogic role, are non-existent in the Singaporean model. Thus teacher education in Singapore exhibits elements of what Winch et al (2015, p. 209) term 'teaching as the application of technical protocols', albeit coupled with high levels of subject expertise. Aspects of teaching that are not seen to contribute to this technical expertise are marginalised. This form of teacher education relies on a tightly controlled recontextualisation process in which knowledge is selected and transformed ready for teachers to apply in the classroom, while teacher educators focus on ensuring that teachers can apply mandated technical protocols to a high standard.

4. In contrast to Singapore, the German, Polish and US programmes show greater variance across institutions. Most German institutions include time on the pastoral and counselling role of teachers, in contrast to all the other countries studied here, while the Polish institutions have the broadest coverage of mathematics pedagogy topics, including work on affective issues (beliefs and attitudes) and selecting instructional materials. Programmes in

the USA repeatedly cover topics taught in the school curriculum and have in comparison with the other countries a more relaxed selection policy. US programmes cover more consistently topics on preparing teachers to address the needs of diverse (underserved) students. There was a wider disparity regarding the field experience/practicum activities that are emphasised in each country, with a higher level of agreement across Poland, Singapore and the USA on 'observing a teacher'.

5. The findings presented here have implications for the form of education studies likely to be seen as relevant for teacher education, the institutional forms in which teachers are educated, and the process of teacher education itself. The forms of teacher education at work here reflect elements of the models of teaching outlined by Winch et al (2015), but with subtle variances that echo the national traditions from which they have emerged and the extent to which the processes of recontextualisation are governed by 'official' and 'pedagogic' stakeholders. A more highly technical model of teacher education may focus on classroom instructional competence, requiring greater input from highly experienced teachers with considerable practical subject-based instructional expertise. Here more disciplinary-based forms of education studies may have a role, but these are likely to be marginalised in the focus on technical competence. In contrast, where broader pedagogic norms persist and there are strong traditions of educational theory that envisage the teacher's role extending beyond instructional competence there may be greater openness to diversity in teacher education, developing a research-capable practitioner and encouraging pastoral and counselling skills. This may suggest involving a rather broader spectrum of academic and professional staff in the process of teacher education, and the contribution of a wider disciplinary-based form of expertise.

Acknowledgement

The authors wish to acknowledge the support of the US National Science Foundation (REC 0514431), and are grateful to Dr Kiril Bankov and colleagues in the participating countries for their work in analysing curriculum documents. The in-depth analysis of the curriculum was a national option within the TEDS-M study. Any opinions, findings, and conclusions or recommendations expressed in this chapter are those of the authors and do not necessarily reflect the views of the National Science Foundation, or of others mentioned in this acknowledgement.

References

Bernstein, B. (1990) *The Structuring of Pedagogic Discourse*. London: Routledge.
https://doi.org/10.4324/9780203011263

Bernstein, B. (1999) Vertical and Horizontal Discourse: an essay, *British Journal of Sociology of Education*, 20(2), 157-173. https://doi.org/10.1080/01425699995380

Bernstein, B. (2000) *Pedagogy, Symbolic Control and Identity*, rev. edn. New York: Rowman & Littlefield.

Carr, W. (2006) Education Without Theory, *British Journal of Educational Studies*, 54(2), 136-159. https://doi.org/10.1111/j.1467-8527.2006.00344.x

Cochran-Smith, M. & Lytle, S.L. (1999) Relationships of Knowledge and Practice: teacher learning in communities, *Review of Research in Education*, 24(1), 249-305. https://doi.org/10.3102/0091732X024001249

Ertl, H., Zierer, K., Phillips, D. & Tippelt, R. (2015) Disciplinary Traditions and the Dissemination of Knowledge: an international comparison of publication patterns in journals of education, *Oxford Review of Education*, 41(1), 64-88. https://doi.org/10.1080/03054985.2014.1001350

Evans, K., Guile, D., Harris, J. & Allan, H. (2010) Putting Knowledge to Work, *Nurse Education Today*, 30(3), 245-251. https://doi.org/10.1016/j.nedt.2009.10.014

Furlong, J. (2013) *Education – an Anatomy of the Discipline: rescuing the university project?* London: Routledge.

Hogan, D. & Gopinathan, S. (2008) Knowledge Management, Sustainable Innovation and Pre-service Teacher Education in Singapore, *Teachers and Teaching*, 14(4), 369-384. https://doi.org/10.1080/13540600802037793

Hordern, J. (2014) How is Vocational Knowledge Recontextualised? *Journal of Vocational Education and Training*, 66(1), 22-38. https://doi.org/10.1080/13636820.2013.867524

Hordern, J. (2015) Teaching, Teacher Formation, and Specialised Professional Practice, *European Journal of Teacher Education*, 38(4), 431-444. https://doi.org/10.1080/02619768.2015.1056910

Le Métais, J. (2003) *International Trends in Primary Education*. London: Qualifications and Curriculum Authority.

McCulloch, G. (2002) Disciplines Contributing to Education? Educational Studies and the Disciplines, *British Journal of Educational Studies*, 50(1), 100-119. https://doi.org/10.1111/1467-8527.t01-1-00193

Muller, J. (2009) Forms of Knowledge and Curriculum Coherence' *Journal of Education & Work*, 22(3), 205-226. https://doi.org/10.1080/13639080902957905

Schriewer, J. & Keiner, E. (1992) Communication Patterns and Intellectual Traditions in Educational Sciences: France and Germany, *Comparative Education Review*, 36(1), 25-51. https://doi.org/10.1086/447080

Shulman, L. (1987) Knowledge and Teaching: foundations of the new reform, *Harvard Educational Review*, 57(1), 1-22. https://doi.org/10.17763/haer.57.1.j463w79r56455411

Stuart, J. & Tatto, M.T. (2000) Designs for Initial Teacher Preparation Programs: an international view, *International Journal of Educational Research*, 33, 493-514. https://doi.org/10.1016/S0883-0355(00)00031-8

Tatto, M.T. (Ed.) (2013) *The Teacher Education and Development Study in Mathematics (TEDS-M). Policy, Practice, and Readiness to Teach Primary and*

Secondary Mathematics in 17 Countries: Technical Report. Amsterdam: International Association for the Evaluation of Student Achievement.

Tatto, M.T., Schwille, J., Senk, S., Ingvarson, L., Peck, R. & Rowley, G. (2008) *Teacher Education and Development Study in Mathematics (TEDS-M): conceptual framework*. East Lansing, MI: Teacher Education and Development International Study Center, Michigan State University, and IEA.

Tatto, M.T., Schwille, J., Senk, S.L., Ingvarson, L., Rowley, G., Peck, R., Bankov, K., Rodriguez, M. & Reckase, M. (2012) *Policy, Practice, and Readiness to Teach Primary and Secondary Mathematics in 17 Countries. Findings from the IEA Teacher Education and Development Study in Mathematics (TEDS-M)*. Amsterdam: International Association for the Evaluation of Student Achievement.

Whitty, G. (2014) Recent Developments in Teacher Training and their Consequences for the 'University Project' in Education, *Oxford Review of Education*, 40(4), 466-481. https://doi.org/10.1080/03054985.2014.933007

Winch, C. (2004) What Do Teachers Need to Know about Teaching? A Critical Examination of the Occupational Knowledge of Teachers, *British Journal of Educational Studies*, 52(2), 180-196. https://doi.org/10.1111/j.1467-8527.2004.00262.x

Winch, C. (2012) For Philosophy of Education in Teacher Education, *Oxford Review of Education*, 38(3), 305-322. https://doi.org/10.1080/03054985.2012.693299

Winch, C., Oancea, A. & Orchard, J. (2015) The Contribution of Educational Research to Teachers' Professional Learning – Philosophical Understandings, *Oxford Review of Education*, 41(2), 202-216. https://doi.org/10.1080/03054985.2015.1017406

Zulijan, M.V. & Vogrinc, J. (Eds) (2011) *European Dimensions of Teacher Education: similarities and differences*. Ljubljana: University of Ljubljana.

Part 4. Afterword

CHAPTER 12

Futures of the Field of Education

DAVID F. LABAREE

SUMMARY This chapter begins with a brief overview of what the book's authors say both about the national variations in education knowledge production and also about three core tensions that run through the field as a whole, looking at the changes in these tensions over time. Second, the chapter introduces a fourth tension that infuses the field, the disagreement about what social goals education should serve. It argues that these four tensions are a necessary and healthy component of schooling and the research about schooling. As a result, any efforts to resolve the tensions one way or the other would be detrimental to the broader role that schooling needs to play. Unfortunately, however, such a narrowing of the vision of education is very much in process in the current policy climate, spread by a global educational reform movement (lovingly referred to as GERM), which relentlessly seeks to remake education into an efficient machine for the production of human capital. The chapter also discusses an alternative vision of education and educational knowledge, which is not driven by educational policymakers but instead by individual education consumers. From this perspective, education is all about providing social access and preserving social advantage. The chapter closes by exploring the implications of this analysis for the future of educational research.

This book is an ambitious effort to characterize at a global level the current condition of the field of educational research. I don't know of anything quite like it in the literature. The idea is to examine the mix of variation and convergence in educational research practices through a series of national case studies, while at the same time attempting to explore central tensions that are endemic in the field. In this final chapter, my assigned task is to synthesize the analyses from the first 11 chapters and then use this synthesis to project the futures facing educational researchers. Good luck with that.

So let me begin with a brief *caveat lector*. Trying to develop a succinct summary of this book is either a fool's errand (impossible on the face of it) or, if possible, then well beyond my limited abilities. And even trying to do this would be grossly unfair to the empirical and analytical richness of the wide array of contributions to the book. In addition, I'm a historical sociologist not a futurist, so trying to spell out the futures of the field is something I would not even attempt.

What I decided to do instead is something less ambitious but possibly more useful – to write a reflective essay spelling out some of the thoughts that these 11 chapters provoked in me as a reader. As I tell my students, the best research is a provocation. It compels you to think about familiar issues in fresh ways; and that is certainly the effect that this book has had on me.

My plan, therefore, is to do the following. First, I give a brief overview of what the book's authors say both about the national variations in education knowledge production and also about three core tensions that run through the field as a whole, looking at the changes in these tensions over time. Second, I introduce a fourth tension that infuses the field, the disagreement about what social goals education should serve. I argue that these four tensions are a necessary and healthy component of schooling and the research about schooling. As a result, any efforts to resolve the tensions one way or the other would be detrimental to the broader role that schooling needs to play. Unfortunately, however, such a narrowing of the vision of education is very much in process in the current policy climate, spread by a global educational reform movement (lovingly referred to as GERM) which relentlessly seeks to remake education into an efficient machine for the production of human capital. I also discuss an alternative vision of education and educational knowledge that is driven not by educational policymakers but instead by individual education consumers. From this perspective, education is all about providing social access and preserving social advantage. I close by exploring the implications of this analysis for the future of educational research.

The authors show that the global field of educational research is a complex mix of nationally distinctive forms of knowledge and sites of knowledge production. Each national case study shows some knowledge characteristics that are peculiar to that context, such as the tradition of *Bildung* in Germany and of pedagogical science in Latvia. In addition, there is wide variation in the organizational setting of educational research, varying from the radically specialized institutions in France to the more standardized setting of the university in the USA and China.

Cutting across these national differences, however, are broad patterns of commonality. In trying to understand these common elements, I find it useful to frame them as chronic tensions that run through the field at a global level. The tensions are omnipresent, but the relative emphasis within the tensions varies from country to country. The authors focus on three tensions in particular. One is the tension between the normative and the objective. On the one hand, education is a value-laden enterprise focused on shaping the young, fusing them with the norms and values we want them to embody as adults. On the other hand, education is a machine for providing knowledge and skills that are needed by society. Educational research, therefore, needs to balance elucidating educational goals and engineering an efficient machinery for skilling.

A second tension is between knowledge that is embedded in the context of educational practice and knowledge that is abstracted from this context. The issue here is whether teachers produce and own their own knowledge of practice or whether this knowledge is generated in the different zone of practice known as educational research and then transferred to the teacher. The question this raises is how we should balance practical knowledge and theoretical knowledge, school-based knowledge and university-based knowledge.

A third tension is between two different ways of organizing educational knowledge. One approach sees the field of education as consisting of a multiplicity of individual university-based knowledge disciplines (sociology, psychology, economics, philosophy, history), each of which is bounded by and imbued with the spirit of that discipline. From this perspective, the field is multidisciplinary in nature. The other approach is to see educational knowledge as a discipline of its own or as an interdisciplinary arena for exploring the institutional setting of the school.

The authors show how the emphasis in these tensions varies across national settings, a variation that accounts for much of the richness of the analysis in the national case studies and the conceptual chapters. But they also point to patterns of historical change in these tensions that are global in character. One is that, in nearly all settings, educational knowledge production began in some form of normal school, a secondary institution focused on training teachers. But over time, the locus of knowledge production shifted from the normal school to the university, sometimes as a shift between institutions and sometimes as an evolutionary process by which the former turned into the latter. Another related change across different contexts was the shift from educational knowledge that was embedded in the practice of teaching to knowledge that was produced in the more distant setting of the university. In recent years, however, the authors show these two change processes in a number of national settings seem to be moving in reverse. Especially in the UK, but also in the USA and elsewhere, there is a movement to move teacher preparation and educational knowledge production out of universities and closer to the site of pedagogical practice in schools.

I label these common characteristics of education as tensions because I see these tensions as fundamental to the educational enterprise. These are not conflicts that need to be resolved one way or the other but intrinsic complexities that animate the field of education and give it much of its vitality. No social institution is free of such fundamental tensions. In fact, the effectiveness of an institution is measured not by its ability to eliminate these tensions but by its ability to manage them. If you look at any healthy school, college, department or institute of education in the world, you are likely to find these three tensions playing themselves out in daily practice. You will find the normative vs. the objective, theory vs. practice, and disciplinarity vs. multidisciplinarity or what some of the contributors here term singular vs. region. These conflicts pop up in every effort to develop programs, evaluate candidates for hiring and promotion, admit students, and assess what constitutes good research.

In fact – and here comes the futures part of my story – one of the biggest problems facing the field of educational knowledge production today, I suggest, is the growing global pressure to resolve these tensions. Doing so, I argue, will diminish both the scope and the social benefits of education as an enterprise.

But before developing this point, I would first like to introduce a fourth unresolvable tension that infuses education and educational research. This one focuses on purpose. A key part of the complexity, contradiction and apparent inefficiency of education is that we cannot agree on what goals we want it to accomplish. Let me point to three social goals in particular. One is nation building. The primary reason that modern societies developed universal systems of public schooling was to support the emergence of the nation state. Schooling was the mechanism for turning subjects into citizens. This is the role that schooling played in the long nineteenth century: forming the imaginary community of the state, providing citizens with the skills and values they need in order function in the new polity, and supplying a common experiential basis for considering fellow citizens as peers.

A second goal for schooling is economic development. This vision emerged later historically, after the state was secured and the national economy was developed. The issue from this perspective is less the need to transmit the values required for social solidarity than the need to provide useful skills that will meet the workforce demands of a growing economy. Thus schools become engines for the production of human capital, whose primary mission is to increase the gross domestic product, increase wealth and the standard of living, and enhance national power.

A third goal for schooling is status attainment. This vision of schooling has always been hovering in the background as a rationale for why individuals might want to pursue education for their own personal gain. By the mid-twentieth century it became explicit and central to the understanding of schooling: if you want a good job, get a good education. In modern societies, individuals gain social positions through their jobs, and schooling is the mechanism for allocating people to specific jobs in the occupational hierarchy based on academic achievement and attainment. School is the way societies help outsiders gain social access, and it's also the way societies help insiders preserve social advantage.

Consider the tensions that persist in the interaction among these competing goals. The first is political, the second economic and the third individual. The first two see education as a public good that benefits everyone in society and not just the individual receiving the education. We all benefit from having competent fellow citizens and economically productive workers, so we have an incentive to educate other people's children. The third sees education as a private good. If I gain more education than you have, it gives me an advantage in the competition for better jobs. As a result, I don't want an egalitarian system of schooling but prefer one that is highly stratified, one that creates winners and losers.

In the twenty-first century, we have seen the educational policy discourse converge on a single overarching goal for education. From the global education reform movement to its policy apparatus in the Organisation for Economic Co-operation and Development (OECD) and its policy police in the Programme for International Student Assessment (PISA) testing program, we have seen one goal trump the others. Nowadays, the uniform message is human capital *uber alles*. The convergence of purpose is strong, consistent and pithy; so my colleague Gay Hoagland refers to this policy discourse as an incestogram.

The rush toward consensus has created the push for a radical form of social utilitarianism, which threatens to rationalize both schooling and the production of educational knowledge around improving economic productivity, raising PISA scores and eradicating a rich array of national differences in educational form and function. This includes what at first looks like a shift in one of the core tensions within education, from the normative to the objective, as education is pressured to focus on the efficient production of job-relevant skills. But in fact this change is best understood as a shift from one set of values to another, from character and citizenship to economic utility.

At the same time, the human capital push fosters a shift in another core tension in the field, by tightening the link between theory and practice. Increasingly practice in schools is under pressure from a rationalized and decontextualized form of knowledge production produced by universities, which seeks to impose uniformity on the earlier relative autonomy of teachers and schools and to tighten the coupling of educational systems. Rather than creating closer mutual connections between theory and practice or shifting the locus of control to the arena of practice, this change increases the power of epistemic knowledge from the center over the ecologies of schooling on the periphery. Far from being liberated by the stronger role that knowledge production plays in the educational system, university knowledge producers find themselves bullied and bribed to confine their efforts to the development of applied knowledge for an economistic educational vision. Practical application trumps basic research and randomized control trials become the gold standard.

Lost in the rush toward the one best goal for schooling are the rich and historically productive national traditions of educational knowledge production that are spelled out in this book. Also lost is the long-time vision of schooling as nation building, citizen formation, character development and liberal learning.

At the same time that the policy establishment has converged on human capital production as the prime goal for schooling, educational consumers have been focusing more intensely on education as the key way to get ahead and stay ahead in the race for social position. Like the economistic goal, the consumerist goal is frankly utilitarian. But unlike the former, the latter views schooling as an intensely private good. The consumer's aim is not to pursue a broad social dividend from schooling but instead to seek personal gain. For some this means going to school to gain access to the social opportunities that evaded their parents; and for others it means using school to preserve social advantages that their parents already have.

One result of this approach for schools is to sharply exacerbate the stratification of a system in which everyone wants to be above average. Another is to increase competition in schools, where winning becomes more important than learning. Yet another is to increase the pressure on schools to emphasize form over content. The aim for the student is to accumulate grades, credits and degrees rather than to pursue learning. As a consequence, education becomes not only a private good but also an exchange value, whose primary worth is as a kind of currency for buying access to a good job and a good life. The OECD approach serves to narrow the learning outcomes of schooling and educational knowledge production to whatever is in service to economic development. But the consumer approach is even more radical, since it undermines the role of schooling as an institution for learning.

What does growing consumerism mean for educational knowledge producers? In many ways it leaves them simply irrelevant. The economic development goal is the expression of educational policymakers and school reformers, who then provide strong incentives for educational researchers to harness themselves to the economistic bandwagon to help engineer the desired outcome. Consumerism, however, is a matter not of public policy but of individual ambition. Consumers are seeking not to change the system but to improve or reinforce their own social status. Their impact on the system – promoting stratification and competition at all levels – is not the result of a social movement with explicit demands but the result of a series of individual choices in the educational market place, reinforced at the ballot box as consumers vote to keep the system expanding to meet their demand. Economism needs educational researchers as social engineers who are imbued with the what-works spirit, but consumerism doesn't need them at all. It operates through market mechanisms rather than policy mobilization and social engineering, so research knowledge is largely irrelevant to it.

Where, then, does this leave us in thinking about the possible futures of educational research as a field of practice? The good news is that the growth of the economistic approach to education provides a lot of funding for educational researchers who are willing take the bribe for performing service in creating a more efficient system for producing human capital. The bad news is that this structure of incentives extracts the heart from educational research just as economism does from educational practice.

One answer to this problem is for educational researchers to push back against the trend toward social engineering, which focuses on determining what works for economic development. Instead they can embrace basic research in education, which directs attention to the broader aims of schooling, reminds people of the rich history of the institution, and plays up the value of particular national traditions of research that offer alternatives to OECD World. They can work to develop university-school partnerships that offer mutual enlightenment in place of colonial rule. And they can provide students, teachers, parents and policymakers with alternative visions of what schooling has been and can still be.

Notes on Contributors

John Furlong is an emeritus professor and former director of the Department of Education at the University of Oxford. He is currently adviser to the Welsh government on Initial Teacher Education and a former president of the British Educational Research Association. His research interests centre on both teacher education and educational research policy and the links between them.

Susan Groundwater-Smith is an honorary professor in the Sydney School of Education and Social Work at the University of Sydney. She has a long history in relation to teacher professional learning at both the pre-service and in-service levels with an emphasis upon action research. Most recently she has been engaged in facilitating children and young people to become participatory in school-based inquiry.

Jim Hordern is a senior lecturer at Bath Spa University. His research interests focus on educational knowledge and practice, particularly in higher, professional and vocational education.

Dina Kuhlee is a senior lecturer at Carl von Ossietzky University of Oldenburg in the Department of Vocational Education and Professional Studies. Her research focuses on teacher education, further education, and educational policy and governance from an international and comparative perspective. She recently co-edited *Governance in Initial Teacher Education: perspectives on England and Germany* (Springer, 2015) and a special issue on vocational education in England and Germany for the journal *Research in Comparative and International Education* (RCIE).

David F. Labaree is Lee Jacks Professor at the Stanford University Graduate School of Education. He is former president of the History of Education Society and former vice president of the American Educational Research Association. His most recent book is *A Perfect Mess: the unlikely ascendancy of American higher education* (University of Chicago Press, 2017).

Gary McCulloch is Brian Simon Professor of the History of Education at the UCL Institute of Education. He is currently vice president and president-elect of the British Educational Research Association and editor of the *British*

Journal of Educational Studies. His recent work includes a book on the social history of educational studies and research.

Régis Malet is Full Professor of Comparative Education at the University of Bordeaux – Ecole Supérieure du Professorat et de l'Education (ESPE) of Aquitaine. He is the director of the Laboratoire Cultures, Education, Sociétés (LACES EA4140) of the University of Bordeaux and the deputy director of the ESPE of Aquitaine, in charge of international development and research. He has been the director of the Faculty of Education at the University of Lille and also the president of AFEC (French-speaking society of comparative education), as well as the editor of *Éducation Comparée* for almost a decade. His fields of research include comparative and international education, education policy, teachers' education and youth identity and citizenship, domains in which he has an extensive publication record.

Nicole Mockler is a senior lecturer in the Sydney School of Education and Social Work at the University of Sydney. She is currently editor-in-chief of *The Australian Educational Researcher*. Her research interests are in education policy and politics, particularly the role of education policy in shaping and framing teachers' work, the relationship between education and the media, and the global commercialisation of education.

Lynn Paine is Professor of Teacher Education and Assistant Dean for International Studies in the College of Education at Michigan State University. Her work focuses on comparative and international education and the sociology of education. Much of her research has involved the comparative study of teachers, teaching and teacher education. Most recently she has been exploring the influence of globally circulating discourses on policy and practice in teacher preparation.

Jürgen Schriewer is an Emeritus Professor of Comparative Education at Humboldt University, Berlin, where he acted both as dean of the Faculty of Education and as a co-coordinator of research networks on cross-cultural studies in historical and social sciences funded by the German Research Agency. A former president of the Comparative Education Society in Europe, he was invited as a visiting professor to universities in Paris, Stockholm, Tokyo, Beijing, Mexico City and Buenos Aires. His research interests centre on the comparative history of education; world society theory and region-specific structural elaboration processes; as well as on the history and methodology of comparative social enquiry.

Maria Teresa Tatto is the Southwest Borderlands Professor of Comparative Education at the Mary Lou Fulton Teachers College, and Professor in the Division of Educational Leadership and Innovation at Arizona State University. She is the principal investigator for the Teacher

Education and Development Study in Mathematics, and for the First Five Years of Mathematics Teaching Study, both designed to explore the connections between pre-service preparation and what is learned on the job during the first years of teaching. She is a former president of the Comparative and International Education Society, and studies the effects of educational policy on school systems.

Weihe Xie, PhD in philosophy, is currently the vice president of the academic council and the dean of the Institute of Educational Research, Tsinghua University. His research interests focus on educational theories, higher education and sociology of education. He has published extensively on education policy, education equity, and employment of college graduates. Professor Xie's academic achievements have been widely recognised internationally. He was invited to give lectures as a specialist in Chinese education at Harvard University, Columbia University, Oxford University and other universities across the world.

Wen Wen is an associate professor at the Institute of Educational Research, Tsinghua University, China. She received her bachelor's degree in liberal arts and master's degree in education from Tsinghua University. She worked with the Directorate for Education, OECD in the summer of 2007. In 2010 she received her PhD in Education from the University of Oxford. Her research interests include teaching and learning in higher education, higher education policy, and internationalisation of higher education.

Christopher Winch is Professor of Educational Philosophy and Policy in the School of Education, Society and Communication at King's College London. He was Chair of the Philosophy of Education Society from 2008 to 2011. His interests lie in the area of philosophy of education, professional and vocational education and teacher knowledge. His latest book, *Teachers' Know-how*, was published in 2017.

Geoff Whitty is Director Emeritus of the UCL Institute of Education in London. He currently holds a research professorship at Bath Spa University in the UK and a Global Innovation Chair at the University of Newcastle, Australia. He is a former president of the College of Teachers and of the British Educational Research Association. A sociologist of education by training, his current research interests are in education policy with particular reference to teacher education and widening participation in higher education.

Irēna Žogla, Dr. habil. paed., is Emeritus Professor of the University of Latvia and senior researcher of the Institute of Research in *Pedagoģija*. Her academic and research profile includes the process of teaching-learning and teacher education. Currently she is an expert at the Council of Sciences of

Latvia and Chair of the Council for Promotion in *Pedagoģija*. She runs a master's programme in *Pedagoģija*, delivers classes in *Pedagoģija* for doctoral and master's students and is a scientific adviser for doctoral research.